Studies in Rhetorics and Feminisms

Series Editors, Cheryl Glenn and Shirley Wilson Logan

WOMEN AND RHETORIC BETWEEN THE WARS

Edited by
Ann George,
M. Elizabeth Weiser, and
Janet Zepernick

Southern Illinois University Press
Carbondale and Edwardsville

Copyright © 2013 by the Board of Trustees,
Southern Illinois University
All rights reserved
Printed in the United States of America

16 15 14 13   4 3 2 1

Library of Congress Cataloging-in-Publication Data
Women and rhetoric between the wars / edited by Ann George, M. Elizabeth Weiser, and Janet Zepernick.
 p. cm. — (Studies in rhetorics and feminisms)
Includes bibliographical references and index.
ISBN 978-0-8093-3138-3 (pbk. : alk. paper) — ISBN 0-8093-3138-1 (pbk. : alk. paper) — ISBN 978-0-8093-3139-0 (ebook) — ISBN 0-8093-3139-X (ebook)
 1. Women—Language. 2. Women in public life—United States—History—20th century. 3. Feminism—United States—History—20th century. 4. Feminism—Language. I. George, Ann, 1957– II. Weiser, M. Elizabeth. III. Zepernick, Janet.
P120.W66W66 2013
306.44′082—dc23   2012028053

Printed on recycled paper. ♻
The paper used in this publication meets the minimum requirements of American National Standard for Information Sciences—Permanence of Paper for Printed Library Materials, ansi z39.48-1992. ∞

To our mothers—
  Betty, Yvonne, Judy Mary—
and our daughters—
  Katie, Sophia, Kari

Contents

List of Figures ix
Acknowledgments xi

Introduction 1
Ann George, M. Elizabeth Weiser, Janet Zepernick

VOLUNTARY ASSOCIATIONS FOR THE CIVIC SCENE

1. Continuous Mediation: Julia Grace Wales's New Rhetoric 19
   Wendy B. Sharer

2. The Hope for Peace and Bread 32
   Hephzibah Roskelly

3. Gertrude Bonnin's Transrhetorical Fight for Land Rights 48
   Elizabeth Wilkinson

4. A Rhetor's Apprenticeship: Reading Frances Perkins's Rhetorical Autobiography 63
   Janet Zepernick

5. Working Together and Being Prepared: Early Girl Scouting as Citizenship Training 79
   Sarah Hallenbeck

POPULAR CELEBRITY IN THE EPIDEICTIC SCENE

6. Reading Helen Keller 97
   Ann George

7. Dorothy Day: Personalizing (to) the Masses 114
   M. Elizabeth Weiser

8. The Shocking Morality of Nannie Helen Burroughs 129
   Sandra L. Robinson

9. Bessie Smith's Blues as Rhetorical Advocacy   143
    Coretta Pittman

10. Traditional Form, Subversive Function:
    Aunt Molly Jackson's Labor Struggles   159
    Cassandra Parente

11. Sweethearts of the Skies   175
    Sara Hillin

ACADEMIA AND THE SCENE OF PROFESSIONALISM

12. Field Guides: Women Writing Anthropology   193
    Risa Applegarth

13. "Have We Not a Mind Like They?":
    Jovita González on Nation and Gender   209
    Kathy Jurado

14. "Exceptional Women": Epideictic
    Rhetoric and Women Scientists   223
    Jordynn Jack

15. "Long I Followed Happy Guides":
    Activism, Advocacy, and English Studies   240
    Kay Halasek

Works Cited   263
Contributors   283
Index   287

Figures

4.1. Frances Perkins   70
6.1. Helen Keller   111
7.1. Dorothy Day   119
8.1. Nannie Helen Burroughs   133
9.1. Bessie Smith   147
10.1. Aunt Molly Jackson   170
11.1. Amelia Earhart   179
11.2. Bessie Coleman   180
12.1. Ann Axtell Morris   204

Acknowledgments

We want to thank the many individuals and institutions whose moral, intellectual, and financial support has made possible this collection. In that light, we acknowledge series editors Cheryl Glenn and Shirley Wilson Logan for their helpful encouragement and advice to make this a stronger book, as well as all the team at Southern Illinois University Press. Our institutions—Texas Christian University, Ohio State University, and Pittsburg State University—provided us time and assistance in various forms over the years, and we appreciate their support of this project. We particularly thank Ohio State student Terry Gomes for his editorial assistance in 2010, TCU administrative assistant Lynn Herrera for her assistance in tracking down copyright holders in 2011, and Julie McDowell of Hal Leonard for her assistance with copyright permissions for Bessie Smith's lyrics. We thank the following archives and estates for permission to quote from their materials: The Elsie Clews Parsons Papers, American Philosophical Society, Philadelphia, PA; National Archives of Canada, Ottawa; George Palmer Putnam Collection of Amelia Earhart Papers, Purdue University Libraries, Archives and Special Collections, West Lafayette, IN; Elizabeth Ann Morris and the Morris Family Collections, Bayfield, CO; the Ninety-Nines Museum of Women Pilots Collection, Oklahoma City, OK; Julia Grace Wales Papers, State Historical Society of Wisconsin, Madison; and the Archives and Special Collections, Hunter College Libraries, Hunter College of the City University of New York. Finally, we thank the colleagues in our various writing groups for their expert advice and support: Theresa Gaul, Charlotte Hogg, Melanie Kill, Carolyn Skinner, and Cassandra Parente. As always, our families' patience and understanding was a boon throughout the production experience.

Permission to quote from records of the Carolina Low Country Girl Scout Council in chapter 5 was granted to author Sarah Hallenbeck by the Girl Scouts of Eastern South Carolina.

ACKNOWLEDGMENTS

Quotations from the following songs appear in chapter 9:
Backwater Blues
By Bessie Smith
© 1927 (Renewed), 1974 FRANK MUSIC CORP.
All Rights Reserved
Reprinted by Permission of Hal Leonard Corporation
It Makes My Love Come Down
By Bessie Smith
© 1929 (Renewed), 1974 FRANK MUSIC CORP.
All Rights Reserved
Reprinted by Permission of Hal Leonard Corporation
Young Woman's Blues
By Bessie Smith
© 1927 (Renewed), 1974 FRANK MUSIC CORP.
All Rights Reserved
Reprinted by Permission of Hal Leonard Corporation
Dirty No-Gooder's Blues
By Bessie Smith
© 1929 (Renewed), 1974 FRANK MUSIC CORP.
All Rights Reserved
Reprinted by Permission of Hal Leonard Corporation
Soft Pedal Blues
Words and Music by Bessie Smith
© 1925 (Renewed) FRANK MUSIC CORP.
All Rights Reserved
Reprinted by Permission of Hal Leonard Corporation
Mama's Got The Blues
Words and Music by Sarah Martin and Clarence Williams
Copyright © 1923 UNIVERSAL MUSIC CORP.
Copyright Renewed
All Rights Reserved   Used by permission
Reprinted by Permission of Hal Leonard Corporation

Quotation from the following song appears in chapter 10: "DREADFUL MEMORIES," Alpha Music Inc. All Rights Reserved. Used by Permission. Also in chapter 10: "I Am a Union Woman," written by Molly Jackson; "Death of Harry Simms," written by Jim Garland; and "Hungry Ragged Blues," written by Molly Jackson, © Figs. D Music (BMI) / Stormking Music (BMI). Under license from The Bicycle Music Company, all rights reserved, used by permission.

ACKNOWLEDGMENTS

Chapter 11: Permission to quote from the essay "On What a Pilot Eats," by Amelia Earhart, is provided courtesy of Purdue University Libraries, Virginia Kelly Karnes Archives and Special Collections Research Center.

Chapter 12: Permission to quote from a letter by Alfred Kroeber to Elsie Clews Parsons, 13 April 1929, archived in the Elsie Clews Parsons Papers, American Philosophical Society, Philadelphia, PA, was granted by the Bancroft Library, University of California, Berkeley. And permission to quote from a letter by Ann Axtell Morris to Dorothy Bryan, 18 March 1933, was granted courtesy of Elizabeth Ann Morris and the Morris Family Collections, Bayfield, Colorado (temporary curator, Inga Calvin).

Chapter 15: Permission to quote from various works owned by Hunter College and detailed in this book's list of works cited was granted by the Hunter College Archives and Special Collections.

WOMEN AND RHETORIC BETWEEN THE WARS

Introduction

Ann George, M. Elizabeth Weiser, Janet Zepernick

The 1920s and 1930s represent a tremendous breakthrough for women into American public life. Secretary of Labor Frances Perkins served out the Depression as the first woman cabinet secretary. Nellie Tayloe Ross and Miriam Ferguson became state governors in 1925. Arkansas Democrat Hattie Caraway was the first woman elected to the U.S. Senate (1932), and South Dakota Republican Gladys Pyle joined her a few years later. Elizabeth Gurley Flynn, the Wobblies' original "Rebel Girl," went on to help found the American Civil Liberties Union, while Mary Anderson began her quarter century as director of the Department of Labor Women's Bureau. Meanwhile, Marjorie Merriweather Post took the Postum Cereal Company public in 1922, and Martha Matilda Harper, owner of more than five hundred hair salons, created the modern retail franchise. Hattie McDaniel won what would be the only Academy Award for an African American actress for sixty-three years, Dorothy Parker regaled *New Yorker* readers with her wit, and Betty Robinson became the fastest woman in the world at women track athletes' Olympic debut in 1928. Jane Addams and Dorothy Day were household names if your household believed in peace and social justice. Dr. Florence Sabin was named the first female lifetime member of the National Academy of Sciences, and National Council of Negro Women president Mary McLeod Bethune became the first African American to head a federal agency.

Yet that promising beginning did not yield the flood of women into public and professional life that might have been expected. Indeed, the opening of the twenty-first century, with its striking array of women's "firsts," presents a surreal echo of women's activity in the 1920s–1930s and illustrates powerfully the extent to which women's role in public life has been rendered largely invisible for the period between the passage of the Nineteenth Amendment in 1920 and the latter half of the century—an invisibility we aim to both examine and dislodge in this book. Wendy Sharer writes in the essay on Julia Grace Wales that opens the collection:

> I wish to put forward, both as a lens for studying the past and as a perspective on the present, the idea that rhetorical theories and practices articulated through alternative channels . . . deserve as much attention from scholars and teachers as the rhetorical theories and practices elaborated in more commonly studied forums such as scholarly publications and widely available textbooks.

Women and Rhetoric between the Wars moves the study of gender and rhetorical practices of women entering public and professional life into the period immediately following suffrage, in a broad-based analysis that weaves together feminist cultural criticism, gender studies, historiography, and rhetorical theory.

The Need for Our History

Feminist scholars have repeatedly demonstrated the public activities of women at times and in places where the more superficial gaze of cultural memory tells us women's activities were confined to home and hearth. In spite of this enormous body of richly documented evidence, the culturally shared "memory" of U.S. women's history is that women didn't participate in public life after suffrage or work outside the home until the 1960s advent of "women's lib." A closer look at the history of women's engagement in public life, however, shows a cycle of increased participation in public life followed by increased repression of women's voices, with the result that women in contemporary politics, corporate and union leadership, the sciences, and academia continue to face all the obstacles and hardships of the true pioneer, in spite of the many generations of women who have pioneered much of this same territory in the past.

In part, as feminist historians such as Wendy Sharer and Nancy Cott note, the invisibility of women in public life in periods and activities outside those defined by the woman suffrage movement of the 1860s–1910s and the women's liberation movement of the 1960s–1970s can be understood as a consequence of the shorthand version of women's activism that has come to dominate our thinking. According to the broad brushstrokes of this model, all the activities of women intellectuals, abolitionists, and suffragists of the nineteenth and early twentieth centuries are grouped under the heading of "First Wave Feminism," which culminates in the passage of the Nineteenth Amendment in 1920. A decades-long gap ensues, followed by "Second Wave Feminism," which begins with the publication of *The Feminine Mystique* in 1963 and the founding of the National Organization for Women in 1966. Yet the record clearly shows that after First Wave Feminism, during the 1920s and 1930s, women were remaking the political, scientific, and cultural landscape in monumental ways.[1] This suggests that the "waves" model is fundamentally flawed. In Burkean terms, it acts as a "terministic screen," preventing us from seeing an alternate interpretation of reality ("Terministic Screens" 45). In emphasizing periods of highly visible political activism and anchoring the history of women in public life to these events, the waves model deflects attention away both from the rich history of women's public participation outside the narrow confines of politics and from the ways in which women's contributions have been systematically erased from public memory. Historian Lori D. Ginzberg has argued that "the historical focus on the radical demand for the vote as women's only significant political act . . . has had the effect of both foreshortening and distorting the history of women's participation in the political process" (qtd. in Mattingly 29). In *Women and Rhetoric between the Wars*, therefore, we present examples of women's rhetoric that move us away from the "waves" model toward a more accurate understanding of women's role in the development of both contemporary rhetoric and life.

Creating a Usable Past: Traces of Women in the History of Rhetoric

Like the rhetorical theory that became the New Rhetoric, women's rhetorical practices of the interwar period were influenced by a variety of contemporary forces: reactions to World War I and its failure of political action; an increasingly vocal workers' movement and the intellectual appeal of communism; the turn to the hard sciences both in the academy and for solutions to real-world problems; the emergence of the social sciences and the resultant shift toward psychology, anthropology, and economics to account for human behavior; and of course the possibilities brought about by suffrage. Little of this has been studied for its impact on rhetoric.

This absence of women from the centers of rhetorical activity is unsurprising, for, as Nan Johnson writes, "The boundaries around rhetorical space have been actively patrolled for as long as it has been undeniably clear that to speak well and write convincingly were the surest routes to political, economic, and cultural stature" (2). When women could not be prevented from participating in public discourse, they have been erased from its memory, often so effectively that each generation of women appears to be charting completely new territory as they infiltrate the barriers and navigate the checkpoints at the borders of rhetoric.

Cheryl Glenn's description of the early stages of her work on *Rhetoric Retold: Regendering the Tradition from Antiquity through the Renaissance* illustrates clearly the absence of any history of women's rhetorical practice:

> When I initiated this project, I was told that there were no women in the history of rhetoric, but that, if I wanted to do "negative research," that might be OK. When my archival and library research revealed only brief glimpses of women (glimpses that eventually took me several years to bring into rhetorical focus), I was warned that my project might not unfold as anything but a series of cameo appearances. (173)

Of the impossibility (or at least the extreme difficulty) of creating anything of value from the erasure of a past, American literary critic Van Wyck Brooks writes, "There is a kind of anarchy that prevents growth because it lays too great a strain upon the individual. . . . [I]t results from the sudden unbottling of elements that have had no opportunity to develop freely in the open; it signifies . . . the lack of any sense of inherited resources" (337). The project Glenn undertakes in *Rhetoric Retold* is precisely this work of discovering for women rhetors, in the language Brooks uses, "a usable past" (339), with the early skepticism Glenn reports a clear sign of how much women's voices had been erased from their own rhetorical history.[2] Indeed, what we find is that repeatedly in the twentieth century women's voices are erased and recovered and then erased *again*, in a cycle that makes inaccessible to each new generation the work of those who have gone before.

We need, therefore, to move beyond the (re)recovery that is the traditional focus of feminist historiography and to place the emphasis on creating a *usable* past, one that informs our present and future discipline.³ In a recent CCCC panel on the future of feminist rhetorical scholarship, Glenn advocated the development of new methodologies ("Rhetorics and Feminisms") for rhetorical research. Thus, in addition to our emphasis on the rhetorical significance today of the work of those women we recover, we include in our collection Kay Halasek's work toward just such a method, a more dialogic, ethnographic/contextual, "sidelong" approach to historiography. As she writes:

> I found it necessary to construct both a research methodology and narrative form that could simultaneously account for and was accountable to . . . the women about whom I was writing. I did not find these women using the conventional historical methods I'd learned in graduate school . . . and, as it turned out, I could not adequately represent them using conventional historiographic narrative structures.

To not only recover but to build upon those erased voices, allowing them to change the way we look at both past and future—our history in stereo, as Shirley Wilson Logan put it at the same CCCC panel—is the goal of our collection.

First Findings

The collaboration of the scholars in this collection, then, has shed new light on the rhetoric of the early twentieth century in order to influence rhetoric in the twenty-first century. Women's rhetorical practices of the interwar period, and the theoretical stances underlying their actions, were influenced by a variety of contemporary ideological, geopolitical, macroeconomic, and biographical forces. Each rhetor engaged in persuasive dialogue to live theories whose ramifications impact us today. Our new understandings of women's role in public life and thought of the 1920s–1930s—and hence of the canonical theories we call the New Rhetoric that grew out of this time period—coalesce around three main points: the movement from agency to action, the anticipation of New Rhetoric, and the ultimate underestimation of hegemonic definitions of "women's place."

Moving from Agency to Action

Women's rhetorical practices during the interwar period often—though not always, particularly for women of color—take rhetorical agency as a given and move directly into rhetorical action. Yet the very fact that our cultural memory of public women is largely blank for the period between Carrie Chapman Catt and Gloria Steinem indicates the extent to which that first generation of "entitled" women failed to leave a lasting mark on the public imagination in spite of, or—as several of our contributors argue—because of their success during their own lives.

In the nineteenth century, white middle-class women were indeed trained in rhetoric, as Nan Johnson documents in *Gender and Rhetorical Space in American Life, 1866–1910,* but it was a domestic rather than a public rhetoric, requiring a particular model of feminine behavior that eschewed public display. The postbellum pedagogies targeting women demonstrate the era's uneasiness about women claiming agency to speak in the public sphere as well as men's desire to keep women "domesticated." Yet, as Carol Mattingly demonstrates in *Well-Tempered Women,* female activists (this time from the temperance movement) extended this sense of the domestic sphere into public space, claiming agency by using their domestic personas to argue that social issues were, in fact, family matters and thus the purview of women. As she puts it, the temperance movement was a "tremendous coming to voice" for women in the nineteenth century (6).

Like their white sisters, African American women in the nineteenth century, as Shirley Wilson Logan argues in *"We Are Coming": The Persuasive Discourse of Nineteenth-Century Black Women,* advocated for abolition, temperance, and women's rights, but they also campaigned against mob violence and embarked upon the fraught task of "racial uplift," urging black audiences to work for "empowerment from within" (157). These women, Logan argues, attended to audience accommodation most carefully, employing persuasive strategies that theorists of New Rhetoric would define as presence, association and dissociation, and identification as they negotiated agency through complex "same but different" positions with respect to black men, white women, white men, and less privileged black women.

By the late nineteenth–early twentieth centuries, women both black (e.g., see Royster, *Traces*) and white (see Sharer, *Vote*; and Hollis, *Liberating*) exerted power as agents primarily by shaping public opinion via "rhetorical practices of collaborative, widespread persuasion" (Sharer, *Vote* 16), working through literacy, religious, and reform organizations that enabled networking and built solidarity; establishing their ethos by framing political issues as moral or domestic; drawing upon the increasingly persuasive power of statistics; and establishing presses and public libraries to circulate otherwise ignored views.

INTRODUCTION

What happened to women's rhetoric in the years from the end of the Civil War to the passage of the Nineteenth Amendment, in other words, was a growing subversion of the parlor rhetoric (or outright lack of training) designed to keep women in their place. Working often together in groups, employing domestic tropes in new more public settings, and advocating for social reforms designed to enhance communal life, women opened up what Nan Johnson calls the "rhetorical space" toward "political, economic, and cultural stature" (1–2). That is, in a movement very broadly culminating in suffrage, women by their actions advocated for agency and the right to speak.

Women in the 1920s and 1930s, however, frequently pursued a different agenda. Having won the "official" right to speak with the passage of the Nineteenth Amendment in 1920, and seeming to have won unofficial sanctioning of her place in the public sphere simply by virtue of so many of her sisters joining her there, the woman of the 1920s spent less time demanding a right to speak and more time proving her right to act (and be judged) in accordance with the norms of her chosen field, be it piloting a plane or preaching the gospel or teaching medical students. This purposive identification with a professional ethos owes less to the voluntary associations model and more to the scientific professionalization movement of the late nineteenth century, as Carolyn Skinner documents among women medical professionals of the time. That is, communal activism, while continuing—and we open our collection with chapters arising from this rhetorical scene—was increasingly tempered by professional or broadly social development. As Susan Faludi writes of the era, "The daughters of the suffrage generation were so beyond the 'zealotry' of their elders, Harper's declared in its 1927 article 'Feminist—New Style,' that they could only pity those ranting women who were 'still throwing hand grenades' and making an issue of 'little things'" ("Second-Place Citizens"). Faludi, like the suffragist "elders" of the time, despairs the lack of continued attention to agency. But rhetorically, the assumption of agency meant the assumption of a right to act that led to a plethora of new topics for speaking and writing on the part of women rhetors. As Karyn Hollis argues, for instance, the working-class women studying at the Bryn Mawr Summer School developed an astonishing range of "transgressive reading and writing" practices (117)—labor dramas, resistant autobiographies, poetry, even statistical studies for the U.S. Labor Department—that "took them out of the silence imposed on women and the working class and into the public discursive arena, where they made assertions in a strengthened voice on matters previously denied them," particularly the "erased discourse of dangerous factory work and its toll on their bodies" (118–19, 8).

To be sure, for women of color the postsuffrage era did not offer the same access to public space, as Coretta Pittman argues in "Black Women Writers and the Trouble with Ethos." Various contributors in this volume likewise illustrate that many women either continued to address "the ethos trouble" or publicly flouted its double standard, and their ability to move to action relied in part on the models and mentors for women's public participation found in their own communities. In the main, however, the majority of women in the postsuffrage decades would see at least a relative opening of the public sphere when they compared themselves to their immediate foremothers.

Anticipating the New Rhetoric

The canon of twentieth-century rhetorical theory is dramatically and almost exclusively male until the last two decades of the century. With the exception of Ann Berthoff and the mysterious Lucie Olbrechts-Tyteca,[4] the New Rhetoric might have been developed in a world entirely devoid of women. And yet the women represented by this collection demonstrated a range of rhetorical practices and reflections that equal the New Rhetoric in technical sophistication.

In the New Rhetoric developing during and after World War II, the Aristotelian belief that "audiences are moved by means of language" became a tripartite focus on *language* as symbolic action for persuasion that united divided humans, on *dialogue* as the preeminent means by which such persuasion should occur, and on *communally constructed truths* as the aim of dialogue. The silencing (and temporary failure) of public discourse during the war, in other words, provided theorists with the exigency to turn their inchoate beliefs into the full-fledged theories that continue to shape our sense of contemporary rhetoric.

Women, however, were absent from the theoretical discussions shaping these rhetorical developments. As both Patricia Bizzell and Jane Donawerth observe, sometimes women's theory looks very much like that of canonical men, but, more often, it looks very different, perhaps not even directly addressing persuasion (Bizzell 51; Donawerth xv–xvi)—and, we would add, perhaps not being contained in a verbal text at all. We see this lived rhetorical theory again and again in the stories of the women of 1920–1940.

Women in many fields were, first, using the rhetorical power of *language* to change perceptions of themselves and of those for whom they advocated. Thus, while I. A. Richards lectured on the interinanimation of words, Dorothy Day's religious rhetoric juxtaposed concepts from multiple genres to promote an identifiable space for social action. While Kenneth Burke argued with the general semanticists as to whether the bias inherent in human attitude could be overcome with scientific language, women scientists' and social scientists' experience demonstrated that science was far from neutral, and Gertrude Bonnin and Jovita González demonstrated that, indeed, purposive subjectivity and persuasive identification were often called for. And while literary critics across the political spectrum, from John Crowe Ransom to Granville Hicks, debated the role of poetics in politics, Bessie Smith and Aunt Molly Jackson used aesthetic experience as a platform from which to voice the silenced, and women aviators fused themselves with their planes to create symbolic platforms from which to promote a changed social reality.

Many of the women in our collection, particularly the women educators and peace activists such as Julia Grace Wales and Helen Cone, were also living—and writing and promoting—the focus on ongoing *dialogue* that became the second hallmark of the later New Rhetoric, and the erasure of their written theorizing is particularly noteworthy.

Finally, the women in our collection, forging their way in this new public rhetorical space, often had an intuitive affinity for the third aspect of the New Rhetoric, *communally constructed truths* as the aim of rhetorical dialogue—and we end our collection with a series of chapters demonstrating what Risa Applegarth terms this community-formation strategy in professional situations. While Stephen Toulmin and the team of Chaim Perelman and Lucie Olbrechts-Tyteca analyzed probabilistic arguments to determine ways that communities could reasonably determine what they "knew" to be true, groups of women from Girl Scouts to professional anthropologists were carrying on the tradition of voluntary associations in public life, deliberating together just what it meant to become co-equal members of public society.

Underestimating Hegemony

Powerful women of the interwar period were not exceptions to the rule. However, though they often recognized the challenges of a rhetorical situation still dominated by a largely male audience, they were not fully aware of the emotional power of the status quo, and their attempts to demonstrate the fitness of women for all forms of public action often failed to account for the incredible power of a pietistic hegemony, according to which women were "by definition" understood not to play certain "inappropriate" roles.

The failure of individual women's successes—and we include in this collection a selection of chapters demonstrating both the power and the pitfalls of this individual popularity—to translate into broad-based or institutional success should give us pause. What has kept these women's achievements from playing a role in the larger history and theory of their era? Certainly, in both the nineteenth and twentieth centuries, war and its aftermath prompted the erasure of women's roles through the silencing of their voices in the public sphere. Nan Johnson argues that the post–Civil War distress of a nation that had lost its moorings produced a powerful need to reorient American life around an ideal and idealized home. Essential to this process was a reassertion of the purely domestic and arhetorical nature of American womanhood (19–20). A similar erasure of women's public influence occurred after World War I, when the opposition to women's peace activism reappeared with great force—an erasure that picked up again with the beginning of U.S. involvement in World War II. The Cold War era, in turn, brought forth a desire for hearth and home that would have been recognizable to women activists from the Civil War.

Thus, America has managed to forget many of the women of this era, and their lived rhetoric did not translate into the rhetorical canon. Our contributors often point to the contradictory public identities these women constructed for themselves—such as Amelia Earhart's "sweetheart of the skies," Bessie Smith's "empress of the blues," or Frances Perkins's representation of herself as the political novice in Roosevelt's cabinet. Most of all, though, the women of this generation, in believing that their own door-opening movement into public life represented a sustainable change in the status quo, erred in overestimating the power of example and underestimating the power of what Burke called *piety*— the deeply seated devotion to a way of being in the world, "the sense of what properly goes with what" (e.g., a woman's place is in the home), the "scrupulous sense of the appropriate" (*Permanence* 74, 77). Many women from the interwar period, like the culture at large, adopted a scientific worldview, becoming skilled makers of data-driven arguments, confident in the persuasive power of evidence-based inductive reasoning to counter gender or racial stereotypes. Thus, for instance, the early-twentieth-century historiographer Mary Beard founded the

INTRODUCTION

World Center for Women's Archives to document the range of women's activity throughout history; as Julie Des Jardins explains, if anyone questioned women's fitness for a particular occupation or position of authority, Beard wanted to be able to point to specific precedents to refute the challenge (226). It is clear that many of the women discussed in this volume saw themselves (and specific other successful women) as examples that "disproved" cultural preconceptions about women's interests and capabilities. However, facts never speak for themselves; they are always interpreted through existing cultural pieties, including gender roles, such that "even something so 'objectively there' as behavior must be observed through one or another kind of terministic screen, that directs the attention in keeping with its nature" (Burke, *Language* 49). Culturally, that is, arguments about women's work proceed not inductively but deductively: if, "by definition," women are not powerful politicians or CEOs or mechanics, then one example or a hundred or even a thousand will be perceived merely as individual exceptions, especially when separated by distance or time. While a successful individual showed what *one* woman could do, multiple examples did not suggest what women in general could do, nor did they dislodge larger cultural beliefs about what women *should* do. After all, gender itself is a socially agreed upon definition rather than an "objective description of inherent traits" (Scott qtd. in Glenn 2), a term existing only in relation to other social ideals. As a social category, "women should" is fraught with long-standing cultural limitations that in the 1920s and 1930s led to an undervaluing of the symbolic action of successful women, with the result that rhetorical theory is only now gaining an understanding of the performative, conservative, bodily, and other rhetorics composed and practiced by these women.

In short, if the scholars of contemporary canonical rhetoric exist in the conversational parlor envisioned by Kenneth Burke, then the careers of the women collected here demonstrate decisively that after World War I women entered that parlor in ever greater numbers. They were standing in the conversational knots that discussed current events, economic and academic policies, and ethical choices. However, when it came time to turn those conversations into theory, it was as if the men left the room to go smoke cigars together. Women may have moved from the parlor rhetoric of the nineteenth century to the rhetorical parlor of the twentieth, but their undeniably feminine bodies still served to screen their words from incorporation into the rhetorical memory of the written canon.

A Return to Invisibility: Why This Matters

It is not then surprising that the major gains made by women in the years between the wars would be so quickly erased and then forgotten. To be feminist in the 1940s and 1950s was to be "radical"—and radical during wartime is unpatriotic. It would take two decades until a woman's theoretical insights—Betty Friedan's *The Feminine Mystique* (1963)—would jumpstart what would become Second Wave Feminism, but by then a generation of idealized domesticity had obscured the gains of women in the postsuffrage era, as Friedan's opening chapter points out:

> [Women] learned that truly feminine women do not want careers, higher education, political rights—the independence and the opportunities that the old-fashioned feminists had fought for. Some women, in their forties and their fifties, still remembered painfully giving up those dreams, but most of the younger women no longer even thought about them. (16)

Lest we think that such silencing is finally a thing of the past, Susan Faludi documents a similar threat to women's public voice in the years immediately following the attacks of 9/11. In *The Terror Dream*, she makes a convincing case from innumerable examples that, just as in the Cold War, the anxiety of an attack on American soil became perceived as an attack on American manhood, and therefore "the illusion of a mythic America where women needed men's protection and men succeeded in providing it" became a controlling metaphor.

Even a decade after 9/11, we still see the backlash to women's 1970s reentrance into public life, and we are once again at a point at which it would be easy for women's participation in public life to be erased. Women's public gains are frequently embattled, and they are not matched by gains in domestic equality. We are living today in an era when too many of us are complacent at a time we cannot afford to be—and our forgotten grandmothers and great-grandmothers of the interwar years show us why. In *Women and Rhetoric between the Wars*, then, we aim to recapture often unexpected women rhetors of the postsuffrage era, to examine their often unexpectedly radical and unexpectedly successful rhetoric, and to consider the cultural conditions that limited their own achievements and the achievements of women in general, not merely to recover the past but to learn from it.

We do not offer this collection as an exhaustive treatment of women's rhetoric between the wars—indeed, we celebrate the fact that many,

many more women contributed to the history of rhetoric in this time period than this collection could begin to cover. Politicians and activists such as Eleanor Roosevelt, Mary McLeod Bethune, Molly Dewson, Ellen Sullivan Woodward, and Ella Reeve ("Mother") Bloor; education reformers such as Lucile Spence, Gertrude Ayer, and Layle Lane; social scientists like Margaret Mead, Ella Cara Deloria, Mary Beard, and Zora Neale Hurston; writers and editors such as Muriel Rukeyser, Josephine Herbst, Harriet Monroe, and Marguerite Tjader Harris; artists and performers such as Dorothea Lange, Hallie Flanagan, and Bette Davis; and so many others—and so many communal enterprises (among them, the Women's Trade Union League, Women's Speakers' Bureau, Women's National Democratic Club, National Association of Colored Women, Daughters of the American Revolution, American Association of University Women)—represent a vast uncharted territory for the field of rhetoric. We fervently hope this collection sparks interest in both the women and their remarkable era.

There is much work to be done because—more than recovery of individuals—what we aim for in this collection is to begin the reexamination of the rhetorical tradition that has placed these women's insights outside the mainstream, to consider the uncredited ways they may have influenced that mainstream, and to posit a revised sense of just what "rhetoric" is all about. Women between the wars were not only "using" rhetoric; they were also creating rhetorical theories to produce their work. They were speaking new theories, enacting them, and even writing them down—but they were writing in ways the mainstream either did not see or did not acknowledge as "theory." Thus our ultimate goal is to spark changes in our methods, our thought, and our canon when we add these women's lived rhetoric into our common history.

A Brief Overview of the Collection

We divide our chapters among three scenes that shape the type of rhetoric possible, framing the rhetorical situation for women rhetors as they defined and were defined by audiences whose expectations determined who could speak, what types of speech were possible, and what were the allowable goals and purposes. We begin with a familiar scene for women's public voices at the time, that of women's voluntary associations. This scene produced many of the highest-profile women of the abolition movement, suffrage, peace activism, and the campaign for industrial safety; and until the 1930s, this was the context for women's discourse that had the most immediate contact with and influence on the still almost exclusively male scene of legislative action. Within this scene, Wendy Sharer's "Continuous Mediation: Julia Grace Wales's New Rhetoric" analyzes Wales's plan for collaborative negotiation of international conflict and her pedagogy for democratic citizenship, arguing that the rhetorical principles Wales developed bear striking similarities to later Burkean and Rogerian rhetoric. Hephzibah Roskelly continues the focus on peace activism in "The Hope for Peace and Bread," a study of Jane Addams's two memoirs from the interwar decades that together create a rhetoric that helps test and develop pragmatic thought. Elizabeth Wilkinson writes in "Gertrude Bonnin's Transrhetorical Fight for Land Rights" that Bonnin/Zitkala-Ša's bi-cultural life experience as a Native American woman educated at elite schools gave her the materials from which to create a juxtaposition of indigenous and sentimental tropes in an influential congressional study of Indian land probate. Janet Zepernick rereads Frances Perkins's memoir of the Roosevelt administration, *The Roosevelt I Knew*, as an autobiographical introduction to the micro-rhetoric of participation in any loosely hierarchical, goal-directed organization. And Sarah Hallenbeck's "Working Together and Being Prepared: Early Girl Scouting as Citizenship Training" demonstrates that the Girl Scouts likewise sought to open the civic arena to young women by instilling the attitudes and behaviors that prepare young men for participation in public life.

We then move to the scene of popular or celebrity status, which allowed entry into public life for many women from less inherently privileged backgrounds. This is the only scene in which the audience is in any sense "the public" or "the masses," with the result that agents in this scene have the greatest reach, yet its scenic expectations limit its functional scope to the realm of the epideictic. In "Reading Helen Keller," Ann George shows the limitations of celebrity as a source of rhetorical agency and argues that Keller's disabled body both enabled her rhetoric (her body made her famous) and constrained her rhetoric by "persuading" the public to read her one-dimensionally. In "Dorothy Day: Personalizing (to) the Masses," Elizabeth Weiser shows how social activist Day translated radical concepts of social theory for her mainstream American audience, inviting an identification with others in ways later theorized by her brother-in-law Kenneth Burke. Sandra Robinson, in "The Shocking Morality of Nannie Helen Burroughs," analyzes the Baptist educator's strategic violations of decorum in the cause of racial uplift. Coretta Pittman's analysis of the legendary blues singer in "Bessie Smith's Blues as Rhetorical Agency" examines Smith's use of her lyrics and behavior to claim an unconventional, sexual self who opposed both race- and class-based forms of oppression. Meanwhile, folksinger Aunt Molly Jackson, as Cassandra Parente shows in "Traditional Form, Subversive Function: Aunt Molly Jackson's Labor Struggles," forges the inscribed communal *doxa* with her body to speak authentically to/for an audience identifying with the self she constructs through her music. And Sara Hillin in "Sweethearts of the Skies" demonstrates how early pilots Amelia Earhart, Bessie Coleman, and Florence Klingensmith fused their bodies with their planes to create an aerocyborg identity that allowed them to challenge the limitations imposed by race and gender.

The final scene, academia, represents a professional path newly emergent for large numbers of women between the wars. It is in some ways even more exclusive than the scene represented by women's voluntary associations, yet it also offered more opportunity for professional advancement by women who were able to subvert those exclusionary practices. Risa Applegarth's "Field Guides: Women Writing Anthropology" argues that women anthropologists responded to the gendered obstacles of their field by creating alternative opportunities using the paired strategies of popularization and community formation. Kathy Jurado demonstrates the subversive nature of scholarship in "'Have We Not a Mind Like They?': Jovita González on Nation and Gender," which brings to light the Tejana folklorist's reframing of the border narrative to position Mexican Americans as natives and teachers of their Anglo counterparts at a time of expanding Latino activism. Jordynn Jack's "'Exceptional Women': Epideictic Rhetoric and Women Scientists" sounds a cautionary note, examining career guides and popular media reports of women in the sciences to argue that the praise of exceptional women promoted a "bootstraps" rhetoric that made individual women responsible for their success and attributed failure to lack of ability. And finally, Kay Halasek in "'Long I Followed Happy Guides': Activism, Advocacy, and English Studies," looks at the texts of Helen Cone and Adele Bildersee, who used their positions as English professors to teach generations of students to translate ideals of dialogue into action long before such later textbooks as *Rhetoric: Discovery and Change*. At the same time, Halasek uses her own position as a rhetorical scholar exploring new methodologies for historiographic research to teach future scholars how to foreground methodology as we continue the work of feminist scholarship into the next generation.

Taken together, the collection both paints and complicates the picture of this understudied era. Yes, women and rhetoric forged a partnership between the wars that led to many stunning successes and trailblazing accomplishments. But their erasure from both memory and the rhetorical canon should give us pause as we look with clearer eyes at our own new successes and accomplishments in the opening of this century, which so eerily echoes their own.

Notes

1. Susan Ware's *Beyond Suffrage: Women and the New Deal* and *Holding Their Own: American Women in the 1930s*, for instance, document the wide range of women's contributions to Depression-era politics and culture.

2. Jacquelyn Jones Royster's *Traces in a Stream* and Carolyn Skinner's "Medical Interventions" document that women professionals of the nineteenth century were also repeatedly trying to recover their own "usable pasts."

3. Weiser discusses the contribution of historical work to contemporary theory formation in "'As Usual I Fell on the Bias': Kenneth Burke's Situated Dialectic."

4. Barbara Warnick spoke on "Lucie Olbrechts-Tyteca and *les Couples philosophiques*" at the National Communication Association annual meeting, Chicago, IL, Nov. 2007.

VOLUNTARY ASSOCIATIONS for the CIVIC SCENE

Continuous Mediation:
Julia Grace Wales's New Rhetoric

Wendy B. Sharer

Frustrated by the inability of traditional diplomacy to prevent war, representatives of various suffrage and women's peace organizations from around the globe gathered at The Hague in 1915 to form the International Congress of Women for Permanent Peace (ICWPP). One particularly important participant in that first meeting of the ICWPP was Julia Grace Wales, an instructor (and later professor) of English at the University of Wisconsin. Wales presented to the new organization her proposal, "Mediation without Armistice: The Wisconsin Plan," which articulated methods of international communication that might end the Great War before the utter defeat of either side. Wales called for and explained the rhetorical groundwork of an international conference of nondiplomatic experts (economists, scientists, scholars, religious leaders, etc.), drawn from neutral countries, which would write and revise terms for peace until those terms were acceptable to the belligerent nations. The Wales Plan was robust and practical enough that, four months earlier, members of the Wisconsin state legislature had approved a resolution endorsing it and recommending it to the U.S. Congress for consideration.

The Wales Plan was heartily endorsed by the women gathered at The Hague. The ICWPP then elected committees of leading women, including Wales and ICWPP president Jane Addams, to present the plan to the governments of Europe, where it was received with high praise. No country's leader, an article in the *Woman Century* explained,

> objected to this [plan] . . . being tried and several gave hearty commendation. Sir Edward Grey [British Foreign Secretary] said he certainly could not object as he had tried a somewhat similar plan to end the Balkan War. The neutral Governments of Europe approved the plan, but were afraid to call the conference without the aid of the United States. Two of them offered to call it in their countries if the United States would agree to send a representative. (Lawrence)

In an effort to respond to these urgings for the United States' involvement, the Wales Plan was presented to President Woodrow Wilson on November 12, 1915, by David Starr Jordan, noted peace activist and first president of Stanford University, and Louis P. Lochner, peace activist and foreign correspondent who would go on to win the Pulitzer Prize and serve as the director of the Berlin Bureau of the Associated Press ("White House Interview" 1).

Despite its favorable reception among European leaders and despite widespread calls for the U.S. government to become officially involved in such a model of mediation—in November 1915, "10,000 telegrams were sent out . . . asking that the plan be adopted [and] meetings were held all over the country[;] in Boston alone there were eight in one day" (Lawrence)—President Wilson remained hesitant to commit the United States to this kind of negotiation. Although official endorsement from the United States was not forthcoming, the Wales Plan did receive significant financial support from Henry Ford. With Ford's funding, Jane Addams explains in *Peace and Bread in Time of War*, a Neutral Conference of Experts—including Julia Grace Wales—commenced work in Stockholm in late January 1916. That conference put the Wales Plan into action and, Addams suggests, elevated Wales's ideas to the point that they would be echoed in the famous Fourteen Points speech delivered by President Wilson in 1918:

> At Easter, 1916, the Conference issued an appeal to "The Governments, Parliaments and People of Belligerent Nations." This was the result of much study, and was founded upon an intelligent effort to obtain the various nationalistic points of view. An enormous correspondence on the subject had taken place, and representatives of many nationalities had appeared before the Conference. . . . This official appeal to the belligerent nations, foreshadowing the famous fourteen points, was also widely published. (42–43)

Yet American popular opinion shifted during the latter part of 1916 and early 1917, and as the country moved closer to its April 1917 entrance to the war, Ford ended his support and the work of the Neutral Conference came to a halt. Still, the Wales Plan, as enacted in the Neutral Conference, had brought the idea of continuous mediation to the world stage, and that idea would continue to influence structures of international negotiation for decades.

In the remainder of this chapter, I will examine some of the main rhetorical principles Wales articulated in her 1915 plan and some ways in which she modified her rhetorical approach to international negotiation over the next several decades. One of my goals is to articulate the value of the largely unheralded work that Wales accomplished. This is, then, a recovery effort. But beyond bringing attention to a woman who, I believe, deserves recognition in the histories of rhetoric, I wish to publicize Wales's work for at least two other reasons. First, I wish to put forward, both as a lens for studying the past and as a perspective on the present, the idea that rhetorical theories and practices articulated through alternative channels—such as the publications and conferences of women's organizations and adult education materials—deserve as much attention from scholars and teachers as the rhetorical theories and practices elaborated in more commonly studied forums such as scholarly publications and widely available textbooks. To this end, I weave throughout this chapter a discussion of how Wales's perspectives on argument and negotiation parallel the work of some well-known, well-respected scholars and teachers of the New Rhetoric in the latter part of the twentieth century. Second, I hope that this chapter will encourage others to engage in the hard but important work of finding and publicizing rhetorical contributions such as Wales's and that it will help historians of rhetoric remain attuned to the difficulties that women—with the possible exception of a very few well-known and, in their time, widely recognized rhetors such as Jane Addams—have faced in trying to be heard (see Hephzibah Roskelly's chapter in this collection on Addams's own difficulties advocating for peace).

Wales's New Rhetoric of Continuous Mediation

The cessation of talks between warring parties, Wales argued in 1915, was an onerous tradition. The longer belligerents fought without any attempts at discussion, she explained, the greater the likelihood that "the fighting peoples [will] get up theories about each other by which each contrives to think of the other as something not human, as 'barbaric' or 'satanic' or something, so that each begins to act inhumanely without being itself inhumane'" (Letter to Committee 4). Lack of communication, in other words, allows countries to dehumanize one another, which allows for violence to continue in the mode of "winner take all" international relations.

Wales recognized that the winner/loser dichotomy that informed warfare also informed the practices of diplomatic discourse that had failed to prevent international violence. In her "International Plan for Continuous Mediation without Armistice," a slightly revised version of the original Wisconsin Plan, Wales asserts that, because traditional methods of diplomatic dialogue—or, more accurately, diplomatic silence—during times of international crisis had failed to prevent large-scale violence, "the situation calls for a conference cast in a new and larger mould." Conventional diplomats, Wales argues, are too accustomed to protecting their nation's interests to lead innovative, productive negotiating sessions ("Appendix" 169). Rather than a meeting of heads of state in which each participant would consider primarily the interests of his nation, Wales proposes a meeting of "persons drawn from social, economic, and scientific fields who have genuine international experience" ("Appendix" 164). What makes international experience "genuine," according to Wales, is its basis in globally defined criteria that value not national greed but international human livelihood. Continuous mediation among this group of experts would begin "as an attempt to discover those principles which underlie the welfare of all and which would constitute a foundation for permanent peace." Among this group of experts from neutral nations, Wales asserts, the sources of international disagreements "will be approached from the standpoint of world citizenship" ("Continuous Mediation" 6). Criteria for any proposal to resolve diplomatic disagreements would be based on principles of "international righteousness," would emanate from "an international political faith," and would "restore the shaken faith of humanity and enable it to set its face with new hope toward the goal of ultimate World Federation" (*Mediation* 5). While Wales does not provide specifics about what constitutes "international righteousness," she does explain that "the initial standing proposals [offered by the group of experts] . . . should be based on some universal principles . . . which govern the welfare of all" (12). As a result of the truly international principles from which their rhetorical practices derive, Wales maintains, "the words of the neutral conference will not be the words of neutral or warring powers. They will be the voice of a world striving to utter itself" ("Mediation"). Wales recognized that nationalist perspectives colored interpretations of the war and the events that led to it. She believed that, in order for international negotiation to succeed, the shared purposes of the negotiators needed to derive not from local but rather global interests. Higher principles of human goodness needed to replace more provincial understandings of advantage, and peoples the world over had to be made to see that the interests of the world population should coincide with the interests of a given class, group, or nation.

Although her ideas have not achieved similar scholarly acclaim, Wales's focus on finding commonality in the face of international crisis appears similar to the focus of work by scholars of the so-called New Rhetoric in the 1950s and 60s. Explaining the rise of the New Rhetoric, Doug Brent suggests that the violent and tumultuous events of history greatly influenced these "new" approaches to rhetoric: "The advent of nuclear weapons ha[d] made conflict resolution not just an ideal but a matter of human survival. In response to these social forces, the speech communication specialists of the 50s and 60s began to shift their interests from persuasion, the traditional goal of rhetoric, to the promotion of mutual cooperation" (453). This shift away from antagonistic debate and toward collaborative conflict resolution is remarkably similar to what Wales proposed in 1915 in *Mediation without Armistice*.

Brent further explains that, for the promoters of the New Rhetoric, "the traditional tools of rhetoric no longer seemed fully adequate" to perform cooperative functions or achieve cooperative ends. The developers and practitioners of the New Rhetoric, like Wales nearly half a century earlier, recognized that the assumption of shared perspectives that informed Aristotelian argument, while perhaps usable in the homogeneous society of classical Greece, did not hold up to the myriad backgrounds and assumptions brought to bear on twentieth-century communication. Like Wales, the New Rhetoricians realized that alternative rhetorical frameworks were needed to navigate the many sites of difference in the modern world. Kenneth Burke's notion of "identification," as elaborated in *A Rhetoric of Motives*, was part of his attempt to develop such an alternative framework. For Burke, identification is "any of the wide variety of means by which an author may establish a shared sense of values, attitudes, and interests with his readers" (243). Gregory Clark explains that Burke viewed the rhetorical principle of identification as an important counter to the more traditional principle of persuasion. Persuasion, for Burke, is the motif of the old mode of rhetoric, a mode characterized by "invective, eristic, polemic and logomachy" (*RM* 20). These old ways of operating, Clark explains, simply did not seem usable to Burke by the late 1940s, after he had "witnessed the contentious first half of the 20th century that culminated in the Nazi holocaust and the invention of nuclear warfare." *A Rhetoric of Motives*, according to Clark, is "a 333-page attempt to offer a survivable alternative" to the aggressive rhetorical model of agonistic persuasion, a model that history had proven to be very, very dangerous. Burke's comments in *A Rhetoric of Motives* support this characterization:

> [W]e need never deny the presence of strife, enmity, faction as a characteristic motive of rhetorical expression. . . . We can be on alert always to see how such temptations . . . are implicit in the institutions that condition human relationships; yet we can . . . always look beyond this order, to the principle of identification in general, a terministic choice justified by the fact that the identifications in the order of love are also characteristic of rhetorical expression. (20)

Moving beyond the narrow scope of national identity to the broader one of international identification based on the common good—two of Wales's primary goals in her plan for "Continuous Mediation without Armistice"—are clearly akin to the rhetoric Burke proposes.

Alternative Means: Educational Sites for Rhetorical Innovation

Just as Wales's theories have not received serious consideration from historians of rhetoric to date, her ideas about negotiation and peaceful rhetoric, despite their merit, were not given serious consideration in many "official" channels in her time. The lack of official support from President Wilson, the demise of the Neutral Conference, and the entry of the United States into World War I convinced Wales to seek alternative means to put her rhetorical principles into practice. In fact, Wales saw the university as uniquely positioned to build the foundations required for international identification and rhetorical change. Throughout her writings, she infused her work as an educator and an academic with a rhetorical spirit of cooperation and constructive interaction. In a typescript of an article called "Some By Ways of Peace Work," Wales suggests that teachers are perhaps most valuable as rhetorical conduits for the development of a peaceful internationalism:

I want to stress just one thing, and that is that a teacher can do much with the mere *turn of phrase*. *With the turn of a phrase one can kill or one can make alive.* One can emphasize difficulties, discords, cynicism and pessimism, human weakness, failure, hatred, selfishness, and by emphasizing them tend to strengthen or even create them. Or one can bring in to the strong light those more positive things of harmony and the larger altruism that create courage and hope and the will to constructive action. (1)

Instructors of composition, Wales argued in "The Legitimate Uses of Reading and Discussion in Freshman and Sophomore Composition," an article submitted to *College English* in 1946, can be particularly important to the development of the cooperative, dialogic rhetorical attitudes and practices that foster understanding rather than agonism:

> The student should learn to respect other opinions as his own, to state them fairly, to try to understand them sympathetically. I think one reason why students often turn away from new materials almost with fear is that they have the notion that it must be either swallowed whole or rejected; naturally—and rightly, if this is the only alternative—they have an impulse to reject it. . . . He is less afraid of new ideas when he finds at the end of any piece of reading, he is privileged and encouraged to sort up its ideas tentatively into *Yes, No,* and *query*. He must learn to analyze, accept, reject, combine, draw tentative conclusions, be undogmatic, have the courage of his own convictions, take in new data, make new tests, revise, suspend his judgment, come to working conclusions, and go ahead with them. (5)

One can hear Wales teaching the same curriculum to the stubborn diplomatic leaders who would not support the Wales Plan for Continuous Mediation. Unfortunately, *College English* never published the article.

The rhetorical principles of continuous mediation, Wales believed, might also be found in graduate education, where the conversations of academic research should embody the rhetorical principles of continuous revision and negotiation. In the rhetorical mechanisms of specialized academic research, Wales explains in a 1941 article in the AAUP bulletin,

> there is perpetual checking and testing, perpetual challenge, defense, and modification. . . . All conclusions are forever open to re-examination, inch by inch. The case is never closed. And out of the whole process comes the steady and vast growth of knowledge. The duty

> to seek publication, once results have been reached, rests squarely upon this principle. Publication is the only means of sharing results and bringing them to critical test; it is the only way that composite work can be carried on adequately. ("Graduate Study" 436)

In other words, publication of ideas in scholarly outlets is akin to the public presentation of proposals for resolving international conflicts. The process of research, like the process of international negotiation, must be conceived of as a continuous dialogue, one in which all points are open to revision, the outcome of which is continued advancement on a much broader scale.

In many ways, Wales's attitude toward the teaching of reading, writing, and research in the university mirrors a germinal work of the New Rhetoric in the field of composition studies: Richard Young, Alton Becker, and Kenneth Pike's textbook, *Rhetoric: Discovery and Change* (1970). According to Brent, it grew, as did Burke's *A Rhetoric of Motives*, out of a perceived need to change rhetorical practices to better suit the international climate of communications. Young, Becker, and Pike point directly to contemporary globalizing tendencies in explaining the impetus for their work in the book's first chapter:

> Profound changes are taking place in the system of Western values that has for centuries guided conduct and provided social stability and continuity between generations. Thus it becomes more and more difficult to reason from ethical assumptions that are generally accepted. . . . As a result of rapid and mass means of communication and transportation, our world is becoming smaller, and all of us are learning to become citizens of the world, confronting people whose beliefs are radically different from our own and with whom we must learn to live. It has become imperative to develop a rhetoric that has as its goal not skillful verbal coercion but discussion and exchange of ideas. (8)

Young, Becker, and Pike also focus on listening or reading in a nonjudgmental way. Brent explains that *Rhetoric: Discovery and Change* was steeped in the so-called Dialogic Rhetoric movement, described thus by Richard Johannesen: "The essential movement in dialogue is turning toward, outgoing to, and reaching for the other. And a basic element in dialogue is 'seeing the other' or 'experiencing the other side.' One also does not forego his own convictions or views, but he strives to understand those of the other and avoids imposing his own on the other" (qtd. in Brent 453–54). In Brent's words, "Young, Becker and

Pike lead their audience to internalize an idea that . . . there are many ways of seeing the world, each with its own areas of validity" (456). Young, Becker, and Pike also emphasize cooperative and collaborative rhetoric through their construction of "Rogerian Rhetoric." As they explain it, Rogerian Rhetoric "attempts to do these three things: (1) to convey to the reader that he is understood, (2) to delineate the area within which [the writer] believes the reader's position to be valid, (3) to induce [the reader] to believe that he and the writer share similar moral qualities (honesty, integrity, and good will) and aspirations (the desire to discover a mutually acceptable solution)" (275). The goal of these steps is to "reduce the reader's sense of threat so that he will be able to consider alternatives that may contribute to the creation of a more accurate image of the world and to the elimination of conflict between reader and writer" (274–75). The goal, in other words, "is thus not to work one's will on others but to establish and maintain communication *as an end in itself*" (8).

Wales's theories of cooperative, collaborative communication were clearly informed by similar principles. Writing in *New Age* in August 1940, for instance, Wales advocates methods of cooperation and compromise that begin with constructive, supportive listening and reading. In "Pro, Not Anti: A Principle of Integration," she laments that "this has been an age of criticism, especially of challenging and adverse criticism, when the faults of nations, races, and institutions of all kinds have had more emphasis than their good qualities" (9). In contrast with these destructive approaches to critique, Wales urges a more positive method that she called "free cooperation without compromise":

> The technique that may afford a way out is to work with emphasis on pro the right rather than on anti the wrong. If we work pro the right, the wrong will tend to take care of itself. Criticism itself can be thrown into a positive, constructive, and co-operative form. If half the energy that now goes into telling what ought not to be done could be put into suggesting what ought to be done, we should begin to go forward and not back. (9)

Perhaps motivated by beliefs similar to those that moved Young, Becker, and Pike to write *Rhetoric: Discovery and Change* twenty-five years later, Wales decided in 1942 to put her rhetorical theory into the form of a textbook to teach future generations how to avoid the ineffectual models of communication that had failed to prevent war. In *Democracy Needs Education*, Wales explains that she wished to present "a practical instrument that anyone can use in carrying on the moral fight for democracy . . . designed for reading and discussion in the home and in all kinds of youthful and adult study groups." The book, she continues, "puts the stress on constant human aspects, and the questions point the way to individual study of changing conditions, local, national, and international" (n. pag.).

Much of *Democracy Needs Education* espouses the same kind of rhetorical principles that informed the Wales Plan. The textbook teaches, for instance, that a constructive attitude is critical to a successful democracy on any scale: "It is best to take trouble or the threat of trouble not with fault finding and self-pity but in the most positive and constructive spirit. Instead of using all our energy being anti this and anti that . . . we shall be wise to turn our eyes steadily toward the goal ahead, pull a strong oar, and cut the waves as best we can" (7). Not only is a constructive spirit essential, so too is an orderly procedure that moves from the presentation of multiple ideas, to the winnowing down of those ideas, to the selection of the best possible ideas. Once again, the progression of thinking, discussing, and revising follows the rhetorical steps set out in "Continuous Mediation."

Throughout the book, Wales also reminds readers to focus on broader sites of identification and to consider the international perspective. A truly democratic citizen must, she instructs, keep "an intelligent view of his own interests." In other words, citizens must put their interests in proper perspective: "The smaller interest must always be put second to the larger. . . . No family is safe in an unhealthy and corrupt community; no community is safe in a badly governed and disorganized nation; no nation has much security in a war-like world." Thus, she explains, "the individual voter needs to keep a national and world-wide view in mind" (36). To keep both views in mind, Wales recommends that citizens read from various news sources, both national and international, along with "perhaps a church weekly." Other publications to promote the rhetorical features of careful listening to and reading of various viewpoints within democratic life, she explains, will need to be developed. She advocates, for instance, "a non partisan publication" that, like the texts produced by the conference of neutral experts she had proposed over twenty-five years earlier, would include "both programmes together with the best arguments to support them, *under one cover*, so that the voter will be sure to have both sides before him at once" (37).

The final chapter of *Democracy Needs Education* deals with what Wales perhaps saw as the ultimate goal of the book and, indeed, of her life's work: "Democracy and World Citizenship." She begins the chapter with the assertion that "it is the plainest of all facts that no nation can live a life that is safe and sound if it lives only unto itself" (100). Accordingly, a citizen of a democracy should "know the history of efforts toward international organization," international economic policies, "and the great problem of how to overcome racial prejudice and promote mutual respect and good will among all peoples" (101). Citizens should also be responsible for teaching future generations a perspective that sees all problems as connected and in need of collaborative address:

> The most important work is to teach the children and young people to think in world terms. There must be a habit of thinking of the problems of all peoples as bound up together and of their welfare as one thing. Only as international understanding grows and as the desire for universal justice and good will becomes the mental habit of a whole generation, can adequate ways be found to meet the technical problems of world intercourse. (102)

The questions Wales poses for readers at the end of this final chapter suggest that she still has faith in the ideal of continuous mediation and that she wishes, even near the end of her career, to pass along this faith to her students and to have them consider how that ideal has, or has not, been met in the practices of contemporary diplomacy: "What efforts have been made in the past," she asks, "to establish permanent instruments on international justice, conciliation, etc.?" Understanding the history of rhetorical methods of international negotiation can then inform responses to her next question about the failure of these efforts to prevent a second world war: "In what ways has the League of Nations been useful? What were the factors that kept it from being an effective instrument for the prevention of war?" The final two questions of the chapter shift to the positive, asking students to consider what to do next to promote her rhetorical ideal: "What are the hopeful elements in the international situation at present? How can we as individuals best help to develop and spread the spirit of world citizenship?" (107).

Conclusion

After the publication of *Democracy Needs Education*, throughout World War II and the settlements that followed, Wales continued to advocate for the principles of continuous mediation, but despite her persistence, her fervent and repeated calls for new principles and modes of rhetorical interaction in international affairs seemed to go unheeded by official governmental bodies. Indeed, her lack of faith in the ability of official governmental organs to embody the rhetorical mechanisms she felt were essential to successful international negotiation proved valid. When she reviewed the Charter of the United Nations in 1945 at the request of Howard E. Wilson, associate professor of education at Harvard and editor of the *Harvard Education Review*, Wales pointed out that "there does not seem to be as direct a provision as one could wish for the free scientific study of conflicts and the advancement of proposals for dealing with those." She identified several aspects of the UN charter that she felt were rhetorically flawed, including the fact that "(1) The Security Council has to condition its work with a view to national obligations and diplomatic adjustments and is necessarily somewhat preoccupied with these; (2) The Assembly is under restrictions with respect to discussing any dispute during the time that it is being dealt with by the Security Council; [and] (3) The Assembly is not in continuous session" ("Letter to Howard E. Wilson" 1). In short, she recognized that the channels of communication embodied in the Charter of the UN privilege the national interests of some nations while limiting the contributions of others. These channels, she pointed out, also allow for secretive dealings within the Security Council while disallowing the continuous discussion and revision that Wales understood as critical to preventing future warfare.

Doug Brent ends his discussion of Young, Becker, and Pike's construction of Rogerian rhetoric by asking if the concept is worth saving. He concludes that it is: "This attractiveness, I believe, stems from the fact that we still do not have anywhere else such a well-articulated combination of dialogic principles combined with a practical set of techniques for implementing them" (462). In many ways, however, Julia Grace Wales provided such a combination in the "New Rhetoric" she articulated between 1915 and her death in 1957. Wales deserves attention for her important contributions to the conversations that would resurface in both Burke and Young, Becker, and Pike. She had proffered a model of what Brent calls "a rhetoric that has as its goal not skillful verbal coercion but discussion and exchange of ideas" (8) almost as soon as the First World War commenced. She had recognized that traditional tools of rhetoric were inadequate to address the extensive, international disputes that drove world conflict. This recognition, however, proved to be either before its time or too much coming from a woman.

That women were not believed capable of making significant contributions to the rhetorical principles of international negotiation can be seen in the response Wales received to her initial plan from Lucy Gay, a colleague in the Department of Romance Languages at Wisconsin: "I thank you for sending me a copy of 'armistice without mediation' [*sic*]," Gay wrote. "I am so proud a woman could conceive and write so fine a thing, whatever its fate." Gay's closing remark suggests that she fully recognized the uphill battle faced by Wales's plan, perhaps in part because it was penned by a woman. Wales herself recognized the difficulty of this battle, particularly within the American political system, and opted to have prominent men—Louis Lochner and David Starr Jordan—present her plan to President Wilson. As reported in the University of Wisconsin's newspaper in 1916, Wales "did not [initially] disclose her identity because she thought it would be more difficult for a woman to get the plan before President Wilson than for a man to do so" ("Discover Author"). Students and scholars of rhetoric today, however, might well grant to her ideas the credit they did not receive in her lifetime.

2

The Hope for Peace and Bread
Hephzibah Roskelly

When Jane Addams stepped onto the stage at New York's Carnegie Hall on 9 July 1915, she was undoubtedly the most respected woman in the United States and arguably the most famous woman in the world. The social settlement she had cofounded with Ellen Gates Starr in Chicago in 1893, Hull House, had proved a vibrant, successful effort to help immigrants prosper in their new country and had brought Addams acclaim from civic leaders, social activists and philosophers, and the public. After the publication of *Twenty Years at Hull House* (1910), she was increasingly sought after as a speaker on issues of economy, social justice, and peace in both national and international forums. In 1907, she had been named a delegate to the first National Peace Conference, and in 1915 she had attended the first gathering of what was to become the Women's International League for Peace and Freedom at The Hague. Her friend and frequent lecturer at Hull House, John Dewey, had by 1915 collaborated with her often as he worked to develop the action-oriented philosophical pragmatism for which he, along with William James and C. S. Peirce, had become famous.[1] She had become so recognizable and appealing to the American electorate that in 1912 Theodore Roosevelt asked her to second his presidential nomination on the Progressive Party ticket, with a platform partially devoted to peace.

Her long experience as a speaker, her rapport with audiences across the globe, and her deep belief in the cause she was to speak on no doubt gave Addams reason for confidence as she began the talk that was soon to become infamous as the "Bayonet Charge Speech." She had returned weeks before from a trip across Europe with the International Congress of Women for Permanent Peace (ICWPP—see Wendy Sharer's chapter in this collection for more on the outcome of that congress). Visiting battlefields, and meeting with world leaders, soldiers, and citizens, Addams and her colleagues had heard testimony about the horrors of the Great War that had begun the year before and had already cost thousands of lives; they themselves had witnessed the privation, the violence, the futility of the conflict. Addams was convinced that the United States should not enter the war. Still, though passionate about her topic, Addams was a deliberate thinker and speaker, not given to elocutionary excess, and the opening lines of her speech were characteristic of her careful rhetoric as she cautioned her hearers against over-reaction: "One gets afraid of tall talk," she admitted, "and one does not know where words may lead the people to whom one is speaking" ("Bayonet" 328). Her speech worked against tall talk, even as it described the devastation, the starvation, and the soldiers' hatred of the violence they performed.

But tall talk was soon to become the rhetorical strategy of the day as the nation moved to war; Addams's very reasonableness in the face of the emotionalism surrounding American calls to arms was to prove part of her undoing. In the weeks after she delivered the Bayonet Charge Speech, Addams suffered a dramatic reversal of fortune. For the duration of the world war and for at least a decade afterward, Addams lost much of her prestige and her platform, was taunted by the press for being at best a busybody and at worst a traitor, and was shunned by the public who cancelled her speeches, wrote her hate letters, and ignored her attempts at responding to their criticism. Roosevelt, who only three years before had stood with her to accept his party's nomination for president, would criticize her in 1917 as "the most dangerous woman in America" (qtd. in True n. pag.).

Addams's work for peace and justice during and after the war in the face of sometimes virulent attacks was more than simply courageous perseverance. The methods of action and the rhetoric she employed in her work are well documented, especially in her books *Peace and Bread in Time of War* (1922) and *The Second Twenty Years at Hull House*

(1930), and they reveal Addams's involvement with and development of the pragmatic philosophy that Dewey made famous at Chicago's School for Social Work. Pragmatism's basic tenets, as suggested by James and Peirce and expanded by Dewey, included binding meaning-making to experience rather than theory, relying on observation rather than *a priori* belief, and testing conclusions. This reliance on experience entailed an acknowledgment of context and a belief in the possibility of change. Addams's wartime speeches and books—recounting experience, carefully testing ideas and considering alternatives, looking toward the future as well as the past—create a rhetoric of pragmatism. Her work does more, in fact; it tests pragmatism's methods and provides new directions for pragmatic thought.[2]

Addams bore witness to the consequences of war in much the same way she had exposed the consequences of privation and ignorance in Chicago's tenements. Increasingly, as observation continued to teach her, she became convinced of the link between social justice and international stability, between peace and bread, and it became her life's work to expose the connection and work for one so that the other might flourish. This essay examines how Addams links peace and bread as both writer and activist, how she employs a rhetoric of pragmatism to negotiate the hostility to that work and to continue to renegotiate concepts of justice, citizenship, and humanity toward the hope of peace. As she practices it, pragmatism's rhetoric emphasizes the observational, the experiential, and the experimental; it establishes a voice characterized by speculation, reason, and acknowledgment of others; and it maintains a belief in the possibilities of communication and change as it asserts its arguments. Addams follows pragmatism's methods in her activity for social justice and peace, and she creates a pragmatic rhetoric that applies those tenets to discourse.

The "Bayonet Charge" and the Failure of Reason

The "Bayonet Charge" speech—which Addams herself had titled "The Revolt against War"—was in some ways the first public test of Addams's ideas about peace and bread. When it was delivered, the United States had not yet entered the Great War, and its president, Woodrow Wilson, had preserved a pacifist stance. He ran for reelection the next year, in fact, on the platform "He kept us out of war" (*Peace and Bread* 34). Yet, even though many citizens in 1915 hoped the United States could avoid entering the war, sentiment for the Allied troops already ran high, accompanied and fed by patriotic rhetoric. In her speech, Addams deliberately attempted to avoid such rhetoric, the tall talk of glory and conquest, and chose instead to concentrate on what she and other delegates from the Peace Conference at The Hague had seen and heard in their travels to every war-wracked country in Europe. A reliance on experience, a pragmatic concept, was deeply a part of her rhetoric in all her speeches and essays. In this speech, as someone coming directly from the frontlines of war, her words carried the immediacy and the weight of eyewitness evidence. In addition, as the founder of Hull House, her ethos had long been established as honest, authoritative, and successful. But she refused to take advantage of either the emotional drama of the scenes she had witnessed or the persona of "savior" of thousands of the poor at Hull House. Employing reason rather than drama, she hoped to encourage rationality rather than sentiment, adopting the reasonable tone of almost all her previous speeches and writing.[3] Her descriptions of interviews with widows and orphans, discussions with political leaders, and touching talks with soldiers were offered quietly, careful illustrations of her contention that everywhere "the people say, 'We do not want this war'" ("Bayonet" 340). Addams understood emotional appeal well, of course; her *Long Road of Woman's Memory*, which was to be published the next year, documented the effects of rumor and the appeal of sentiment among groups of women at Hull House. But in part because she had seen the sometimes frightening effects of rumor on communities, she believed in the need for logic, evidence, and reasonable conversation in the face of inflamed passions. She trusted her audience to hear her as a trustworthy observer and to draw sensible conclusions.

As Addams discovered, however, careful reasoning pales next to appeals to the comforting certainties of patriotic action. At the moment she delivered it, the speech that described Addams's hope for peace in Europe received resounding applause. But the approval was short-lived. Richard Harding Davis, a journalist and adventurer who wrote popular accounts of his travels, had been in the Carnegie Hall audience and the next day wrote a letter to the *New York Times* protesting one bit of evidence Addams had offered as an indictment of the war. Near the end of the speech, she spoke of soldiers' horror of the bayonet charge: "We heard in all countries similar statements in regard to the necessity for the use of stimulants before men would engage in certain bayonet charges. . . . They all have to give them the 'dope' before the bayonet charge is possible. Think of that" ("Bayonet" 333). Addams finds in the soldiers' reluctance proof of "the humane impulse of the soldier of any nation who wishes not to kill so gruesomely even his enemy" (333), and her quiet *Think of that* indicts all sides and all leaders who knowingly work against the soldier's impulse. But Davis proclaimed himself incensed at her conclusion: "Miss Addams denies [the soldier] credit of his sacrifice. She strips him of honor and courage. She tells his children, 'Your father did not die for France or for England or for you; he died because he was drunk.'" His outrage builds to the last sentence: "I have heard no statement so unworthy or so untrue or ridiculous. . . . [T]he crudity and ignorance it displays are inconceivable."

It wasn't long before Davis's attack was picked up by newspapers across the country. Headlines about the speech continued for weeks as did published letters abusing Addams. In *The Second Twenty Years*, Addams admits being stunned by this reaction: "I was presenting data which to my mind indicated a revolt against war taking place in the midst of war itself" (131). In her earlier war memoir, *Peace and Bread*, she writes: "Dr. Hamilton [Alice Hamilton, her partner in the effort at The Hague] and I had notes for each of the statements with dates and names of the men who had made them, and it did not occur to me that the information was new or startling" (78). To Addams, the fact that humans had to be coerced to get them to eviscerate other humans was unremarkable, and she counted on the reasonableness of that fact and the strength of her evidence to sway her audience. She had erred; reason couldn't compete with the tall talk of heroism.

The *Wall Street Journal* was one of the many newspapers that continued to attack Addams for her actions on behalf of peace and bread. Two years after the "Bayonet Charge" speech, the newspaper accused her of being a naïve and dangerous agitator when she spoke out against the Allied naval blockade that was starving thousands in Germany and throughout Europe. Claiming that it is "particularly important during war that our bankers should bring before the wide public . . . the seriousness and purpose of war" and "discourage sentimental peace talk," the editors charged Addams with prolonging the war's misery with her false sentiment: "Miss Jane Addams furnishes an example of this kind of agitation, unconsciously bringing out the typically illogical position of the pacifist." She might be "incapable of falsehood" herself, but "this is much more dangerous because it is half-truth." Addams cares only about starving enemy women and children, the editorial claimed. "She does not hesitate to starve the women and children of Belgium, or of Poland, or Rumania. Evidently these are not the women and children in the mind of Miss Addams" ("Starvation"). In an editorial later that year, the *New York Times* was even more scathing, suggesting that Addams's pacifism was driven by a desire for celebrity: "Miss Addams has gone to bizarre extremes in her advocacy of weird measures and her championship of impossible people, apparently capitalizing on a reputation honestly won in a worthy work to keep herself constantly in the headlines." Affirming the damage to her reputation, the *Times* concludes, "She has sacrificed fame for notoriety and a place in the public heart for a place in the spotlight" (Editorial).

Addams's anguish and frustration at being so misunderstood, deliberately as often as not, is obvious in *Peace and Bread*. The malignity of public mischaracterizations throughout the war was, she writes, "rather overwhelming" (77). She remarks that soon after the "Bayonet Charge" speech, she attempted to clarify her statement about soldiers and stimulants but again found it so garbled by the press "that I gave up in despair" (80). Late in 1915, she became ill with pneumonia, the beginning of several years of semi-invalidism, made worse by the depressing knowledge that she had been made a pariah. Her rhetorical failure in the Carnegie Hall and later speeches discouraged her. Evidence made little difference to inflamed emotions, and because she was a woman, reporting from the front line, her evidence could easily be discounted as irrelevant or naïve or womanishly squeamish. As her war memoirs demonstrate, the lessons she learned were hard to bear even years later since they revealed not only the failure of reasoned argument but also the ragged tears in the fabric of the democracy she believed in. "Many people had long supposed liberalism to be the freedom to know and to say, not what was popular or convenient or even what was patriotic, but what they held to be true," she reflects in *Peace and Bread*. But when it comes to war, she finds, all democratic bets are off. "We found that any attempt at bold and penetrating discussion was quickly and ruthlessly suppressed" (104). Addams ruefully admits being slow to recognize this "ruthless" silencing as what she calls the "war technique," one element of which was to make "pacifist activity or propaganda so absurd that it would be absolutely without influence and its authors so discredited that nothing they might say or do would be regarded as worthy of attention" (77). Silencing was both the rationale for misrepresentation and the result of it.

Pragmatic Inquiry

But Addams refused to remain overwhelmed or silent. Instead, she begins to use others' questioning of her motives as an opportunity to examine them herself; self-examination becomes a primary strategy in the war memoirs. She wonders at her earlier contention against the terrific force of the majority, admitting her deep desire for community—"at moments . . . one secretly yearned to participate in 'the folly of all mankind'" (*Peace and Bread* 80)—and describing her self-doubts: were she and her colleagues too arrogant? "Who were we to differ with able statesmen?" (82). Might she be led to fanaticism in the cause of peace? This admission of uncertainty became part of Addams's rhetoric and her pragmatic approach to locating what pragmatists like Dewey termed "usable truths." Throughout both war memoirs, Addams acknowledges continually her own limitations. It is no false humility. She believed in her own doubt, realizing that her refusal of certainty enabled continued inquiry and connection with others. As she records her doubts, she also reflects on the benefits of facing opposition. Although her Hull House activism had met with great approval, she notes that this approval came partly from public ignorance of the settlement's radical experiment in democracy. Those who understood that the settlement was not charity work, that Addams and Starr were not missionaries, were, as Addams says, quite critical. Addams quietly faced down the opposition with proofs of its success at what she called "civic housekeeping" (Elshtain 60).

Equally important for public approval was the familiarity of Hull House activity as woman's work—the cleaning, feeding, and nurturing of others that women performed in a home. By contrast, Addams's pacifist activity and rhetoric appeared to move her into a male preserve of munitions, international law, and combat. For Addams, the connection between one sphere and another had become as unexceptional as it was inescapable: bread and peace both reduce suffering. It was no doubt the common sense of the connection that prevented her from understanding public disapproval of what seemed a new and dangerous role for her as peace activist and therefore meddler in the male affairs of state. But for Addams the roles of social settlement worker and peace worker were not just compatible; they were inseparable. Her memoirs and speeches after 1915 reveal her growing sense of how peace and war depend on plenty and want, and this understanding helped her act on behalf of bread and peace even when she was being roundly criticized for the "Bayonet Charge" speech and her peace activity, even when silence seemed the better part of valor.

She began to affirm in detail the connection between deprivation and violence in speeches for the federal Department of Food Administration in 1917. Desperate to be of use after the United States entered the war, despite public dismissal of her, she spoke across the country about food conservation and production. Her mission was more than informational: "I firmly believed that through an effort to feed hungry people, a new and powerful force might be unloosed in the world" (*Second Twenty Years* 144). The powerful force is peace, unloosed when the hungry are fed. Her talks about food as a civic issue met with a variety of responses, as her wry reflection indicates: "Some towns would consider me too pacifistic to appear; others apparently had never heard of my deplorable attitude and still others, bent only upon the saving of food, were indifferent" (145). At a Woman's Clubs convention in Hot Springs, Arkansas, she was disappointed not to find women who recognized the connection she strived to make: "I had hoped to find some trace of woman's recognition of her obligation to feed the world and of her discovery that such a duty was incompatible with warfare" (146). Negative response notwithstanding, Addams's sense of woman's role as breadgiver and thus peacemaker was increasingly unwavering. "As I had felt the young immigrant conscripts caught up into a great world movement, which sent them out to fight, so it seemed to me the millions of American women might be caught up into a great world purpose, that of conservation of life; there might be found an antidote to war in woman's affection and all embracing pity for helpless children" (*Peace and Bread* 47). But her insistence on connecting the spheres of woman's and man's work through the idea of peace and bread was radical. Perhaps it was recognizing the implications for social change in Addams's peace actions that made her erstwhile supporter Theodore Roosevelt find her "dangerous." The link between peace and bread is Addams's most important pacifist idea, and, as Roosevelt might have understood, her single most provocative rhetorical trope.

For the pragmatist, always interested in expanding experience and in using it to reconsider old beliefs and consider new practices, the need to remain tentative and to admit the importance of contingency were hallmarks of the method's effectiveness. Addams's ideas were grounded in experience and evidence but qualified by admission of alternative possibilities. The result in her war memoirs is a persona at once authoritative and humble. She typically refrains from being definitive about what others thought or even about her own opinions and memories from the early days of Hull House and from the war years. "I venture to believe" (10) she says, or "As I recall" (12). Her memoir retains her insistence on calm reason rather than bombastic tall talk, as when she discusses her dismay at President Wilson's altering his pacifist position to support American entrance into the war: "We seemed to have come to an impasse therefore . . ." (17). Her rhetorical questions exhort readers to examine the possibility of alternative action even after that possibility has been closed off, as in this line reflecting on the harsh terms of the Treaty at Versailles: "What might have happened if President Wilson could have said in January, 1919, what he had said in January, 1917—'A victor's terms imposed upon the vanquished . . . would leave a sting'" (39–40).

By the time she wrote *The Second Twenty Years* in 1930, Addams's questions had often become contingent statements that lead to future as well as past possibility, a recognition of how what Cornel West calls the pragmatist's "usable past" connects to a "future-oriented instrumentalism" (ix). Addams looks forward and back as she writes, "Perhaps the international associations represented in Geneva will gradually form the beginnings of a wider sense of unity" (148) and "Perhaps it was our preoccupation with actual starvation that constantly drew us back to an examination of ultimate aims" (149)—both these reflections discussing the International Women's League for Peace and Freedom and its refutation of the Versailles Treaty. She uses the word *seemed* or *possible* continually in both her war memoirs: "It seemed reasonable to hope for world order" (*Peace and Bread* 51) or, with humorous self-mockery, "Possibly, as a foolish pacifist" (38). The avowal of uncertainty builds Addams's ethos and strengthens her message: readers see her trying out alternative explanations or outcomes, reframing her own positions, questioning her sureness, and searching for points of truth, points of connection. She asserts uncertainty as a principle of right action, understanding, like pragmatist jurist Oliver Wendell Holmes, that certainty leads to violence. "When you know that you know," Holmes said in 1929, "persecution comes easy" (qtd. in Menand 62). For both Addams and Holmes, veterans of wars and pragmatic thinkers, a rhetoric of peace requires doubt as well as affirmation.

Although in part it is this habit of contingency and qualification in the "Bayonet Charge" speech that made her words appear weak to her 1915 audience already thirsty for action, she retains the rhetorical strategy throughout her writing during and after the War, suggesting that she finds it useful as a way to demonstrate her beliefs in mediation and possibility as well as to underscore her reliance on pragmatism as a method for investigating the truth of her assertions. Sustained inquiry allows Addams to test her beliefs pragmatically, weighing consequences and alternatives. In the process, she finds her belief in peace and the means toward it strengthened. Because she continues to question, Addams allows herself to remain tentative about her conclusions, to the degree that her belief could be altered if inquiry necessitated it. As she writes about her doubts and questions her actions, Addams demonstrates how important the process of challenging belief is to sustaining it.

And yet the stress of her isolated position made her vulnerable during and after the war. The deaths of many older pacifists, she suggests, were caused, at least in part, by the emotional and psychic strain of taking the unpopular path: "More than the normal amount of nervous energy must be consumed in holding one's own in a hostile world" (*Peace and Bread* 85). In her typical quiet, modest style she may downplay it, but the nervous energy Addams had to expend as she tried to hold her own in the hostile world of wartime America exacted its cost, a cost she admitted to occasionally. Writing *The Second Twenty Years*, Addams has accepted the fate of one who champions unpopular causes: "Perhaps, because nothing save love stirs the imagination like hatred, there was a necessity for some object upon which the hatred stirred up during the war could vent itself. What so near at hand as the pacifists whom the newspapers had systematically identified with the enemy" (151).

Especially after the war, Addams's direct knowledge of the plight of starving European women and children, many of them German, gave her strength to refute the attack from the press and public of being "pro-German." Almost defiantly for her, she reflects: "Public approval or disapproval came to seem of little consequence compared to the tragic suffering we had seen face to face" (151). One experience she records in *Peace and Bread* is her "first view of starved children." Traveling through France shortly after the Versailles agreement had been signed, she and a group of representatives from the Friends' Service Committee visited a school in Lille, where children were lined up to be tested for tuberculosis:

> As we entered the door of a large school room, we saw at the other end of the room a row of little boys, from six to ten years of age, passing slowly in front of the examining physician. The children were stripped to the waist and our first impression was of a line of moving skeletons, their little shoulder blades stuck straight out, the vertebrae were all perfectly distinct as were their ribs, and their bony arms hung limply at their sides. (96)

Similar little "winged shoulder blades" haunt her in Vienna and Berlin, Frankfort and Leipzig, and lead her to criticize the newly formed League of Nations for ignoring the problem of starvation and thus losing a possibility for peace: "Could it have considered this multitude of starving children as its concrete problem, feeding them might have been the quickest way to restore the divided European nations to human and kindly relationship" (98).

In spite of—indeed, because of—her questioning spirit, an underlying strength of purpose is evident in all her postwar writing, a strength that feeds the need to speak in order to bear witness through memory. The symbolic, educative dimension of memory had been powerfully demonstrated in *The Long Road of Woman's Memory* (1916), her account of women's lives at Hull House and how the stories they shared helped them survive tragedy and grief. *Twenty Years at Hull House* (1909) had also been a memoir and, like *The Long Road of Woman's Memory,* one concerned primarily with documenting how memory and experience enhance learning—especially, perhaps, for the memoirist herself—to create occasions for better, more effective action. The voice in both of Addams's war memoirs sounds still bewildered about war's effects on public reason but resolute about the need for remembering those effects, for speaking with clarity: "With all our errors thick upon us," Addams says in *The Second Twenty Years,* "we may at least be entitled to the comfort of Plato's intimation that truth itself might be discovered by honest reminiscence" (273). Memory, honestly recaptured, becomes a way to understand the importance of the past, which as her accounts firmly demonstrate, lives in its effects on the present and the possibilities it offers to the future.

Democracy and Dissent

Addams's work for peace became the focus of her life in the decades after the war, and she gave speech after speech about the need for conversation with and respect for immigrants, who were increasingly suspected of harboring anarchist or communist sympathies. The Russian Revolution in 1917 had filled Americans with a fear that surfaced completely only after the end of the war. So paralyzed and panicked was the general population that a deep distrust of all change marked local and national politics. Addams sees this postwar mindset as a twin desire to forget and to be certain. New ideas led to uncertainty and so were suspect: "To advance new ideas was to be a radical, even a Bolshevik," she says (*Second Twenty Years* 154). Addams perceives the flaw underlying this desire for stasis: "The nation forgot that nothing is so dangerous as to prohibit social changes, nothing so unnatural to the very structure and function of society as to forbid its growth and development" (154–55). As she had observed in her Hull House work, she recognizes that change is both natural and necessary to expand democracy.

As before the war, Addams became the target of the fearful. And as before, the press played a role in making Addams a suspicious character. In 1920 and beyond, her membership in the fledgling Civil Liberties Union was "proof" of disloyalty, and her public support for immigrants' right to dissent became evidence of her sympathy for the "Reds"—or of being a Red herself. Silence and fear made the warring past seem to the American public a better, even safer, time than the changeable present: "In the minds of many good men and women the war itself thus became associated with all that was high and fine and patriotism received the sanction of a dogmatic religion which would brook no heretical difference of opinion" (*Peace and Bread* 110). Postwar fear made Addams's peace work, and her insistent linking of peace to bread, even more difficult. But Addams continued to argue, in her nondogmatic way, for the necessity of respecting different opinions. In a 1924 speech supporting Chicago factory workers' rights, she used democratic ideals as evidence for the benefits of dissent: "Free speech is the greatest safety valve for our United States," she claimed. "Let us end this suppression and spirit of intolerance." The next day the *Chicago Tribune*'s headline read "Reds Upheld by Jane Addams as Good Americans" (qtd. in Eblen and Kelley 261). By this time, she was no stranger to misrepresentation by the press and perhaps was unsurprised.

Addams's memoirs record instances that reflect the fear of difference and free speech that characterized the times: arrests of immigrants, some of them former Hull House residents for whom she posted bail; the trial of I.W.W. workers for sedition and the horrible conditions of their imprisonment; the notorious deportation of dissidents. For some, her postwar activity on behalf of the Women's International League (WIL) bordered on sedition itself. Addams was stripped of her honorary membership in the Daughters of the American Revolution ("I supposed at the time it had been for life, but it was apparently only for good behavior") when the DAR published what was famously called a "spiderweb chart" showing the consequences of the "poison of liberalism" that spun from organizations like the WIL who, they claimed, were "aiming to destroy the government of the United States" (*Second Twenty Years* 180–81). Always, there was the desire to keep the "foolish pacifist" from speaking. Yet the harassment Addams faced as peace activist and women's advocate only led her to reflect on the enormous costs of war even more deeply. She had seen the privation of the millions of war survivors and knew the grim accounting of loss of life. Now she observed the terrifying warping of the national consciousness: "Survival of war psychology is an unaccountable thing; it constitutes a new indictment, if one were needed, of the devastating effects of war upon human character" (174). Understanding the "war psychology" that continued to operate in the minds of many Americans no doubt helped her bear the loss of friendly relations she wished for.

Addams's reflections on pacifism in a time of postwar fear and frenzied nationalism included the importance of Hull House for her as refuge and the pragmatic testing ground for the workability of her ideas about both peace and bread. As a "professor in the University of Chicago" (likely John Dewey) whom she quotes in *The Second Twenty Years* wrote about the connections between her peace work and the settlement house: "Jane Addams may not have discovered the principles of internationalism through her experience at Hull House, but it is easily within the bounds of truth to say that she could not have lived there without practicing them" (113). Hull House helped people who spoke more than a hundred different languages, who needed work for bread and hope for change. Knowing that the many who came to Chicago's South Side looked for opportunity and the freedom from fear that the country promised, Addams had fed the hungry, found work for the needy, taught home economy and hygiene, seeing her work as an instance of the democratic experiment of America itself.

Hull House helped Addams realize clearly the link between sustenance and peace because she learned to see that the settlement house was a microcosm of life itself. "In time," she says near the end of *The Second Twenty Years*, "we came to define a settlement as an institution attempting to learn from life itself" (408). Life itself, she didn't say, can learn lessons from the settlement house as well, lessons of mutual cooperation, the conditions that stimulate growth and change, how humans might settle—and respect—differences. But, although she doesn't make that claim directly, she does quote from an article on Hull House in wartime published in the magazine *The World Tomorrow* that suggests what Hull House has to teach political leaders: "How is it that this company preserves its ranks so staunchly unbroken? The reason is their profound conviction of the worth and sanctity of the opinions of other people" (202). For Addams at Hull House and at work for peace, that was a fair definition of democracy itself.

Rhetoric for Future Action

In reading Jane Addams's memoirs and speeches after the Great War, it is impossible not to be struck by the sustained energy in her voice. Her resilience and humor, her generosity, are evident in all her work, a feat especially notable given the public scorn she endured nearly until the end of her life. Addams stayed open-hearted and optimistic in great measure because she believed in youth and in the responsibilities and worth of the old to teach and to change. She often ends her talks with a call to both generations to find paths toward better action. Both, she argues, must be open to new conceptions "of the social forces which come from integration in the sphere of activities rather than in that of ideas. What we want is not mere argument, certainly not suppression of any sort, but the release of energy and the evocation of new powers in common action" (*Second Twenty Years* 202). Addams emphasizes action rather than abstraction as the task of old and young alike, claiming that in action lies the hope for communication and thus for more effective democracy. She makes new action her central claim, using pragmatism's "core tenet," as West calls it (5). Addams's belief in action is part of her future-oriented rhetoric and her hope for youth.

Continually and insistently, Addams argued for new understandings among humans and nations, a new consciousness that recognizes our increasing links to others no matter how different they appear to be. In 1930, she finds these understandings not in a distant future but in the almost realized present: "the modern world is developing an almost mystic consciousness of the continuity and interdependence of mankind" (*Second Twenty Years* 7). It is in the near future, the potentially possible, where her optimism and strength lie. "It lies with us who are here now to make this consciousness—as yet so fleeting and uncertain—the unique contribution of our time to that small handful of incentives which really motivate human conduct" (8–9). What we need for a new consciousness to awaken, she argues in a 1933 speech on "Our National Self Righteousness," is "humility of spirit, a willingness to reconsider existing institutions" as well as "a recognition of our national misjudgments." She pleads for uncertainty: "We are so fully convinced of our own righteousness" (380). In great measure because of Hull House, Addams believed in the truth of experience and, as a pragmatist, understood how experiences multiplied and varied gave humans access to better truths. Hull House had also taught her to believe in and act on reconciliation, which requires the painful admission that frailty and fault are never the sole property of one human or one side. Just as peace and bread are inseparably linked so, too, are individual humans and the nation state. As C. S. Peirce contended that "society is but a loosely compacted person" (191), she claimed, "We forget that politics are largely a matter of adjusted human relations" (*Second Twenty Years* 23). To repair the community, we must repair our relationships with one another, she believed. Our understanding of one another, what Addams called "affectionate interpretation,"[4] could only be had by knowing one another and sharing experience in mutual good will and common cause. In that enterprise arises the new consciousness she speaks of, and knowing and telling become part of what the old and young communicate.

Addams's death on 21 May 1935 occurred on the very day that Hitler defiantly announced an unprecedented German military buildup, effectively destroying the agreement made sixteen years before at Versailles. Another war would soon eclipse the war to end them all that Addams had fought so hard to end and to prevent from reoccurring. Addams would no doubt have fought to prevent that much more terrible war as well, would have attempted again to end it, spoken after it to alter the conditions that would bring another war in its wake. From this distance, one could say that all of Addams's work, the constant writing and speaking and listening, failed to make much of a dent in the national passion for militarism, for slogans instead of reasons, and for intolerance of dissent. But the lessons she has to teach seem ever more cogent and more insistent. When she won the Nobel Prize for peace in 1931, the first American woman to do so, she had finally begun to be reclaimed by the country that had so often tried to silence her. Seldom has the meaning of an award seemed so appropriate: "War is not a natural activity for mankind," she asserted in *Peace and Bread*. "It is instead a natural tendency to come into friendly relationships with ever larger and larger groups and to live constantly a more extended life" (139). Addams's rhetoric of experience and testing, her searching reflection, her pragmatic plan for mediation and friendship, and most of all her example of quiet perseverance might still secure us methods that take us toward peace, toward our own more extended life.

Notes

1. See Charlotte Haddock Siegfried, *Pragmatism and Feminism*, for a discussion of Dewey's debt to Addams as an activist, philosopher, and practitioner of American pragmatist thought.

2. See Robert Danisch's *Pragmatism, Democracy, and the Necessity of Rhetoric*, which argues that the pragmatic method itself insists upon rhetorical understandings and practices.

3. By 1915, Addams had published six books and dozens of essays in popular magazines and journals. She had been a much sought after speaker at local, national, and international events for over twenty years.

4. Addams first used the phrase in "A Modern Lear" (1896, 1912), her analysis of the Pullman Strike in Chicago in 1893. Affectionate interpretation requires that the stronger, more powerful or wealthy, have responsibility to locate common principle and communion with others in everyday life.

3

Gertrude Bonnin's Transrhetorical Fight for Land Rights
Elizabeth Wilkinson

In the summer of 1923, the Philadelphia-based Indian Rights Association (IRA) began to realize the scope of the corruption surrounding Indian land probate in Oklahoma. In response, the president of the IRA, Herbert Welsh, called for an investigation by a three-member team consisting of Matthew Sniffen from the IRA, attorney Charles H. Fabens from the American Indian Defense Association, and Gertrude Bonnin,[1] a Yankton Dakota woman, representing the Indian Welfare Committee of the General Federation of Women's Clubs. Bonnin, Fabens, and Sniffen spent five weeks in eastern Oklahoma during November and December 1923, and by February 1924 they had completed their report, *Oklahoma's Poor Rich Indians: An Orgy of Graft and Exploitation of the Five Civilized Tribes*[2]*—Legalized Robbery*. The thirty-nine-page document describes what they found: an almost unimaginable situation in which unprincipled businessmen and state officials used legal loopholes and illegal tactics including kidnapping, rape, and murder to strip Native landholders, male and female of all ages, of their rightfully allotted land. The report, which would eventually go to Congress, led to an investigation by the Department of the Interior, the findings of which paved the way for the 1934 Indian Reorganization Act.

This chapter argues that the effectiveness of *Oklahoma's Poor Rich Indians* is due in large measure to the strategies adopted by Bonnin in writing the section of the report that details individual cases of abuse and exploitation. In introducing Bonnin's account of the demoralizing victimization of peoples forced into legal and social powerlessness and individual vulnerability, the joint authors write, "There are some phases of our investigation that can be presented best by a feminine mind, and we leave it to Mrs. Bonnin" (Bonnin, Fabens, and Sniffen 23). However, Bonnin's special qualifications for writing this section derive not merely from the fact of her feminine sex, which, in the minds of her male coauthors and in the eyes of society at large, would make her especially sympathetic to the weak and vulnerable, but also from her own embodied status as a Dakota woman, who through her cultural upbringing assumed both the right and responsibility to speak publicly and politically. In writing this report, Bonnin operated under the double marginalization of being both female and Native American at a time when it was still sociopolitically restrictive to be either when acting from within Euro-American society. (See Kathy Jurado's chapter on Jovita González in this collection for another example of a non-Euro-American academic negotiating the borderlands).

However, in this chapter I would like to present the possibility that rather than functioning as obstacles, Bonnin's gendered and cultural identities become tools. Instead of suffering from the disadvantages usually associated with a hybrid identity, Bonnin intentionally and strategically *trans*ports and *trans*mits elements from one identity location into another in a form of rhetorical positioning, or agency, that I have labeled *transrhetorical*. She moves among the rhetorical locations that are defined by gendered and cultural constructs, and what she brings to those rhetorical scenarios, and what she adopts from them, constitute her transrhetorical agency.

Becoming Transrhetorical

I have coined the term *transrhetorical* as an alternative to customary labels such as *hybrid* and *bicultural*, terms that describe the sociopolitical and subsequent rhetorical results of colonization. Many critical responses to Native writings, especially Indigenous-authored texts published before the mid-twentieth century, center on the internal conflicts inherent in an unasked-for cultural amalgamation experienced by Native peoples due to forced assimilation. A number of scholars have assessed Bonnin in terms of her discordant cultural identity. Dexter Fisher writes of Bonnin's "conflict between tradition and acculturation" (ix). When she chose (or was coerced) in 1884, at eight years old, to go to White's Manual Technical Institute in Wabash, Indiana, Bonnin rushed from a solidly Dakota life headlong into Euro-American ways of speaking, dressing, learning, and living. Thus, much of Bonnin scholarship focuses on her search for and creation of what Fisher calls her "position between two alien worlds" (xii). Accordingly, scholars center on her fiction, semi-autobiographical writing, and letters that protest against the assimilative boarding schools—the mechanism by which alienation and loss of identity occurred—and highlight the negative results of her forced acculturation. Rarely does Bonnin's rhetorical power gained from time spent behind enemy lines, so to speak, come into play. To label Bonnin's identity position merely as hybridity is to acquiesce to the associated sense of loss that term now carries: loss of language, culture, community, and identity. To deem her bicultural undervalues the rhetorical maneuvering power she claimed and constructed out of her situation. Using the descriptor *transrhetorical*, I place the focus on how the subject makes use of the condition rather than on the condition itself, allowing for the possibility of a conscious, active deployment of sociopolitical agency.

In Gertrude Bonnin's case, three cultural and intercultural situations provided the experiences through which she created her transrhetorical agency: a Dakota-based understanding of gender roles; her position as already "Other" and therefore outside of the Euro-American constructs that defined and restricted a (white) woman's place; and her knowledge of Euro-American rhetorical resources associated with white womanhood, specifically the sentimental, which she could then deploy to make herself legible to her white audience. I don't seek, here, to enter into the debate about either the complicity or subversiveness of sentimental fiction in the cause of women's rights, the on-going "Douglas-Tompkins" debate. Like many Native literature scholars, for instance Cari Carpenter in her 2008 text *Seeing Red: Anger, Sentimentality, and American Indians*, I take as a given that the sentimental is a weapon for Native authors such as Bonnin. Through her use of sentimental tropes, she "reinvents the enemy's language," to paraphrase the title of Joy Harjo and Gloria Bird's anthology of Native women's writing, and uses it for her own purposes.

Bringing in sentimentalism, a largely mid-nineteenth-century genre, may seem interestingly out of place in a discussion about early-twentieth-century women's writing. However, the very educational system in which Bonnin learned to wield a pen was justified by and saturated with the rhetoric of sentimentalism. Indian boarding schools, including the one Bonnin attended, both grew from and imbued students with sentimentalist ideals. The largely well-intentioned notion that "orphaned" Indian children—many, as young as five, were forcibly taken or coerced to leave their families, clans, and reservations—could, through the power of Christian education, learn to act morally and through right action succeed dovetailed beautifully with humanist desires to solve the Indian problem by saving each poor heathen from his or her savage state. Furthermore, the Dawes Act and corollaries that aimed to "'Americanize' the Indian" were pushed through Congress because of and in response to genuine concerns often raised by white, sentimentalist female writers. Individual land ownership, as set out in these federal acts, purported to turn Native peoples into Christian, domestic, American farming families, white picket fences included. Susan Bernardin points out that as "the first literary response to the era's Indian education system, Zitkala-Ša's [Bonnin's] stories selectively use the language of domesticity to scrutinize sentimental ideology's foundational role in compulsory Indian education as well as its related participation in national efforts to 'Americanize' the Indian" (213).

While it is imperative to avoid overgeneralizing when writing about gender practices and beliefs of Native peoples, it is safe to say that the Dakota—which includes Dakota, Lakota, and Nakota (the branch that Bonnin belonged to)—respected women's roles as integral in all aspects of life. White Buffalo Woman, a primary spiritual figure, remains important and omnipresent in Bonnin's time and today (Palmer 185–87). Traditionally, both women and men acted as healers. Women acted as educators, instilling a Dakota worldview. Bonnin relates in "Impressions of an Indian Childhood" a memory of a female elder telling a story of a magical woman whose powers came from the tattooed crosses on her cheeks; she writes that though she heard the story when she was a young child, the "impression was so acute that the picture still remains vividly clear and pronounced" (Zitkala-Ša, "Impressions" 71). In one Dakota story, a woman elder is made chief, and in another, a woman guards the path to the afterlife and judges all those who might enter (Palmer 188–89). Being a Dakota female did not and does not keep a woman out of tribal politics; in fact, it requires her to participate. What we know of Gertrude Bonnin, particularly through her correspondence with one-time fiancé Carlos Montezuma, reflects this mindset of Dakota female agency. Exhibiting what Ruth Spack calls "the traditional power and prestige of Sioux women," Bonnin formed her transrhetorical ethos by resisting the traditionally expected norms of a white, middle-class woman and wife foisted on her and other Native American girls at Christian-run boarding schools (183). Spack offers interesting insight in her text "Dis/engagement: Zitkala-Ša's Letters to Carlos Montezuma, 1901–1902," highlighting moments when Bonnin refuses to trade her intellectual pursuits and political activism for a life as Montezuma's stereotypically "white" wife. In letters to him, Bonnin writes, "I require food for the intellect and spirit quite as much as my meals each day" (qtd. in Spack 179) and asserts that she "know[s] so little about keeping a house in running order that the under taking [sic] is perfectly appalling" (qtd. in Spack 181). Spack shows that Bonnin "declares her independence repeatedly by stating that she has no interest in being merely a city doctor's wife, [and] that she 'would not like to *have to obey* another'" (181).

Bonnin carried an embedded idea of female strength into the non-Dakota world she entered upon leaving her reservation home for White's Institute, the Quaker-run boarding school for Indians. At White's, Bonnin confronted a system that required Indian girls to learn Euro-American domesticity. While Laura Wexler constructs Bonnin as being a passive recipient acted upon by "the codes of sentiment" inherent in her boarding school experience, Jessica Enoch argues that Bonnin's scathing semi-autobiographical trilogy, a series of three articles that appeared in the *Atlantic Monthly* in January, February, and March of 1900, show her rejecting prescribed gender roles and critically condemning Indian boarding schools' sentimentalist agenda. Wexler writes that "by the time that she came to write these autobiographical stories" Bonnin's "self-conception had been so effectively ensnared with the codes of sentiment that there was no Indian in them that was left untouched by Western codes" (32–33). Jessica Enoch agrees that female, Indian boarding school students were exposed to "domestic values and activities" and "were also introduced to tenets of true womanhood that dominated the era" (87) but states that Bonnin "refused to carry out the gendered role Carlisle prescribed for her as an Indian female teacher" (74). I move the analysis one step further. Bonnin, during her non-Dakota education, was asked to mimic the white model of domestic femininity. However, as I will discuss below, she describes in her February 1900 installment in the *Atlantic Monthly* a sharp lesson that taught her she would never be allowed to fully become that feminine model. As a result of these cultural interworkings, I argue that she did not simply refuse the gender constructs foisted upon her; she learned the cultural codes expected of white, middle-class women and, because she was not constrained by them and was instead embedded with notions of Dakota-based gender norms, manipulated them to her rhetorical advantage.

While she resisted the assimilative goals of boarding school, Bonnin excelled as a scholar: after White's, she attended Earlham College where she distinguished herself as a writer and orator. However, an experience during her college days solidified the dominant culture's perception of her as always and already "Other." Bonnin writes in the February *Atlantic Monthly* piece, "School Days of an Indian Girl," that while competing in an oratory contest, she was subjected to racist comments from students at competing colleges. She reports:

> After the orations were delivered a deeper burn awaited me. There, before that vast ocean of eyes, some college rowdies threw out a large white flag, with a drawing of a most forlorn Indian girl on it. Under this they had printed in bold black letters words that ridiculed the college which was represented by a "squaw." Such worse than barbarian rudeness embittered me. (Zitkala-Ša, "School Days" 102–3).[3]

Rather than silence her, this attitude, I argue, emboldens her. Because of her outsider position, she can freely speak without the risk of losing status in a way white women cannot.[4] Despite this transrhetorical knowledge and freedom, however, she must tread that line carefully so as to be acceptably legible to the same white world that "others" her.

After Earlham, Bonnin began to publish to a wider audience, deploying elements of the sentimental but twisting those elements for political ends. She placed the aforementioned *Atlantic Monthly* trilogy in 1900; in 1901 and 1902 other politically savvy and sentimentally moving pieces followed.[5] In each of these, Bonnin manipulated elements of sentimental, domestic fiction—for example, the tropes of the saving grace of religion and of the helpless, young victim. However, in "The Soft-Hearted Sioux," Christianity destroys the family rather than saves it; and in "A Warrior's Daughter" the male sweetheart is in distress, and the warrior's daughter does the saving. For over two decades, allowing for some gaps presumably due to work and family constraints, Bonnin wrote and published prolifically, and her numerous poems, articles, essays, rewritten song lyrics, an opera, and even her foreword to a collection of retold children's stories all served as mediums for her political protest. These writings provided a more than adequate training ground for her most explicit and vitriolic statement, her emotional descriptions in *Oklahoma's Poor Rich Indians* of the horrors experienced specifically by Indian women and children. My study of this report cannot do justice to its scope and impact, and I find it remarkable that, to date, Bonnin's contribution is not easy to access. To my knowledge, *Oklahoma's Poor Rich Indians* is not included in any anthology of her work, and only approximately fifty libraries and historical societies own copies of the original text. Yet, in her sentimentalist descriptions of real-life horrors, Bonnin finds just the weapon with which she can wage her political war.

Bonnin's embodied identity includes at least three socially constructed markers: female, Dakota Indian, and political activist. As a well-educated, politically active woman, Bonnin belongs to the expanding corps of influential women activists from all walks of life whose work is represented throughout this collection. However, from a Euro-American perspective, because of her Dakota body, she is already and always outside of the constructs of white, middle-class womanhood. Bonnin borrows from each of those identities, changing her rhetorical garb to suit the demands of the situation. In *Oklahoma's Poor Rich Indians* she adopts the dress of "a feminine mind," donning the domestic and private sentimentalist apparel necessary to establish a respectable white womanly persona. Bonnin then develops the ability to slip into the persona that best allows her to deliver her message and simultaneously affords the most positive reception of her as rhetor delivering that message. Like many other Native authors, Bonnin's transrhetorical manipulations indicate an active and positive affirmation of agency in the midst of continued colonizing forces, and her literary output over the course of her lifetime is a tangible example of this. Bonnin had a history of publishing polemical literature under the Dakota name Zitkala-Ša (including an article with the outrageously provocative title "Why I Am a Pagan" published in *Atlantic Monthly* in 1902), but as a champion for Indian rights in a white, male political world, when she wrote *Oklahoma's Poor Rich Indians* she chose to revert back to her Christian, married name, Gertrude Bonnin. She slipped off the dress of angry Indian woman and donned that of impassioned, but measured, female activist.

Attacking the Orgy of Graft and Exploitation: Transrhetorical Means to an End

Relying on some of the linchpins of sentimentalist fiction as can be seen in such diverse texts as Harriet Beecher Stowe's *Uncle Tom's Cabin* and Dickens's *The Old Curiosity Shop*, Bonnin draws on a sentimental paradigm that resonated well into the twentieth century. Bonnin plays on the tropes of the helpless, innocent girl-child; the virtuous poor (female) assaulted by the cruelties of the (male) world; the missing or failing guardian; and the use of ample tears, those emanating from her characters and those she hopes to solicit from her audience. Dickens's illustration of the sentimental through the character of Little Nell and Stowe's similar construction of Little Eva are easily compared with Bonnin's descriptions of Millie Neharkey, an eighteen-year-old Indian girl, and Ledcie Stechie, "a Choctaw minor, seven years old" (26). It is crucial, however, to remember that whereas Nell and Eva are fictional creations, Millie and Ledcie suffered all the physical and mental torture that Bonnin depicts. And, as seen in her earlier works, rather than serve up sentimentality that entertains and provides audiences with the expected, satisfying moral moment of closure, Bonnin employs her own transrhetorical narrative ethos and uses sentimental tropes to awaken her fellow Americans, especially those in power, to the public, political, present and continuing horror being enacted within their borders, in the hopes that through her rhetoric they might be moved to help save Native culture, land, and lives.

Although Bonnin describes a number of cases, her transrhetorical agency is most fully evident in descriptions of Millie and Ledcie. Bonnin presents shockingly brutal evidence to her audience but also uses Millie's case to shore up her own authoritative ethos. This then allows her an even more forceful voice when she next details Ledcie's tragedy. In just over three pages of information about Millie, two and a half are excerpts from the *Muskogee Phoenix*, a familiar and credible source for many of Bonnin's readers. Even so, she shapes this section by the excerpts she chooses and by the framing information she provides. In the opening sentence, Bonnin creates Millie as the stock sentimental character, a helpless child victim, who was "kidnapped a few days prior to reaching her legal age" and endured "unbelievable brutality" (23). Bonnin taps into the sentimental notion of the virtuous poor, stating that though Millie is "wealthy in her own right," "she is living upon charity" while "her property is tied up in litigation through no fault of hers" (23). After tapping into her audience's emotions, Bonnin launches into clips from the *Phoenix* that provide the facts of the case: the value of Millie's land ($150,000); the names of corrupt attorneys and businessmen implicated in her kidnapping (in particular Grant C. Stebbins, president of the Gladys Belle Oil Company); the details of the kidnapping, including use of alcohol and accusations of "white slavery" (interstate transport of women for the purpose of prostitution); an allegation of check forgery on Millie's account; and a charge that Millie's father also had been robbed by Stebbins. Bonnin ends the portion quoted from the *Phoenix* with a statement from Superintendent of the Five Civilized Tribes Shade E. Wallen, who declares, "The case is one of the most revolting in the history of Indian service" (26). By channeling the accusation through the mouth of a prominent white official, Bonnin shrewdly allows a white male to make the claim for her. Here is the transrhetorical at work: Bonnin, a Dakota woman with a "feminine mind," puts on a sentimental bonnet and gives the audience the titillating emotional introduction into Millie's story; then she slips on a masculine overcoat and provides facts and figures, and even a male voice, all the while working toward her cultural responsibility, wielding a political pen in defense of Indian peoples.

After the last newspaper excerpt, Bonnin's firsthand description of Millie Neharkey turns even more pointedly to a sentimental characterization of the girl, whom, Bonnin states, "I personally met" (26). This is not hearsay her readers are getting; this is primary information. Millie, eighteen when Bonnin meets her, is described as being so small and slight as to look "in every way to be a girl of only thirteen or fourteen years" (26). Bonnin, "struck by her smallness of stature, her child's voice, and her timidity," relates that she was "in the sixth grade prior to the time she was kidnapped" and calls her "decidedly immature" (26). Presenting her as childlike heightens the sentimental rhetoric and call for help that follow. Bonnin presents Millie as a "victim of an unscrupulous, lawless party" who is "mutilated by a drunken fiend" (26). She, a terrified child, "is assaulted night after night," but her screams "brought no help"; no moral, law-abiding, warm-hearted soul helps her. Using the phrase "assaulted" in conjunction with the time setting of "night after night" invokes, without explicitly stating, the crime of rape. The "fiends" Bonnin writes of have not simply stolen money from an Indian woman not crafty enough to see through the graft; they have, couched in Bonnin's rhetoric, *raped a little girl*. Here is Bonnin writing transrhetorically. Although she does not use the word *rape*, she, a woman, delivers explicit and shocking information to a male audience about the sexual assault of a child. Within the passage, Millie becomes, like the sentimental characters of Nell and Eva, helpless; however, after priming her audience first with a safe sentimentalist ethos and then switching to the protestations of an official male voice, she creates a space for herself to overstep the bounds of proper (white) female rhetoric to report on an Indian girl *raped* by greedy white men. Using particular word choices to create a tone of desperation, Bonnin asks her audience to become emotionally attached and then to hear and react to her request for political action.

Bonnin presents Millie as not just an innocent victim, but one who is without a voice to protest the exploitation, nor a guardian to protect her from it. Using a quotation from the *Phoenix*, Bonnin informs readers that Millie was "kept in a state of fear and prevented from communicating with her former guardian" (24), a situation reminiscent of Nell's in Dickens's *Old Curiosity Shop*. Millie's case reaches its emotional climax when Bonnin underscores an inability to communicate and signifies to her audience that the situation she writes of is so shocking as to be almost unspeakable. Upon hearing Millie, Bonnin writes, "*I* grew dumb," "there was nothing *I* could say," and "Mutely *I* put my arms around her" (26; emphasis added). The enormity of the crime makes Bonnin, in that moment, seemingly as mute and helpless as Millie; she is, here, enacting the demure sentimentality of the white woman by declaring her inability to speak of such proscribed things, but is also occupying a political (white male and also Yankton female) position *by speaking out*. The conversation between herself and Millie is long, but "private." For Millie it *is* unspeakable and horrendously private, just what Bonnin's audience would expect; women cannot publicly speak about being raped, so Millie suffers silently until Bonnin makes her private, emotional tragedy political and public. In this transrhetorical instance, Bonnin assumes an eyewitness position available to her only because of her cultural status. Her Indianness allows her to hear and narrate the repeated rape of Millie without experiencing scandal or loss of status—she is already other. This position breaches the prophylaxis of sentimental fiction in particular, while retaining the sentimental tone necessary for rhetorical effectiveness.

In the lines that follow, Bonnin reenters into vital communication on behalf of Millie and many other voiceless Indian peoples suffering in Oklahoma. Weaving the sentimental element into the report, Bonnin's rhetoric is potentially not simply heard, but felt, specifically by members of Congress who had the power to act by taking over the administration of land policies in the corruption-ravaged state of Oklahoma. However, the information that she presents is not simply emotional and anecdotal; it carries the weight of lawful testimony as part of the "official record at Union Agency, Muskogee" (26). With that phrase, Bonnin lends herself greater authority and strokes the ego of her audience; they warrant the "official record" of Millie's story. Bonnin's rhetoric appears to attempt to alter the reaction of an audience that might be predisposed to disregard the emotional stories that a simple woman writes about the unfortunate circumstances of an Indian. The three elements—sentimentality, eyewitness reportage, and authority as a Native informant—do not necessarily comprise a coherent, fully integrated, rhetorical identity. Instead these are components of a syncretic strategy Bonnin deploys—rhetorical moves more customarily affiliated with incommensurate positions and subjectivities, especially racialized and gendered ones. But Bonnin's transrhetoricity allows for this syncretism.

Bonnin ends her presentation of this case with this appeal: "Her terrified screams brought no help then,—but now, as surely as this tale of horror reaches the friends of humanity, swift action must be taken to punish those guilty of such heinous cruelty against helpless little Millie Neharkey, an Indian girl of Oklahoma" (26). She then asks for "*action, immediate action* by the honest and fair-minded Americans of this 20th century," adding the italics to emphasize the urgency of the situation (26). She plays perhaps to a sense of American post–World War I patriotism and perhaps to an Easterner's (congressman's) assumption that the West is indeed still in need of being civilized by telling her audience "the power is in [your] hands to redeem not only the helpless Indians, but a sister state of the Union from the petty thieves that infest her" (26). This ending reinforces her ethos as one of the "honest and fair-minded" and as a right-thinking American working for justice, but it also positions her as ostensibly helpless without the efforts of her readers. They must hear, and they must act. In positing this ending to Millie's story, Bonnin primes her audience to now hear "the smothered cries of the Indians for rescue," the line that starts her next section, "A Seven-Year-Old Victim."

In describing the case of Ledcie Stechie, Bonnin uses the sentimental tropes of the helpless, innocent child victim; the virtuous poor little rich girl; the failing and, in this instance, also evil, guardian; and the shedding of tears from both the grieving grandmother and, potentially, from Bonnin's sufficiently affected audience. The first two tropes lead importantly to the third: that the child is both rich and vulnerable makes her easy prey for the evil, would-be guardian. The latter tropes constitute Bonnin's call to action. She attempts to pathetically move her audience to an emotional tipping point, but, unlike in sentimental fiction (Bonnin's audience, in contrast with Stowe's, must do more than just *feel right*), tears are not enough. Children are being raped and murdered, and Bonnin's audience must act to protect them. Ledcie's story provides even more impact than Millie's because, sadly, like Stowe's Little Eva and Dickens's Little Nell, Bonnin's "Little Ledcie Stechie" dies as a result of a cruel and greedy world. Bonnin's visceral depiction is designed to elicit shock and lead to action. Analogous to Tompkins's assertion when describing the death of Little Eva, Ledcie's death taps into "a pervasive cultural myth which invests the suffering and death of an innocent victim with [a] just kind of power . . . to work in, and change, the world" (130). One could assume that this is the hope of Bonnin: by changing the hearts of her readers, she will provoke a just change for the Native peoples of Oklahoma. Ledcie's death is horrific and tragic, but Bonnin uses it, as Stowe and Dickens did with their tragic sentimental heroines, to show a path of redemption to her fallen audience.

As Bonnin describes in the report, Ledcie is a seven-year-old (and, the reader can infer, an orphan), living with her "old grandmother in a small shack in the hills" despite the fact that she has inherited land from her mother that includes a twenty-acre, oil-producing plot (26). Ledcie's initial guardian, her uncle, is coerced into giving up guardianship to "Mr. Jordan Whiteman, owner of the First National Bank of Idabel" (27). Here, buoyed by the authoritative ethos she has created, Bonnin herself names names rather than relying on the newspaper excerpts. Notwithstanding a monthly allowance of $200 owed to Ledcie and her grandmother because of non-Native use of their allotted land, Bonnin shows them to be living in a state of poverty and starvation. Instead of that allowance, Whiteman gives them $10 a month and provides for $15 worth of food, but only at Blake's store, a two and a half mile walk from their home. Bonnin writes that in April 1923, "they were brought to Idabel, the County seat. The rich little Choctaw girl, with her feeble grandmother, came to town carrying their clothes, a bundle of rags in a flour sack. Ledcie was dirty, filthy, and covered with vermin. She was emaciated" (27). The Indian Service recognized Ledcie's poor health (undernourishment and malaria), administered five weeks of medical treatment, and then placed Ledcie in a nearby boarding school. Within twenty-four hours, Whiteman removed her from the school, and no one reported seeing the child again until one month later when "word was brought to the hills that Ledcie was dead" (28).

Here, Bonnin strategically places information about the girl's wealth (money that Ledcie and her grandmother do not know she has) in a manner that highlights the sentimental trope of "poor little rich girl," such that no reader can escape sympathizing with the "rich little Choctaw girl," whose only protector, her "feeble grandmother," can, in actuality, provide no protection at all (27). Bonnin presents Ledcie as "living in dire poverty, without proper food or clothing and surrounded by filth and dirt" for two years (26–27). Here then is the unsuspecting prey for grafters, who are ready to wring money out of her and then casually dispose of her.

In the mode of a sentimental novel, despite the dire circumstances of the child and grandmother, the audience is given a breath of hope for their survival: Indian Services takes over Ledcie's care; she gains eleven pounds and is sent off to school. But that brief glimmer is snuffed out quickly when Whiteman demands the child's return, and in the very next paragraph she is reported dead. At this point Bonnin truly pulls at the sentimental heartstrings triggered by the trope of the helpless, innocent victim and uses the scene to display tears in her narrative and present the pathos engineered to elicit tears from her audience:

> Greed for the girl's land and rich oil property actuated the grafters and made them like beasts surrounding their prey, insensible to the grief of and anguish of the white-haired grandmother. Feebly, hopelessly, she wailed over the little dead body—its baby mouth turned black, little fingernails turned black, and even the little breast all turned black!" (28)

The grandmother, fearing the child has been poisoned, asks for an examination of the body, but Whiteman commands that the corpse be buried immediately; subsequently, the court appoints, "against her vehement protest," a guardian for the grandmother as well.

In popular variations of the sentimental plot, the guardian figure is benevolent albeit incompetent, and this unfortunate condition dooms the innocent child to become the victim of unscrupulous characters. In this real life instance, Bonnin shows layers of benevolent semi-guardians, the uncle and the grandmother, who are victimized along with the helpless child. She then illustrates how, in this instance, the storyline is rewritten: the appointed guardian, coincidentally named "Whiteman," is also the proverbial wolf in sheep's clothing. It may be just this image Bonnin was hoping to evoke when she writes of the grandmother, "She, too, will go the way of her grandchild, as sheep for slaughter by ravenous wolves in men's forms" (28). Alternatively, Bonnin might be implying a Christian connection in an alignment with Jesus, the sacrificial Lamb of God. Whatever the case, this tragic circumstance brings about the "wailed" tears of the grandmother and potentially elicits tears from Bonnin's readers that, she is quick to remind them, are not enough. This will happen again, she tells them, "unless the good people of America intervene immediately by remedial Congressional action. Such action is the duty of all loyal Americans for the protection of America's wards" (28). Through her transrhetorical agency, Bonnin has effectively deployed the sentimental figures of white womanhood and white childhood in the defense of Indian land rights and peoples.

Bonnin's efforts produced immediate response and, arguably, eventual change for Native peoples. The report's publication triggered a congressional hearing; Deborah Welch writes of "the hostile reaction of the subcommittee's chairman, Congressman Homer P. Snyder, to the emotional indictments contained in 'Poor Rich Indians'" ("Zitkala-Ša" 190). According to Welch, Snyder's "opening remarks at the Hearings make his unfriendly stance clear: 'We do not want hearsay evidence; we do not want long stories or legends about Indian lore or anything of that sort. We want specific cases and specific testimony'" (190). Of course, Bonnin's contributions *are* "specific cases and specific testimony"; however, due perhaps to harsh criticism received previously when testifying against peyote use, Bonnin allowed her cowriters to present their report to Congress.

The Senate subcommittee, after hearing the evidence provided by Sniffen, Fabens, and Bonnin's investigation, exonerated the Oklahoma county courts, declaring them "lily white" (49). Still, Snyder was right to be fearful; despite the congressional whitewash, Bonnin's rhetoric produced tangible change. The congressional committee "did confirm the presence of 'unconscionable attorneys and persons who make it a profession to obtain appointments as guardians'" (Welch, "Zitkala-Ša" 191). Newspaper editors across the country saw through the blatant dissimulation and published scathing reviews of the proceedings. Finally, the Oklahoma Bar Association "passed a resolution denouncing its colleagues who had acted unscrupulously in Indian wardship cases and volunteered to assist in devising yet another bill calling for investigation," and the Oklahoma legislature "passed the Frye Bill which placed maximum limits on the fees attorneys and guardians could collect from Indian wards" (190–92). Bonnin's transrhetorical maneuverings, then, worked to push the United States to restore at least a small part of the land, life, and culture that, for hundreds of years, it had robbed from "Oklahoma's Poor Rich Indians."

Notes

1. Bonnin is more widely known by her chosen Dakota name Zitkala-Ša, which she used when publishing her earlier literary works.

2. The United States labeled the Cherokee, Choctaw, Creek, Seminole, and Chickasaw nations the "Five Civilized Tribes" in the mid-nineteenth century.

3. Barbara Chiarello notes that the March 1896 edition of the college magazine *Earlhamite* reported that "Earlham was represented by an overdrawn caricature and 'Humility' [was] painted in large letters" (2). The "caricature," one can only assume, was as Bonnin described, "a forlorn Indian girl" or stereotypical "squaw."

4. Bonnin won the right to advance to the intercollegiate contest with an essay called "Side by Side" arguing for woman suffrage. However, in the regional contest, Bonnin changed the entire content of the essay to focus on the situation of Indians, retelling American history from the perspective of Native Americans.

5. "Impressions of an Indian Childhood" appeared in *Atlantic Monthly* in January 1900; "School Days of an Indian Girl" followed in February; and "An Indian Teacher among Indians" was published in the March issue. Her other stories and articles included "The Soft-Hearted Sioux" and "The Trial Path" in *Harper's Monthly Magazine* in 1901; "A Warrior's Daughter" in *Everybody's Magazine*, 1902; and "Why I Am a Pagan" in *Atlantic Monthly*, 1902.

4

> I said to myself, "That's the way to get things done. So behave, so dress, and so comport yourself that you remind them subconsciously of their mothers."—Frances Perkins in an interview, c. 1951

A Rhetor's Apprenticeship: Reading Frances Perkins's Rhetorical Autobiography

Janet Zepernick

Frances Perkins (1880–1965), secretary of labor from 1933 to 1945 and the first woman cabinet member, has received surprisingly little scholarly attention, given her pivotal role in the Roosevelt administration and her status as chief architect of the heart of New Deal legislation: Social Security. Recently, that has begun to change, as work by public administration scholars DeLysa Burnier and Meredith Newman, as well as biographers Kirstin Downey, Emily Keller, Penny Colman, and Naomi Pasachoff, has begun to draw back the veil of historical neglect and (as Burnier argues) active marginalization that effectively obscured Perkins's monumental accomplishments. One of the important contributions of recent scholarship has been to demonstrate convincingly that Perkins's own estimation of her role as a member of Roosevelt's inner circle was in no way exaggerated. The very fact that such outside corroboration seems necessary is a powerful illustration of the ease with which women's past accomplishments have been rendered invisible for future generations. Nevertheless, recent vindication of Perkins as a reliable chronicler of her own life opens up a fascinating area of research in the form of Perkins's insightful and thoughtfully rendered account of her rhetorical education and the successful application of the principles she learned and espoused.

The essential starting point for any study of Perkins as rhetorical theorist is her 1946 political memoir of the Roosevelt administration, *The Roosevelt I Knew,* and the posthumous *Al Smith, Hero of the Cities: A Political Portrait Drawing on the Papers of Frances Perkins.* In form, *The Roosevelt I Knew* is an insider's account of Franklin Delano Roosevelt and the New Deal, with particular emphasis on the period from his campaign for governor of New York in 1928 to the end of his first term in the White House in 1937. In texture, it has the lively, personal style and immediacy of memoir; and the voice, the rhetorical lens, and the interpretative, analytical approach all create a strong sense of Perkins's presence. Although its nominal focus is Roosevelt, the political man, read across the grain, it forms a sort of rhetorical literacy narrative or autobiography of Perkins herself, in which she frames her own continuing political education as a sequence of discrete moments—events, conversations, and observations—that emerge as reference points in her recollection of Roosevelt's administrative style and the larger interactional context within which the work of the New Deal administration occurred. In that sense, *The Roosevelt I Knew* is a work of political exegesis that takes the invention and implementation of the New Deal as its text and reads it as a series of lessons in rhetorical practice. The work that became *Al Smith: Hero of the Cities* was begun in a similar vein. With the working title "The Al Smith I Knew" (Martin 486), it was intended as a political biography of the New York governor (1919–20 and 1923–28) whose career in politics was closely intertwined with Perkins's career in social reform. Although Perkins herself was unable to complete the manuscript, her presence is very evident, and it is in many ways the companion volume to *The Roosevelt I Knew.*

Together, I argue, the two works form what I call Perkins's autobiographical rhetorical theory: a first-person, narrative textbook on the micro-rhetoric of "the great game of politics" (*Roosevelt I Knew* 137) as it is played out in any loosely regulated, hierarchical organization, including the bureaucratic governance of a representative democracy but also including the departmental structure of higher education and many large corporations. The result is what we might expect to see if, say, Plato wrote about a character called Plato who was the student of a teacher named Socrates. It is an engaging series of pedagogical vignettes, like the *Phaedrus* in its affectionate and intimate depiction of its characters, and like Cicero's *De Oratore* in its detailed depiction of rhetorical best practices for a very specific and narrowly defined scene. Like Cicero, Perkins herself was both a theorist and expert practitioner of the rhetorical principles her treatise represents, and she brings theory to life by illustrating it with some of the most exciting and game-changing events of twentieth-century American political life.

My analysis of Perkins's rhetorical autobiography traces the three broad themes that appear most frequently and that Perkins herself identifies as the foundation of effective rhetorical action:

1. Learn to fit seamlessly into any setting and to be on easy terms with any interlocutor. Listen to everyone, and keep lines of communication open, even with opponents.
2. Live always as an apprentice: be humble, seek mentors, seek the lesson in every experience.
3. Harness the power of information. Learn how to get the information you need and how to make it useful to others.

The Progressive Democrats of New York: Smith, Perkins, and Roosevelt

As a representative of the National Consumers' League, the women's political organization founded to translate, via collective action, women's private status as consumers and experts in domestic matters into leverage for social reform, Perkins found a valuable ally in Albert E. Smith (1873–1944), a Democratic member of the state assembly whose roots in the New York City immigrant working class gave him a personal commitment to the social reforms advocated by the Consumers' League. When Perkins and Smith first met in 1910, Perkins was already an accomplished (if rather newly minted) professional in the field of social reform. She had completed a master's degree at the premier graduate program in social work, the New York School of Philanthropy (now the Columbia University School of Social Work), where she had undertaken the kind of scientifically conducted fieldwork that was to serve as the basis for all her future work. Her rigorous program of graduate study had taken Perkins from what was essentially an internship at Hull House to a paid position as secretary of the Philadelphia Research and Protective Association while she studied economics and sociology at the Wharton School of Finance and Commerce, and finally to a full-time, paid position as secretary of the New York City Consumers' League. Meanwhile, Smith had spent the years since 1904 in the state assembly, pursuing his own political apprenticeship and working his way into the locus of power in New York State politics. From Smith and other influential Democratic members of the Assembly,

Perkins learned how political operators navigate the legislative process and how to work effectively with the men who wielded power. From Perkins, Smith learned the power of research-based evidence, which the generation of American social workers trained by Jane Addams had learned to bring to bear on social problems. At the beginning of his first term as governor, Smith appointed Perkins to the New York State Industrial Commission and opened the door to a political career that lasted until 1953.

Perkins's collaboration with Roosevelt began in 1928, when he was the newly elected governor and she was the more experienced continuing appointee in the New York State Labor Department. However, Perkins's and Roosevelt's connections had begun long before in the complicated and interwoven relationships among the woman suffrage movement, the women's movement in industrial reform, the state and national Democratic party conventions, New York State politics, and the social circle to which both Perkins and the Roosevelts belonged. While Roosevelt's standing in national memory has as much to do with his international leadership during World War II (in which Perkins played no part) as with the invention of Social Security and programs such as the National Recovery Administration and the Works Progress Administration (in which Perkins played a pivotal role), it was the popularity and effectiveness of those latter programs that made possible Roosevelt's reelection—and therefore set the stage for his role as the leader of the free world during World War II. It seems reasonable to suppose, therefore, that Roosevelt owes his status as one of the most important figures in the history of the twentieth century in large measure to Frances Perkins.

Style and Substance: Reading *The Roosevelt I Knew* Across the Grain

George Martin, in *Madame Secretary, Frances Perkins* (still the definitive biography), reports that *The Roosevelt I Knew* was a collaborative effort between Perkins, who dictated for transcription, and Howard Taubman, who collated, organized, and edited the transcribed material (473). The fact that Perkins composed orally is apparent in the style of the finished product: short sentences, uncomplicated syntax, emphasis on illustrating principles through first-person narrative of eye-witnessed events, and an argument structure indicative of following a single train of thought to its logical conclusion. This passage, in which Perkins explains how Roosevelt, then governor, established his national reputation as a leader and problem-solver on matters of employment, illustrates both Perkins's conversational style and her treatment of the events she narrates as though they are primarily to be understood not merely as significant moments in Roosevelt's career but as concrete demonstrations of rhetorical principles:

> In 1931 there was no federal labor legislation, and attempts at labor and social legislation on a federal basis had been declared unconstitutional by the Supreme Court. It seemed wise to explore the unemployment problem with other eastern industrial states which had similar problems and which were aroused over the conditions of people in their own states. . . .
>
> The governors assembled. Here was one of the tests of Franklin Roosevelt's powers of leadership. For the most part he did not know them. They were willing to come at his invitation because they were in the same predicament. However, no man in politics likes to acknowledge the leadership or superiority of any other person of equal rank. . . . Roosevelt understood that his first problem was to disarm these governors, to present himself to them as truly disinterested, a public official charged with a grave duty, honestly trying to find an answer and asking their help and cooperation. (103–5)

As this passage shows, very little imagination is required to read *The Roosevelt I Knew* as an autobiographical textbook in practical rhetoric for participants in a representative democracy. In true textbook method, Perkins explains each principle while presenting an incident that illustrates it in action. The effectiveness of the principles she teaches is apparent in the staggering domestic success of Team Roosevelt (including Perkins herself) in the period before Roosevelt became a war president.

In obvious, external ways, the text is framed as a straightforward portrait of the great man written by a humble admirer from his inner circle. The typography of the title, The *Roosevelt* I Knew, foregrounds Roosevelt and clearly reduces the first-person author to a subordinate position, while on the facing page, a portrait of the man himself, in classic presidential solemnity and captioned "President Franklin D. Roosevelt," emphasizes his elevated status. The table of contents reinforces this impression, with four sections that progressively indicate Roosevelt's sphere of influence: the Man, the State, the Nation, and the World. Perkins's introduction, too, is consistent in style and focus with the framing of this text as a "portrait of the great man": its first two words are "Franklin Roosevelt," and Roosevelt himself—or an aspect of his character or work—is the subject of nearly every sentence, creating a strong impression that the text is to be a work of homage.

One paragraph, however, breaks this pattern and in doing so clearly indicates an alternate possibility, which Perkins herself points to when she says that "this book about Roosevelt is not a biography" (*Roosevelt I Knew* 4): "This book . . . is biased in his favor. I agreed with most of his positions and policies and worked for many years to help develop, spread, and establish them in action. . . . Despite his shortcomings, I, on the whole, respect the methods he used to handle his problems and develop his strength" (4). The tone here, though positive, is more evaluative than celebratory, and by placing herself in the subject position, Perkins identifies herself as neither objective biographer nor unquestioning admirer, but judge: an arbiter of both policy and procedure, whose expertise allows her to comment on Roosevelt's shortcomings and pronounce an authoritative verdict on his strategies. In a subsequent paragraph, Perkins identifies the "problems" mentioned in the passage above as "his handicaps, both physical and intellectual"[1] and adds that "he was not born great, but he became great" (5). In other words, Roosevelt is of interest, not just because he was a good and powerful person, but because his life exemplifies the process by which "a rather unpromising young man" could become "a great man—not merely a President, but a man who so impressed himself upon his time that he can never be forgotten and will be loved as a symbol of hope and social justice long after his generation and his works have passed away" (5). "He grew to greatness," Perkins continues, "by a full utilization of all his talent and personality; he began where he was and used what he had" (5), and it is this process, rather than the man himself or his accomplishments, which is the focus of the text. At heart, that is, Perkins's text is a New Deal interpretation of the classical notion of rhetorical education for citizenship; it is her autobiographical textbook of rhetorical theory, whose three central themes I now examine in detail.

Fitting In and Being One of the Boys

On the importance of fitting seamlessly into any context and learning to be on easy terms with any interlocutor, Perkins is emphatic, both in her assessment of its place as the essential first lesson for anyone hoping to play the game of politics and in her explicit demonstration that this is a skill—or at least a habit of mind—that can be learned. In accounting for Roosevelt's rhetorical effectiveness, Perkins repeatedly points to his ability to connect with people from all social strata and from all walks of life. This ability to appeal to his audience's values, to anticipate their emotional needs, and to create a vision that many Americans could embrace is certainly evident in his written speeches and radio addresses, but Perkins demonstrates a very different aspect of this skill when she explores its role in the micro-rhetoric of face-to-face conversation. In the passage below, in which she explains how Roosevelt learned to talk to labor leaders, Perkins illustrates the strategic value of learning to converse easily across class boundaries:

> Roosevelt's principal social talent lay in making people feel at ease in his society and in getting them to talk about the things they knew. He was soon learning from these girls [trade unionists Rose Schneiderman and Maude Schwartz] a great deal about the trade union movement. . . . Later on he became acquainted with other labor leaders. . . . When he talked with them, relying upon the knowledge he had gained from these girls, he appeared to have a real understanding of the trade union movement. A labor leader once said to me, "You'd almost think he had participated in some strike or organizing campaign the way he knew and felt about it." (31–32)

According to Perkins, Roosevelt learned the importance of easy sociability only after his first term in the New York State Senate. Recalling this period (which she herself witnessed), Perkins says, "I have a vivid picture of him . . . going in and out of committee rooms, rarely talking with the members, who more or less avoided him, not particularly charming" (*Roosevelt I Knew* 12). Although it is tempting, in the peculiarly American way of reading hardship as a source of personal growth, to assume that Roosevelt became more socially adept through his illness and as a result of his subsequent paralysis, Perkins identifies Roosevelt's experience as Woodrow Wilson's assistant secretary of the navy as the initial formative period during which he recognized the importance of being "one of the boys":

> Roosevelt noted Wilson's personal difficulties with the politicians, his remoteness and isolation from them. Taking state committeemen to luncheons to listen to and mollify their grievances was one of the chores Roosevelt undertook. He gave up the notion of strictly formal and professional relations between political associates. He unbent, laughed with them, swapped yarns, and began to be as easy and natural as with old friends and neighbors. (20)

Fig. 4.1. Frances Perkins after testifying before the Senate and House labor committees to endorse the Black-Connery Wage and Hour Bill, eliminating sweatshop conditions and child labor, with the bill's sponsors, 4 June 1937. Photo courtesy of Library of Congress, Prints and Photographs Division, photograph by Harris and Ewing, LC-DIG-hec-22822USZ62.

For Perkins herself, becoming one of the boys was complicated by her social class and education, but far more by her sex. At about the same time that Roosevelt was learning to swap yarns with the boys as assistant secretary of the navy, Perkins had the epiphany that was to shape her public persona for the rest of her life: "I said to myself, 'That's the way to get things done. So behave, so dress, and so comport yourself that you remind them subconsciously of their mothers'" (Perkins interview, 232).

In spite of the natural disadvantage of being female, Perkins learned (first from Jane Addams at Hull House, and then from Florence Kelley in the National Consumers' League and from her many friends in New York State government) to treat every interlocutor as an equal. As a result, she found herself treated as an equal by the men she encountered, not just in public, but in private as well. Describing her experience as a member of the Roosevelt administration, Perkins says, "The men in the cabinet, from the beginning, treated me as a colleague and an equal. . . . I recall once that Claude Swanson, the Secretary of the

Navy, wondered whether he should tell a certain story since there was 'a lady present.' 'Go on, Claude,' said the President, 'she's dying to hear it'" (*Roosevelt I Knew* 153). Notably absent from Perkins's description of this exchange is any reference to her actual feelings about hearing Swanson's racy story. This omission helps to focus readers' attention on the pedagogical implications of the incident: what matters is not Perkins's taste in conversation but the fact that Roosevelt was able to see in Perkins a reflection of the other men present—a quality that transformed her from token woman in the cabinet (a ceremonial and essentially powerless role) to one of the boys.

This strategy must have succeeded outside the narrow and unusual confines of Roosevelt's cabinet as well, for early in her Washington tenure, while New York politicians, businessmen, and labor leaders would have been her most recent male associates, Perkins gave this evaluation of her experience working with men: "the American man is accustomed to dealing with women in business and does it very well. I really believe most people make the mistake of over-estimating the difficulties a woman meets" (qtd. in Hagee). Clearly Perkins herself did not share Rose Feld's view—expressed with the passion of experience in her 1935 *New York Times* article "Back to the Kitchen?"—that anti-woman sentiment was rife in the workplace. Although Perkins was in many ways a clear-eyed observer of the world, this may be one area in which her inability to see herself as unusual blinded her to the experience of others. While hardly unique in her ability to go anywhere and command respect from anyone, Perkins certainly benefited from the accidents of birth, education, and social background that characterized the leaders of the women's movement in her generation.

Like Roosevelt, Perkins learned empathy as part of her rhetorical apprenticeship, and it remained one of her most essential traits. Perkins illustrates this in describing an incident with General Hugh S. Johnson, who had been named to direct the National Recovery Administration and learned at the last moment that his authority was to be much less than he originally expected. Having informed Johnson, whose association with the program was deemed essential but whose leadership style was highly erratic, that the National Recovery Administration would be supervised by a cabinet board to whom Johnson would report (rather than by Johnson alone reporting directly to the president as Johnson expected), Roosevelt recognized Johnson's incipient revolt and instructed Perkins to "stick with Hugh. Keep him sweet. Don't let him explode" (*Roosevelt I Knew* 202). As Johnson recalled the incident,[2]

> She asked me to get in her car and, while we drove slowly around, she pointed out to me that what I proposed doing would make a great upset and interfere with the President's vacation; said that I had an absolute duty to stay at least until his return; conjectured that, perhaps, some coordination could be worked out; observed that there was an immense social service to be required any way, and was generally so understanding, friendly, kindly, and persuasive that there was hardly a choice but to agree with her. ("Gen. Johnson Takes Fling at Richberg")

Johnson's account shows Perkins touching on all of the points that would have been salient for General Johnson: his sense of duty to his commanding officer and his country, his hope that the position might be at least somewhat negotiable, and—on a purely personal level—his need to feel accepted and valued by his peers, as represented by Perkins herself. The potential catastrophe was averted, and Perkins adds that, "the next day, I think, he told a group of people, 'Frances Perkins is the best man in the cabinet'" (*Roosevelt I Knew* 204), a comment that reflects both the effectiveness of Perkins's empathic response to Johnson's distress and the extent to which Perkins's habitual representation of herself as somebody's mother allowed her to take on that nurturing role without complicating her status as one of the boys.

This incident with Johnson illustrates another aspect of Perkins's first principle, as well: the importance of keeping lines of communication open and the potentially disastrous consequences of failing to do so. While Johnson was being considered for the NRA position, Perkins reports:

> Baruch came to my house socially once and in the course of the conversation asked me, "What's this I hear about Hugh Johnson being considered for administrator of the Recovery Program?"
> I replied that I thought it likely.
> Baruch went on, "He's been my number-three man for years. I think he's a good number-three man, maybe a number-two man, but he's not a number-one man. He's dangerous and unstable ... do tell the President to be careful."
> Baruch wasn't seeing the President then. I forget why. Some disagreement about the fiscal and gold policy, I believe. I reported this conversation, but it was too late. Johnson had been told he was to be appointed. (*Roosevelt I Knew* 200–201)

Perkins's emphasis on the importance of keeping lines of communication open is further illustrated in her treatment of William Green, the president of the American Federation of Labor. When Perkins's cabinet appointment was announced, Green's immediate reaction was to declare that "labor can never become reconciled" to Perkins as secretary of labor ("Approve and Oppose Her"). In response, Perkins said that "Mr. Green and the American Federation of Labor are entirely within their rights. . . . I am glad they expressed themselves openly and frankly. It creates a more wholesome situation and I do not in any way regard it as an expression of ill-will against me" ("Miss Perkins Cool under Green's Fire"). If Perkins failed to regard it as an expression of ill will, she was the only one to do so; however, her emphatic refusal to accept Green's offered insult (and perhaps also the rather maternal style in which she framed her reply) left room for valuable future collaboration between Green and Perkins.

Green appears in another incident on the same theme, although this time he figures as the one who is willing to cross lines to talk with the enemy. As Perkins describes the incident, she had planned a meeting between Green (as labor representative for the steel industry) and the operators of the steel companies:

> Green was entirely willing. When the heads of the big steel companies and executives of the smaller companies came into my office, Green was sitting there. I started the introductions.
>
> Most of them did not permit themselves to be introduced to Mr. Green. They backed away into a corner, like frightened boys. It was the most embarrassing social experience of my life. I had never met people who did not know how, with hypocrisy perhaps but with an outward surface of correct politeness, to say how-do-you-do even to people they detested. (*Roosevelt I Knew* 221–22)

Perkins's own social relationship with Green, which had begun after his initial rebuff, fortunately survived this meeting, with the result that the line between labor and management in the steel industry was eventually crossed, again with Perkins's assistance.

The Perpetual Apprentice

As a result of her ability to meet with anyone at all on equal terms, Perkins made excellent friends and allies in surprising places and created for herself an invaluable program of mentorship. Here, for instance, she describes what was to become the pattern of her political education:

I later came to realize that this was part of a plan, and some of our Democratic friends by indirection had agreed to it. It was taken for granted that the friends of the bill would condemn it as amended and that it would be dropped without a roll call in the Senate. I didn't figure this out for myself. Tim Sullivan, the senator from the Bowery, told me. It was hard to believe, for I hadn't yet learned about "practical politics." (*Roosevelt I Knew* 13)

Perkins herself plays multiple and shifting roles in *The Roosevelt I Knew*, and noticeable slippage occurs among various representations of Perkins as author, narrator, and character. As author, she is the voice of theoretical expertise that identifies and interprets the "teachable moments," and it is Perkins's work of interpretation, informed by the backward gaze of experience and reflection, that draws theory from practice. At the same time, Secretary Perkins is a centrally located first-person observer—and often main character—of the unfolding drama. Like Plato's Phaedrus, Perkins as character is occasionally cast as the wide-eyed innocent, a political novice who observes the world with close attention and recognizes in every new experience an opportunity to extend her practical knowledge and deepen her political savvy. In the scene below, for example, Perkins reveals how she came to recognize the possible funding mechanisms for Social Security at a time when the Supreme Court took a largely oppositional stance on federal programs designed to promote social welfare:

> I drew courage from a bit of advice I got accidentally from Supreme Court Justice Stone. I had said to him, in the course of a social occasion a few months earlier, that I had great hope of developing a social insurance system for the country, but that I was deeply uncertain of the method since, as I said laughingly, "Your Court tells us what the Constitution permits."
>
> Stone had whispered, "The taxing power of the Federal Government, my dear; the taxing power is sufficient for everything you want and need."
>
> This was a windfall. I told the President but bound him to secrecy as to the source of my sudden superior legal knowledge. (286)

For readers with experience of the federal payroll tax withholding labeled "FICA" (Federal Insurance Contributions Act), the idea of a tax to support the old-age pension known as Social Security might seem to be so obvious as to have no imaginable alternative. To get a sense both of the continuing usefulness of this lesson and the strategic breakthrough it represented for the committee charged with identifying a practical funding source for Social Security, readers might consider as a comparison the apparent novelty of this approach when used to account for the insurance premiums that will be collected under the Health Care Reform Act of 2009 (see Pear).

Harnessing the Power of Information

Perkins's professional training in social work, during which she learned the social scientist's technique of combining firsthand observation of individual cases with numerical data drawn from studies of large populations, was one of her most important tools as a lobbyist and reformer. Both her training at Hull House and her subsequent experience in lobbying for social and industrial reforms in Philadelphia and New York had taught her the enormous power of being able to speak from what she herself had witnessed. As a disciple of the rhetorical value of firsthand experience, she created as many opportunities as possible for the politicians with whom she worked to see for themselves the conditions their proposed bills would try to remedy. About her education of Al Smith and Robert Wagner, she says:

> we used to make it our business to take Al Smith to see the women, thousands of them, coming off the night-shift on the rope walks of Auburn. We made sure that Robert Wagner personally crawled through the tiny hole in the wall that gave egress to a steep iron ladder covered with ice and ending twelve feet from the ground, which was euphemistically labeled "Fire Escape" in many factories. (*Roosevelt I Knew* 22)

From Al Smith, Perkins learned to see information from the perspective of the legislator who would have to rely on that information as the basis for writing a bill and arguing for it in committee and on the floor of the assembly. Unlike Perkins, whose training emphasized information as a way to represent existing conditions and the harm they caused, Smith's information-gathering focused on the more strategic elements: "'What are the facts?' he would ask. What do experts propose to remedy the situation? How can their proposals be carried out?" (Josephson 137). Perkins's ability to provide evidence that would make both problem and proposed solution readily understandable to legislators and voters—including the kinds of eyewitness accounts these site visits made possible—was a significant factor in Smith's initial appointment of Perkins to the position of labor commissioner ("Senate Confirms") and in Smith's own success as governor.

For Roosevelt, who also believed in the value of seeing things at firsthand but was unable to make the physically demanding journeys that would have required, Perkins became something like a camera lens through which he could observe, at the next best thing to firsthand, whatever she herself had seen. Here again, Perkins's academic and practical training in social work was the foundation for her rhetorical practice. Her ability to create a "thick description" of accurate, relevant, and compelling detail enabled her to provide precisely the kind of memorable information Roosevelt needed in order to understand the dynamic and human elements of the economic problems it was his responsibility to solve. In describing this process, Perkins says, "I learned in that period that Roosevelt could 'get' a problem infinitely better when he had a vicarious experience through a vivid description of a typical case.... In this way he got the economic and human problem all at once" (*Roosevelt I Knew* 97).

Her tenure as New York State industrial commissioner gave Perkins valuable opportunities to hone her skills in gathering and making effective use of large quantities of statistical data, but more importantly, she was able to use that time as something like a "proof of concept" for the importance of accurate, up-to-date, and detailed quantitative data as a means of understanding the overall state of labor and industry. In this respect, the fact that New York had the largest state economy and labor market in the nation meant that her experience in the New York State Labor Department was excellent preparation for her role in Washington. While Perkins's use of data in New York served as an apprenticeship in data-driven policy making for both Perkins herself and the Progressives of the Democratic Party, it also gave Perkins an opportunity to introduce the concept to a larger audience. Here Perkins describes the moment in which she catapulted not only herself but also the idea of labor statistics onto the national stage:

> On January 21, 1930 . . . I read a story out of Washington . . . that President Herbert Hoover had told the press that there had been a gain in employment in the past week. He indicated that things were much better.... I surmised that misleading figures from the United States Employment Service had been given to him and that he, the President, an educated and intelligent man, had not taken the precaution of checking them.... The next day I sent for the press and issued a statement that the President was wrong. Unemployment was increasing, I said . . . and things were worse. (*Roosevelt I Knew* 95–96)

For Perkins herself, this moment was the beginning of a brilliant career of social reform that carried Perkins and Roosevelt, but also the many, many other participants in the New Deal, to heights of effectiveness that have yet to be equaled in American government.

Conclusion

In the annals of American rhetoric, much attention has been paid to Roosevelt's public addresses for the obvious reason that the words of a leader spoken to the people represent the rhetorical corpus of both an individual and an era. In that sense, then, the rhetoric of the New Deal is rightly represented by the speeches, radio addresses, and op-ed pieces of Roosevelt, the members of his cabinet, and his political and philosophical allies throughout the country. In a representative democracy, however, addresses to the people can never be anything but epideictic. The truly deliberative discourse of a representative democracy occurs within the chambers of its legislative body and, with far less fanfare, in the offices of the appointed officials whose responsibility it is to carry out the will of the Congress. Even congressional sessions, however, represent only the most visible portion of the deliberative process. Before a bill is ever proposed in Congress, it is planned and negotiated in much smaller, less public settings, working its way from aides to work groups to committees and back again. It is here that executive-branch proposals become formulated policies ready for debate, and here again that the intricate negotiations of rule-making and eventual enforcement of the new laws are undertaken. It is in these conversations that alternatives are considered, decisions are made, and obstacles are overcome. In a very real sense, the interpersonal interactions of individuals and small groups during this part of the political process are at least as significant as the public addresses that capture—or fail to capture—the public imagination.

In many ways, Frances Perkins's life story embodies the two most compelling historical narratives that are told about women in the interwar period: the professionalization of social work as a driver of domestic policy and the progress of women from the periphery of civic action to the legislative assembly and—equally important—to the private offices in the halls of government where the real work of representative democracy is done. Perkins's insider account of the micro-rhetorical processes through which the New Deal came into being also serves as a continually relevant textbook for any of us who occupy a position in which responsibility, authority, and power are distributed across a dynamic network of individuals and committees. Little has changed about "the great game of politics" since Perkins wrote this text.

Notes

1. Roosevelt's physical handicaps are a matter of historical record. The intellectual handicaps to which Perkins refers were the limitations of not having a scientific mind (*Roosevelt I Knew* 163–65) and not having been trained as an economist (225–26), two limitations that Perkins herself did not share. Perkins argues that Roosevelt's polio and subsequent paralysis were instrumental in making him a more humble, thoughtful, and empathic individual (12, 29), all qualities that she places among Roosevelt's greatest strengths.

2. This is an especially informative incident because both Johnson and Perkins described it in print. The description here is from Johnson's account, but it matches Perkins's (*Roosevelt I Knew* 203) in nearly every particular.

5

Working Together and Being Prepared:
Early Girl Scouting as Citizenship Training

Sarah Hallenbeck

According to popular mythology, the American Girl Scout movement began in early 1912 with a phone call. Fresh from a tour abroad in which she had befriended British Boy Scout founder Lord Robert Baden-Powell, wealthy Savannah socialite Juliette Gordon Low telephoned her cousin and ordered her to "come right over. I've got something for the girls of Savannah and all America, and all the world, and we're going to start it tonight." That "something" that Low had to offer was inspired by the newly formed British youth organizations, the Boy Scouts and Girl Guides. Within a decade, Low's American movement had ballooned to more than fifty thousand members across the country, including not only girls ages ten to eighteen, but also thousands of "lieutenants" and "captains" in their late teens and twenties who served as troop leaders. By the mid-1940s, the organization boasted over a million members from all fifty states and offered girls and women opportunities to explore the outdoors, develop practical and professional interests, and hone their leadership skills.

Certainly, the scope of the Girl Scouts' influence makes the organization a valuable location from which to consider American girls' and women's unprecedented forays into public life in the aftermath of World War I. Indeed, the Scouts constitute one of the "alternate publics" (Gere 13) of the period, within which members, youth and adult, engaged in embodied, literate, and rhetorical practices that they felt would contribute meaningfully to the well-being of their nation. In the first days of suffrage, in particular, they saw their organization as instrumental in transforming women's present and future societal roles—an important extension of the work done during those years by women's clubs and voluntary associations (see, e.g., Gere, Sharer, and Scott). As one Girl Scout movement leader put it in 1921, the organization had become "a great volunteer school of citizenship in which the women of the country share with their younger sisters the results of their own experience in ideals and practical working knowledge of community living" (Bryant 8). Bryant's description indicates the extent to which the early Scouting organization was animated by the sense that it could prepare girls for a lifetime of meaningful and productive civic involvement.

Nonetheless, in looking back at the origins of the movement, feminist scholars have since had difficulty characterizing Scouting's precise contributions to the experiences of early-twentieth-century girls and women. Some scholars (historian Sherrie Inness and literary critic Sally Mitchell, for instance) have been troubled by the early movement's promotion of domesticity and homemaking as patriotic acts. These scholars suggest that the Scouts, as well as their British sisters, the Girl Guides, used more adventurous activities—such as camping, military signaling, and basketball, among others—to attract members but emphasized domestic activities instead. Although the nationally distributed Scouting reading materials, as well as the high completion rate of the Cooking and Home Nurse badges during the 1920s (Bryant 13), demonstrate that homemaking skills were part of the Girl Scout program, other scholars have begun to locate places within the Girl Scout program that complicate this characterization. Literary critic Laureen Tedesco, for instance, argues that the language and images within the early handbook, *How Girls Can Help Their Country*, helped girls to envision themselves as assertive and adventurous. Historian Susan A. Miller, meanwhile, examines Low's efforts to emphasize camping and outdoor living in order to differentiate her Scouts from the comparatively domestic-themed Camp Fire Girls (6).[1]

While all of these readings are compelling, I believe that much work remains to be done to assess the early Scouting organization's role in educating the young women who grew up during the years after suffrage. Rather than calling upon the specific activities—domestic, outdoors, or otherwise—in which the Girl Scouts participated for retrospective evidence of whether the organization challenged or reinscribed the gender order within which it was working, we might look instead at the pedagogical goals and strategies that animated early Scouting and that underlie these activities. For instance, Low framed her organization not as a site for recreational or even vocational training, but above all as a place "to train girls for citizenship in the broadest sense" (3), suggesting the organization's commitment to providing young women with a political and rhetorical education that would allow them to respond to the diverse contexts—domestic, social, professional—in which they would likely find themselves. I argue that Girl Scouting not only offered girls a sense of themselves as citizens capable of enacting change within these contexts, it also reframed the very concept of citizenship to include collective rather than only individual engagement and civic participation contingent on broad knowledge rather than "expert" status attainable only through higher education. Low's comment indicates that, like the women's organizations of the day, the Girl Scout organization provided members with a "protected enclave" (Sharer 163) in which they could learn to undertake the duties of active citizenship in preparation to act within larger community conversations.

In this chapter, I examine a variety of local and national Scouting texts in order to reconstruct the goals and strategies that animated the early Girl Scout movement. Specifically, I consider two of the recurring arguments, or topoi, that Scouting texts share and that represent the organization's major pedagogical goals during Scouting's first fifteen years of existence (1912–27)—formative years for the women who came of age in the period between the two world wars.[2] First, I consider the Scouts' goal of providing a location in which girls could learn how to behave in a democracy, a skill that, leaders asserted, boys and young men gained through sports, military training, and political and business negotiations—all of which Girl Scouts could replicate in their own procedures and operations. Next, I consider their second goal of emphasizing universal preparedness, which the Girl Scouts derived and modified from Baden-Powell's "Be Prepared" Boy Scout motto, linking it to productive citizenship as well as to the expansion of girls' knowledge base. And finally, I assess the legacy of Scouting for women who grew up in the years during and after World War I and the lessons that these women's experiences might offer feminists today as we continue to struggle to make our voices heard in the political arena.

Citizenship, Cooperation, and Collaboration

Among the concerns that feminist scholars have expressed in their readings of the pre–World War II Girl Scout organization is the apparent emphasis that leaders placed on members' obedience and submission as part of cooperation. "A Girl Scout Obeys Orders" was, in 1920, the seventh directive within the Girl Scout Law.[3] Although in retrospect this law seems intended to suppress members' active participation in decision making both within and beyond the organization, I suggest here that the directive for Girl Scouts to "obey orders" stemmed largely from leaders' perceptions that girls needed the discipline of group membership that boys and men already possessed. Learning to obey orders, these leaders thought, was for girls a necessary indoctrination into communities that had long been charged with the forging of strong citizens. And although the Girl Scout organization did demand a great respect for obedience, its emphasis on the need for girls to work together effectively in groups also facilitated opportunities for decision making and action.

In her 1921 report written for the U.S. Department of the Interior entitled "Educational Work of the Girl Scouts," Girl Scout secretary Louise Stevens Bryant indicates that helping girls to "develop community interests of an impersonal sort" was "perhaps the greatest contribution of the scouts toward the training of girls for citizenship"(6). This emphasis on moving girls into public, "impersonal" realms, of pushing them to collaborate in a systematized fashion, emerges consistently throughout Bryant's report as a central justification for the organization's existence. Whereas boys and men had long shared in defining common public interests, she argues, "girls have had in the past no such common interests" because their games had been "either solitary or in very small groups, in activities largely of a personal character" (7). Girl Scouting, Bryant suggests, was uniquely situated to assist girls in making this transition from "personal" to "impersonal" interests by teaching them to act effectively and efficiently in groups representing the larger interests of a community. As she put it, "If women are to be effective in modern political society, they must have from earliest youth gregarious interests and occupations" (6–7). Her statement illustrates her sense, in common with women's organizations such as the League of Women Voters, that the demands of suffrage would offer women new responsibilities for which they required citizenship training that paralleled the cooperative experiences shared by boys and young men.

By enforcing military-style obedience, Bryant asserts, the Girl Scouts could teach girls the need to submit to authority when necessary. "Following directions given to a group is quite a different matter from doing something alone, and most of us need special training in this" (8), she notes, describing military organization as "the best way men have found of getting a number of persons to work together" (7–8). Bryant's borrowing of military terms and metaphors is echoed in the 1920 Girl Scout handbook, *Scouting for Girls*, in which the narrator advises girl readers of the importance of obeying orders: "a small, well-trained army can always conquer and rule a big, undisciplined mob" because the army knows how to "obey and to act in units." In addition, the individual soldier obeys "by instinct, in a great crisis, only because he has had the long practice of obeying when it was a question of unimportant matters" (Bacon 8). By practicing obedience to orders in their daily lives, this argument suggests, and by envisioning themselves as part of an army or government, Girl Scouts could mobilize as citizens whose realm extended beyond the home and whose collective action might even contribute to the national well-being.

In addition to aligning themselves with the military in order to illustrate the importance of following orders, the Girl Scout organization employed military terms and practices to familiarize members with the public group membership that leaders perceived as masculine. The use of military-inspired terms such as *commissioning* and *captains* (rather than *leaders*), as well as activities such as marching and signaling, trained girls to think of themselves as part of a military unit, which, presumably, would help them to work more "impersonally," as Bryant puts it. As one camper newsletter from South Carolina's Camp Agnes Ann begins, "We're in the army now! We're in the army now! We must be healthy soldiers, so drink your milk!" ("Ravelings"). The playful tone here suggests that individual groups often made use of Scouting's military alignment as a rhetorical strategy for encouraging girls to complete even the most mundane tasks. So, too, as Bryant notes in her report, did the wearing of uniforms serve as a pedagogical tool—a "novel experience to many an overdressed doll who has been taught to measure all worth by extravagance of appearance"—that gave the girls "a sense of belonging to a larger group" by reminding them that "they represent a community to whose laws they have voluntarily subscribed, and whose honor they uphold" (Bryant 8).

If girls could learn to take a more "impersonal," civic-minded view of their interactions with others by envisioning themselves as part of a well-trained army, they could also do so by learning through their participation in Scouts how to behave within a democratic organizing body. According to Bryant, the Scouting movement was itself structured with this end in mind: "The basic organization of the girl scouts into the self-governing units of a patrol is in itself an excellent means of political training. Patrols and troops conduct their own meetings, and the scouts learn the elements of parliamentary law. Working together in groups, they realize the necessity for democratic decisions" (6–7). Bryant's description suggests the degree to which early leaders intended for Scouting to offer girls training for citizenship. In addition, it indicates the possibilities that leaders envisioned within the movement for girls' autonomy and decision making. Similarly, author Ellis Butler writes in the "Weekly Feature" column issued by the Girl Scout News Bureau that "Girl Scouting teaches tolerance of other people's opinions" and "gives group training," which is "the beginning of civilization" (2). And *Scouting for Girls* notes that patrols of eight girls within troops serve as "the ideal unit and cornerstone of the organization," charged with learning "through practical experiment" the workings of "democratic team-play" (Bacon 13). The captain-led troop, meanwhile, is merely "the administrative unit of the organization" (14), while the more distant, adult-led National Council oversees from afar and generally only at the captains' request. This explanation, like Bryant's and Butler's, emphasizes the empowerment of the girls, rather than the adults, in governing the organization, and it points to the need for girls to learn to interact with one another in new ways. The early Girl Scouts saw a fundamental connection between their own organization and democratic government: in each of these configurations, the former serves as a practice ground for the latter, in which the girls may someday participate.

    Within this practice ground, too, the Scouts modeled for girls impersonal, democratic processes of group consensus-making through the organization's careful delineation of appropriate behavior—including language, organization, and topics for discussion—for troop and patrol meetings. A chapter in *Scouting for Girls* is dedicated to this topic; readers follow the text through a sample troop meeting in which members introduce motions, conduct votes, and interact in language that echoes *Robert's Rules of Order*—a handbook that many women's organizations of the time were also using to structure their own meetings (Scott 83). The "Business Chairman," for instance, asks, at different points: "Will the Secretary read the minutes of the last meeting?," "Will anyone make a motion?," "The motion is carried," and so forth (Bacon 58–59). This formal language provides girls with an introduction to parliamentary procedure and encourages them to view Girl Scouts as a serious political undertaking in which they are empowered to make and carry out decisions that will affect others as well as themselves.

In addition to providing activities that modeled existing parliamentary processes, Scout leaders encouraged girl members to reflect upon their own involvement in the group decision making and negotiating that were inherent to the organization's structure. A 1925 editor's page within the national Girl Scout magazine, *American Girl*, for instance, requests letters from girls on the topic of "the most difficult problem our troop has met during the past year and how we solved it," directing prospective writers to reflect on "just what good suggestions were made by the various girls, and how the troop came to decide as they did" ("Along the Editor's Trail" 50). This assignment encourages girls to articulate their difficulties in an impersonal manner and to problem solve, placing the decision-making power in the hands of the troop members rather than their leaders. In addition, it encourages individual groups to think of their struggles as having larger relevance to other troops around the country. As the editor notes, "Girl Scouts and Captains exchange ideas and plans. What is successful with one troop is quite likely to be successful with another" (50). Such a perspective extended the emphasis on collaboration beyond the individual troop to include the organization as a whole. (See Risa Applegarth's chapter on women anthropologists in this collection for an example of women applying these same collaborative and universalizing lessons to their professional lives.)

Meanwhile, local organizations, such as the Charleston County Council of Girl Scouts, sponsored contests among members, inviting girls to respond to queries about group problem-solving and rewarding published essay writers with a free week of camp. One girl's response, though not offering the specified solution, demonstrates the writer's recognition of the need to articulate the issue in impersonal terms: "I am going to put before you a problem I cannot see into. There is a certain girl in our troop who tries to be boss all the time. She is ex-patrol leader and is useful in our troop in all ways but that one. When she is asked to do a thing, she always thinks she has a better idea and goes by it. What shall we do?" (qtd. in Butler 43). This writer describes the offending Scout as "useful" to the troop despite her problems accepting direction from others; she keeps her comments general rather than offering specific situations that would lessen the applicability of the advice she seeks to other Scouts. And the advice given is couched in military terms—the editor of *American Girl* offers a Civil War anecdote in which Abraham Lincoln submits humbly to the orders of a young sentry, demonstrating the appropriateness of obedience even for the most powerful leader and suggesting that young girls, like young Civil War sentries, are on occasion deserving of the respect of such leaders.

Because the ages of girls and their leaders were often close and because Scouting perceived itself as offering training that had not previously been available to women, opportunities for civic training were not limited to the organization's youngest members. In order to enact the methods of democratic collective action that Bryant describes in her report, the Scouts offered leadership schools and even college fellowships for its captains, aged twenty-one and over, and lieutenants, aged eighteen and over. Girl Scout Fellows during the late 1910s and early 1920s were required to take part in both college study and field work; in addition, they spoke before other women's organizations, participated in captain training and recruitment, and worked to develop Girl Scouting's budding educational philosophy. Like the girls themselves, these young leaders understood their role in the organization as central to its development. As Helen M. Keller, a fellow from Boston University, put it in an article entitled "What It Means to Be a Girl Scout Fellow" in the Girl Scout publication *Rally*: "co-operation will be the great power of the coming generation of American women. To find means to develop this power and to train girls in its use is the problem I am trying to solve.... Conclusions drawn from this work, in addition to a self, trained in theory and in practice, are what I, as a Girl Scout Fellow, hope to make acceptable to scouting" (5). Keller, like Bryant, emphasizes cooperation as an important skill for women to learn and represents herself as capable of solving the "problem" she sees for the Girl Scouts to address. Similarly, Louise M. Hall of Columbia's Teachers' College reports in the same article that she is taking such classes as Philosophy of Education and Advisors for Girls as part of her fellowship curriculum; the latter class, she notes, addresses specifically "the many problems with which a leader is confronted in her relation to girls and their relation to the different features of community life" and is helping her to "work out a scheme for the greater efficiency of troop organization and troop discipline" (5). Both fellows are engaged with questions of managing and developing the movement through bottom-up leadership skills, and both understand their contributions to its development as significant.

In addition to the nationally sponsored leadership schools and fellowships, captains formed their own communities within their local councils in which they conducted leadership-training sessions and negotiated local policies at monthly meetings. The "Captain's Club" of Charleston, S.C., for instance, coordinated its own training week at Camp Agnes Ann, for which Local Director Alice Wagoner polled captains to determine the training topics, including "girl motivation" and "troop management." During regular meetings, the Captain's Club operated according to the same policies of businesslike collaboration as were recommended for younger Scouts—voting on motions for instituting a uniform salute, for instance, and brainstorming, at one meeting, ideas for any "civic work" to which the area Scouts could dedicate themselves. The work of the Captain's Club suggests the degree to which the aims of the early Girl Scout organization defined the experience not only of its girl members, but also of the young leaders who volunteered their efforts in support of those aims.

Overall, the central emphasis on cooperation and collaboration within Girl Scout practices, animated through its perceived connection to military organizational strategies and, paradoxically, to democratic processes, played a central role in the organization's goals as an extracurricular educational ground within which girls could learn skills for citizenship. While this emphasis included mandates for militarism and obedience that in retrospect may seem unsettling, it also demystified for members methods of communication and cooperation from which they had long seen themselves as excluded. And perhaps most importantly, it resituated citizenship as a collaborative act within which even girls—seemingly among the most powerless members of society—could participate effectively, given the right training and reflection.

Being Prepared for Anything

If scholars have been concerned about the early Girl Scouts' emphasis on militarism and member obedience, so, too, have they expressed dissatisfaction with the Girl Scouts' appropriation of the Boy Scouts' "Be Prepared" motto. Indeed, the notion of preparedness, though for Boy Scouts a fairly unambiguous concept rooted in traditionally masculine outdoors activity, generated questions when applied to girls' Scouting education: for what might girls need to be prepared? In what ways could their preparedness translate to community and national betterment? In many cases, the organization seemed to answer these questions by applying the concept of preparedness to the home or to traditional volunteer activities for women. During World War I, for instance, khaki uniform-clad Girl Scouts received public commendation for helping the wives of soldiers with chores around the house, conserving food by canning vegetables, compiling and sending scrapbooks and packages to soldiers overseas, and selling over $9 million in war bonds. While these activities demonstrated, both to members themselves and to others, that these forms of "preparedness" could benefit the nation just as soldiering could, contemporary scholars have complained that they also applied the Boy Scout motto to seemingly conservative ends. Nonetheless, the notion of preparedness—whether expressed explicitly in the form of the motto, paraphrased, or suggested tacitly—remained powerful and versatile in Girl Scout texts even after the war's end, and in this section I suggest that it succeeded both in expanding the scope of girls' knowledge and experience and in conveying to girls that, through reading and practice, they could demonstrate their usefulness and effectiveness as citizens, regardless of their age, gender, or lack of official educational credentials.

The notion of preparedness was the very engine that powered the early Scouting movement on both sides of the Atlantic. Derived from Baden-Powell's concerns, while serving in the British Army in India and Africa, that young soldiers were losing their resourcefulness and their ability to think on their feet, the "Be Prepared" motto[4] signified a universal readiness to act that, Baden-Powell suggested, could help the British Empire maintain its status in the world. As Miller notes, Baden-Powell's own youth had been spent learning to move silently in the woods while tracking animals, cooking game, and avoiding teachers at the prestigious Charterhouse public school he attended (Schultz and Lawrence 295). These skills, as legend has it, proved useful in his military exploits, including the Siege of Mafeking during the Second Boer War, in which he led a small and ill-equipped army in withstanding attacks from over eight thousand Boer soldiers. Baden-Powell, then a colonel, became famous in Britain and America for employing such tactics as planting fake minefields and instructing soldiers to avoid fake barbed wire when moving among the trenches. In an era when people could not help but speculate on the effects of modern technologies, increasing professional specialization, and mass consumption on human behavior, Baden-Powell's humble but wily strategies for survival seemed particularly ingenious, just as his complaints that his charges in the British Army were unable to replicate them seemed a special cause for concern. Were modern youth becoming weak and intellectually lazy? Originating within Baden-Powell's own organization, the notion of "preparedness" offered an apparent solution to the problem, attractive to both adults and youths: Scouting would help its young modernized members regain their inner wiliness and thus strengthen their nation and defend it from attack.

Appearing repeatedly in the Girl Scout handbooks, internal correspondence, and public documents, the idea that Scouting could help members "be prepared" for whatever came their way, combined with the suggestion that this was an educational goal that modern living had somehow failed to meet, generated a kairotic sense of urgency and possibility for members. The motto's persuasive effects were twofold: it both justified the group's existence as an organization that could educate competent citizens in ways that were being otherwise neglected, and it encouraged girls themselves to look upon their training as a rewarding activity with potentially significant results in an emergency or disaster. Readers of *Scouting for Girls* are told that British Girl Guides and the Boy Scouts are already preparing themselves for this skill-based brand of citizenship—that these groups have learned that they must "be ready for any kind of duty that may be thrust upon them, and what is more . . . know what to do by having practiced it beforehand in the case of any kind of accident or any kind of work that they may be asked to take up" (Bacon 20). This statement captures the versatility of the "Be Prepared" trope, as it refers to "any kind" of accident, duty, and work and directs the readers to a variety of merit badges, ranging from Citizenship to Cyclist to the aforementioned Home Nurse.

Whereas the Girl Scouts advanced the notion that collaborative citizenship was a response to the new civic demands of modern womanhood, they suggested that preparedness was a lost art. As *Scouting for Girls* explains, American pioneers had exhibited the resourcefulness that modern Girl Scouts ought to possess: "In the old days of this great country of ours, before telephones and telegrams, railroads and automobiles made communication of all sorts so easy, and help of all kinds so quickly secured, men and women—yes, and boys and girls, too—had to depend very much on themselves and be very handy and resourceful, if they expected to keep safe and well, and even alive" (Bacon 17). The young reader is connected to a past in which safety and survival were part of a high-stakes enterprise and in which the conventions of gender, age, and class went apparently unnoticed because of necessity. Each person had to "depend very much on [herself]" to learn the skills necessary for survival—skills that were universally useful to both the individual and the society in which she lived. By regaining these skills through careful study, the handbook suggests, the Girl Scout could regain this resourcefulness, making herself more useful to her country in whatever way was needed.

This argument possessed infinite flexibility in encouraging girls to have a "can do" attitude toward all challenges, whether domestic, professional, or related to emergency situations. Just as the Scout who "keeps her head and shows herself steady, reliable and willing, when called upon for help in illness or emergencies," shows herself "to be a true Scout who is living up to the Scout motto of 'BE PREPARED'" (17), so, too, does the Scout capable of fulfilling her role as business chairman at a Girl Scout meeting. As *Scouting for Girls* notes, "The idea is to have every Scout in the troop learn to be a Chairman so that any and all could act in the capacity of a Business Chairman at any kind of meeting" (58); this language hints at future meetings outside of Girl Scouting that might require a Scout's leadership. Often texts would suggest extreme instances in order to demonstrate to girls the ways that their universal preparedness might be of use. One article from the Girl Scout News Bureau even suggested that "equipped only with a jack-knife, ingenuity and a knowledge of nature lore, a pioneer Girl Scout might be cast away on a desert island for a month and be none the worse for lack of the usual food and shelter" ("Jack-knife" 1). Whereas modern technology had apparently made others soft, the Girl Scout could reclaim the skills of her ancestors by reading about and developing whatever skills might be necessary for her situation, no matter how dire (or unlikely) her circumstances might be. This emphasis on universal readiness and self-reliance suggests the organization's recognition that girls during this time period were eager for opportunities for adventure and challenge.

Overall, the "Be Prepared" motto served as a valuable source of rhetorical force for the early Girl Scout movement: one that could authorize its work in communities and inspire members to look upon their merit badge and troop activities—related to civic, domestic, emergency, or professional duties—anew. Similar to the emphasis on collaborative civic engagement, the mandate for universal preparedness called upon girls to think of themselves as agents capable of bringing positive change to their communities. (See Sandra Robinson's chapter on Nannie Helen Burroughs in this collection for a similar approach to African American activism.) Like her pioneer ancestors, the prepared Scout might know how to survive in times of emergency; like a trained nurse, she might be able to treat patients at home or in the hospital; and like the modern business person conducting a meeting, she might be able to lead groups of individuals in reaching consensus. The Girl Scout's citizenship was defined by its own versatility; ungendered, unclassed, and capable of possessing wisdom beyond its years, this identity multiplied the realms into which the Scout might tread, encouraging exploration rather than modern, exclusive expertise and suggesting empowerment through resourcefulness.

Conclusion

During its first ten years, the Girl Scout organization conceived of itself as a citizenship training ground for girls defined by two distinct but intersecting goals: that, collectively, girls needed special practice learning teamwork and cooperation so that they could wield civic influence and that, individually, they needed to "be prepared" to show their skill in whatever situations they encountered. Together, these two tropes united in the Scout the self-reliance of her ancestors with her hitherto undiscovered leadership skills, thus allowing her to demonstrate both her adaptability and her ingenuity. As a girl citizen, she could make herself useful to society in two ways: by demonstrating her individual skill in some untold but needed setting and by working seamlessly and impersonally with her Scout sisters toward an equally untold greater good.

Significantly, the Girl Scout movement's insistence that modern women were both losing old skills that had helped to sustain previous generations and introducing new ones in order to elevate their status in society generated a sense of kairotic urgency, justifying the organization's objectives and motivating members to plunge into their Scout work. Although the "Be Prepared" motto remains to this day within Scouting, it no longer commands this urgency, as modern Scouts are no longer motivated to envision their preparedness as central to the well-being of the community or nation. Even in the opening pages of the 1947 Intermediate Scout handbook—now nominalized as simply *Girl Scout Handbook* rather than the more adventurous, less gendered *Scouting for Girls*—girls are asked, simply: "Do you like to do interesting and useful things with other girls your own age? Do you like to camp, and to explore, and to make things with your hands? Do you like stories and games and songs and dances? . . . Girl Scouting is a club for you where all these things are waiting for you to enjoy them" (Chapman and Gaudette 3). In contrast to the tone in *Scouting for Girls*, Girl Scouting here has become a club for young hobbyists, in which activities are to be enjoyed rather than mastered and in which the reader is asked to account for her hobbies and interests rather than to develop her potential or prepare to meet her responsibilities as a citizen. Similarly, in the aftermath of World War II, the concepts of "captain," "lieutenant," and "patrol" were replaced simply with "leaders," who are now generally mothers of the girls rather than young women from within the community. While the organization still encourages girls' participation in troop decision-making, it no longer does so with such a deliberate intention that this strategy will translate into civic action beyond scouting. It is no wonder, then, that contemporary scholars have not considered early Girl Scouts' role in providing citizenship training for its members as this earlier purpose has largely been effaced by Scouting's present-day goals and activities.

Regardless of the fate of the organization's initial goals or its early alignment with militaristic, domestic, or essentialist models of citizenship, the size and scope of the early Girl Scout movement suggests the continued importance of women's voluntary associations during the interwar years. Similarly, the collective effort made by Low and thousands of other American women to introduce modern citizenship to their youngest sisters demonstrates the significance of rhetorical training and activity that rested not with the exceptional individual or the individual act, but with the flexibility and resilience of organized groups of women. These women—adult organization leaders and captains alike—persuaded their young charges that their efforts mattered and that their work would have immediate and lasting consequences within both individual communities and the nation as a whole.

Notes

1. Camp Fire Girl founder Luther Gulick saw it as "fundamentally evil" (qtd. in Tedesco 24) to ignore sex differences while his wife Charlotte complained that the Girl Scouts did "not sufficiently recognize that first grand division of labor which arose when man went forth while women guarded the fire of the household" (qtd. in Miller 6). When the two organizations briefly tried to merge interests in 1913, their efforts came to halt when Low insisted that the Gulicks adopt the Girl Scout laws, closely derived from Baden-Powell's own laws.

2. The organization changed rapidly after Low's death in 1927 and is, thus, difficult to characterize over a longer period.

3. The Law in 1920 included the following: "A Girl Scout's Honor Is to Be Trusted, A Girl Scout Is Loyal, A Girl Scout's Duty Is to Be Useful and to Help Others, A Girl Scout Is a Friend to All, and a Sister to Every Other Girl Scout, A Girl Scout Is Courteous, A Girl Scout Is a Friend to Animals, A Girl Scout Obeys Orders, A Girl Scout Is Cheerful, A Girl Scout Is Thrifty, A Girl Scout Is Clean in Thought, Word and Deed" (Bacon 20–21).

4. Interestingly, Baden-Powell liked to point out that "Be Prepared" was a derivation of his own initials (Miller 25).

POPULAR
CELEBRITY
in the
EPIDEICTIC SCENE

6

> If ever there was a superwoman that woman is Helen Keller. By her indomitable will she wrought a miracle, and when one ponders over her achievements, the brain is dazzled by the possibilities of the human mind.—Hattie Schlossberg, *Call* magazine, 4 May 1913

Reading Helen Keller

Ann George

In 2010 the ultraconservative Texas State Board of Education approved sweeping changes to the K–12 social studies curricular standards. Among other changes, these standards include a revised roster of women who merit study: Carrie Chapman Catt and Harriet Tubman are out; Phyllis Schlafly is in, as are legendary exemplars of selfless service Clara Barton and Helen Keller. But in Keller's case, the board didn't do its homework: Keller was a radical feminist and lifelong socialist, who in 1913 declared herself "the determined foe of the capitalist system, which denies the workers the rights of human beings. I consider it fundamentally wrong, radically unjust and cruel. . . . It must, therefore, be . . . destroyed" ("Blind Leaders" 64). A large red flag hung in Keller's study, where she penned articles for *Solidarity*, the *Toiler*, and the Socialist Party organ the *Call*. By 1916, Keller left the too-tame Socialist Party to join the Wobblies, exclaiming, "I don't give a damn about semi-radicals!" ("Why I Became" 84). When asked whether she was "committed to . . . education or revolution," she replied, "Revolution. . . . We can't have education without revolution. We have tried peace education for 1,900 years and it has failed. Let us try revolution and see what it will do now" (84).

The board's inaccurate image of Keller is not so surprising when one considers that Keller battled such public misperceptions throughout her life. As the epigraph suggests, in the public mind, Keller was an iconic figure—a miracle girl, "a marvel of attainment," who could overcome any hardship ("At 50"); she was seen as selfless, indefatigable, unfailingly optimistic. Indeed, she was less a person than "a symbol of the heights to which mankind can soar" ("Miss Keller Seen"). Her public image was decidedly hagiographic. Henry James called Keller "a *blessing*" (qtd. in Braddy xxii), and H. G. Wells, "the most wonderful being in America," as if she were quite incorporeal (qtd. in "Wells"); she was, by turns, an angel or the "'patron saint' of the handicapped" ("Miss Keller Seen"). Keller, however, chafed at being "hailed as . . . a priestess of light" (H. Keller, *Midstream* 153), certain that her desires and abilities could not be so narrowly defined.

In this chapter, I use Kenneth Burke's concepts of *piety* and *boring from within* to examine Keller's attempts to complicate her saintly image in her 1929 autobiography *Midstream: My Later Life* published by Doubleday when Keller was forty-nine. My purpose is twofold: first, I wish to recognize Keller not just as a radical but as a radical rhetor,[1] one who was simultaneously voiced and silenced in multiple ways and who, as a result, developed a remarkable repertoire of rhetorical strategies. Second, by putting Keller in conversation with Burke, I seek to demonstrate her contribution to modern rhetorical theory. Reading Keller in light of Burke throws into relief the extent to which Keller is doing more than rhetoric; she's doing rhetorical theory—a theory lived as much as written and one that often rivals Burke's in sophistication. Moreover, reading Keller in light of Burkean (written) theory ultimately reveals the importance of reading Burke in light of Keller's (lived) theory. Like other women discussed in this volume, and the untold others still to be recognized as theorists, Keller has a lesson for and about Burke—and, by extension, the canon of new rhetoric.

I begin, then, by explaining Burkean piety and its role in public resistance to Keller's early attempts to embody a radical identity. Then I analyze the rhetoric of *Midstream*, which, I argue, functions as a primer, presenting lessons on how to "read" Keller—as a decidedly human woman whose commitment to socialism could be appreciated, even emulated. That *Midstream*'s reading lessons failed says less about Keller's rhetorical strategies, I contend, than about the enduring power of Keller's public persona—her verbal rhetoric (especially her 1903 *Story of My Life* and celebrated fund-raising) and highly visible bodily performance—which constrained her ability to enlarge or complicate the public meaning of her life. (Hephzibah Roskelly's chapter on Jane

Addams in this collection records another misunderstood activist's response in memoir.)

Burke's and Keller's Piety

During the 1930s, Burke, who, like Keller, advocated socialism, studied the psychology of transformation in order to explain why people resist change, clinging to a system (such as capitalism) even when it fails them. In *Permanence and Change* (1935), Burke calls this reason *piety*, the psychic and physical devotion to a habit of being. Piety, he claims, is "a much more extensive motive"—both broader and deeper—"than it is usually thought to be" (69), extending beyond "churchliness" to include the entire range of human behavior (75). For Burke, the term captures the often inexplicable, unarticulated, religious intensity of people's attachment to behavior or beliefs—exercising *religiously*, *worshipping* a musician or sports team. Such devotion is not a matter of goodness but of completeness or thoroughness, taking an idea or role to the nth degree. "Piety," Burke explains, "is a system-builder, a desire to round things out, to fit experiences together into a unified whole. Piety is *the sense of what properly goes with what*" (74). Burkean piety is also "extensive" in its intensity: it is "the *yearning* to conform with the 'sources of one's being'" (69; emphasis added). People have individual pieties, but those are formed within (and constrained by) larger, cultural pieties—etiquette, nationalism, ideology, and, of course, gender roles (traditional concerns for women's propriety, purity, etc. are all demands for piety). Challenging a socioeconomic system, even when motivated by social justice, is an impious act.

Burkean piety, designed to analyze the interinanimation of identity and culture, is a particularly useful tool for examining Keller's conflicting pious and impious representations. Generous since childhood and deeply religious, Keller clearly embodied traditional "feminine" virtues that constituted her pious public image, but she just as clearly wanted to be more: her socialism, her "yearning" to shatter what she called her "plaster saint" image (qtd. in Brewton n. pag.) are also deeply pious urges on her part, expressing, in Burke's terms, "loyalty to the sources of [her] being" (*Permanence and Change* 71); these latter desires, of course, are marked culturally as impious. Keller, like all radical rhetors, thus faced the rhetorical dilemma Burke called the "piety-impiety conflict" (87). As Burke famously explained in *A Rhetoric of Motives*, "You persuade a man only insofar as you can talk his language by speech, gesture, tonality, order, image, attitude, idea, *identifying* your ways with his" (55). An effective rhetor appeals to her audience's pieties, drawing upon established beliefs, framing her arguments in existing vocabulary; however, a radical rhetor is inherently impious, ultimately seeking to overturn her audience's pieties. How then to be an effective, radical rhetor? The inflammatory leftist rhetoric of the 1930s, Burke argued, would never work: "Zestful antagonism has been the bane of radicals in America. They court resentment. . . . America is the country of 'boring from within'" ("Boring from Within" 327). Boring from within—working within the system, using the master's tools—is a common political strategy; "if you want to attack the Republican party, become a Republican," Burke says (327). As a rhetorical strategy, boring from within enables rhetors like Keller to negotiate the piety-impiety conflict, not by resolving or ignoring it, but by embracing it—claiming an insider ethos to advance controversial arguments, identifying them with existing cultural values. The more radical—the more impious—the change, the more pious an activist's appeals must be.

Culturally conservative people and institutions, of course, fight back when their pieties are threatened. Keller's celebrity—created in part by her disability—provided her with enough of a platform to be perceived as a threat, but, paradoxically, that same physical disability (often equated with a mental one) along with her gender made it easier for opponents to dismiss or silence her. One revealing example of such public dismissal appears in a 1913 *New York Times* report that ran under the double headline, "Miss Keller Tells How Blind Progress" / "Socialist and Likes Beer" (20). The *Times* story, a mix of genuine wonder and freak show curiosity, opens by noting that Keller was "dressed in a becoming evening gown of pink and pink satin slippers, with her dark hair arranged in waves down either side of her face and tied low on the back of her neck." The questions were finger-spelled into the "blind girl's palm"—Keller was then thirty-three but still frozen in the public mind as the seven-year-old at the water pump. "Miss Keller likes to talk," the report continues, "and she sent back gay, crisp answers" to questions about whether she can tell colors by touch (no), whether she most regrets being deaf or blind (deaf), whether she picks out her own clothes (yes). When politics came up, Keller confirmed that she was a Socialist, and then added, "and I am not a teetotaler either, for I drink beer"—which, the reporter notes, drew a huge laugh at "the thought of the little woman in pink drinking beer." When the headline links Keller's beer drinking and socialism, the radical politics of the girl in the pink party dress become equally laughable.[2]

Such treatment pushed Keller to adopt a rhetorical strategy few Keller scholars discuss: humor, a double-edged tool that simultaneously accommodated and subverted conventional perceptions of gender and disability. (Humor, as Keller uses it, is thus a form of boring-from-within rhetoric.) Her self-deprecation did invite critics to be dismissive, but it also allowed her to push back, serving up a triple-impiety: humor is traditionally a male strategy, and no one expects a deaf-dumb-and-blind woman—or a saint—to crack jokes. Thus, when some men sought to dismiss her socialist critiques by asking, "How can one deaf and blind from infancy know about life, about people, about affairs?" Keller shot back, "I must plead guilty to the charge that I am deaf and blind, although I forget this fact most of the time. Occasionally I come into sharp collision with the stone wall out in my back field, and for a second or two there is not the slightest doubt in my mind that I am blind" ("Blind Leaders" 55–56). Keller honed her humor when she and her teacher Anne Sullivan Macy traveled the cross-country vaudeville circuit in the years 1919–24; along the way, Keller collected seventeen pages of frequently asked questions and her snappy retorts—the original Helen Keller joke book:

> Q: Do you think any government wants peace?
> A: The policy of governments is to seek peace and pursue war.
> Q: What is your definition of a Bolshevik?
> A: Anyone whose opinions you particularly dislike.
> Q: Do you think the voice of the people is heard at the polls?
> A: No, I think money talks so loud that the voice of the people is drowned.
>
> (H. Keller, "Vaudeville Circuit" 106–7)

These are not quite the "gay, crisp answers" reported earlier in the *Times*. Here, Keller reveals her astute political analysis and circulates an alternative representation of herself, more mainstream (read pious), certainly, but also more assertive and incisive.

Her rhetorical situation changed drastically, however, in 1924 when the financially strapped Keller became a lobbyist for the American Federation for the Blind (AFB), and as her rhetorical options narrowed, the gap between her public and private images widened. Her livelihood now depended upon her ability to project a thoroughly pious image to politicians and donors. But although the AFB shut down most of her left-wing activism, she continued to self-identify as a radical. Hence, Keller increasingly relied on humor and boring from within.[3]

Midstream, published just five years after her AFB employment, is a prime example of Keller's "new rhetoric," illustrating both her attempt to revise her saintly image and the public's continued resistance to her impious redefinition.

Reading and Writing *Midstream*

Keller acquiesced in the main to Doubleday's insistence that *Midstream* be about her personal life rather than her politics. Over the course of 350 pages, Keller presents loosely strung together reminiscences about her love of family, dogs, and books; her fundraising and lecture tours; her writing and religion; her relationships with an astonishing cast of characters, ranging from Mary Pickford to the emperor of Brazil; and her life with Anne Macy, to whom the book is dedicated. Newspaper archives offer telling details about how *Midstream*—and, hence, Keller—was read: reviews omit her radical politics, highlighting Keller's miraculous achievements and the personal anecdotes "appropriate" for women's pages.[4] M. Grant Cook, writing in the *Times Literary Supplement*, finds Keller's "grateful appreciation" of her Teacher and friends and the "vivid power" with which she describes her home life and travels "moving" (39). *Time* magazine's review emphasizes Keller's meetings with famous men, notably, Mark Twain, Henry Ford, J. D. Rockefeller, and Andrew Carnegie, who, the reviewer chuckles, "once threatened to take Miss Keller over his knees and spank her soundly for being the fervent Socialist and birth-controller she still is" ("Three Senses"). The review, in other words, cashes in on Keller's celebrity and, while noting her radical politics, dismisses them by infantilizing Keller. The *New York Times* reviewer admires the book's portrayal of Keller's "unique inner world" (one whole column details how she "hears" a whippoorwill) ("Helen Keller Continues") and praises her commitment to serving the blind; no mention is made of her political activism. The book, the reviewer concludes, is "full of engaging little comments" and is "completely revelatory"—this last because Keller confesses to a secret, short-lived engagement when she was thirty-six.

Midstream is, indeed, a revealing book. These notices and reviews, however, give no hint that what *Midstream* reveals is a Keller whose beliefs are as radical as ever, that it contains biting comments on Fordism and class. Nor do reviews indicate that alongside the "engaging comments" about travel and friends run Keller's attempts to revise her public identity by giving voice to censored, impious parts of herself.

Although Keller declares that she has "not attempt[ed] to . . . give a special message in these pages" (*Midstream* 1), repeated comments about public misperceptions of her and about the difficulties of shaping the book attest to Keller's awareness of the rhetorically fraught task of self representation at this point in her career. In a series of what I call reading lessons, Keller instructs her audience in (re)interpreting the text that is her life; using boring-from-within rhetoric, Keller encourages readers to identify both with her as a fellow human—"I want whoever is interested to know that I am a mere mortal, with a human being's frailties and inconsistencies" (177)—and with her radical politics.

Keller's reading lessons begin in the opening pages when she discusses the difficult process of writing autobiography:

> Into the tray of one's consciousness are tumbled thousands of scraps of experience. That tray holds you dismembered, so to speak. Your problem is to synthesize yourself . . . into something like a coherent whole. The difficulty multiplies when you find that the pieces never look the same to you two minutes in succession. . . . I put together my pieces this way and that; but they will not dovetail properly. When I succeed in making a fairly complete picture, I discover countless fragments in the tray, and I do not know what to do with them. (3)

Here, Keller impiously asserts that her life can be read in multiple ways, many of which are "true" but none of which is complete. "I wish I were made of just one self—consistent, wise, and loving—a self I should never wish to get rid of at any time or place, which would move graciously through my autobiography, 'trailing clouds of glory.' But . . . [d]eep within me I knew nothing of the kind would happen. . . . It is no use trying to reconcile the multitude of egos that compose me" (333). In this, she insists, she is no different from readers: "We are all complex" (333). By acknowledging her "frailties and inconsistencies," she encourages readers to acknowledge her humanity and her multiple, sometimes-inconsistent selves.

In a chapter called "I Capitulate," for instance, Keller recounts her reluctant decision in 1913 to accept an annuity from Andrew Carnegie: "I cannot pretend that it was not humiliating to surrender, even to such a kind and gracious friend" (147); in addition to her shame, she is no doubt aware of the inconsistency of preaching socialism while taking Carnegie's money. Keller seems most troubled by the apparent conflict between her pacifism and her militant socialism—"I preach love, brotherhood, and peace, but I am conscious of antagonisms, and lo! I find myself brandishing a sword and making ready for the battle" (333)—a conflict she reconciles uneasily by arguing that even a violent socialist revolution is justifiable since it is the surest way to bring lasting peace. An episode recounting Keller's exams by doctors studying the nature of sensations offers readers another example of her complex character. Her "scientific tormentors," she writes only half-jokingly, use instruments of "appalling ingenuity" that "pinch, prick, squeeze, press, sting, and buzz. One counts your breaths, ... another tries ... if you know when to cry and laugh, and how fear and anger taste, and how it feels to swing round and round like a large wooden top, and if it is pleasant being an electric battery, and shooting out sparks of lightning" (257–58). Clearly, Keller does know how fear and anger taste. Nevertheless, she ends the episode by taking back her criticism—"I am glad I have had ever so small a share in researches which are pregnant of results"—implying that she was being "flippant" only to entertain her readers (260). And they *are* entertained. Keller is nothing if not witty. But it's a mistake to dismiss her critique; the Keller angry at her medical dehumanization and the Keller eager to serve can co-exist, two genuine if contradictory parts of her character.

Although Keller teaches readers that there are many "real" Kellers, she also insists her saintly public image is a myth, perpetuated by wildly inaccurate press reports

> that I had educated myself, that I could distinguish colors, hear telephone messages, predict when it was going to rain, that I was ... never discouraged, ... that I applied myself with celestial energy to being happy, that I could do anything that anybody with all his faculties could do. They said this was miraculous—and no wonder. We supplied the particulars when we were asked for them; but we never knew what became of the facts. (153)

In *Midstream*, Keller does not hide her annoyance with public ignorance; indeed, that she feels annoyed like anyone else is part of the point. Whatever patience Keller has felt obliged to show in public, she admits here, has been an act: "I have become quite expert in simulating interest in absurdities[,] ... [p]utting on my Job-like expression" (153).

Keller's chapter on the 1919 film of her life, *Deliverance*, presents her most sustained reading lesson, illustrating the media's role in constructing Keller as symbol—a symbolism she then impiously deflates with mock-heroic description and behind-the-scenes commentary. Keller finds it difficult to take her cinematic self completely seriously—or, rather, her rhetorical maneuvers make it difficult for *Midstream*'s readers to take that self seriously. A *New York Times* review describes *Deliverance* as "a succession of wonders, of strange, mysterious, awe-inspiring things at which ordinary human beings"—i.e., not Keller—"can only marvel" ("The Screen"); Keller, however, describes the succession of "absurdit[ies]" created when, like reporters who ignore information, director George Foster Platt abandons "matter-of-fact narrative" in favor of what she wryly calls a "mystical unfoldment of my story" (*Midstream* 195). Keller debunks the first "awe-inspiring" scene by interrupting her hyperbolic description with comic asides: "Ignorance, a hideous giant, and Knowledge, white and panting, wrestled on the hillside for the spirit of the infant Helen. I held my breath when Ignorance hurled Knowledge over the cliff"—and, here, readers almost imperceptibly hold their breath, too, as Keller sets up the bathos—"wondering what insurance we should pay her if she was dead" (195–96). The high drama of this battle ends with a slapstick image of Knowledge defeating Ignorance when "her floating garments . . . entangled him and [threw] him to the ground" (196). The scene's melodramatic resolution—"The evil genie then departed with a madman's glare of hate into the shadows of the earth, while Knowledge covered the infant with her mantle of conscious light" (196)—is punctured when Keller spells out the point: "It was now clear to the dullest of us that there was no limit to what might be wrought into the Helen Keller picture. Why waste time on a historic picture when the realm of imagination was ours for the taking?" (196).

Midstream's version of other "mystical unfoldments" similarly undercuts the film's heroic posture by showing readers how the scenes—and, hence, her symbolic stature—were constructed. In one case, "someone suggested that it was foolish to be making the picture of a mortal woman when we might as well be depicting a mystical Mother of Sorrows wandering lonely, and grieving for the blind, the wounded, and the fallen of humanity" (201–2). What Keller shows readers, instead, is a gritty scene: "a great crowd of strange creatures—men and women of all races, colours, ages, and degrees of deformity . . . wait[ing] . . . to be disinfected (the influenza was in full swing, and everyone who entered the studio had to have his nostrils and throat sprayed). . . . The noise was demoniacal, and the smells were nauseating" (202, 204).

Of the film's grand finale, Keller remarks that it was "such a curious fantasy. I was supposed to be a sort of Joan of Arc, fighting for the freedom of the workers of the world" (207). Again, Keller starkly contrasts the director's vision of Keller/Joan astride a grand white horse with her actual experience on the set: "It was a motley swarm of people dressed in all sorts of queer costumes to represent all the peoples of the earth, and there was a dreadful confusion of horses, . . . waving banners, and trumpets blown loud and long. . . . Out there in the fierce California sun I grew hotter, redder, and more embarrassed every second. The perspiration rolled down my face, and the trumpet tasted nasty" (207–8). Keller concludes the chapter happily abandoning her symbolic role: "I was glad when it was all over, and my quaint fancy of leading the people of the world to victory has never been so ardent since" (208). Indeed, the film, Keller implies, runs counter to her own reading of *Deliverance*'s point: to "show the public in a forceful manner *how I had been saved* from a cruel fate, and how the distracted, war-tortured world we were then living in could be saved from strife and social injustice" (186; emphasis added). The director casts Keller in the role of Deliverer; Keller had cast herself as one of many who were delivered.

Keller describes one moment, however, when she actually became the symbolic Mother of Sorrows; as the camera rolled, the crowd of extras portraying the world's downtrodden spontaneously fell to its knees, and Keller "reached out . . . and touched the bowed heads. . . . The contact smote my soul, and the tears rolled down my cheeks. . . . All the love and pity which until that moment I had been trying to simulate suddenly rushed over me like a tide. I thought my heart would burst, so overcharged was it with longing to lift the weary load of misery beneath my hands" (205). Examples such as this suggest that Keller does not intend to completely disrupt her public image. As here, Keller's piety is often genuinely felt; she also needs it professionally and politically—her public piety is what enables her to both make a living and bore from within to advocate change. But paired with her stated desire to step out of the saintly role, this example also shows a Keller determined to faithfully represent her own felt experience of herself (or, her *selves*) by circulating alternate, often impious, identities.

Reading the American Dream

As Keller teaches *Midstream*'s audience how to read her multiple selves, she also teaches them how to read—and critique—American culture, taking them with her, textually, on cross-country travels, encouraging them to look behind the scenes of industrial capitalism as she has done. After a stop in Detroit, for instance, Keller remarks, "A visit to the Ford plant gives one much to meditate upon. I have tried to imagine what the world would be like if it were all run like the Ford plant" (292). Initially, she claims,

> the Ford idea looks wonderful. It seems as if this "hard-headed" businessman had found the high road to Utopia. But memory flashes a picture on the mind of the thousands of men at the Ford plant working in perfect unison, like a marvellous mechanism, each man a tiny cog or screw or shaft in the machine, and one wonders if, when the machine is dismembered, the human parts will be capable of enjoying the blessings of Utopia, or will their brains have become so mummified that they will prefer to remain parts of the machine? (292–93)

Similarly, Keller's impious lessons about America in her "On the Open Road" chapter show readers how "new ideas kept crowding into my mind, and my attitude changed as different aspects of civilization were presented to me" (156). For example, Keller reports that visiting mining or factory towns brought her face to face with "the ugly facts" of class inequality (158): "I had once believed that we were all masters of our fate.... I had overcome deafness and blindness sufficiently to be happy, and I supposed that anyone could come out victorious if he threw himself valiantly into life's struggle" (156–57). But the poverty she witnessed taught her—as she now hopes to teach readers—"that the power to rise in the world is not within the reach of everyone, and that opportunity comes with education, family connections, and the influence of friends"; without them, she asserts, thousands of working-class Americans are condemned to "hopeless drudgery ... to create comfort and beauty in which they could never have a part" (157). Keller *did* believe that obstacles could be overcome, but only with help, with education, food and housing and health care, equal opportunity and power—in short, with a kind of help that requires wholesale transformation of the economic system. To hear, as the public had, only half of Keller's message—we can overcome—was to turn a deeply radical message into a deeply conservative one. As Liz Crow argues, Keller's "image of resilience and courage serve[d] the status quo" by "keep[ing] the focus on the individual; they are responsible for their own destiny" (853). Keller, in essence, had become an American trope; she was used to embody and, thus, validate a piety she did not believe in—the bootstrap mentality of the American dream—and she presses readers to see that as a gross misreading of her life and of capitalism.

The book's penultimate chapter, "Thoughts That Will Not Let Me Sleep," presents Keller's most complex rhetorical performance: neatly sidestepping Doubleday's order to avoid politics, Keller makes them personal by teaching readers the difficult lesson that radical politics is an essential part of her identity—and the even more difficult lesson that "true" (pious) Americans should also embrace those politics. In doing so, she demonstrates great rhetorical savvy, boring from within, slipping in and out of her pious womanly role in order to advocate birth control and revolutionary socialism. Keller begins with a rhetorical feint, warning readers that she's about to launch what is likely to be an ineffective tirade; she remarks that she feels too deeply and has too little skill to make readers feel culpable but not offended: "delicate banter," she confesses, "is not one of my strong points" (329). Here Keller adopts a "proper" feminine humility and something like a hostess's concern for her guests' entertainment. When she deplores modern industrialism, she avoids antithetical rhetoric by not placing blame; instead, she uses relatively unaggressive "I statements" ("I have gone through ugly dark streets . . ." [330]; "I have been appalled . . ." [331]) and bores from within, using emotionally drenched descriptions of impoverished children and patriotic appeals. The passage is short on leftist rant, offering, instead, pitiable portraits of children "born in ill-smelling, sunless tenements, whose hunger drove them early to the sweat-shops and mills and mines" (331), implicitly drawing upon her own symbolic motherhood ("Mother of Sorrows") and appealing to readers' maternal feelings.

Only after demonstrating her piety via pathetic appeals does Keller introduce a brief plea for birth control. With classic boring-from-within rhetoric, Keller reframes the argument: birth control is not a feminist or even a socialist issue, but a patriotic one; it's about protecting children and, finally, about maintaining a working democracy: "these [impoverished] children, who in body and soul have become dwarfed and misshapen, are not fit citizens for a republic. They are at once a danger and a reproach" (331). Upright, patriotic Americans concerned about the souls of their children and their country, Keller argues, must either limit the number of children born or provide for their wellbeing. Americans uphold a strange, illogical order that makes it a crime to teach the prevention of conception and yet fails to provide decent living conditions for the swarms of babies that come tumbling into the world. O America, beloved of my heart! The worst that men will say of you is this: You took little children out of their cradles, out of the sun and dewy grass, away from play and their toys, and huddled them between dark walls of brick and cement to work for a wage, for their bread. For their heart-hunger you gave them dust to eat, and for their labour you filled their little hands with ashes! I love my country. . . . But my love for America is not blind. Perhaps I am more conscious of her faults because I love her so deeply. (332)

When advocating radical causes, Burke argues, "We will be strongest if we can change the situation for the better while leaving people's minds exactly as they were. To be immediately effective, we must promote changes which can be put into effect by utilizing the mentality already at hand" ("Boring from Within" 327). Keller does exactly that, bookending her birth control argument with pious appeals to patriotism and child welfare.

Keller also uses the "mentality at hand" when she identifies socialism with American (William Penn, Walt Whitman) and Christian icons. Keller's Lenin is not a godless Communist; he is a Christian prophet: "Where our dull eyes see only ruin, his clearer sight discovers the road by which we shall gain our liberty. Revolution, he sees, yea, and even disintegration which symbolizes disorder is in truth the working of God's undeviating Order" (335). A socialist revolution, in short, is God's will. Keller argues, "Men vanish from the earth leaving behind them the furrows they have ploughed. I see the furrow Lenin left sown with the unshatterable seed of a new life for mankind, and cast deep below the rolling tides of storm and lightning, mighty crops for the ages to reap" (335). She concludes with a general Christian appeal, tied only implicitly to socialism, leaving readers with the image of Keller as a devout rhetor/teacher:

> I believe that every question between man and man is a religious question, and that every social wrong is a moral wrong. I believe that we can live on earth according to the fulfillment of God's will, and that when the will of God is done on earth as it is done in heaven, every man will love his fellow men, and act towards them as he desires they should act towards him. (340)

In Burkean terms, Keller identifies "her way"—socialism—with readers' ways—patriotism and Christianity. She teaches readers that the seemingly impious is actually the pious.

Reading Keller's Pious Body

Given the prominence of Keller's "reading lessons," the question then becomes why readers failed to acknowledge her continued radical critique of American pieties and her public image. Certainly, celebrity lends itself to one-dimensional media portrayals, and Keller's story was particularly easy to label miraculous or saintly. But another factor may be that as strong as Keller's verbal rhetoric was, her body carried even more suasive force. By all accounts, Keller had a powerful physical presence, the loveliness apparent in photographs plus something the camera couldn't capture—an extraordinary expressiveness, a luminous aura. Michael Anaganos, head of the Perkins Institute for the Blind, was struck that, even as a child, she projected "an unconscious eloquence of the whole body" (qtd. in Cohen 15). AFB advocate Robert Barnett reported, "If she walked into a room, it was like an angel" (qtd. in Nielsen, *Radical Lives* 51), an observation echoed by Van Wyck Brooks, who wrote that he had seen Keller wear "a look of seraphic happiness such as I had never seen on a human countenance" (qtd. in Cohen 15). The AFB, of course, had a vested interest in maintaining the image of a saintly Keller and, hence, forbade publication of Keller photographs without permission. Crow notes that the AFB archive of over two thousand Keller photos contains only one image that shows Keller "looking strained and tearful" and that bears the note, "Too tense. Just throw away" (853). Added to her extraordinary story, Keller's bodily eloquence created an irresistible image for public consumption. Because her initial fame stemmed from disability, her body was the focus of the public's gaze, described or shown in constant press reports and in her books. Keller's body, in fact, may be her most publicly read "text," and through her body, Cohen argues, Keller "came to mean more than she could ever say" (19). And because Keller was hard to understand in public lectures, the audience didn't listen to her words so much as read her presence. Einhorn similarly notes, "Even before she opened her mouth, she was considered successful. Her very presence conveyed a message of strength and inner power; she herself functioned as proof. Here was a miracle people could literally see and hear. A living symbol. An epideictic person" (73)—the embodiment of piety.

Fig. 6.1. *Midstream* frontispiece—the pious Helen Keller planted in readers' minds as they begin her memoir. Photo by Nickolas Muray, © Nickolas Muray Photo Archives.

However, because Keller's body served as such a potent enthymeme for piety, it could overpower her radical verbal arguments; when the public read Keller's verbal texts, they read through the lens of her pious body. Even when Keller was not physically present, Cohen argues, "simply knowing of Keller's handicaps transfigures the words she wrote" (18). In other words, Keller's body acts similarly to what Burke called a terministic screen, a linguistic filter that reflects, selects, and deflects reality ("Terministic Screens" 45). In Keller's case, Burke's concept has to be stood on its head: Burke theorizes how words shape our perception of the material world; Keller demonstrates how material bodies shape our perception of words (including *Midstream*). Keller's body reflected, as terministic screens do, truths about her character: her extraordinary strength and benevolence. It also selected those characteristics as her essential nature—the one true Keller—while deflecting her radical message, one that was deeply impious, partly because incongruous (piety is a sense of what goes with what), for whatever image Americans have of a radical, it is neither a disabled or radiant woman nor a child (the image of Keller with her hand under the water pump was, and is, nearly indelible). So, even as Keller deployed verbal piety to argue for leftist causes, her bodily piety defined her as simply the miracle girl. The public didn't "see" *Midstream*'s arguments about politics and public image because those arguments didn't "go with" the pious picture they had of her.

Burke's social psychology suggests that, given the power of piety, the public was almost certain to resist Keller's impious challenges: readers acted piously not just in dismissing her radical politics but also in refusing her a complex identity. If piety encouraged readers to see a unified Keller and if her highly visible body was quintessentially pious (and what can be more pious than a pitiable, virginal, virtuous woman who has overcome tragedy?), then the public would read her verbal texts piously as well. As miracle girl and Mother of Sorrows, Keller's pious public image was completely "round[ed] out" and, as such, nearly impregnable to her own impious desire for multiple, radical selves.

But if Burkean piety helps us account for public resistance to Keller's radical critiques, Keller's deft handling of the piety-impiety conflict and her through-the-looking-glass revision of Burke's theory of terministic screens reveal what canonical new rhetoric doesn't account for. Burke writes that "even something so 'objectively there' as behavior"—writing for socialist magazines, supporting strikers, posing demurely for the camera—"must be observed through one or another kind of *terministic screen*, that directs the attention in keeping with its nature" ("Terministic Screens" 49). What Keller shows through her lived theory, however, is that even something as objectively there as words on a page is observed through a bodily screen. It could be argued that the idea that women's bodies shape responses to their words is a truism; it's certainly the experience of all the women discussed in this book. And yet where in canonical new rhetoric, with its too-quick turn from the material to the terministic, can we find this critical precept that bodies screen terms?

I suggest, then, that *Midstream* offers one more reading lesson, this one for rhetoricians: whether we read Keller as beatific body, impious radical, pious public servant, or complex collection of pious and impious selves, we should also read her as a vital contributor not just to women's rhetoric but to rhetorical theory.

Notes

1. To date, Keller's radicalism has been studied by scholars in history (Foner), education (Quicke), English (Brewton; Cohen), disability and women's studies (Crow; Nielsen). Lois Einhorn's groundbreaking *Helen Keller, Public Speaker* is the sole rhetorical study.

2. Keller complains bitterly about the press's insistence on keeping her in her (pious) place: "It seems to me difficult to imagine anything more fatuous and stupid than their comments on anything I say touching public affairs. So long as I confine my activities to social service and the blind, they compliment me extravagantly, calling me the 'archpriestess of the sightless,' 'wonder woman,' and 'modern miracle,' but when it comes to a discussion of a burning social or political issue, especially if I happen to be, as I so often am, on the unpopular side, the tone changes completely" (*Midstream* 172–73).

3. See, for instance, Keller's hilarious 1932 satire of Fordism, "Put Your Husband in the Kitchen."

4. This is especially true in local papers: one reports *Midstream* was discussed at a Woman's Club luncheon in Garner, Iowa ("Here and There"), and the *Aniston (AL) Star* Society page excerpts three paragraphs describing "Miss Keller's Garden." The *Kansas City Star* elevates Keller's story to high art: beginning from a "triply tragic basis of blindness, deafness and muteness," Keller's life, it claims, is "unbelievably epic in character" ("At 50").

7

Dorothy Day: Personalizing (to) the Masses
M. Elizabeth Weiser

"Is it not possible to be radical and not atheist?"

Hearing that question today, social activists can think of "radical" Christian Americans like Rev. Martin Luther King Jr., or Sr. Helen Prejean, groups like Witness for Peace or Bread for the World or, indeed, their own church's likely participation with homeless shelters or refugee resettlement or green projects or anti-war demonstrations. In 1933, however, when social activists asked that question at a crowded May Day rally in Union Square, the circle of American religious radicals was much smaller. Among Roman Catholics, the circle was smaller still: some bishops inspired by a late-nineteenth-century papal encyclical, and Dorothy Day, radical journalist, recent convert, and founder that May Day of a newspaper and a lay movement, both named the *Catholic Worker*. Within a few years her message would reach hundreds of thousands, and by now, eight decades later, her work has changed millions of lives around the world. Day's brother-in-law Kenneth Burke[1] would have called her "radical nonatheist" stance a falling on the bias across dichotomous beliefs, uniting what seemed to her to be the best of both religious conservative and liberal progressive ideals. And she brought her readers along with her: Seventeen years before Burke theorized identification as the prerequisite to persuasion in *A Rhetoric of Motives*, Day urged middle-class Americans toward a rhetorical identification with radical movements, foreign ideologies, and immigrant others through structured, personalized reflection that translated abstractions into everyday concrete experiences.

Rhetoricians such as Sharon Crowley are today legitimately concerned that the liberal foundation of American public life is being eroded by an antagonistic religious value set. In her award-winning book *Toward a Civil Discourse,* Crowley labels this stance *fundamentalism,* which she defines broadly as belief in any nonnaturalistic explanation for creedal doctrines (the virgin birth, the resurrection) (Crowley 9). Fundamentalists *may* hold liberal political beliefs, she concedes, but most do not because (as she quotes Jason Bivens) liberalism "is associated with representative democracy, has tended to privilege individual over collective rights, favors negative liberty (freedom from coercion) over positive liberty (freedom to participate in politics in active, constructive ways), and seeks to protect moral and religious pluralism by separating public from private realms of society" (10). By implication, most Christian activists would have difficulties with democracy, individualism, freedom from coercion, and privacy—and this ideology not surprisingly "seems bizarre when measured by the standards of secular politics" (11). Crowley's aim, as she states in her book's title, is to forge dialogue between academicians and religious activists. I applaud her effort and share her concern for an erosion of the value of civil discourse, but I question her stark categorization of "fundamentalist" Christians and their "seemingly bizarre" beliefs. Dorothy Day, I believe, provides both a helpful bridge between religious and activist beliefs and a complicating alternative to Crowley's liberal secular/conservative fundamentalist dichotomy.

In this chapter, I examine Day's newspaper columns and books from the 1930s to demonstrate how Day articulated two key strategies of Burkean rhetorics—falling on the bias and identification—to produce shifts in perspective among her middle-class audience. These shifts toward radical ideas Burke theorized but could not, without a mass movement such as Day's, put into practice. In addition, my analysis shows that Day's bias-falling stance complicates the view of today's academic rhetoricians toward religious activists, while her personalized approach offers opportunities for dialogue among these often antagonistic communities.

Day's Rhetorical Stance

In some ways, Day's rhetoric followed an established path: Like many women engaged in social service during the Depression, she carried the pathos of the poor across a social divide to middle- and upper-class donor/volunteers upon whom the success of her work depended. Like many political activists, she carried Marxist ideas of capitalist inequities across an ideological divide to the masses of poor workers who might be prolabor but were not pro-Communist Party. Like many social reformers in immigrant communities, she carried "foreigner" stories from her Bowery neighborhood across the geographic divide to white Anglo middle America. But Day's brand of Catholicism also posed unique challenges: Her belief in the dignity of the individual above all made her antagonistic to radical communism as well as to mainstream capitalism. "*The Catholic Worker* stands opposed to Communism, Socialism, and Fascism," Day declared in her April 1934 column ("Days with an End"). Her belief that true change began in the soul and radiated outward to the world made for a complicated maneuvering between what Burke would soon describe in *A Grammar of Motives* as materialism (the belief that changing the scene will change the agents) and idealism (the belief that agents are radically responsible for themselves regardless of scene). This maneuvering across seemingly opposing viewpoints epitomizes Burke's *falling on the bias*, which, as I describe elsewhere,[2] was his term for an expansive stance incorporating the best of all sides into an ambiguous unity. Burke saw falling on the bias as a dynamic, more radical stance than mere compromise, and it was this position that Day adopted as a "non-atheist radical."

Unlike Burke, however, Day had rhetorical agency as the founder of a mass movement, and therefore she used her "falling on the bias" stance to do more than describe her position. Through her personalizing rhetoric she encouraged others to identify with her bias-falling radical nonatheism. In her first memoir, *From Union Square to Rome*, she recalls her time in jail as a suffragist, reading the Psalms and finding that, through them,

> I was no longer myself. I was man. I was no longer a young girl, part of a radical movement seeing justice for the oppressed, I was the oppressed. . . . I was that mother whose child had been raped and slain. I was the mother who had borne the monster who had done it. I was even that monster, feeling in my own heart every abomination. . . . [M]ost people instinctively protect themselves from being touched too closely by the suffering of others. They turn from it, and they make this a habit. . . . But one who has accepted hardship and poverty as the way in life in which to walk, lays himself open to this susceptibility to the sufferings of others. (6–7)

That this story is more rhetorical than memoir she makes clear, insisting that "this [book] is not an autobiography" (1) and titling its first chapter "Why"—as in both "why me?" and also "why not you?"

The story of Day's life is always told the same way: All sources emphasize Day's "bohemian" existence as a young adult in 1920s New York City, her conversion in 1927 after the birth of a daughter, and her resultant Catholic "devotion" that led in 1933 to her cofounding, with the transplanted French peasant Peter Maurin, the Catholic Worker movement, which promoted solidarity with the poor as a return to Christian roots. This hagiographic narrative—the bohemian-conversion-devotion cycle—originated with Day herself, carefully narrated in a series of memoirs starting with 1938's *From Union Square to Rome* and culminating most famously in her 1952 *The Long Loneliness*. As Dana Anderson points out, Day from her earliest work was well aware that her personal narrative was a powerful rhetorical tool in the construction of a mass movement[3] and therefore, to borrow the feminist slogan, for Day the personal was *always* political.

Origins of a Mass Movement

Day and her friends unveiled the first issue of the *Catholic Worker* on World Labor Day, 1933. In Day's New York City, both the Socialists and the Communists held what were expected to be extensive parades that ended in rallies in Union Square. New York City's entire police force of nineteen thousand was on active duty to prepare for riots, with one thousand of them in the immediate vicinity of the square. They were armed with tear gas, rifles, and machine guns, according to the next day's *New York Times*. Distribution of "radical literature" was prohibited. By late afternoon, fifty thousand Socialists and Communists were united together in the hot square to pledge a United Front for better working conditions and against fascism ("May Day"). This was the crowd through which Day and a few others moved, selling copies of the *Catholic Worker* for a penny. Day's first column announced that the paper was "printed to call their attention to the fact that the Catholic Church has a social program. . . . The fundamental aim of most radical sheets is the conversion of its readers to radicalism and atheism. Is it not possible to be radical and not atheist?" ("To Our Readers"). The paper's title was surely meant to evoke the Communist Party's *Daily Worker* and thus to offer readers that bias-falling stance between religiosity and radicalism.

Because the hagiography of Day (she is currently in the first stage of canonization in the Roman Catholic Church) emphasizes her conversion to Catholicism as a break with her "bohemian" past, the preconversion training Day received in using print to move the masses is often overlooked. Before the *Catholic Worker*, Day had been a reporter for the socialist *New York Call* and Max Eastman's radical paper, the *Masses*, where she was also an assistant editor. When Mike Gold reopened the paper in the 1920s as the Communist Party's organ, *New Masses*, Day wrote occasional pieces. After her conversion, she wrote for the most progressive Catholic journals of the time, *Commonweal* and *America*. (Piehl 91–92; Day, *House of Hospitality* v–xiii). From its beginning, then, Day's *Catholic Worker*, which she edited for forty-seven years, sought to syncretize the moral philosophies of Day's early Marxist perspectives with those of her adopted Catholicism, and it did this using the methodology she had learned from her years in the radical movements—public education via print journalism aimed largely at the working class. As she would write years later of this time, "My whole life had been in journalism and I saw the world in terms of class conflict.... I did not want to increase what was already there but to mitigate it" (*Long Loneliness* 181). Day's journalistic background prepared her to respond actively to poverty by, as she wrote in the same passage, "enlightening the ignorant and rebuking the unjust"—activities she would identify as Catholic works of mercy (see "Long Editorial").

Combining reportage and commentary on current events affecting the poor and unemployed with quotations from Church documents and prominent Catholics, *Catholic Worker* promoted the social program of the Church as it fell on the bias of progressive and conservative movements. She not only sold the paper but also gave it out to parishes around the country, quickly making it a staple of the church literature racks and, not coincidentally, providing parishioners with a channel for both their charitable giving and their active service. Half a year after it began, twenty thousand copies of the *Catholic Worker* were being printed; by 1940 the figure was 185,000.

Intellectual Underpinnings of the *Catholic Worker*

The Catholic Worker movement took for its economic vision the early church doctrine of communal property ownership "according as every one had need" (Acts 2:45) that Marx had famously reformulated in his *Critique of the Gotha Program*, "from each according to his ability, to each according to his needs" (18). The vision of Day and her cofounder Peter Maurin was one of agrarian radicalism that fell on the bias of urban-worker-based Marxism and conservative, anti-industrial trends of Southern Agrarianism.[4] The volunteers and homeless guests in the House of Hospitality on Mott Street shared together the living space and the work—indeed, guests and volunteers were often one. And on the farms, as Day explained, "there are untilled acres, there is room for every kind of employment where the single unemployed can pioneer and lead the way for the family, thus serving not only himself but the common good" ("Farming Commune").

Fig. 7.1. Dorothy Day (*far right*) and colleagues at the Catholic Worker office, ca. Sept. 1934. Photo by Henry Beck, courtesy of the Department of Special Collections and University Archives, Marquette University Libraries.

The Catholic Worker movement also adopted—and adapted—other Marxist perspectives. They fought evictions just as did the Communist Unemployed Councils. Their newspaper covered strikes and its members joined picket lines. When William Randolph Hearst used his newspapers to congratulate "the Catholic press" on their "militant fight against Communists" in the winter of 1936, Day wrote a scathing attack in response, noting that "the Catholic fight on Communism is one based on philosophies, not on economics. And by the same token your brand of Americanism, your bourgeois Capitalism, your class war, your militaristic attitude come in for the same condemnation as does the philosophy of Marx and Engels" ("Catholics Have No United Front"). Day wrote later that in starting the paper they thought particularly of "the poor, the dispossessed, the exploited" (*Long Loneliness* 204)—a significant sequence that included not just "the poor," a term of existential reality for Depression-era America, not just "the dispossessed," a term redolent of Christian teachings of exile, but also "the exploited," those being victimized by the unacknowledged class war. For Day, it was the Communists, "those poor unfortunate ones who have not the faith to guide them," who were paradoxically "apt to stand more chance in the eyes of God than those indifferent Catholics who sit by and do nothing for 'the least of these' of whom Christ spoke" ("Why Write?"). The Communists, in other words, were providing the ethical model that Day and Maurin believed Christians should emulate.

The Catholic Worker movement itself, though, was far from communism in Lamb's clothing. "Here is my attitude towards Communism now," Day wrote in 1938. "I consider it a heresy, a false doctrine but, as St. Augustine says, there is no false doctrine that does not contain certain elements of truth. I believe it is the failure of Christians which has brought about this heresy" (*From Union Square* 147)— and the Catholic Worker, therefore, aimed to restore to Christianity the path it had lost. As it vociferously pointed out, the movement sprang from a Catholic tradition of social activism going back at least a generation:

> This month I've been reading the Encyclicals of the Holy Father.... They are the best kind of spiritual reading because they are directed to us now, at the present time, for our present needs. The Encyclical on labor is perhaps the best known, but they are all pertinent, deep and searching in their analysis of the present day and our conduct at this time. (*House of Hospitality* 184)

Anderson writes that "papal pronouncements dating as far back as Leo XIII's *Rerum novarum* ("The Condition of the Working Classes" [1891]) and Pius XI's *Quadragesimo anno* ("On Reconstructing the Social Order" [1931]) explicitly declare the Catholic Church's devotion to the needs of working men and women" (58). With *Rerum novarum* (para. 51–55), the hierarchy of the Catholic Church officially endorsed both labor rights and the regulation of business practices, even as it strongly supported private property and private acts of charity rather than broad social programs. And according to *Quadragesimo, both* capitalist individualism and communist collectivism were dangers that it was the Church's duty to judge and correct (para. 46). This was the worldwide tradition out of which Day could write with confidence in 1939, "Far dearer in the sight of God . . . are these hungry ragged ones, than all those smug, well-fed Christians who sit . . . cowering in fear of the Communist menace" (*House of Hospitality* xiii).

This global social tradition was not, however, the Catholic Church as it often lived out its role in America in the 1930s—a church that was perhaps more than any other large denomination at the time an institution of recent immigrants, in a period dominated by such charismatically anticommunist and isolationist figures as Father Coughlin, whose weekly radio addresses drew millions of listeners with a firebrand American populism that attacked political leaders but did not encourage direct local action (Kennedy 227–40). "Where was the Catholic leadership in the gathering of bands of men and women together, for the actual works of mercy that the comrades had always made part of their technique in reaching the workers?" Day wrote (*Long Loneliness* 165). And yet, as a church of working-class immigrants, it felt viscerally the privations of the Depression. What Day tapped into with her newspaper was a church ready for social action but unsure how to go about it. "'People are reading pamphlets on social doctrine now,' the girl who is the rack tender at a large church uptown said," Day wrote in a September 1933 column. "People ask for *The Rights and Duties of Citizenship, The Civics Catechism*, and this last month or so they've called for *The Ethics of War*. I have to order more of those. I have the two encyclicals on labor, by Popes Leo XIII and Pius XI too" ("Listener" 5). Catholics were seeking out their own traditions, and the *Catholic Worker* aimed to educate them.

Day and Maurin, then, critiqued the American Catholic Church for not supporting its own social teachings. At the end of a column urging true "Catholic Action" in the reaching out to one's neighbor, for instance, Day listed the medieval church's corporal and spiritual works of mercy (feed the hungry, instruct the ignorant, etc.)—and then noted in a pointed "PS": "Not one of the ten prayer books we went through around the office listed these works of mercy, though they listed the seven deadly sins" ("Long Editorial"). Maurin's oft-repeated maxim, which Day first published in the second edition of the newspaper, said that "Catholic scholars have taken the dynamite of the Church, have wrapped it up in nice phraseology, placed it in an hermetic container, and sat on the lid. It is about time to blow the lid off so the Catholic Church may again become the dominant social force" ("Easy Essays").

At the same time, they critiqued institutional communism for its antireligious stance, its urban technological bias, its advocacy of violence, and its rigid doctrinism. Day advocated studying the communist position from a Catholic perspective:

> Take the Daily Worker, the Communist newspaper.... Study the Communist criticism of the present system. What is the Catholic criticism? What remedies do the Communists offer? What is the Catholic solution?... If you study Communist theory and practice, and Catholic theory and practice, and then uphold the latter, you will be doing a constructive piece of work in combating the materialist philosophy of the present day. ("Long Editorial")

Most of all, Day and Maurin criticized the communist belief that organized class warfare could bring about social change, or as Day put it, "whether or not a man believes in God, the fact remains that we are all the children of one Father.... The work we must do is strive for peace and concordance rather than hatred and strife" (*House of Hospitality* 180). It was at the level of collective strategies that Peter Maurin's original training, passed on to and popularized by Day, ran up most sharply against Marxism.

Maurin was a disciple of personalism, which in his native France was an ongoing spiritual renewal that brought the sense of personal engagement with the world to thousands of otherwise disaffected churchgoers. Personalism emphasized each individual's fulfillment in personal responsibility to the poor. Its primary advocate at the time was Emmanuel Mournier, the editor of *L'Esprit*. Personalism can be seen as a radically conservative counter to the "rights of man" philosophy of public human rights, and Mournier called upon personalists to "patiently, cooperatively, *remake the Renaissance* after four centuries of error" (10). He was opposed to the Marxist ideal of collectivism, arguing that the human person "can never be considered merely as part of a whole, whether of family, class, state, nation, or even humanity.... No collective whole ... can legitimately utilize the person as a means to an end" (69). But it was a radical—not a status quo—conservative response, in that its call was for reformation, re-forming of the person. Unlike the American religious response to Marxism—Father Coughlin and his growing attachment to fascism—the French response included Mournier, philosopher Jacques Maritain (later on the drafting committee of the Universal Declaration of Human Rights), and Christian existentialist Nikolai Berdyaev encouraging religious and laity, intellectuals and the masses, to work together as persons for the good of other persons.

When Maurin moved to America from France, then, he brought with him Maritain-Mournier's radical-conservative personalism and the Popes' cautious support of labor rights, which Day used to critique the rugged American individualism that she saw leaving the less fortunate to starve: "The age of individualism, laissez faire industrialism and self-seeking capitalism is dead and gone.... Men are beginning to realize that they are not individuals but *persons* in society, that man alone is weak and adrift, that he must seek strength in common action" ("Liturgy and Sociology"). Maurin and Day spoke out against what they saw as attacks on the personal spirit from all sides—collectivist communism, tyrannical fascism, exploitative capitalism, and hedonistic liberalism. They saw the crisis of the age as both an economic and a spiritual crisis and, therefore, saw the first step in the revolution as a change in one's heart: "We do not believe that [New Deal] legislation is going to bring us out of the morass we are floundering in. We do believe that the problem before us, of working for a social order in which the way of life will enable man to save his soul, is a moral one that must engage the minds and energies of all Catholics," Day wrote on the movement's fourth anniversary ("Catholic Worker Celebrates").

Translating the Foreign into American

It was Maurin who, in his aphoristic "Easy Essays" that Day published in the second issue of *The Catholic Worker,* laid out the philosophical underpinnings of the movement. It was Day, however, who interpreted the philosophy and made it real for an audience of everyday, churchgoing Americans who thought the system wasn't quite working for much of America and heard the Gospel message on Sunday of "as long as you did it to one of these my least brethren, you did it to me" (Matt. 25:40), but who were not necessarily ready to debate Rousseau, emulate medieval monasticism, or advocate the international solidarity of the worker in class struggle. It was Day who articulated and responded to the characteristically American fear of giving to the poor:

> I have heard people say, in coming in contact with need: "If I supply them with groceries this week, they will be expecting me to keep it up." But I do not think it works out this way. It has not with us, here at THE CATHOLIC WORKER office. In fact when we have made gifts of food, clothing, a bit of money (though that seldom) it has usually been the other way around. The recipients have come back to see what they could do for us. ("Long Editorial")

Maurin might have the ideal of a perfect society, but it was Day who showed America how it might be lived.

Most specifically, Day decoded the radical European thought in which Maurin was steeped into her editorial columns, titled in the

1930s "The Listener" and later "Day by Day." In these columns, she took the philosophy of Maurin and the personalists, the social teachings of the Church, and the policy statements of the Marxists, and transformed them into stories about real, recognizable people with whom all Americans could identify. For instance, while Maurin wrote the poetic statement, "People would become better / if they stopped trying to become better off. / For when everybody tries to become better off, nobody is better off. / But when everybody tries to become better, everybody is better off" ("Easy Essays"), Day wrote about their Italian neighbor Mr. Rubino, who could no longer afford to buy autumn grapes and make wine that he then shared with the *Catholic Worker* staff. "For the long hard winter is before us. Evictions are increasing. . . . We must work, and we must pray, and we meditate as we write this that it would be so much easier for all our Italian friends to work and pray, to have courage to fight and also to be patient, if they could make as usual their fragrant and cheering grape wine" ("And Now a Note of Melancholy" 15). In another 1933 column, the Communists' indictment of the bourgeoisie becomes Day's story of Mary, a young "mother's helper" who earned two dollars a week doing childcare and cleaning and slept on a board on her employers' bathtub, not really mistreated but not at all loved, with "nothing to look forward to in the future of the present social system" ("Mary Is Fifteen" 6).

Each of Day's stories had a clear point, often stated directly in its conclusion. A midwinter editorial from 1935, for instance, recounts a day's work distributing clothes to various ragged, homeless people, remembers the poor around the world, and ends with the personalist message, "There is no use looking for a revival in business, a return of prosperity, until the hearts and minds of men be changed. If we wish for a program, let us look into our own hearts. The beginning is there" ("Editorial—Mid-Winter" 19). The story of a baby born to a single homeless woman living at the Catholic Worker house in 1941 ("Baby Is Born") and the story of the first calf born at the Catholic Worker farm in 1936 ("Mysteries") both serve as "holy mysteries" that Day links to the line of hundreds of hungry men outside her door each day.

That each homely story was carefully crafted can be seen in the arrangement of items within a column, particularly in those which appear to be merely a chronology of current events. For instance, a 1937 column that begins with the story of an unemployed porter who contributes $2 goes on to juxtapose his story with that of the society women before whom Day speaks in Palm Beach, who tell her they would "give their very souls to help the poor," but "birth control and sterilization" are the only solutions. They contribute nothing, not even a speaker's fee, and the column concludes with Day's pointed reflection:

> We are told always to keep a just attitude toward the rich, and we try. But as I thought of our breakfast line, our crowded house with people sleeping on the floor, when I thought of cold tenement apartments around us, and the lean gaunt faces of the men who come to us for help, desperation in their eyes, it was impossible not to hate, with a hearty hatred and with a strong anger, the injustices of this world. ("Michael Martin, Porter")

A 1933 story that begins by juxtaposing people's concern for trapped animals to their lack of concern for families trapped by poverty goes on to note that the newest game in high society is the scavenger hunt, yet every day, the poor scavenge through the garbage for food and clothing: "If the several hundred guests at the Waldorf had to scavenge night after night and morning after morning, the hunt would not have had such an enthusiastic response" ("Scavengers").

Personalizing the Abstract

Wendy Sharer writes that women who worked with the poor during the early part of the twentieth century often saw themselves as a bridge between the people with whom they worked and the members of their own social class, and they were used to couching their appeals in the language of emotion. "Through their settlement work," she recounts, "women who would [in the 1930s] lead the Women's Bureau learned that statistics alone could not convince legislators to support progressive policies that might benefit working women. Thus, the textual forms their research took often relied on pathos for their persuasive effects" ("Genre Work" 13). (See Elizabeth Wilkinson's chapter on Gertrude Bonnin and Janet Zepernick's chapter on Frances Perkins in this collection for other examples of the use of this trope.) Day also utilized pathetic appeals but in a unique manner, narrating the stories not only of the poor but also of herself and her companions. From the beginning, Day let readers into the everyday life of the house on Mott Street, in the Bowery, that served as the *Catholic Worker* office, its soup kitchen, its social work office, its education center, and the communal living space of both workers and homeless. It was a radical lifestyle, but by personalizing not only the life of the poor but her own, Day made it a recognizable lifestyle.

This first number of *The Catholic Worker* was planned, written, and edited in the kitchen of a tenement on Fifteenth Street (*By Little* 51). . . . Every morning about four hundred men come to Mott Street to be fed. The radio is cheerful, the smell of coffee is a good smell, the air of the morning is fresh and not too cold, but my heart bleeds as I pass the lines of men (80). . . . Two of the girls in the House of Hospitality have been fighting constantly. Today I felt so bad about it I could have wept (67). . . . During the summer when things were going especially hard . . . , I grimly modified grace before meals: "We give Thee thanks, O Lord, for these Thy gifts, and for all our tribulations, from Thy bounty, through Christ our Lord, Amen" (76).

Kenneth Burke was arguing at just this time that to persuade, leftist activists had to couch their philosophies in the word-values of ordinary Americans. His famous speech at the First American Writers' Congress, in which he called for translating the terms *the masses* or *the workers* as *the people* in proletarian writing is the best-known example of his thought (George and Selzer 17). As he told the Congress, "I believe the symbol of 'the people' makes more naturally for *propaganda by inclusion* than does the strictly proletarian symbol [of the worker], . . . which makes naturally for a *propaganda by exclusion,* a tendency to eliminate from one's work all that does not deal specifically with the realities of the workers' oppression" ("Revolutionary Symbolism" 272). Day's columns, in these terms, were clearly propaganda by inclusion. Uniting Catholic doctrine, French social change, Marxist economic imperatives, and daily personal encounters with the urban poor—many of them immigrants—Day not only Americanized the Other, but also brought the ideals of men like Maurin into the material reality of an everyday faith journey of individual, fully realized people. A 1939 column, for instance, described a few summer days on Mott Street during a six-day Italian *festa*, during which she and a Lithuanian guest attempted to explain to an equally homeless Japanese Buddhist what that night's Jewish Day of Atonement symbolized. The whole column was written as if readers were sitting on the house porch with Day and these friends, and ends with a mention of the war, recently erupted, and the reflection "but here on Mott Street daily life is so hard, there is murder and sudden death, there is imprisonment and illness, hunger and pain always. That is life for these poor. And when there is a fiesta and dancing and music and the joy of children and family life, then they will take that too, and be happy while the moon shines down over all ("San Gennaro Festa").

The work of the Catholic Worker movement—putting out a monthly paper, daily feeding four hundred, collecting and giving away clothing, preventing and easing evictions, serving as de facto social workers to the desperate and sick, running a cooperative farm and programs for children, advocating on social issues, all the while living in community with the poor, providing shelter to the homeless in their own home, and then, astonishingly, attempting to sustain a decentralized movement of similar houses and farms that sprang up across the country—this work was not done by saints, Day's columns demonstrated, but by ordinary people taking seriously their understanding of the Gospel. Because they were ordinary people, other ordinary people could join the movement. Because what they served was not "the cause" or "the poor" but Mr. Rubino or Barbara and her baby or the family evicted from 13th Street, then reaching out became not a radical choice but a personal one, one human reaching out to another.

Conclusion: Personalizing an Essence, a Third Way toward Civil Discourse

Burke would write in *A Rhetoric of Motives* (1950) about classifying an essence, an eternal presence, into a temporal framework "by conceiving of its kind according to the perfection . . . of which that kind is capable" (13–14). For Day, the Kingdom of God was this kind of essence, a clear vision of perfection that colored the everyday world as it was lived out daily in radically unexpected ways. Placing the essential into time, Burke wrote, meant translating one's personal narrative into abstract idea (the role for Day of religious reflection), and then translating it back into a new, persuasive narrative now larger than oneself (the role of her columns and memoirs). This making of the essential into narrative, placing abstract thought into time, "provides for a *personalizing* of essence," Burke would write (15)—precisely the personalizing that Day set out to accomplish. People flocked to the *Catholic Worker*, and it became a movement, because Day's columns turned abstractions into concrete stories about ordinary people trying their hardest to respond to extraordinary and dehumanizing situations in an ordinary human way—a temporal instance of a promised perfection. "You persuade a man [or a woman] only insofar as you can talk his language by speech, gesture, tonality, order, image, attitude, idea, *identifying* your ways with his," Burke would write in 1950 (55). Day's lived example of identification as the principal tool for persuasion through her columns in the *Catholic Worker* brought her readers into this potentially frightening new world of radical personal responsibility for the impoverished and made that world, falling on the bias between religiosity and progressivism, seem familiar enough to be acted upon.

In Sharon Crowley's terms, Day's nonatheistic radicalism would indeed be a kind of fundamentalism, but one that would, like Crowley's liberalism, enable "disagreement without necessarily incurring incivility, intimidation, or violence" (17). Crowley suggests that there are two ways to change fundamentalist values: one is "to demonstrate the superiority of alternative values" and the other is to demonstrate how given values are contingent or might logically be connected to liberal values (200–201). I would argue that showing fundamentalists that their values are either inferior or unstable is hardly "civil" discourse. Day's "fundamentalist" rhetoric points toward a third way, one indeed that Crowley briefly points toward. That way is expansion upon (Crowley's word is "rewriting") the given values, redefining "narrowly defined" notions of "family, God, and nation" (200) to demonstrate, as Day wrote, that "we are all of us children of one Father." As one human family, we all—Marxists and Catholics or secularists and fundamentalists—owe each other not the abstract correction of superior ideologies but the practical love of consubstantial beings.

Notes

1. Burke was married to first Lily and then Libbie Batterham, whose brother Forster was Day's common-law husband before her conversion and the father of her daughter Tamar. Letters in the Burke archives indicate an ongoing, if casual, relationship with the Burke family—Tamar's cousins—as well as contact with Burke's best friend Malcolm Cowley.

2. See Weiser.

3. With the exception of Anderson, much of the work on Day focuses not on her rhetorical strategies but on her personal qualities—her commitment and endurance, if one is inclined to be favorable (Cornell, Ellsberg, and Forest; Jablonski; Mize), or her obedience and orthodoxy, if one finds her problematic (K. Johnson).

4. Like Burke, Day maintained friendships both with members of the Left, such as Eastman and Cowley, and with conservative Agrarians such as Allen Tate.

8

The Shocking Morality of Nannie Helen Burroughs

Sandra L. Robinson

Nannie Helen Burroughs, race worker and founder of the National Training School for Women and Girls, adopted for the school's motto the promise that "We specialize in the wholly impossible." Reflecting Burroughs's own recognition of the enormous obstacles facing her students, this motto also signifies the complexities and contradictions inherent in being black and female in America during the first decades of the twentieth century. The notion of specializing in impossibility denotes a profound paradox: How could black women believe in their own agency despite the virulent forces of racism? How could they overcome disempowerment as white and black men stripped them of power, authority, and influence? All black women faced the daunting challenge of countering the effects of scurrilous representations and multifaceted oppressions that resulted from entrenched American racism. Burroughs's response to this exigency was to fly in the face of adversity, go against the grain of conventional wisdom, and establish a shocking platform for agency: the moral superiority of the Negro girl and woman. While contemporary readers have found her difficult—political activist Angela Davis, for instance, called Burroughs's remarks on Negro woman superiority "glaring"—the rhetorical strategies she used to build this platform for agency introduced a new paradigm within Negro discourse for women that uniquely responded to the failure of political action in the wake of World War I and continuing intraracial and interracial oppression of black women. Burroughs's three key strategies are rhetorical linchpins that link religion, politics, education, and gender into a seamless discourse:

- She consciously acted as a "moral entrepreneur" (Gilkes 146), using the opportunities created by her roles as corresponding secretary of the Woman's Convention Auxiliary of the National Baptist Convention and founder of the Nannie Helen Burroughs Press to "market" her strategies for racial uplift.
- She asserted that Negro virtue resided in the Negro woman; therefore, she elevated Negro women and girls to a morally superior status, consciously counterpoising the interests of Negro women to those of Negro men while emphasizing the importance for women of policing their own behavior.
- She used strategic violations of decorum to draw attention to her arguments and to make them more emphatic.

Becoming a Moral Entrepreneur

Nannie Helen Burroughs was born 2 May 1879 in Orange, Virginia, to former slaves who purchased farmland just after the Civil War. She received her education at the M Street School in Washington, D.C., a four-year colored high school known for its academic excellence. Administrators included social and political activist Mary Church Terrell; Anna Julia Cooper, who became principal in 1902 and was at the time one of only four black women who held a PhD; and Francis Lewis Cardozo, who won scholarships in Latin and Greek and studied at the University of Glasgow and in Edinburgh before going on to the London School of Theology. Not surprisingly, M Street School offered a college preparatory classical arts curriculum. A business major, Burroughs excelled academically and, according to Lolita Perkins, "develop[ed] her oratory skills" (231) as a founding member of the Harriet Beecher Stowe Literary Society. In 1896, she graduated with honors as class valedictorian. Despite her qualifications, however, Burroughs encountered the same intraracial discrimination based on class and skin tone that Coretta Pittman, in her essay in this collection, finds illustrated in Bessie Smith's lyrics. The African American newspaper *Washington Bee* poignantly wrote that the administrators and teachers of the District of Columbia's Colored schools "constituted a self-conscious elite that held itself aloof from Negroes outside its charmed circle"

(K. Johnson 56). Education and personal excellence were not enough to allow her the earned privilege of meaningful employment, and this incident transformed Burroughs's future. According to biographer Aurelia Downey, "Nannie's disappointment became God's appointment for her life" (4). Burroughs, stung by the racial disdain of her own community, proceeded to reinvent herself as someone who would never be overlooked again and who could overcome the ontological impossibility of her skin color. She invented an alternate career path, becoming an organizational genius, a prolific writer, a civil rights activist, and a dynamic orator, as well as school founder.

For race activists, this nadir of American race relations early in the twentieth century was a competitive arena, dominated by educated and well-known leaders who had the ear and the pocketbook of the American public and the Negro press. Burroughs's strategies, therefore, were as much about capturing a following and being heard as about being effective in her mission. To that end, she began her career by creating her own rhetorical venues and platforms for her message. Burroughs's agency was triply amplified by her roles as corresponding secretary to the National Baptist Convention Auxiliary Women's Convention, founder and president of the National Training School for Women and Girls, and, in 1934, founder and editor of the *Worker*, a monthly school newspaper that she developed into a quarterly magazine designed for missionaries, leaders, and workers. By 1908, she had her own publishing company: Nannie Helen Burroughs Press. Gilkes describes Burroughs as a "moral entrepreneur who consciously, at times militantly, sought to define and clarify appropriate values and modes of behavior within the black experience. As an activist, Burroughs publicly combined perspectives on raising women with the uplift of the entire black community" (146). Using the rhetorical venues she created for herself, Burroughs quite literally marketed the idea that women are morally superior and that agency could be acquired through appropriate training.

With publication of the *Worker*, Burroughs expanded her sphere of influence to include the "Woman's Missionary Union (WMU), an association of White Baptist women . . . [whose mission was] to assist Burroughs 'in any way that is feasible'" (Easter 38). Burroughs stated the purpose of the magazine in an editorial in the first issue:

> We need this magazine for our women's organizations that they may be more efficient in their work in the churches. The best missionary writers will contribute material that will be of tremendous help to all women who are seeking light. . . . If our leaders will only

cooperate with us, read the magazine, use the material, study the lessons carefully, it will not be long before the local societies will take on new life and the local leadership will do better work, know more about God's work, win more souls, and work more earnestly for the salvation of a lost world. (qtd. in Easter 37–38)

Burroughs's monthly editorial (for every issue of the *Worker* until her death) allowed her to reach a large audience of African American women. The quarterly circulation goal was 50,000, but actual circulation rose as high as 103,000 per quarter; according to Easter, "the magazine boasted one of the largest circulations of any magazine for Negro church women" (38–39). As corresponding secretary to the Women's Convention, Burroughs had access to "nearly a million women from every part of the country" (33).

Burroughs's publications created a shared context with her readers and served as portable vehicles that allowed her to speak to a national audience. Moreover, Burroughs had every confidence not only in the immediate relevancy of her work but in its usefulness for future generations, and she included in her marketing strategy a strong argument for continuing financial support:

> Your Corresponding Secretary believes profoundly in the moral and spiritual value of self help. She believes that the hope of the race is in the masses. She believes that the Negro church woman is their rock in a weary land. For that reason, we must provide for the continuous publication of materials such as *The Worker, How, Making Your Community Christian*, etc., long after we are gone. Unless we provide for the propagation and perpetuation of the basic ideals for which we have given our lives, much of the good that we do will not live long enough to send its roots deep to bear fruit in the life of the race. (qtd. in Easter 39)

In this passage, Burroughs makes a visionary connection with future generations and argues that for their sake, financial support of her press and continual publication of her instructive pamphlets is a moral imperative for her readers.

The Moral Superiority of Negro Women

According to Burroughs, Negro virtue resided in the Negro woman. She promoted and marketed the moral superiority of Negro women as a strategy to uplift the race in order to achieve agency for everyone. Although this notion may seem shocking to twenty-first century readers,

Fig. 8.1. Nannie Helen Burroughs, date unknown. Photo courtesy Library of Congress, Prints and Photographs Division, LC-USZ62–79903.

in the context of the years between the wars it was not shocking at all; rather, it was a creative trope designed to turn negative representations of Negroes on their head. Burroughs's platform of moral superiority was "molded and constrained by prevailing conventions and traditions," as Shirley Wilson Logan notes (xiv). Burroughs and her contemporaries responded in various ways to the virulence, contradictions, and complications of racism and sexism. According to Burroughs's biographer Evelyn Higginbotham, the primary strategy used by black Baptist women, led by Burroughs, was the "politics of respectability" (185–229). Higginbotham argues that by asserting their adherence to a self-imposed social code of respectability, these women simultaneously rejected and transcended negative representations of black women as inherently inferior. For such women—disempowered and oppressed in politics, wage-earning, and family structure—control of their personal lives as reflected in an almost-militant respectability was the one tool they could unquestionably use to counter negative stereotypes. The respectability of black women, then, was a tool used "to expose race relations as socially constructed rather than derived by evolutionary law or divine judgment" (Higginbotham 192).

Black women's sexual vulnerability to rape and domestic violence during the interwar years influenced them to further develop a "culture of dissemblance," asserts Darlene Hine ("Rape and the Inner Lives" 912–20). Hine defines this culture as a self-imposed secrecy and invisibility that black women constructed to "protect the sanctity of inner aspects of their lives" (915). They would create the appearance of openness about themselves and their feelings but remain an enigma. "Only with secrecy, thus achieving a self-imposed invisibility, could ordinary Black women accrue the psychic space and harness the resources needed to hold their own in the often one-sided and mismatched resistance struggle" (915). Consequently, the culture of resistance fostered the "development of an image of Black women as being super-moral" (920). Burroughs brought this concept into sharp relief by turning "super-moral" into morally superior in her effort to counter the negative images that surrounded black women.

Scurrilous public representations of Negro women proliferated in cartoons that reflected white America's fear, distrust, and hatred of Negroes. Cartoons provided a way to establish stereotypes of Negroes as dangerous *others*. Thus the *Montgomery Advertiser's* 1916 caricature of a Negro maid depicts her as a crow carrying in her "beak" a pail containing a white man and stolen food scraps that she is bringing home to her shiftless husband lounging in a nest (Hunter 146). Despite the fact that servants were deemed "indispensable" (144) to the white families who could afford them, fear of their servants gave cartoonists fodder. A similar *Atlanta Constitution* cartoon entitled "Sanitary Precaution" depicts a Negro maid, surrounded by flies, leaving her filthy home traveling to the clean "average white home" (144). Hunter describes this demonization of Negro servants, their use as a scapegoat, and their association with fears of disease and contamination:

> Black women were vilified not only because of their preponderance in white households, but also because of the stereotypes of libidinous women and the connotations of TB. As one white southern physician stated, "Their girls early learn evil ways." Whites considered African-American women as promiscuous by nature and saw their bodies as receptacles for dangerous, unspeakable germs.... "Many Negro women have gonorrhea, and pay little attention to it. This is a very real menace to our white boys, and through them, after marriage, to our innocent daughters also. For, despite our best efforts, many boys are going to sow wild oats," stated a physician. Despite the fact that white men sexually exploited black women, these women, the very objects of their scorn, were depicted as the seducers of innocent white boys. (197)

Negro women also had to contend with the lingering nineteenth-century notion of the Cult of True Womanhood. Race women believed that the perception of the super-moral woman (the *superior* woman in Burroughs's rhetoric) was needed to overcome extremely oppressive conditions, particularly sexual exploitation. "The true woman ideology prescribed moral guidelines of conduct for the white native born middle-class female that essentialized her role as a paragon of feminine virtue and morality. The ideal woman exhibited qualities of innocence, modesty, piety, submissiveness and domesticity," writes Karen Johnson (22), who goes on to assert that the concept of the "true woman" did not apply to black women. Feminist historian James Oliver Horton, however, disagrees. Domestic work was open to black women, who could acquire steady work and take their children with them to their jobs, unlike their male partners, who were in competition with white people for laborer's jobs. It was difficult for one salary to support a family, and "under these circumstances, it was unreasonable to expect that black women could at the same time be model housewives, yet that was exactly what they were urged to do in the pages of black newspapers. Unrealistic or not, these black women were also expected to be 'true women'" (Horton 60). A black woman was expected to keep her house neat and clean, to insure that her family always had clean clothing to wear, to be sensitive to her children, plan nutritious and delicious meals . . . and devote eight to twelve hours a day as a wage earner. Black newspapers, including Burroughs's *Worker*, urged black women to do even more, thereby reinforcing an impossible agenda: "A woman should rise early . . . so that she might prepare breakfast for her husband, allowing time to listen to his conversation, express interest in his work, and provide sympathy for his problems" (60). Further, the black woman should always attempt "to cook her husband's favorite food, never gossip about him, keep his secrets, and 'always receive him with a smile'" (60).

Burroughs and other prominent leaders had the uphill task of tackling two critical issues regarding black women's sexuality. One was the negative stereotype of black women's sexuality, such that "many black women felt compelled to downplay, even deny, sexual expression" (Hine, *Hine Sight* 45). The second issue undergirds one of Burroughs's primary motivations for founding the training school for women and girls: "The determination to save young unskilled and unemployed black women from having to bargain sex in exchange for food and shelter motivated [Burroughs and others] to provide black women with protection from sexual exploitation and with dignified work" (45). Burroughs's "ironic" decision to train young women to be "better maids" (114) may have inadvertently signaled to future generations that she was somehow complicit in limiting young black women's potential, but this would be an unfair conclusion. In fact, as Burroughs herself discovered in her initial attempt to obtain work, even for an educated black woman, more often than not, the only employment available was as a maid. The alternative was sexual bartering. Training better maids was, therefore, actually a strategy to teach young women specific practical skills and morality as protective devices while simultaneously establishing their moral superiority. During the 1920s Burroughs caustically and repeatedly reminded her audiences of the role of the Negro woman in family life in her editorials in the *Pittsburgh Courier*:

> The Negro woman "totes" more water, grows more corn, picks more cotton, washes more clothes, cooks more meals, nurses more babies, mammies more Nordics, supports more churches, does more race uplifting, serves as mudsills for more climbers, takes more punishment; does more forgiving, gets less protection and appreciation than do the women in any other civilized group in the world. She has been the economic and social slave of mankind. (qtd. in E. Brooks 21)

Indeed, far from limiting black women's potential, Burroughs's first public declaration of Negro woman's moral superiority, printed in the August 1915 issue of *Crisis*, one of the oldest African American periodicals in America, coincided with a forum of leading Negro intellectuals such as Charles Chestnutt, Francis Grimke, and women from the National Association of Colored Women (NACW) to advocate woman suffrage. Some more recent African American activists have dismissed her logic—Angela Davis, for instance, wrote in 1983 that Burroughs was the only woman who "assumed a position which rested on the convoluted argument that women were morally superior implying, of course, that they were inferior to men in most other respects" (*Women, Race, and Class* 147). However, Hine's identification of the "culture of dissemblance" places Burroughs's zeal in an appropriate rhetorical context. Black women acquired this "psychic space" to harness the resources needed to survive their hostile environment and create alternative self-images that shielded them from scrutiny, thus protecting their "private, empowering definitions of self" ("Rape and the Inner Lives" 916). Negro women were keenly aware that they were often accused of inviting sexual attacks or being willing accomplices. At the same time, their desire for personal autonomy and the urgent need for economic stability motivated them to find spaces where they could mobilize, organize, and invent survival strategies—and for this they needed space away from the hostile environments that surrounded them. Dissemblance became a safe space for women who did not have the power to prevent or eliminate the negative social, sexual, and political representations of Negro women that critically affected their lives. The effect of this culture created the appearance of disclosure or openness through strategic respectability.

As scholars have noted, this culture of strategic respectability, this super-morality, found its first political expression in the NACW. Founded to protest the negative representations of Negro women's sexuality, it was "the largest and most enduring protest organization in the history of Afro-Americans" (Hine, "Rape and the Inner Lives" 917). Burroughs's pronouncement of moral superiority, then, was consistent with the strategies of her time. As she wrote in a 1915 article, "Had [the black woman] not been the woman of unusual moral stamina that she is, the black race would have been made a great deal whiter and the white race a great deal blacker. She has been left a prey for the men of every race, but in spite of this, she has held the enemies of Negro female chastity at bay" ("Black Women and Reform" 178). The moral superiority of black women, then, was for Burroughs not an intimation of their intellectual or other inferiority to men, but a shield and a protest against men's incursions.

Further, Burroughs explicitly recognized that upholding Negro virtue for women would also serve as an exemplar and an argument for men. Her 1927 article for the *Southern Workman* simultaneously extols Negro virtue, chides the reader for not recognizing inner virtues, and offers predictions for the future of the race:

> The tragedy in this problem-solving enterprise is that the Negro is not being taught the tremendous achieving power of his virtues. He is not being taught to glorify what he is.... When the Negro learns what manner of man he is spiritually, he will wake up all over. He will stop playing white even on the stage. He will rise in the majesty of his own soul. He will glorify the beauty of his own brown skin. He will stop thinking white and go to thinking straight and living right. He will realize that wrong-reading, wrong-bleaching and wrong-mixing have "most nigh ruin't him" and he will redeem his body and rescue his soul from the bondage of that death.... I believe it is the Negro's sacred duty to spiritualize American life and popularize his color instead of worshipping the color (or lack of color) of another race.... No race is richer in soul quality and color than the Negro. Someday he will realize and glorify them, he will popularize black. Preachers, teachers, leaders, welfare workers are to address themselves to the supreme task of teaching the entire race to glorify what it has—its face (its color); its place (its homes and communities); its grace (its spiritual endowment). If the Negro does it there is no earthly force that can stay him. ("With All Thy Getting" 299–301)

Inner virtue, Burroughs here demonstrates, brings bodily pride, which leads not to individualized quiescence but its opposite, communal power.

Evelyn Brooks identifies Burroughs's three-pronged message as "the prophetic principle of the feminine in the black religious tradition" (21). In 1933 the *Louisiana Weekly* covered Burroughs's speaking to an enthusiastic overflow audience of young people at the Bethel A.M.E. Church. In her speech, "What Must the Negro Do to Be Saved," she instructed her audience in three principles that are central to her discourse: Glorify women, glorify things of the spirit, and raise the race. In particular, Burroughs argues that black women have "made possible all we have around us—church, home, school, business" and that recognizing the contributions of black women is an essential foundation for raising the race. In the face of cultural attitudes that denigrate black women on every side, Burroughs says, "We must have a glorified womanhood that can look any man in the face . . . and tell of the nobility of character within black womanhood." By introducing this new message of spiritually glorifying black women, Burroughs links the glorification of women to a God-centered life and to the life and death struggle of the entire race. Thus, the Negro woman is no longer a figure to be trivialized, maligned, sexually abused, ignored, or pitied. She is now prominently seated in the light of God.

The Shocking Truth: Burroughs's Strategic Violations of Decorum

Burroughs was a challenging speaker. Unlike her contemporaries, Burroughs strategically violated the rhetorical principle of decorum, choosing the manner that is appropriate at the right time and place in rhetorical situations. In order to be effective, the rhetorical act must seamlessly link the circumstances, the speaker, and the audience. Burroughs understood decorum—as a church woman she was aware that if a speaker's ideas are appropriately embodied and presented, the audience would better receive the point of the message. However, Burroughs turned rhetorical theory inside out by practicing antidecorum in her particular rhetorical situations. She was not afraid of going against the grain of commonly accepted notions to prove her points in language her audience would appreciate—and remember. In this dramatic piece of oratory, Burroughs uses brusque comedy and shocking imagery to prescribe what Negroes must do to be spiritually saved, instructing her listeners to "chloroform your 'Uncle Toms'" and "unload the leeches and parasitic leaders who are absolutely eating the life out of the struggling, desiring mass of people" ("What Must the Negro Do to be Saved?" n. pag.). Burroughs's rejection of situational decorum was a central aspect of her rhetorical performance and had a powerful impact on her contemporaries, both for good and for ill. Easter argues, in fact, that Burroughs's rejection of decorum, "her penchant for speaking the undressed truth," may be the reason "she never received national recognition for her accomplishments" even though she was held in high esteem by black church leadership (118).

Unlike other race leaders, Burroughs addressed even the most familiar topics in shocking terms. In 1934, "responding to a poem on lynching published in the *Afro-American*" (Easter 118), Burroughs wrote: "The ballot and the dollar are the shield and the sword for any people in a democracy. If they [Black people] do not learn to evaluate them and use them to protect themselves and to fight their battles, they will always be mud sill, door mats, stepping stones and hound dogs" ("Nannie H. Burroughs Says"). Burroughs employed creative metaphors to urge her audience to use their votes and their economic standing to fight racism rather than "begging the white race for mercy." As she colorfully put it, "The mud sills will be walked over; the stepping stones will be walked upon; the hound dogs will be kicked around; and the bull dogs will get what they go after"—in stubborn tenacity is power.

In a similar vein, Burroughs simultaneously shocks, entertains, and chides her readers in her 1929 speech entitled "What the Negro Wants Politically: You Heard about the Election" celebrating the election of Herbert Hoover. The speech, "reprinted in a number of black newspapers" (Sarkela, Ross, and Lowe 45), lists Burroughs's reasons for supporting the Republican Party. Burroughs, as president of the National League of Republican Colored Women (NLRCW), worked very hard to promote the Republican platform because she and her contemporaries believed that the Republicans offered the best opportunity for Negro advancement. As the references to Tammany Hall show, Burroughs saw the Democratic Party machines—which worked so effectively on behalf of white immigrant workers of the North—as the entrenched enemies of racial equality in the South. In a speech that prefigures the arguments made during the Civil Rights movement in the 1960s, Burroughs argues that what the Negro wants politically is the same thing every other right thinking voter should want: "his rights as an American citizen and not simply jobs for a few politicians. . . . general relief from demoralizing evils, rather than personal rewards for party fealty" ("What the Negro Wants" 46–47).

In this speech, the homely aphorisms ("all the King's Horses and all the king's men") and malapropisms ("it can't be did") in which Burroughs couches her celebration of the defeat of the Democrats create a voice of folksy, natural wisdom, which contrasts strongly with the much more educated language in which she argues for political action grounded in moral elevation and civic preparedness: "Negroes . . . should keep all of their clubs intact, hold regular meetings, carry on a campaign of education and enlightenment and thereby build up a vigorous morale and be ready. . . . The best advice to give our people, politically, is organize and keep organized" ("What the Negro Wants" 46–47). Arguments on specific points are introduced comically, and short memorable phrases are used that could be repeated in future speeches and writings. Despite the comedy, though, Burroughs does not lose sight of reminding her audience of their responsibilities. Although massive change was expected, her readers were to remain constant and vigilant. (See Sarah Hallenbeck's chapter on the Girl Scouts in this collection for another use of preparation and vigilance). What Burroughs excelled at, then, was in breaking the rules of *genre* decorum—the kinds of language expected in a church or in a newspaper—in order to more closely achieve *audience* decorum—the language most appreciated by her listeners and readers.

Her most shocking violation of decorum may be one of her earliest writings. In a 1918 report as corresponding secretary to the Women's Convention of the National Baptist Convention, Burroughs flaunts her impudence as she speaks to power, mocking President Woodrow Wilson for not suspending Jim Crow laws by referring to Wilson's war slogan, "Make the world safe for democracy":

> He likes to write—he likes to say things. He has used up all the adverbs and adjectives trying to make clear what he means by democracy. He realizes and the country realizes that unless he begins to apply the doctrine, representatives of our nation would be hissed out of court when the world gets ready to make up the case against Germany and to try her for her sins. (qtd. in E. Brooks 17)

Her militant demands were repeated in the black press, and her power within black communities across the country was evidenced by her forty-four year tenure as corresponding secretary to the community's most significant church. Thus her personal decorum, or antidecorum, became entwined with her ethos: she spoke and wrote precisely in the manner most appreciated and expected of Nannie Helen Burroughs, whatever the situation.

Conclusion

Burroughs's rhetorical acts live on in the continuing distribution of her pamphlets and training materials. Her 1908 play, *On Their Way to the Slabtown District Convention*, is still performed at colleges and performing arts centers. And most significantly, her school—the National Training School for Women and Girls—lives on, today renamed the Nannie Helen Burroughs School. It is now an elementary school with a website that provides a virtual tour of photographs that record the history of Burroughs's mission and purpose for its founding. The school's staff has updated Burroughs's theme of "We specialize in the wholly impossible" with somewhat more hopeful—if less memorable—themes for the twenty-first century: "Endowing Our Future" and "Preparing for Global Citizenship." Burroughs might tweak the style, but she would surely approve of the message.

9

> Yes, she was terrific, and there's been nobody since that could sing the blues like Bessie Smith. She would come over to my house, but, mind you, she wasn't my friend. She was very rough.—May Wright Johnson, *Hear Me Talkin' to Ya*

Bessie Smith's Blues as Rhetorical Advocacy
Coretta Pittman

The 1920s and 1930s were a period of tremendous intellectual and artistic energy in the African American community, a surge of culture characterized by figures such as W. E. B. Du Bois, Langston Hughes, Marcus Garvey, Jessie Fauset, and Louis Armstrong. Many of these intellectuals and artists sought to erase negative images of African Americans, replacing them with more positive and "respectable" representations. In Jim Crow America, dominant (white) cultural representations of African Americans emphasized racist depictions that reinforced the second-class status of African American people. However, there was hope among the African American intelligentsia that art could be used as a mechanism to improve the African American cultural image. Alain Locke, in his 1925 essay, "The New Negro," illustrates this argument that the artistic contributions of African Americans could propel the masses forward:

> The migrant masses, shifting from countryside to city, hurdle several generations of experience at a leap, but more important, the same thing happens spiritually in the life attitudes and self expression of the Young Negro, in his poetry, his art, his education, and his new outlook, with the additional advantage, of course, of the poise and greater certainty of knowing what it is all about. From this comes the promise and warrant of a new leadership. (5)

Locke and others believed that if art were to have any power to transform the social and material circumstances of the African American masses, then representations of African American life had to be moderate, not salacious.

But while the upwardly mobile and largely male intellectuals of the African American community shaped what came to be known as the Harlem Renaissance, another artistic movement was taking place alongside: African American women blues singers were creating a renaissance all their own. Mamie Smith, Clara Smith, Gertrude "Ma" Rainey, Alberta Hunter, Bessie Smith, and others were writing, recording, and performing blues music and capturing the spirit of a subculture within the African American working classes. Bessie "the Empress" Smith, regarded by many as the greatest classic blues singer and so enormously popular that she became the highest paid African American performer of her time, wowed audiences with songs bearing titles such as "Mean Old Bed Bug Blues," "Jail House Blues," "Gimme a Pigfoot (And a Bottle of Beer)," and "Wild About That Thing." For some key figures in the Harlem Renaissance, however, the blues women's lyrical content (and sometimes public behavior) was viewed not as a valuable artistic expression of the African American experience but as a challenge to the bourgeois norms embraced by their moderate and elite African American contemporaries.[1]

Exhortations to help advance the "Negro" race did not come only from the public intellectuals of the Harlem Renaissance. Long before the classic blues women performed and recorded blues music, African American leaders sought to advance the masses by encouraging them to embrace moderate behaviors that might dispel myths regarding the so-called immoral behavior of the black working class. Before and after the turn of the century, prominent African American women activists such as Anna J. Cooper, Ida B. Wells-Barnett, Mary Church Terrell, and Nannie Helen Burroughs worked to construct an alternate image of African American womanhood. Their rhetoric of social uplift offered tangible models of appropriate public behavior for working-class women to emulate. As Evelyn B. Higginbotham demonstrates, church policies written by women like Burroughs focused on constructing new identities that emphasized "sobriety, honor, and integrity, and every other wholesome virtue" to alter the perception of African American women in the eyes of white society as well as intraracially (192). (See Sandra Robinson's chapter on Burroughs's uplift rhetoric in this collection.) While Wells-Barnett, Burroughs, Terrell, and others stressed the importance of appropriate public and private behavior, however, Smith's and other blues women's music stressed independence, fearlessness, and sexual freedom, implicitly arguing that working-class women did not have to alter their behavior in order to be worthy of respect.

In this chapter, I demonstrate how, bound by different ideological and rhetorical practices, Smith used lyrical content, vocal techniques, and public performances (musical and social) to suggest that individual and group empowerment did not have to be relegated to a narrow vision of African American womanhood that embraced domesticity, piety, and conformity but instead accepted independence, sassiness, and sexual freedom as a means to personal freedom and happiness. Even though Smith did not write pamphlets or speak at the lectern arguing for the rights of working women, I contend that her music was a kind of activism, asserting the right of working-class women to express their pain and discontent, to drink, to fight, to party, and to communicate their sexual needs in a vernacular that helped to soothe their souls. Alongside, but sometimes in contention with, a few public intellectuals associated with the Harlem Renaissance, Smith employed that vernacular as a form of working-class rhetoric steeped in the cultural expressions, values, and traditions of the African American working classes. As a prelude to my analysis of her music, I discuss Smith's "blues self" and the complexities of her ethos in rhetorical contexts where representations of African Americans were particularly contested. I then examine in detail songs Smith wrote and/or performed dealing with poverty and hopelessness, intraracial conflict, and female sexuality.

Smith and the Complexities of Ethos

Writing about ethos in "Self-Structure as a Rhetorical Device: Modern *Ethos* and the Divisiveness of the Self," Marshall W. Alcorn contends that the self is at the center of ethos:

> If *ethos* refers to the character of the speaker or writer involved in persuasive activity, and if an understanding of *ethos* seeks to clarify the role that the self plays in argumentation, an initial goal should be to investigate character and how it can "be" in a text. A theory of *ethos* needs to be grounded in a relatively clear, but also a relatively complex, understanding of the self. (4)

The blues self that Smith's lyrical content defined and described suggests that the self could "be" in the text by representing an authentic self, one that "is" in the text without seeking to be like others with moderate attitudes and behaviors. Thus, the ethos of Smith's blues music belies transformation, instead arguing for experiential truth as a means to agency and credibility: "I am" persuasive and credible because I have told "my" truth. The blues self Smith presented in recordings and performances in the 1920s and 1930s was at once acceptable and unacceptable, depending on her rhetorical situation. As Alcorn articulates, the fact that character acts as a conduit for persuasion is complicated by a number of factors outside the control of the individual: "the self is not something universal but is something deeply crafted by history and by changing social formations" (6).

Historical formations of the African American self were shaped largely by people and standards outside African American communities. W. E. B. Du Bois's theory of double consciousness provides an acute description of the African American self at war with itself and with historical forces:

> It is a peculiar sensation, this double consciousness, this sense of always looking at one's self through the eyes of others, of measuring one's soul by the tape of a world that looks on in amused contempt and pity. One ever feels his twoness—an American, a Negro; two souls, two thoughts, two unreconciled strivings; two warring ideals in one dark body. (102)

It seems probable that Smith, like many African Americans of the early twentieth century, experienced double consciousness. Because of "this sense of always looking at [herself] through the eyes of others," she almost certainly had to reconcile conflicting notions of self. What becomes evident after listening to her music and studying her lyrics is that the self she presents seems to be most connected to a subculture within the African American working classes and to an ethos that demands of its audience respect for the lyrical sincerity of the music she wrote, recorded, and performed.

Smith began her performance career on the streets of Chattanooga, where she was born into a poor family in 1894. Later, Smith left Chattanooga and charted her musical career as a blues singer, performing in the South, North, and Midwest, ultimately becoming the biggest headliner act on the Theater Owners Booking Association circuit (all white owners, all African American performers). Published reports in the *Chicago Defender* indicate that she was a very successful performer; one 1926 article notes that "Bessie Smith . . . and her Harlem Frolics are now touring the Sunny South, packing 'em in at every engagement"

Fig. 9.1. Bessie Smith in 1936, one year before her death. Photograph taken by Carl Van Vechten; courtesy of the Library of Congress, Prints and Photographs Division, Carl Van Vechten Collection, LC-USZ62–100863 DLC.

("Bessie Smith's Revue" 8). In addition, George Hoefer reports that Smith sold "between eight and ten million records before the collapse of the record business" in the 1930s (134–35).

Despite Smith's success, neither she nor her music was accepted in all circles. For instance, she once auditioned for Black Swan records (W. E. B. Du Bois was on its board of directors) and was summarily dismissed because she was considered too rough—she supposedly stopped singing to spit (Hoefer 132). In fact, even her admirers, white and black, considered her a "rough" (i.e., working class or even "low class") woman. In a 1926 *Vanity Fair* article titled "Negro Blues

Singers," the influential (white) critic and patron of Harlem Renaissance writers and musicians, Carl Van Vechten, clearly articulated what he viewed as class distinctions among a number of blues singers, including Smith and Ethel Waters: "If Bessie Smith is crude and primitive, she represents the true folk-spirit of the race. She sings Blues as they are understood and admired by the masses. Of the artists who have communicated the Blues to the more sophisticated Negro and white public, I think Ethel Waters is the best" (106).[2] Although Van Vechten may have considered Waters the better artist, Angela Davis contends that

> To unschooled white ears as well as to successful black people who did not particularly relish musical reminders of their own social roots, Ethel Waters may have appeared to be the most accomplished blues singer of the period. But, as universally recognized today, Bessie Smith was the real genius of her craft. She was not only the greater artist, she also more accurately represented the sociohistorical patterns of black people's lives. (*Blues Legacies* 153)

Even among her peers, although Smith was considered a great artist, her "roughness" and the lyrical content of her music often created, or were seen as, a class distinction between Smith and more "sophisticated" African Americans. As the chapter's epigraph indicates, May Wright Johnson, wife of famous jazz pianist James P. Johnson, would acknowledge that "there's been nobody . . . that could sing the blues like Bessie Smith," would invite Smith to her house, but would not consider Smith a friend because "she was very rough" (241–42). Johnson similarly delineates the class differences she saw between herself, Smith, and their respective audiences when recounting one of her own and Smith's performances: "In 1921, I was playing at the 81 Theatre on Decatur Street in Atlanta, and Bessie Smith was at the 91, just down the street. . . . The 91 was a smaller and rougher theater" (241–42). Johnson continues, "My husband . . . was leading the band at the 81, which was the bigger theater . . . and I was the principal, not just a chorine" (241). In short, despite the fact that blues music was a part of the burgeoning cultural renaissance and that Smith was its most gifted interpreter, Smith and her music (including her working-class subjects and audiences) were "classed" by the African American elite as undeserving of serious recognition. Discussion of blues as an art form and of Smith is conspicuously absent from conversations about great art in the scholarly writings of Du Bois and Locke. For instance, there is no mention of Smith in Du Bois's *Crisis* when her first hit record

"Down-hearted Blues" was released in April 1923 to resounding success (selling an estimated 750,000 copies), and there is no mention of her death in a car crash in September 1937. (See Cassandra Parente's chapter in this collection for the elite's reaction to another "rough" woman, folksinger Aunt Molly Jackson.)

Throughout her musical career, it appears that Smith opposed conceptions of the self that might interfere with her lifestyle and with the rhetorical choices made while composing, recording, and performing. For example, on one occasion, performer and pianist Porter Grainger brought Smith to Carl Van Vechten's apartment (Van Vechten, "Memories" 7). According to Van Vechten, there were a number of important performers there: "George Gershwin . . . Marguerite d'Alvarez and Constance Collier, possibly Adele Astaire. The drawing room was well-filled with sophisticated listeners." While in his apartment, Smith was invited to sing, but before doing so "asked for a glass of straight gin, and with one gulp she downed a glass holding nearly a pint. Then, with a burning cigarette depending from one corner of her mouth, she got down to the Blues, really down to 'em, with Porter at the piano" (7). This is just one story among many that illustrates the extent to which Smith contested the bourgeois role she was supposed to take on as an African American public figure who had the money and fame to be in an elite class but refused to join.

In fact, by all accounts, Smith was a larger-than-life figure in the 1920s and 1930s. Reports suggest she enjoyed having a good time. She drank moonshine, had sex outside of marriage, and was involved in lesbian relationships. Her music embraced behaviors and attitudes that appeared "unseemly." And her on-stage attire was flamboyant. She wore eccentric hats while she performed on stage; a 1924 photograph shows her wearing a "lampshade" style hat (Albertson 69). At a time when African American women in leadership positions were trying to shrug off stereotypes about loose African American women, Smith's music and behavior brought those "bad" African American women into the public sphere. Yet I submit that Smith was more than a caricature of herself and other working-class African American women. In her lyrics, Smith worked out publically the private triumphs and sufferings of a blues woman and a blues people. Some of the people who were drawn to blues music were migrants who had "deserted the rural communities of the South . . . [seeking] work and adventure as solitary wanderers from place to place" (Frazier 272–73). Some of the wanderers moved on to larger Southern cities like "Montgomery or

Birmingham, or Memphis," while others moved to Midwest cities such as Detroit or Chicago, where Alberta Hunter or Bessie Smith helped them deal with the pain of their lives (274).

Eyewitness reports illustrate the powerful bond Smith created with her audiences. Van Vechten describes how Bessie Smith's magnetic voice influenced her audiences' emotions when he saw her perform on Thanksgiving night in 1925:

> Now, inspired partly by the expressive words, partly by the stumbling strain of the accompaniment, partly by the powerfully magnetic personality of the elemental conjure woman with her plangent African voice, quivering with passion and pain, sounding as if it had been developed at the sources of the Nile, the black and blue-black crowd, notable for the absence of mulattoes, burst into hysterical, semi-religious shrieks of sorrow and lamentation. Amens rent the air. ("Memories" 7)

Zutty Singleton, who played for Smith when she performed in New Orleans, especially notes the power of Smith's on-stage personality: "Yes, I remember Bessie Smith, the Queen of the Blues, and man, I'm sure sorry for the folks who missed seeing and hearing her. You don't know what you missed by not seeing and hearing the Queen in person" (11).

Smith connected with her audiences by asserting an ethos that was unapologetic in all of its manifestations: in the lyrical content of the blues, in her social behavior, in her style choices, and in her rhetorical practices. She used the cultural resources of the blues to maintain the rhetorical practices that already existed in the vernacular of the African American working classes. Rather than invent or construct an ethos to suit the needs of the African American intelligentsia, Smith's music suggested that ethos already existed in the authentic stories of her music. Julie N. Christoph calls inventing or "constructing an *ethos*" a strategy of 'moral display.'" I argue, instead, that Smith's moral display did not have to be created or invented; it was always there. Christoph says that moral display

> [is] often used without any specific reference to group membership, but, as with Aristotelian *ethos*, . . . attempt[s] to connect with the moral standards of the community and to establish trust through demonstrating similar values. . . . Moral displays confirm writers' alliances with "particular discursive communities" by enacting the kinds of moral assessments that are part of those community practices. (671)

Smith's popularity suggests that her music reflected the themes, experiences, and desires of a subculture within the African American working classes, which then allowed the moral display of her music to connect singer and audience together in a discourse community; in doing so, the lyrical content of her blues music allowed her to be the living embodiment of a blues people trying to work out their pain, joy, and progress together. Thus, as Angela Davis argues, Smith's blues music "provided a cultural space for community-building among working-class black women" (*Blues Legacies* 44). The following sections demonstrate how Smith used themes of hopelessness and despair, intraracial conflict, sexual satisfaction, and independence to articulate an African American working-class ethos.

The Trouble She's Seen: Hopelessness and Despair

In 1927 Smith recorded "Backwater Blues." In this original composition, Smith describes a flood that devastated parts of Tennessee in 1926. According to reports in the Nashville *Tennessean* and the *New York Times*, "One thousand persons [were] estimated to have been made homeless in Northeast Nashville, many of them negroes" (qtd. in Evans 112). Smith had first-hand experience of this widespread dislocation because she was in Nashville at the time of the flood to perform a series of concerts. Because the flood was so devastating to the region, she was forced to stay in Nashville for about ten days (Evans 111). "Backwater Blues" was written as a first-person narrative account of Negro suffering. In the second stanza, when Smith sings, "I woke up this mornin', can't even get out my door / That's enough trouble to make a poor girl wonder where she wanna go," this is not an imagined experience but her own witnessing of the tragedies caused by the flood. The bleak mood and the slow tempo of the song help to communicate the hopelessness the flood victims experienced as they attempted to make sense of the devastation. Moreover, Smith's careful description of the flood's aftermath signals her commitment to both the importance of narrative and of human life. Her lyrics were powerful laments that articulated the ways the poor Nashville residents dealt with their suffering:

> Then I went and stood upon some high old lonesome hill
> Then I looked down on the house where I used to live . . .
> Backwater blues done caused me to pack my things and go
> 'Cause my house fell down and I can't live there no mo'.

Smith's use of the first-person encourages audiences to identify with the flood victims on a personal level while also acknowledging the scope of the tragedy: standing on that lonesome hill, the narrator sees that "there's thousands of people ain't got no place to go." When Smith begins to hum the final lines of "Backwater Blues," "Mmmmmmmmm, I can't move no mo' / There ain't no place for a poor old girl to go," she raises listeners' awareness as she tries to help them (re)imagine how human beings deal with personal loss. The shared experience Smith creates in "Backwater Blues" links local, regional, and national communities together in ways the poor Negro masses would have been unable to do.

More than mere entertainment, Smith's music provides insight into the lives of the working classes, particularly African American women, who were often an invisible part of the American racial landscape. In the first-person narrative of songs like Porter Grainger and Spencer Williams's "Washwoman's Blues," for example, Smith conveys the emotional and physical essence of life as it was experienced by the working poor:

> All day long I'm slavin', all day long I'm bustin' suds
> Gee, my hands are tired, washin' out these dirty duds
> Lord, I do more work than forty-'leven Gold Dust Twins[3] . . .
> Got myself a achin' from my head down to my shins.

The slow tempo of the song and the sadness in Smith's voice mimic the drudgery of laundry work as well as describe how such difficult work was reminiscent of slave labor. As Angela Davis asserts, and as the first line implies, this work "was, in effect, slavery reincarnated" (*Blues Legacies* 98). And Smith's dynamic interpretation of Williams's lyrics helps to bring singer and audience together. The audience is confronted with and asked to critique the ways labor, racial identity, and self-esteem influence the life attitudes and outcomes for women who have to work hard to feed their families. Smith sings, "Sorry I do washin' just to make my livelihood / Oh, the washwoman's life, it ain't a bit of good." Before the invention of the washing machine, washing clothes was a physically demanding job—so difficult that the narrator claims, "Rather be a scullion cookin' in some white folks' yard / I could eat aplenty, wouldn't have to work so hard." When fans of Smith's blues music heard or watched her perform "Washwoman's Blues," many would have been able to identify with the song's lyrics and mood. Since the jobs working-class African American women could obtain were often difficult and sometimes demoralizing, the song realistically reflected the desperation of their own situations or of someone they knew. Angela Davis believes "Washwoman's Blues" "provides us with an example of the way [Smith] and other blues women addressed gendered social issues that were rarely, if ever, formally acknowledged elsewhere" (*Blues Legacies* 101).

Contesting Intraracial Conflict

As Davis argues, part of what makes Smith's music so rich is the way her "representations of the politics of gender and sexuality are informed by and interwoven with [her] representations of race and class" (xv). This complex intermingling of gender, sexuality, race, and class is beautifully illustrated in "Young Woman's Blues," a song Smith wrote in 1926, in which she takes aim at the mythology permeating African American social life: the racial caste and color system *within* the African American community that had its historical roots in slavery. For some African Americans, lighter skin was prized over darker skin—the lighter the skin, the more "aesthetic" qualities an individual was deemed to possess.[4] Smith's young woman flatly rejects this idea that self-esteem should be based on racial hue. On this level, the song is about racial pride: the young woman insists, "I'm as good as any woman in your town. / I ain't no high yella, / I'm a deep killer brown." The young woman's "man had gone away," but her blues are temporary, for the young woman's "deep killer brown" skin does not stop her from getting any man she wants: "See that long lonesome road, / Lord, you know it's gotta end and I'm a good woman and I can get plenty men." Skin color, of course, is also a gender issue: in the day-to-day realities of life in the 1920s and 1930s, dark skin could be a liability to women who were considered unattractive by some African American men.

On another level, then, "Young Woman's Blues" is about female independence. Not only does Smith empower the woman in her song to be proud of her "deep killer brown" skin; she also allows the woman to contest the rules of the domestic space. The domestic space was a place where women, including working-class African Americans, could acquire respectability both in the eyes of the broader society and intraracially. However, in "Young Woman's Blues," the narrator does not seek marriage and domesticity; she unabashedly claims, "I ain't gonna marry, ain't gon' settle down, / I'm gon' drink good moonshine / and run these browns down." In this song, women have a chance to decide for themselves. The choices they make may not be "morally appropriate," yet Smith allows them a kind of agency. That she was willing to create scenarios in her music where women were empowered to make their own decisions is an important part of her rhetorical advocacy.

Bessie Smith addresses the problems of racial caste systems again in "Mama's Got the Blues." With a unique ability to use her voice to combine secularity with religiosity in her blues music, Smith lends her masterful vocals to this song about love, racial conflict, and personal heartache. The song's narrator has lost her man and thinks that her skin color may have been the cause of their breakup. Smith sings, "Brownskin's deceitful but a yella man is worse / I'm gonna get myself a black man and play safety first" (qtd. in A. Davis, *Women, Race, and Class* 310). In the racial mythology, African American males with a fair complexion were sometimes considered "pretty men" who cared more about their good looks than being a good boyfriend or husband. The racial mythology also suggested that fair-skinned African American men were highly desirable to some African American women. Their desirability sometimes caused them to be arrogant and perhaps more inclined than their darker-skinned brothers to "mistreat" their women. However, by publically articulating the mythology through a defiant narrator, Smith works to undermine the racial myth. Rather than accept poor treatment, the woman in "Mama's Got the Blues" moves on and finds plenty of men: "I got a man in Atlanta, two in Alabama, three in Chattanooga / Four in Cincinnati, five in Mississippi, and six in Memphis, Tennessee / If you don't like my peaches, please let my orchard be" (qtd. in A. Davis, *Women, Race, and Class* 310). Although Smith's music addresses problems such as poverty, physical abuse, and imprisonment that might be considered more serious, her songs about intraracial strife merit attention here because they illustrate an essential part of Smith's blues ethos: an unflinching, multifaceted portrayal of the lived experiences of working-class African Americans during the 1920s and 1930s. Songs about intraracial conflict connected to skin color accurately reflect a part of that experience and would resonate with African Americans, many or most of whom had first-hand encounters with the racial categories that designated some of them better than others.

Sexual Freedom and Exploration

Like other classic blues women, Smith's music also explored working-class women's relationships to sex and empowerment. The open celebration of women's sexual choices, needs, and behaviors is an indication of the indomitable spirit Smith created in the women of her blues songs, who left home when they were ready, who engaged in sexual practices outside of marriage, who left men who treated them poorly, who committed acts of violence against men and women who mistreated them, and who found relief in sexual relations. One of Smith's most famous compositions about sexual fulfillment is titled "It Makes My Love Come Down." The lightness of Smith's voice, along with the playful piano accompaniment, masks the sexual content of "It Makes My Love Come Down." In this first-person, up-tempo song, Smith's narrator catalogs the ways intimate contact gives her sexual satisfaction—each of the song's eight stanzas tells her "red hot papa" a different way he can arouse her, including voyeurism—"when I see two sweethearts spoon, / underneath the silvery moon, / it makes my love come down"—cuddling in the dark, "actin' like a clown," kissing "nice," being "loveland bound," going for a ride:

> When you take me for a ride
> When I'm close up by your side,
> It makes my love come down, ridin' all aroun'
> Easy ridin' makes my love come down.

The narrator is, by turns, playful and passionate: "When I get my toodle-oh / It makes my love come down, want every pound / Hear my cryin', it makes my love come down." In short, Smith creates a picture of a sexually assertive woman who demands pleasure from her man and who not only is unashamed of her desires but "can't help from braggin'" about them.

While "It Makes My Love Come Down" is one of Smith's more descriptive, provocative songs about sex, it is only one of many songs in which she explicitly addresses sexuality. In her song, "Dirty No Gooders Blues," the narrator describes the sexual pleasures that "no good men" can offer: "the meanest things he could say would thrill you through and through / And there wasn't nothing too dirty for that man to do" (qtd. in A. Davis, *Blues Legacies* 272). In a J. C. Johnson composition titled "Empty Bed Blues Part I," Smith sings, "he's a deep sea diver with a stroke that can't go wrong / He can touch the bottom and his wind holds out so long," and in "Empty Bed Blues Part II," she sings, "he give me a lesson that I never had before / when he get through teachin' me, from my elbow down was sore."

Smith is no less shy about alluding to sex and fun in her original composition "Soft Pedal Blues," in which the narrator wants to extend a party to the early morning hours:

> There's a lady in our neighborhood who runs a buffet flat
> And when she gives a party, you know just where she's at
> She give a dance last Friday night that was to last till one
> But when the time was almost up, the fun had just begun.

Chris Albertson, Smith's biographer, writes that buffet flats "offer[ed] a cornucopia of pleasures: bootleg liquor flowed freely, though not inexpensively, gambling was a popular feature, and each room had a different 'show.' The aim was to satisfy every known sexual inclination, and patrons who wished to partake in pleasures of the flesh were welcomed to do so, for an added fee" (140–41). Ruby Walker, Smith's niece and confidante, told Albertson they had visited a buffet flat in Detroit (140). The woman in Smith's song is not ashamed of enjoying herself there. In fact, she admits she is having a good time: "I'm drunk and full of fun, / Go spread the news, 'cause I've got those soft pedalin' blues."

Of course, Smith's descriptions of sexual fulfillment could only serve to reinforce the stereotype of African American women's licentious character that some middle-class African American leaders worked tirelessly to erase. Given her direct violation of middle-class notions of propriety, it seems likely they would have disapproved of Smith's sexually charged music so out of sync with their vision of a moderate, respectable African American womanhood. But Smith's song choices indicate that she was not willing to stop singing about controversial subjects to placate some of her peers. Her music argues, instead, not that working-class African American women should *become* "respectable" (observing middle-class norms), but that they already *are* respectable (deserving of respect on their own terms). The popularity of "It Makes My Love Come Down" and "Soft Pedal Blues," as well as the number of other blues songs celebrating women's sexuality, suggest that many of Smith's fans recognized themselves and their behaviors in Smith's characters and that Smith's music had particular resonance for African American women who valued their newly won sexual freedom.

Conclusion

Sadly, Smith gave few interviews to explain why she wrote and recorded such provocative music. But despite the absence of Smith's account of her musical choices, what becomes clear from an analysis of her music is that she provided a record of the experiences of a blues people unwilling to change their core values to appease members of their own racial group. And some of her peers agreed with what appears to be Smith's own refusal to change. In his famous 1926 essay, "The Negro Artist and the Racial Mountain," Langston Hughes argues that Smith had a right to "be" her authentic self in the "text." He says, "Let the blare of Negro jazz bands and the bellowing voice of Bessie Smith singing Blues penetrate the closed ears of the colored near intellectuals until they listen and perhaps understand" (1271). Hughes hoped they would eventually recognize Smith's genius and understand how she affirmed the existence of a blues people who were often ignored and silenced.

Some of the criticisms Smith received during her lifetime are understandable. In the early twentieth century, African American leaders well knew the extent to which white people judged the entire race based on the "negative" behavior of a few African Americans who behaved "inappropriately." Thus, presenting a united front to help quell the perception that all African Americans were unintelligent, overly sexualized brutes seemed like a smart move politically. Yet as Hughes points out, artists like Smith should be allowed to express themselves in a way that is true to their own ethos. Although prominent figures affiliated with the Harlem Renaissance attempted to address ways to ameliorate the suffering of the masses, they often did so through a middle-class social paradigm. By circulating authentic and sympathetic representations of the lives of working-class African Americans, Smith's music argued for the humanity of the working classes in a distinctly different idiom and genre. As a rhetorical advocate, Smith expressed and validated a working-class ethos, helping to give meaning to their lives.

Notes

1. W. E. B. Du Bois, for example, in admonishing Claude McKay for writing about the underside of African American life in *Home to Harlem*, argues that McKay's book lacked literary merit and that the salacious parts of the book fed the interests of white readers who enjoyed reading sensational stories about African American people. Ideas about what constitutes good and respectable art were, of course, contested among the literary writers of the period. Like McKay, Zora Neale Hurston and Langston Hughes also chose to write about themes and characters that did not always reflect a middle-class version of African American reality.

2. Angela Davis claims that Van Vechten "took a decided interest" in Smith's career and that her place in the Harlem Renaissance scene "is largely due to Van Vechten's desire to count her among the guests at his notorious parties, which

were attended alike by leading black intellectuals and white connoisseurs and consumers of black culture" (*Blues Legacies* 146).

3. Gold Dust was a laundry detergent featuring on its box a picture of two African American boys, who illustrate how to use the product. The belittling image also insinuated that Gold Dust could help alleviate labor-intensive work; however, the laundress in the song (and in reality) worked harder than the Gold Dust twins implied.

4. See E. Franklin Frazier's excellent discussion of the color and caste system with African American communities in *The Negro Family in the United States*.

10

Traditional Form, Subversive Function: Aunt Molly Jackson's Labor Struggles

Cassandra Parente

Born Mary Magdalene Garland in 1880, Aunt Molly Jackson was ten years old and in jail when she discovered her voice. Attempting to avoid a ten-day sentence for playing a prank, Jackson composed her first folk song, "Mr. Cundiff Turn Me Loose," and performed it for the sheriff and his wife. Shrewdly playing on Cundiff's emotions, Jackson portrayed her living conditions as despicable: "The nits and lice they are a-hangin' to the jiste [joists] / I heard one turn over and say 'Jesus Christ'" (qtd. in Romalis 70). The lice, she later admitted, were made up to get the sheriff's attention. They did. Assured that Molly would remove the line, the sheriff invited others over to be entertained. While her protest did not lead to her freedom, it taught her the rhetorical power of song when listeners began leaving gifts and money. As Jackson explains, "At the end of ten days, I had thirty seven dollars and twenty seven plugs of 'tobaker' and the jailer's wife made me a satin dress" (qtd. in Romalis 71). Despite her success, it would be almost twenty years before Jackson composed another original song.

In 1911, when Jackson was thirty-one, the Louisville & Nashville Railroad stretched into Harlan County, and the rural area where she worked as a midwife became a coal-mining mecca with a population that boomed from ten thousand to sixty-four thousand in twenty years' time (Lynch 55). Owning everything from the general store to the church, mining companies defined the entire social world for Harlan's inhabitants and seemed to promise economic stability, but by the late 1920s, profits plummeted due to overproduction and increasing competition from the oil and electricity industries. Workers paid for the market shift with cuts in hours and wages. According to Jackson's biographer, Shelly Romalis, by 1931, Harlan miners worked only three days a week, earning a total of $4 in scrip (34). Far from providing comfort, a miner's wages barely afforded survival. So many children suffered from bloody flux (dysentery) that, as Jackson recalls, "blood was running out of the tops of their little feet.... You could track them to the soup kitchen by the blood" (qtd. in Greenway, *American Folksongs* 266–67).

Throughout the 1930s, similar economic collapses created a *kairotic* moment for Appalachian women such as Jackson. Responding to horrid conditions in mines and mills, they turned to an available means of persuasion commonly used by women in their communities: folk music. Using traditional patterns of rhythm and rhyme to convey a new, subversive message, Jackson and other singers gained center stage at strikes and rallies, exerting their rhetorical power to support local workers. To understand how these women made themselves heard, it is necessary, as Barbara Biesecker argues, to "shift the focus of historical inquiry from the question who is speaking ... to the question what play made it possible for a particular speaking subject to emerge?" (148). This approach is especially valuable for rhetorical studies of folk singing, which, as A. L. Lloyd explains, is less a personal act than a dialectic, a "perpetual struggle for synthesis between the collective and the individual, between tradition and innovation, between what is received from the community and what is supplied out of personal fantasy" (17).

In this chapter, I analyze Aunt Molly Jackson's particular synthesis of tradition and innovation as she uses the rhetorical power of folk music to rally miners and their families and to publicize the dire conditions in 1930s Harlan County. To do so, I first discuss folk music as a rhetorical tradition, then examine its strategies—embodied ethos, adaptation and parody, stock language—at work in Jackson's Depression-era songs. My analysis of her music and career suggests that it was Jackson's rhetorical effectiveness that led, paradoxically, to the undoing of her successful balance between the collective and the individual: attempting to capitalize on her embodied ethos, left-wing activists transplanted her body and voice to urban contexts and her lyrics to print publications—moves that brought her fame but eventually stripped Jackson of the rural, folk ethos that made her part of the communal tradition. Thus, although Jackson became part of public memory, she appears as an individual singer, removed from the larger rhetorical tradition of which she and many other rural women are a part. But it is not only public memory that needs remapping. Jackson's story is important to historians of rhetoric, I argue, because it challenges current understandings of women's rhetoric, first, by redirecting scholars' gaze to folk singing, in particular, and collective rhetorical action, in general, and, second, by countering scholars' default portrayal of working-class women as silent and invisible. (See Risa Applegarth's chapter on community formation among anthropologists in this collection for another example of reading individual accounts more accurately as communal representations.)

More than Tradition: Folk Music as Available Means

Focusing on the individual rhetor and the conventional forms and spaces of rhetoric, scholars of rhetorical history often conclude that *all* women have been silenced, with an exceptional few breaking out of the domestic sphere to disrupt a masculine tradition. Thus, Joy Ritchie and Kate Ronald claim that "women must first invent a way to speak in the context of being silenced and rendered invisible. This is doubly true for poor women" (xvii). However, such generalizations eclipse the experience of some women of color and of working women who were granted access to a larger public and were welcomed into certain rhetorical traditions. Drawing on a history of women's involvement in the creation and transmission of ballads in England and Scotland, Appalachian women such as Jackson, for instance, were encouraged to challenge gender and class inequities through the art of folk singing.

During the eighteenth century, when hundreds of thousands immigrated to Appalachia from England's borderlands, they brought a repertoire of narrative, minstrel, and popular ballads (Cohen and Samuelson xxvii). Many of these songs were used to teach young women about sexuality and provide them with models of female empowerment. For instance, in one of the first songs Jackson recalls learning, "The Gypsy Laddie" or "Gypsy Rover" (Romalis 69), a lady leaves her lord, wealth, and baby to run off with a gypsy. In the two versions published in *English and Scottish Popular Ballads* (1904), the woman prefers poverty to marriage, deciding "if I have brewn good beer, I will drink / of the same, / and my lord shall no more come near / me" (485).

In most versions, the lady commits adultery and escapes her marriage without retribution, countering traditional portrayals of women as the chaste guardians of virtue.

Usually set in the distant past and handed down for generations, folk songs, even with strong feminist undertones, came to be seen as traditional rather than rhetorical, and women, as tradition bearers, were able to perpetuate these songs in America. Jackson recalls that her great-grandmother "took me on her knee and sang the songs to me that my great-great grandmother knew. . . . [She] taught me most of the songs I know" (qtd. in Romalis 62). Since songs were typically passed from woman to woman, Mary Bufwack and Robert Oermann note, "a distinct female point of view was passed through the generations" (xiv). Thus, the cover of Loraine Wyman and Howard Brockway's collection *Twenty Kentucky Mountain Songs* (1920) shows a barefooted woman playing a dulcimer surrounded by children (Filene 19). Supporting this visual, the songs within the collection and those published by three of the foremost collectors—Olive Dame Campbell, Cecil Sharp, Francis Child—are mostly attributed to women.

While functioning as an available means for women, folk songs' rhetorical potential and women's involvement in the tradition have often been dismissed. Like other scholars, historian Benjamin Filene argues that their predominance within collections merely shows that "[women] felt more comfortable than men singing for collectors," "the collectors felt more comfortable with female informants," "many of the collectors themselves were women," and "women may have been more likely to preserve the sorts of songs in which collectors were most interested" (20). While Filene contends that the songs attributed to women interested collectors because of their traceable English and Scottish roots, he fails to acknowledge that these songs were also maintained because they foregrounded women's issues, making folk music an available means for singers and female collectors. In fact, according to Bufwack and Oermann, many of these songs shocked collectors, who "expect[ed] the old song culture to reflect their own repressed sexuality" (6). These songs, as such, served a subversive function: under the guise of "tradition," Appalachian women such as Jackson used ballads rhetorically.

Kentucky's Pistol Packin' Mama as Extension of the Folk Tradition

While the 1930s presented women with access to a larger public stage, *kairos* has always been central to the creation and transmission of folk songs. To be rhetorically effective and survive oral transmission, a song has to be selected by the community as representative of the collective experience and be deemed valuable enough to be committed to memory. In other words, each song needs to derive directly from its local context and to both draw from and impact communal beliefs in that moment. As Lloyd notes, most ballads deal with the struggles of a given era—whether knight versus knight or, later, miner versus mine owner (143). Within traditional folk songs, Bufwack and Oermann suggest, women often battle with lovers and husbands, carrying out aggressive or vindictive fantasies (5) in which the woman triumphs over social convention. Typically these songs served a didactic function, educating and reeducating men and women about gender roles. As English professor Mary Barnacle concluded after conversations with Jackson, "Ballads made clear what a dangerous and tragic thing love must be in the mountains and what a dreary thing it usually was with its early marriages, Puritan conventions, and harsh and violent double standards" (qtd. in Romalis 29).

For example, in a traditional ballad Jackson recorded with Alan Lomax in 1939 for the Library of Congress, "The Farmer's Curst Wife" or "The Devil and the Farmer," a farmer gives his "bad" wife to the devil. In hell, she beats his imps until, fearing her, the devil returns her home. Since the tale often ends with her husband exclaiming, "I am to be cursed: She's been to hell and come back worse" (qtd. in Bufwack and Oermann 11), there is no sense that she is punished; in fact, some versions end with a warning for men: "Now you know what a woman can do, / she can whup out the devil and her husband too" (Lomax and Lomax 154). Far from silent and chaste, the wife is portrayed as a domestic rebel rewarded for her assertiveness, encouraging listeners to step outside the bounds of social convention. Such lessons apparently affected Molly, who, according to Romalis, purportedly married and divorced John Mills before marrying miner Jim Stewart at thirteen (73–82). Shortly after his 1927 death, she married another miner, Bill Jackson, who, according to her brother, was "the only man Molly married whom she couldn't control" (qtd. in Romalis 83). Evidently this was the case, for he divorced her in the early 1930s, most likely, Romalis speculates, because of her union activities (83). Never a passive wife, Jackson's roles in her relationships mimic those characterized in traditional ballads.

As industrial demands transformed Appalachian life, the content of folk songs shifted to reflect the new difficulties women faced: the scorned wife was replaced by the miner's wife or mill worker, who struggles not with a lover, but with a manager; often, the lone heroine became, instead, a united group of women or workers. For example, in 1910, Jackson composed her first protest song in response to a strike at the Hughes mine in Ely Branch where her second husband, Stewart, worked. Addressed to miners' wives, with copies left at the communal spring, Jackson encouraged women to "take your children out of Ely Branch, / before they cry for bread" and accused Hughes of lying to miners to break up the strike (qtd. in Romalis 80). Her song also reached an unintended audience: the mine managers, and, for her actions, Stewart was fired (83). In such ways, songs composed during this period had greater consequences, allowing women to directly confront issues and transforming workplaces and social gatherings into arenas of rhetorical exchange.

To participate in this exchange, the rhetor needed to embody the appropriate ethos, since folk songs must express collective beliefs or struggles in order to survive. As Jackson highlights when defining a folk song as "what the folks composes out of their real lives," folk singing requires an ethos gained through shared experience (Jackson n. pag.). As folk music became more protest-oriented, the singer's ethos took on even greater significance; a protest song coming from one not burdened by poverty and industrial life had little cultural currency. A miner's daughter, wife, and mother,[1] Jackson experienced the economic and domestic strife faced by Harlan's residents and developed an insider status that established her ethos as a folk singer within the community. She quickly grew familiar with the mine's direct dangers, which claimed the vision of her father and the lives of her brother, second husband, and son.

As a young midwife, a career she began at age twelve and continued until 1932, she served as "aunt" to over a hundred miners' children. Traveling from home to home to deliver and care for these children, Jackson shared stories and songs and, not unlike an ethnographer, collected material for the music she composed—stories about starvation, infant deaths, and families doing without. Jackson also extended her midwife duties beyond the child's birth and could be found throughout the 1920s and 1930s helping children scrounge for food or even stealing it from the company-owned store's clerk at gunpoint, earning her the nickname "Pistol Packin' Mama." Thus, Jackson built her ethos as a trusted representative of the collective experience of Appalachian women.

Using the material she gathered, Jackson sang about the suffering of miners' wives. For instance, in 1930 when the mines began laying off workers, cutting wages and operating hours, Jackson composed "Hungry Ragged Blues." Within the song, Jackson's nameless narrator reflects the collective grievances of women within the coal camps. In the first two stanzas, Jackson represents the speaker as an individual miner's wife: "I'm sad and weary, I got these hungry ragged blues; / Not a penny in my pocket to buy one thing I need to use. . . . / I woke up this morning with the worst blues I ever had in my life; / Not a bite to cook for breakfast, poor coal miner's wife!" (Jackson and Greenway 6). In the fourth stanza, Jackson's singer becomes an omniscient narrator, describing the women's living conditions: "All the women in this coal camp are sitting with bowed-down heads; / Ragged and barefooted, and their children a-crying for bread" (6). By shifting to a third-person point of view, Jackson synthesizes her experiences with those of the community; the song is no longer an individual's blues, but the blues of all miners' wives that might be sung by any woman within this context. In a stanza added later, Jackson further emphasizes women's collective experience with first-person plural pronouns: "No food, no clothes for our children, I'm sure this ain't no lie; / If we can't git more for our labor, we will starve to death and die" (qtd. in Romalis 41). Though only men labored in the mines, by using the collective "we" and claiming the work as "our labor," Jackson asserts that women also have reason to protest the unfair labor practices within the mining community.

And protest they did. The song, Jackson claims, was sung by a group of women who marched into the mine together (Romalis 188). In doing so, the song's rhetorical purpose was to instruct husbands/miners and guide their actions. While many traditional ballads serve an indirect didactic function, "Hungry Ragged Blues" directly confronts male listeners, telling them, "Oh, don't go under that mountain with the slate hanging over your head; / And work for just coalite and carbine [sic] and your children a-crying for bread" (Jackson and Greenway 6). Within the song, Jackson even chides men who refuse to go on strike, stating that "[a] man that'll work for coalite and carbide ain't got a lick of sense" (6). As she relayed to folklorist and musicologist Archie Green, through this song, she successfully "urged eighteen men out on strike. . . . They throwed their tools down and . . . I marched them all through the hills and me yelling, 'Sad and weary'" (qtd. in Romalis 188–89). In addition to inspiring women to march and men to attempt a wildcat strike, the song had a third intended audience: sympathetic outsiders.

In the final two lines—"Some coal operators might tell you the hungry blues are not bad; / They are the worst blues this poor woman ever had" (qtd. in Romalis 41)—Jackson uses her authentic experience to proactively counter the mine owners' rhetoric and, thereby, educate outsiders about the hardships within the mining town. For this reason, she often chose to perform this song at strikes and rallies and whenever writers visited Harlan's coal camps.

Jackson's facility with traditional ballads is evidenced not only by the number of songs she later recorded (over one hundred for the Library of Congress in 1939), but also by her understanding of how memory and invention serve integral and overlapping functions within a given folk community, allowing the singer to recall a specific song and revise the lyrics for a different rhetorical situation. Jackson was particularly adept at parodying traditional songs—a technique she used often once the scattered wildcat strikes developed into the massive strike that earned her hometown the nickname "Bloody Harlan." When mine owners announced a 10 percent wage cut in February 1931, the workers, backed by their wives, held a "spontaneous strike" (Duke 27). When the United Mine Workers of America (UMWA) arrived on the first of March, eleven thousand eagerly joined. The next day, they were evicted from their company-owned homes (27). Aid promised by the UMWA never arrived (Lynch 56). Jackson, still working as a midwife at the time, recalls: "Thirty-seven babies died in my arms the last three months of 1931. Their little stomachs busted open; they was mortified inside" (Jackson and Greenway 5). Starvation led to desperation, culminating in the Battle of Evarts on the first of May, which left three deputies and one miner dead and drew in the National Guard. Shortly after, the UMWA withdrew, calling the strike "unauthorized" (Duke 28). The Communist-led National Miners Union (NMU), arriving a month later, found workers who, in John Dos Passos's words, were "so desperate that they'll join anything that promises them even temporary help" (67). To dissuade workers from joining the union, the press in Harlan labeled the NMU irreligious and unpatriotic.

Responding to these charges, Jackson composed several parodies to challenge the mine owners' oppressive practices and dissociate the strike from atheism. In 1931, when the company-owned hospital began refusing service to those who could not pay in advance, for example, Jackson composed "Dreadful Memories," parodying J. B. F. Wright's popular hymn "Precious Memories." The original hymn sentimentally recalls childhood memories that "flood my soul"; the singer, warmed by "sacred scenes" from the past, optimistically looks toward a future in "that lovely land somewhere." Jackson's parody highlights the lack of such memories and hope for mining families:

> Dreadful memories! How they linger,
> How they pain my precious soul!
> Little children, sick and hungry,
> Sick and hungry, weak and cold.   (Jackson and Greenway 5)

As Cohen and Samuelson note, by drawing upon a popular hymn, Jackson "helped establish the righteousness of the union" when it was being labeled an organization of atheists (137). Instead, she painted the coal operators as inhumane:

> I can't forget them coal miners' children
> That starved to death for want of milk;
> While the coal operators and their wives and their children
> Were all dressed in jewels and silk.   (Jackson and Greenway 5)

During the strike, Jackson's parodies of traditional religious hymns not only allowed her to counter claims that union members were irreligious, but also provided her with music that could be taken up quickly by listeners: raised in the Baptist church, her main audience already knew the hymns and could hum, if not sing along, upon first hearing her revision, enabling the songs to easily enter collective memory.

Jackson used the same technique to further distance herself and the strike from the communist movement when the label "Red" became unpopular, even dangerous, in Harlan. Her husband, Bill, for one, was fired because, according to Jackson, she supported too publically the NMU (Romalis 46). Jackson insisted though, "I've been framed up and accused of being a Red when I did not understand what that meant. . . . I got all of my progressive ideas from my hard tough struggles, and nowhere else" (qtd. in Lynch 62). Her lyrics from the 1930s do show that she either did not understand or chose to publicly denounce the relationship between the NMU and the Communist Party U.S.A. (CPUSA). In "I Am a Union Woman," a song written in support of the NMU and based on the tune of a Baptist hymn, "Lay the Lily Low," for instance, Jackson describes herself as "a union woman, as brave as I can be" and uses the power provided her by the union and the folk-song tradition to organize workers, calling on them to "come join the NMU" (Jackson and Greenway 2). However, as the song goes on, Jackson uses her lyrics to linguistically and geographically detach herself from the

Communist Party: "I was raised in old Kentucky, in Kentucky borned and bred; / And when I joined the union, they called me a Rooshian Red" (2). While her diction was a result, in part, of cultural immersion, it was also a conscious choice on Jackson's part: she used an "old Kentucky mountain dialect," she explained, because if she were to use "high-fallutin' words," "they [Appalachians] would have said [she] had a big head and kicked [her] out of the house" (qtd. in Romalis 167). Through her word choice, then, Jackson presents herself as a native Kentuckian and NMU member, not a Communist, separating the two groups and inviting workers to draw the same distinction. In doing so, Jackson, an insider with an established rural, working-class ethos, became an important figure for the NMU, translating their beliefs in a way that was palatable to her fellow Appalachians and in a language and tradition they understood.

From the Hollers to the Big Apple: Jackson as a Cultural Broker

At the age of fifty, Jackson was "discovered" by leftist intellectuals. When Theodore Dreiser's National Committee for the Defense of Political Prisoners came to Harlan in 1931 to hear miners' testimony, Jackson arrived at their door on the third day. After relating her own tale of misfortune, she sang her well-known ballad "Hungry Ragged Blues." According to her half-brother Jim Garland, committee members were so taken with her lyrics and presence that "they thought she was just about the whole Kentucky strike" (qtd. in Romalis 42). Evidencing the impact Jackson had on leftist thinking, the committee printed her lyrics on the first page of their 1932 book *Harlan Miners Speak* and contributors such as Dos Passos peppered their individual sections with quotes from the lyrics. The book became an influential piece of industrial history and firmly established the relationship between the leftist intellectual community and Kentucky's Pistol Packin' Mama.

Jackson's "ordinariness" encouraged the Dreiser Committee to see her as an effective symbol to unite workers in the South and to serve as an authentic representative of Appalachians in the North. Hence, in December 1931, the committee invited Jackson to New York to raise funds for the miners. By some accounts "run out of Kentucky" because of her prounion activities (Jackson and Greenway 1), Jackson accepted the invitation. Performing before an estimated twenty-one thousand at the Bronx Coliseum and another three thousand at New York's Star Casino (Lynch 64–66), Jackson began her concerts with an untitled piece that explained who she was and described the dire situation in

Harlan. The song focuses on hardships that listeners could most easily identify with—namely, the pitiable suffering of the children—and Jackson successfully uses juxtaposition to emphasize the disparity between the lifestyles of owners and workers:

> While the coal operators and their wives
> All went in jewels and silk,
> The poor coal miners' babies
> Starved to death for bread and milk. (qtd. in Greenway, *American Folksongs* 259)

Such juxtaposition was a common folk technique, enabling listeners to quickly grasp important differences. Further, as also illustrated in "Dreadful Memories," stock rhyming phrases ("all went in jewels and silk," "starved to death for bread and milk") function in oral traditions as formula, which Jackson could use and move at will to express differences succinctly and memorably.

As she had at the age of ten, Jackson found her songs capable of eliciting donations. After her first concert, she exclaimed, "I collected hatfuls of bills that night, and my youngest brother, Jim Garland, pulled off his two socks and filled them full of silver, and next morning we sent over $900 to the starving miners and their families" (qtd. in Greenway, *American Folksongs* 260). Jackson's performances also earned her some celebrity. By early December, the *New York Times* described her "Hungry Ragged Blues" (renamed "The Kentucky Miners' Wives' Hungry Ragged Blues" for her urban audience) as "her now famous song" ("Anderson Decries" 24). The *Daily Worker*, official organ of the CPUSA, also consistently cheered Jackson's success: "Wherever she goes the same things happen; the police shift uneasily and take tight hold of their sticks and their guns, and the workers gather in hundreds, in thousands, they sing her songs, listen to her words, take her advice because it's shrewd, courageous and they can trust her absolutely" (qtd. in Romalis 97).

However, accounts of Jackson's rhetorical efficacy in the leftist press may well be hyperbolic. While Dreiser's committee had clearly intended for Jackson to serve as what Romalis calls a "cultural broker" (3), they unwittingly placed her in a context where folk music and its conventions were neither popular nor well understood. Denisoff argues that, far from the hollers of Kentucky, her reliance on southern conventions, colloquialisms, and rural symbols—effective rhetorical tools in an Appalachian setting—proved less persuasive to New York audiences

(4). Ben Robertson, reporter for the *New York Herald Tribune*, found her speech and songs full of "allegory, with frequent idiom and colloquialisms from her section. She drew many similes from the woods and from the Bible" (qtd. in Green 79). Used to drawing on clichés and stock phrases, for instance, Jackson sang, "through the hot part of the summer / our babies died like flies," lyrics that, while perfectly apt within the folk community, could appear insensitive to outsiders.

Further, though she sang of murder, dying children, and worker solidarity, her voice, in keeping with folk tradition, was nasal and unadorned. Folk communities gauge a singer's credibility, in part, by how she avoids modulation when singing; it is a way of showing that the singer is separate from the message—that it is the argument of the people not

Fig. 10.1. Aunt Molly Jackson in New York City in the mid-1930s.
Photo courtesy of Shelly Romalis, Professor Emerita, York University, Toronto, Canada.

one individual. To urbanites and leftist musicians, however, Jackson's emotional and artistic detachment from her music was puzzling and unpalatable. As Charles Seeger recalls, when Jackson later performed for the Composer's Collective, a branch of the Communist-sponsored Worker's Music League, "Aunt Molly's songs left the group more bewildered than inspired" (qtd. in Reuss 53). To be fair, though, Jackson was equally unimpressed by their musical style, and folklorist and labor historian Richard Reuss agreed. In Reuss's view, the Collective's mission of creating music that was "in so unique a form that it would be impossible to imitate and hence remain forever associated with the working masses" left it utterly removed from the workers the Collective sought to inspire (Reuss 45). Thus, when the CPUSA attempted to broaden its base, the Composer's Collective was dissolved and Aunt Molly Jackson revived—though with her lyrics revised to suit a new rhetorical purpose.

The Leftist Transformation of Jackson from Singer to Symbol

Despite her success raising funds and awareness in the North, less than a month after her first New York performance the NMU called an "ineffective strike" on 1 January 1932 in Harlan. Though the failed strike faded from the headlines, Jackson, for a time, thrived in the North. Leftist musician Margaret Larkin helped her complete her first and only commercial recording; folk collector Alan Lomax recorded her songs for the Library of Congress; folk singer Pete Seeger transcribed her lyrics and "credited her as one of his major influences" (Romalis 101); Leadbelly and Woody Guthrie became her companions, the latter describing her as "the best ballad singer in the country" (qtd. in Romalis 139). Slowly, however, Jackson began to survive in the north more as a symbol of—rather than a folk singer from—the southern, rural working class, attractive to intellectuals who found her idiosyncratic ways charming and authentic. As Romalis notes, "Wealthy radicals" such as actress Luise Rainer and playwright Clifford Odets invited Jackson "to their elegant homes [and] lavished food and drink" upon her (95), and Mary Barnacle, professor of English and folklore at NYU, spent hours interviewing Jackson, recording her stories and songs, even inviting her to guest lecture in her courses (101). Yet, Reuss explains, while Jackson "was revered as a militant example of the Kentucky proletariat, admired for her ability to blend class sentiments with old mountain tunes, . . . few radicals . . . really enjoyed the harsh, tense sound of her voice" (184). Thus, after the failed strike, Jackson's lyrics survived mainly in leftist print publications, not in performance.

While throughout the 1930s Jackson embraced the symbolic political role leftists had assigned to her, she later grew suspicious of their revision of her lyrics. According to Greenway, she was especially "concerned about the palpable Communist ideology taken on by some of her songs" (*American Folksongs* 261). In order to appeal to a broader urban audience, leftist writers, such as the Dreiser Committee, often replaced Jackson's Kentucky idioms with those familiar to northern activists, making her a stronger advocate for communism and dismantling her local, communal ethos. For example, in the original lyrics to "Hungry Ragged Blues," Jackson referred to listeners as "friends and workers," while in *Harlan Miners Speak*, her readers become "friends and comrades" (vi)—a communist term. As a result, the song's message is directed toward party sympathizers rather than miners and their families.

As leftist writers continued using Jackson to interest urbanites in the communist movement, more such lyrical revisions were published. Most notably, "The Death of Harry Simms," a song Jackson wrote with her brother in 1932,[2] was transformed from a narrative of working-class resistance to a tale of a murderous upper class as Simms, a young union organizer, is murdered not by the original "some life-stealing gun thug" (Jackson and Greenway 3) or, as in an early variant, "the dirty coal operator gun thugs" (qtd. in Romalis 37) but (as in the 1968 issue of *Sing Out!* magazine) by "the dirty capitalist gun thugs" (qtd. in Greenway, *American Folksongs* 261). When the song "came back to Aunt Molly years later," Greenway notes, it had a new ending that significantly changed the lyric's focus:

Original Lyrics	*Revised Lyrics*
The thugs can kill our leaders	Comrades, we must vow today,
And cause us to shed tears,	This one thing we must do;
But they cannot kill our spirit	We must organize the miners
If they try a million years;	In the dear old NMU;
We have learned our lesson	And get a million volunteers
Now we all realize	Into the YCL[3]
A union struggle must go on	And sink this rotten system
Till we are organized.	In the deepest pits of hell.
(Jackson and Greenway 3)	(qtd. in Greenway, *American Folksongs* 261)

In the revised version, the workers seek to recruit "a million volunteers," broadening the song's audience and purpose so that the call for workers to unite is replaced with a call to train a new generation to sink the entire capitalist system "in the deepest pits of hell."

Communal revision is a defining characteristic of folk music but not when the revisions change the ethos of the singer. Discussing the process of folk re-creation, Jackson admits, "I know how these things is done for I've done 'em myself." Nevertheless, the press's taking of what she called her "honest, true things" and leaving them "messed up" upset her greatly (qtd. in Green 82). While *vocally* Jackson sought aid for Harlan miners and their families and served as a communal voice for rural Appalachians, *in print* she appeared as an ardent supporter of Communism. Though the latter focus made her a more prominent figure in New York's political scene at the time, her symbolic value and ethos dissipated as the New Deal restored faith in capitalism. Over time, Jackson found herself in rhetorical limbo: on the one hand, she was too politicized, too urban, too individualized to be considered part of the folk tradition; on the other hand, her musical style and her radicalized lyrics left her without the public, urban forum she once enjoyed. As a result, Jackson, immortalized in the pages of leftist publications such as *The Little Red Songbook*, was granted a place in distant public memory rather than in a communal rhetorical tradition.

Moving from Individual Rhetors to Collective Rhetorics

Today, Jackson's name is mentioned in almost every collection of strike or labor protest songs and in histories of the Harlan coal strikes. Yet her songs are still often presented without mention of the ballads they are based upon or the many other women folk singers involved in the strikes, such as Ella Mae Wiggins—the minstrel of Gastonia—or Florence Reece, whose "Which Side Are You On" is still sung at rallies today. Even Romalis's definitive biography of Jackson, as one reviewer notes, includes neither an explanation of "what motivated Jackson to compose these songs" nor a description of the "ballads she used as the models for her original compositions" (Huber 114). There still seems to be a sense that notable rhetoric happens in specified locations—the pulpit, the podium, the book, the academic journal—spaces that traditionally require a certain economic and social status to inhabit.

Jackson, though an important figure in the process, marks neither the beginning nor end of women using folk singing as a means of making their issues and voices heard. In addition to the nameless women who sang their husbands onto the strike lines, the Fuller Sisters, Moonshine Kate, Adelyne Hood, Lily May Ledford, Agnes "Sis"

Cunningham, Sarah Ogan Gunning, the Carter Family, Roba Stanley, Samantha Bumgarner, and Almeda Riddle, to name a few, spent the 1920s and 1930s recording, performing, and popularizing ballads. Within Appalachian homes in Tennessee and Kentucky, as Bufwack and Oermann note, Avie Owens and Clara Butcher were learning songs from their mothers that they would pass on to their daughters: Dolly Parton and Loretta Lynn (11). Just because many went unnamed, just because the home is often not seen as a rhetorical platform, does not mean that these women were not heard. It is not by chance that some of the most outspoken feminist/activist singers have chosen folk music as their genre. Artists such as Joan Baez, Hazel Dickens, Alice Gerrard, Odetta, Joni Mitchell, Jean Ritchie, Ani DiFranco, and The Indigo Girls are part of an undisturbed line of female folk singers who continually placed gender and social issues at the core of their lyrics and, in doing so, preserved one of the oldest, though often unrecognized, available means for women. When such women "seep into view," then, we as rhetorical scholars have to avoid "considering [them] exceptional rather than as part and parcel of a pattern" (Royster, *Traces of a Stream* 4). Instead, we need to dig beneath representations, mark the context for their words, and understand that the construction of an individual rhetor involves the work of many hands.

Notes

1. Jackson gave birth to two children, who most likely died in infancy, as little information can be found about them. According to Romalis, Jackson nevertheless considered herself a mother since she raised six children that Stewart and Bill Jackson fathered with other women and even adopted Stewart's son (75–76).

2. Once "The Death of Harry Simms" moved from the folk community to the commercial world, the issue of authorship arose. Though Jackson at first claimed the song as her own, she later acknowledged collaborating with Garland (Romalis 37), who today is credited as the songwriter.

3. Young Communist League.

II

> It is sometimes hard for the man in the street to think of aviation [as an increasingly common means of travel]. Because of its background in war, he regards it as embodying all the hazards of military maneuvers. Because it was kept alive by "stunts" in country fairs in the years after the war, he often sees it only as some variety of circus. The record of ninety-thousand miles flown on scheduled routes every day in the United States is gradually dispelling both ideas.—Amelia Earhart, "Mrs. Lindbergh"

Sweethearts of the Skies

Sara Hillin

The early women pioneers of aviation—women such as Amelia Earhart and two of her contemporaries, Bessie Coleman, a barnstormer who performed before thousands and was the first African American pilot to hold an international license, and Florence Klingensmith, known for her amazing aerobatic feats—faced considerable challenges in their drive to conquer the skies. To meet these challenges, I will argue, Earhart, Coleman, and Klingensmith deliberately cultivated the image of "aerocyborgs"—women literally connected to their aircraft, who exploited this connection rhetorically in order to disrupt culturally constructed norms of American womanhood. Their aerocyborg approach not only opened new fields for women but also offers an early instance of the human-machine link—and one that, unlike many, involves women.

If, as N. Katherine Hayles argues in *How We Became Posthuman*, "the construction of the posthuman is also deeply involved with boundary questions, particularly when the redrawing of boundaries changes the locus of self-hood" (279), then these pioneering women pilots were, in fact, playing with boundaries—redefining their own "locus of self-hood" and actively inviting their audiences to do so along with them. In so doing, they were theorizing, through their lived experience, ways to articulate the interplay between "the signifying power of materialities and . . . the materiality of signifying processes" before a vocabulary of posthuman discourse had even been invented (249).

Embodying the Aerocyborg

According to Donna Haraway in *Simians, Cyborgs, and Women: The Reinvention of Nature*, cyborgs are "creatures simultaneously animal and machine" (149), and this functions well as a definition of these three pilots, who showcased their inseparability from their planes in image and speech/text. Central to Hayles's definition of the cyborg is the perspective of relationality: the cyborg is an interaction or interrelationship between biology and technology. Perhaps more than in any other human relationship with technology, pilots must feel a kind of symbiotic relationship with the aircraft, not simply inducing "motion" in the machine but also becoming a part of it—a relationship that induces "action," in the Burkean sense of purposive symbolic response. Certain things the pilot of a small, propeller-driven aircraft must be almost subconsciously aware of—the slight, left-leaning torque of the plane, the fact that even the most subtle hand or foot movements create significant changes in pitch or airspeed—require profound union between the senses and mental and physical reactions of the pilot and the airplane.

My own brief foray into piloting has given me some insight into this experience. During one lesson, my instructor emphatically told me that I needed to "wear" the airplane,[1] and I did eventually arrive at a sense of embodying the machine in order to act with it in response to forces such as wind. The plane becomes an extension of the human body in the act of flying. As Hayles points out, in the posthuman era there is no clear demarcation between "bodily existence and computer simulation, cybernetic mechanism and biological organism, robot teleology and human goals" (*Posthuman* 3). The pilot's very life depends on this unclear demarcation, as an inability to form this fusion of self and machine leads to a dangerous lack of control over the craft. For early women pilots, however, the aerocyborg identity, which originated in the physically imperative dynamic relationship between the pilot and her plane, became a *rhetorical* device—a "technology of inscription," which, as Hayles argues, enables users to "[insert] themselves into the chain of textual production" (26).

I argue that because these pilots were so closely connected with their aircraft, pilot and plane acted together to create a rhetoric of resistance to the patriarchal dominance of aviation. As the cyborg "is a creature in a post-gender world [and] has no truck with bisexuality, pre-oedipal symbiosis, unalienated labour, or other seductions to organic wholeness" (Haraway 150–51), so these women were a new "breed"—"female/pilots," "girl/flyers," "woman/pilots" (and inevitably they were marked with one of these three labels in the majority of press releases). They were examples of the fact that, as Hayles states, "living in a technologically engineered and information-rich environment brings with it associated shifts in habits, postures, enactments, perceptions" ("Flesh and Metal" 230). This is not to say that the planes were automatically extensions of the humans, directly communicating (like a telephone); rather they were, as Kenneth Burke termed it, "*indirectly* communicative media (in the broad sense that cars, refrigerators, foods, clothing, and guns could be called communicative)" (*Language as Symbolic Action* 416). Earhart, Coleman, and Klingensmith, however, endowed their planes with action, transforming them into dynamic, directly communicative media through barnstorming, transatlantic flights, and races.

Of the three women, Amelia Earhart was the most prolific. Born in Kansas in 1897, Earhart was from a young age drawn to more "tomboyish" activities and was encouraged in her curiosity about aviation by her father. After Columbia and the Harvard extension school, Earhart moved to Boston, where she flew and began to gain publicity. Her "vocal salesmanship" (*For the Fun of It* 111), as she termed her attempts to convince women to take part in aviation, included three best-selling books, eight articles penned for the *New York Times* between 1928 and 1935, a stint as aviation writer/editor for *Hearst's Cosmopolitan* from 1928 to 1930, lectures, and countless interviews, as well as the press's incessant tracking of her exploits. Although today Earhart is most famous for her disappearance, in 1937, on the last leg of an attempted round-the-world flight, in her writing she is careful to distance herself from "stunt flyers" or "thrill seekers," opting instead to represent herself as an aviator par excellence. Earhart's rhetoric is founded on a subtext that insists that she and her plane are collaborators. In *20 Hrs. 40 Min.: Our Flight in the Friendship*, for instance, she insists that the "plane and the engine, of course, are no better than their pilot" (249). This verbal construction of a cyborgian self-image can be seen in the unfinished manuscript "On What a Pilot Eats": "There is little scientific data regarding air travel diet, for either passengers or pilots. Obviously the latter on long flights need the kind of food which will supply concentrated, easily assimilated fuel for the mental and physical machinery" (2). Here, Earhart fuses her body with the plane: she is "machinery," and her "fuel" becomes fuel for the plane; if her stomach/gas tank is not refilled, the plane's performance suffers. They are, essentially, one.

Because the aerocyborg identity hinged on the woman/machine symbiosis, these pilots' aggressive use of their aerocyborg status made impossible any essentialist reality that would allow them to be stereotypically feminine in the public eye. Each of the three women refuted her traditional gender roles, arguing implicitly for a postgender construction of "pilot" that would allow her to make use of her mechanical talents and be recognized for them without constant reference to her marked gender and racial status. As Haraway argues, the cyborg story is about "transgressed boundaries, potent fusions, and dangerous possibilities which progressive people might explore as one part of needed political work" (154). Earhart seems to have borne the brunt of the criticism for her consistently "unfeminine" image. There is, for example, a definite sense of relief expressed by one London journalist who, as the headline declared, spied the "Transatlantic Girl Flyer out Shopping in Borrowed Clothes." He writes that Earhart was unrecognizable save for her "unruly mop of curly hair" and goes on to assert: "Her boyish flying costume discarded in favor of borrowed but becoming and less conspicuous attire, Miss Amelia Earhart . . . appeared in public today as a pretty, smartly gowned and decidedly feminine American girl." Journalists faced with these women in "drag" seemed to want to salvage some vestige of femininity, describing Earhart, for example, as a "slender blonde social service worker" ("Amelia Earhart Weds" 1).

Carefully manipulated image was one powerful way in which the aerocyborg identity was maintained. In many publicity photographs, these women not only appropriated the "masculine" attire of flight suits, leather jackets, and helmets, but also fused themselves visually with their planes. For instance, in the eleven archival photographs of Klingensmith that I examined, all but one show her in clothing related to flying (most often a flying cap), and in five she is pictured in front of her aircraft. Similarly, many photos of Earhart in *Hearst's Cosmopolitan* and various press releases show her and her famously "unruly" hair, sitting or standing atop one of the wings of her aircraft or standing in front of it, with her arms outstretched across the propeller; she poses with the plane in such a way as to make it an undeniable presence in the image. Coleman took the rhetorical potential of flight apparel to a whole different level. Of the six most widely circulated photos of her from the early 1920s, she is pictured next to her plane in two, and in both she is in her flight suit. The masculine, military

Fig. 11.1. Amelia Earhart arrives in Ireland after her solo transatlantic flight in her Lockheed 58 Vega, ca. 12 May 1932. Photo courtesy of the National Air and Space Museum, Smithsonian Institution (SI 86–10744).

outfits she appropriated to constitute herself as a pilot par excellence became as much a part of her performed rhetoric as the aerobatics. Ken Gornstein notes that "to emphasize her spiritual kinship with the fifteenth-century Maid of Orleans, Coleman donned French military outfits for many of her performances" (21); in another performance, she paid aerobatic homage to the black soldiers of the Eighth Illinois Infantry by cutting a figure eight in the sky ("Bessie Gets Away" 2).

While all three pilots faced unique challenges in their rhetorical endeavors, Coleman, who was one of thirteen children born (in 1892) to a sharecropping family in Atlanta, Texas, flew in a culture where both gender and race worked against her—her equipment was often subpar, and she was forced to perform in venues with segregated facilities. Indeed, she had to move to France to find an instructor who would teach an African American woman to fly, earning her license from the Federation Aeronautique Internationale in Lecroty, France in 1921. Ron Edwards believes Coleman saw aviation as a "way to rise above the cotton fields" (8), and according to Philip Handleman, she decided that flying "would be her instrument of success" (20). Gornstein notes that she played to eager audiences and successfully created a rhetorical space in which to promote the place of African Americans in aviation.

Supported and adored by smaller communities (such as the readers of the *Chicago Defender*, which strongly promoted her, as well as the African American audiences to whom she spoke in person), Coleman did not have the mainstream access of Earhart. As an upper-middle-class

Fig. 11.2. Bessie Coleman standing on the wheel of a Curtiss JN-4 biplane. The printing at the bottom reads, "Yours' Aviatrix, Bessie Coleman." Photographer: Dove and Poster, 192[?]; courtesy of Security Pacific National Bank Collection/ Los Angeles Public Library.

white woman, Earhart could better control her own publicity—she was a media darling, and though her mishaps were the subject of a few headlines, by and large she was touted with admiration. Thus, while Earhart specifically eschewed the identity of "thrill seeker," Coleman purposefully cultivated it. She had access to her own film, which allowed her to innovatively exploit an emerging medium to dazzle her audiences. Using a newsreel taped in Berlin that showed her both standing by the plane and, as Doris Rich explains in *Queen Bess: Daredevil Aviator*, "flying over the defeated Kaiser's palace" (46), she displayed her rhetorical savvy by including "clips of the 2,000 feet of film of her performances in Europe and the United States, which she had judiciously preserved and taken with her" (91). While Earhart sought to shed the marked image of the "woman" pilot (an image constructed by the media), Coleman deliberately used the combination of racial pride and her status as a "woman pilot" to boost her ethos. As a black woman exhibiting rhetorical agency in the 1920s, Coleman defied stereotypes of the "unlocated" woman—she used her voice to portray herself as representing the *possibility* of flight for other black Americans.

Coleman's rhetoric continued the project of "racial uplift" begun in the nineteenth century: "the belief," as Shirley Wilson Logan describes it, "that through education, economic independence, and sanitary living conditions, black people could thrive" (151). She always reminded her audiences that the driving force behind her work was the promotion of racial pride rather than her achievements as a woman. Coleman, like activists Ida B. Wells and Nannie H. Burroughs (as Sandra Robinson's chapter in this collection demonstrates), found that promoting "racial uplift" became an exigence that propelled her into pioneering work. In Coleman's case, this was the development of the novel ethos of the black aviatrix as a means of encouraging civic participation among African Americans. She lectured extensively; indeed, her lectures, Doris Rich explains, brought in more money than her stunt flying (91). Jacqueline Jones Royster argues that "rhetorical prowess for African American women gains its deepest meaning and clarity within the context of their particular brand of community leadership" ("To Call" 175). For Coleman, it was through the unusual combination of theatrical stage presence, visual media, and mechanical skill that she blazed her own rhetorical trail, creating solidarity and establishing herself as a leader.

As an African American, Coleman had a particularly embattled position from which to create her public image. Not only was her work often overshadowed in the mainstream press in favor of white aviators, but as Amy Sur Bix notes, while Americans "labeled white female flyers with cute labels such as 'angels,' 'sweethearts of the air,' and 'powder-puff pilots,' press references to Coleman consistently stressed her racial identity" (11). One can see Coleman's doubly marked status in headlines such as the *New York Times'* 1922 "Negro Aviatrix Arrives" (4). "Formed by a double negation [the labels of nonwhite and nonmale]," writes Haraway, "women of color have no positive identity" (283). Coleman was acutely aware of this negation, having been excluded from both male camaraderie and white women's flying clubs. She was, as Bix argues, in the difficult position of making flight seem accessible to African Americans even though she was forced to do so in unsafe, second-rate aircraft, while showing whites that "her accomplishment disproved stereotypes of racial inadequacy" (24). Coleman, therefore, forged her own positive identification by means of her inspirational "pride-in-race" speeches (D. Rich 22) that were in turn "forged" symbolically with her visual attachment to the plane.

The twelve articles related to Coleman that appeared in the *Chicago Defender* between 1921 and 1926 and the two that appeared in the *New York Times* (1921 and 1922) all deal with her as an "aviatrix"—a woman inseparable from her aircraft who exploited an airborne identity that flew in the face of racist and sexist essentialism. She took advantage of her ethos in the African American community to publicize her views on flying and plead for funds to open an African American flight school in the United States. There was a fascinating rhetorical synergy between Coleman and the *Defender*, in which the aviator's every move was depicted through the lens of race. One *Defender* article by Ralph Elliot written shortly after Coleman was injured in a crash allowed her a platform to push the community to action: "Must I," she asks with an impatient gesture, "escape from death to open a school for whites only? Or will the Negro race give it a little coloring? So far cooperation has come from the whites" (3). Coleman was also careful to document the effectiveness of her rhetorical efforts. She explains that during her stay at the hospital, "seven boys of our race have come to see me here and expressed a desire to learn the art of flying" (Elliot 3). Another article gave her the opportunity to sum up her exigence—"I shall never be satisfied until we have men of the Race who can fly"—and to explain why that exigence included *flying* as the agency for achieving her purpose: "I thought it my duty to risk my life to learn aviating and to encourage flying among men and women of the Race who are so far behind the white men in this special line" ("Aviatrix Must Sign"

2). "Everywhere she went," writes Ken Gornstein, "she promoted her belief that blacks could succeed in the world of aviation or in any other endeavor" (21). Coleman's performances—verbal and visual—had a tremendous impact on African American women's introduction to the field of aviation. Her legacy includes the Bessie Coleman Aviators, founded as a memorial to Coleman ("They Take" 88) and, ultimately, the Bessie Coleman Aero Club, opened in 1929 by William Powell, fulfilling Coleman's long-deferred dream of establishing a flight school for African Americans (Edwards 11).

The Ultimate Cyborg

Florence Klingensmith, though far less well known than the other two women pilots, relied most heavily on the nondiscursive aerocyborg image. Born in Fargo, North Dakota, in 1906, she was drawn to adventurous endeavors as a young woman, including riding motorcycles and horses and parachute jumping (Studer 1), and was best known for her participation in air races and for setting the inside loop record in 1931. Unlike Earhart or Coleman, she did not make speeches or write news articles, but what little remains of her own words indicates that she was using her stunts and speed records to argue for equal respect for women in aviation. She passionately promoted her own exhibitions with ingenuity and a sense of situated ethos as a mechanic who knew planes inside and out. When it was suggested that some women might be able to pilot a plane but most had very little idea what was inside a motor or how aircraft were put together, she shot back, "Ask the men if I don't know all about planes. Ask them if I don't do all my own mechanical work.... I'm as good with a plane as any man" (qtd. in Studer 1). Her brief memoir of her flight training (she began in a class with four hundred young men) details her struggle to break into aviation:

> From March until June 1, I worked as a mechanic's apprentice, and through dirt and grease I worked my way to one solo flight out of every six hours of instruction. Still lacking the money to do much flying, parachute jumping was my next move, but it did not prove highly profitable. After spending three months glued to the ground, I promoted a booster's flying club which proved unsuccessful. From that came the idea to promote my own plane. After three months of hard talking, discouragement and persistency I won out with $3,000 in hand. With this and the advance from advertisers, I was able to buy a Monocoupe. (Letter to Unidentified Friend, Feb. 1932)

Klingensmith defied the stereotypical relationship between man and machine (which Earhart also confronted in *For the Fun of It*, where she damns the popular notion that mechanical training was strictly for boys). As an aerocyborg, Klingensmith deliberately exploited the fusion of mechanical talent—yet another aspect of aviation that, in the public's mind, should have remained a masculine arena—with her feminine appearance, her pretty face and diminutive size, which several journalists noted, apparently nonplussed that such a small, attractive woman could be so successful in this field.

Klingensmith's public persuasion was accomplished primarily through her visual displays in which, virtually, she was subsumed into the aircraft. Her *own* rhetoric was primarily one of the sky—she raced and looped her way into recognition, along the way earning the Amelia Earhart Trophy at the 1932 National Air Races held in Cleveland. The press, through its commentary on her accomplishments, played an important part in shaping her aerocyborg identity both during her life and posthumously. Journalists marveled at her speed and aerobatic acuity in various races, including the one that ended with her fatal crash—the International Air Races of September 1933 in which she competed with men (a first for women competitors). Reginald Cleveland of the *New York Times* reported two days after her death that she flew the race "with intrepid skill that outclassed all her men competitors" (1). Headlines such as "Woman Pilot Hits a 200-Mile Clip" fed the public's interest in the excitement of the competition, but the articles also acknowledged Klingensmith's challenge to male pilots. "Miss Klingensmith climbed into Johnny Livingston's little red and yellow clipped-wing monocoupe yesterday," wrote Marion Hopwood of the *Cleveland Plain Dealer* in September 1932, "and before she had landed had shown the men pilots a few things about handling a fast plane" (2).

Klingensmith put on spectacular aerobatic performances, becoming, in June 1931, the first woman to perform 1,078 "inside loops" (a record which still stands for women). Margie Richison reported that for five hours and twelve minutes she kept her plane performing a continuous series of loops before a crowd of ten thousand (9). She also entered numerous air races. Clara Studer, who wrote on Klingensmith for the *Ninety-Niner* right after her death in September 1933, argues that no one who saw or read about Klingensmith's final race would doubt her flying abilities since it was not her piloting but a mechanical error in the fragile wing material that caused her plane to crash.

She died, Studer maintains, "proving that women can fly on an equal basis with men" (1). Studer's commentary assists Klingensmith's mission posthumously, bolstering her reputation as a rhetor by helping to interpret the significance of her courage and sacrifice "in the history of feminism, since her heroic death so concretely points up the tragic psychological situation which comes about when a woman pilot is denied, because of her sex, the chance to compete with men on an equal footing" (1).

While these journalistic accounts recognize Klingensmith's piloting abilities, they also seem to acknowledge something even more significant in her motives: she seized an exigence, and, using her plane as her available means of persuasion, helped pave the way for women to be recognized as equal to or superior to many male pilots in skill and bravery. Frank Phillips, who had sponsored the race in which Klingensmith died, commented that "her death was at once a challenge and an inspiration to carry on in the conquest of space" (qtd. in Studer 2). What is interesting about both these comments is that they attach deliberate rhetorical significance to Klingensmith's career.

The Rhetorical Aerocyborg

Perhaps the most significant written rhetorical contribution by a female pilot during the interwar period was Amelia Earhart's work as aviation editor for *Hearst's International Combined with Cosmopolitan*, a publication that catered to a wide audience of both men and women with diverse interests. *Hearst's*, during the 1920s and 1930s, was a journal of some literary and intellectual significance—in the issues in which Earhart's features appeared, her writing was alongside pieces done by the likes of Edna Ferber, Fannie Hurst, Ring Lardner, Winston Churchill, Sinclair Lewis, and Calvin Coolidge. One clear exigence running through most of Earhart's articles is the need to address the general public's fears about flying, even in pieces that were not devoted to this topic, such as her profile of Mrs. Charles Lindbergh.

The November 1928 issue included an announcement from Ray Long that Earhart, "the charming young woman who is the new member of our staff," would, from that issue onward, frequently write articles pertaining to flying (33). Long justifies the need for these pieces, commenting that flying "is so much a part of life today that whether or not one wishes actually to fly one owes to oneself an intelligent well formed interest in the subject" (33). In this same issue appeared Earhart's article, "Try Flying Yourself," in which she not only delves into basic mechanics of flight (explaining, for instance, what happens in a stall) but also directly addresses women's present and future role in aviation:

> A number of men have urged me to help them interest their wives or women friends in aviation and it is with these men in mind that I write now of women in aviation—a phrase that might well be changed more specifically to women outside of aviation. . . . The more people who fly, women included—the better—but just *using* planes, not being at the controls, also counts almost as heavily. (35)

With this comment, she began to establish an argument echoed in her book-length works as well—that women's role in aviation extended far beyond piloting and into their influence as passengers and purchasers of aircraft in terms of what comforts and amenities needed to be addressed in aircraft design.

The majority of the articles she wrote for *Hearst's* concluded with the journal's address and an invitation to readers to "write to Miss Amelia Earhart" with any questions about aviation. That a publication of such prestige would name Earhart its sole authority on aviation matters speaks to Earhart's ingenuity in maintaining a public image as a competent pilot as well as her gift for writing about aviation through an appealing prose style that illustrated the intricacies of piloting with helpful similes and analogies.

Only one of her editorials was devoted to women's particular apprehensions about aviation: "Why Are Women Afraid to Fly?" (July 1929). The first page includes a photograph of a toddler holding a ragdoll— underneath it, the caption reads, "From doll days, training militates against becoming aviators" (70). Earhart addresses both the prejudices against employing women in aviation careers and the educational system that largely sets girls up to avoid mechanical endeavors. She also addresses a common stereotype lobbed at women concerning their emotional constitution:

> We hear much of women's "nerves." They may be different in some ways, but it seems to me, given a similar education, those differences would tend to disappear. A woman can sew, watch two or three things on the stove, keep an eye on three or four children, and remain unperturbed. Half an hour in a similar situation for a man completely shatters his nervous system. (138)

Hearst's provided a platform for Earhart to celebrate women's ability to multitask—a skill of monumental necessity for any pilot. In "Fly

America First" (October 1929), Earhart echoes her sentiment that flying, like any new technology, is fallible, but certainly not worthy of the anxieties expressed by so many:

> Fear is more or less an emotional attitude. Many experienced pilots are afraid to get on a horse, at least without a parachute. The men who are accustomed to submarines usually distrust airplanes and vice versa. We can't go back to oxcarts because accidents occur in other forms of transportation. Of course, there are sacrifices for the speed which we attain today. But curiously, the faster we travel, the longer our span of life has become. (135)

Earhart's forceful reassurance that we should plug ahead in the name of technological progress despite our fear of the unknown was a familiar staple in her *Hearst's* essays. In her capacity as aviation editor, Earhart took every opportunity to dispel myths about being both a passenger and a pilot.

Another article, "Miss Earhart Answers Some Questions about Flying" (December 1928), offers Earhart's responses to queries from both men and women. In reading her responses as well as her other articles, one might get the sense that she was weary of hearing from women who dodged the opportunity to take up aviation (or prevented their husbands from doing so) for what seemed to be specious reasons. For example, one woman asked the following: "I have never flown. Friends who have, say you are apt to get seasick. I wish you would tell me about it." Earhart reassures the woman, however, that "in the open planes the atmosphere is so exhilarating that even a novice isn't apt to worry about airsickness" (31).

And within those discussions, she often returned to myths about the *sensations* of flying, which she felt were mostly responsible for such fears. In her piece on Anne Lindbergh, she asks Anne if she does not find it to be so that most people avoid flight because they "anticipate some unpleasant sensation rather than because they are really afraid of flying"—Earhart goes on to answer this question by asserting that, indeed, most people simply fear air-sickness and dizziness rather than an actual crash (79). In other articles, such as "Vagabonding by Air" (December 1928), she addresses the sensations a little more casually, explaining, for example, that "air bumps act as do waves in a choppy sea, tossing one about. In a small plane it is a little like riding through rapids or rough water in a canoe" (195). What these explanations do for her readership is demystify and make more appealing both the idea of learning to fly oneself and simply being a passenger on an aircraft.

While she depended to some degree on the media's sensationalizing of her status as a *female* pilot to open up rhetorical spaces, Earhart also expressed the wish that women pilots would *not* be regarded as oddities but simply as pilots. For example, when she was forced to land in El Paso, Texas (an event recounted in "Vagabonding by Air"), she notes that "cars gathered at once, the women seeming especially anxious to see what I looked like. Some day, I dare say, women can be fliers and yet not be regarded as curiosities!" (196).

It is obvious that Earhart's ethos, as well as that of other women pilots whose accomplishments made headlines, impressed the president of *Hearst's*, Ray Long, who wrote a one-page opinion piece, "Powder Puffs for Men" (July 1930). In this brief essay, he denounces the glee with which newspapers referred to the women's cross-continent air race as a "powderpuff derby" and challenges those who found the term funny:

> Well, if they [Earhart and Elinor Smith, another accomplished pilot] are a fair sample of the efficiency, poise and modesty of those air women, I know quite a few fellows posing as he-men who might emulate these women to their own great advantage, and to the advantage of those who pay their salaries—even if they have to buy a couple of powder puffs to accomplish it. (1)

Long's editorial, even if self-serving as *Hearst's* editor, stands out among the many journalistic portrayals of "girl flyers" by men because it attempts to reclaim the women's image as pilots from sexist assumptions that framed much of the commentary about their work.

The Legacy of the Aerocyborg

Tragically, each woman died while flying—Earhart during her highly publicized flight around the globe, and Coleman and Klingensmith during stunt performances. As Burke notes in *Permanence and Change*, "The tragic symbol is the device *par excellence* for *recommending* a cause. How could one better picture an issue in an appealing light than by showing that people were willing to be destroyed in behalf of it?" (196). This idea is particularly applicable to Coleman, who repeatedly stated that it was her mission to risk her life to prove that African Americans could contribute to aviation, though it is also clear that

Klingensmith and Earhart were more than willing to sacrifice their own lives—and did. Their deaths left gaps that would later be filled by new women in aviation (as can be seen by the creation of groups such as the Bessie Coleman Aviators, as well as the still thriving Ninety-Nines Organization for Women Pilots, which Earhart helped to found).

But perhaps what is of more rhetorical significance is the way the aerocyborg persona responded to the overwhelming trend to frame women in aviation within familiar "feminine" imagery. Note, for example, how a *Pittsburgh Press* journalist begins her 1934 article on the contributions of aviator Phoebe Omlie, who earned the prestigious position of Special Assistant for Air Intelligence: "To the casual observer, Phoebe Fairgrave Omlie looks like the kind of woman that a hardworking husband could expect to find waiting home evenings in a ruffled pink apron, apple cheeks flushed from the heat of an oven that was busily browning his favorite roast" (McBride 7). This comment plays on several culturally embedded norms for women: it suggests that anyone observing Omlie would see the domestic wife performing the normative functions of that role—cooking in traditional feminine attire for her "hardworking" husband, who forays freely into the public sphere while she stays safely at home.

The article's tone suggests an uneasiness with Omlie's gender transgression; the journalist, who refers to her as the "little person" and the "feminine special assistant," comments: "come to think of it, her job has a kind of housekeeping angle to it, too. For she is all the time aiding aviation to take stock of itself as a prelude to the thorough straightening-around and cleaning-up that every business as well as every home needs occasionally" (7). By framing Omlie's work in a public and dangerous space in domestic terms, the writer attempts to render benign Omlie's important post. As Robin Lakoff explains, "New perceptions don't make sense, since they cannot be placed in a familiar frame. Within the frame, things are unmarked: normal, predictable, neutral, orderly, natural, and simple" (48). It was only by associating Omlie's work with a predictable, "natural" role that the journalist could describe her career.

This same confusion over how to classify the aerocyborg is evident in the journalistic coverage of Earhart, Klingensmith, and Coleman. But then, as I have shown, much of their persuasion *depended* on disrupting discourses and creating a new identity, no matter how uncomfortable and alien these challenges may have seemed to the mainstream public. They embodied the daring question of why our bodies should necessarily "end at the skin" (Haraway 178). At home in the airborne space of unfixed identity, these pilots wore their planes as they wore their flight suits, writing their messages with their wings.

Note

1. The notion of "wearing" the plane raises the interesting possibility of discussing early women pilots' "masculine" attire and mechanical/piloting skills as a sort of rebellious "drag," which, in Judith Butler's terms, "constitutes the mundane way in which genders are appropriated, theatricalized, worn, and done; it implies that all gendering is a kind of impersonation and approximation" (715). In this light, the pilots' actions serve to overthrow "compulsory" repetitions of female gender performance (718).

ACADEMIA
and the
SCENE OF
PROFESSIONALISM

12

Field Guides: Women Writing Anthropology
Risa Applegarth

Anthropology has long been perceived as a "welcoming science" for women. Margaret Mead, the most famous anthropologist of the twentieth century, suggested in 1960 that it was anthropology's status as a "new science" that made her discipline "kinder to women, to those who came from distant disciplines, to members of minority groups" (5). Certainly this perception has some basis in fact: when anthropology emerged as a field science in the late nineteenth and early twentieth centuries, anthropologists' attempts to construct a complete account of human history seemed to positively *require* women's participation. Otis Mason, speaking to the Anthropological Society of Washington, a forerunner of the American Anthropological Association, asserted in 1882: "Who may be an anthropologist? Every man, woman and child that has sense and patience to observe, and that can honestly record the thing observed" (26). Two years later, Edward Tylor, founder of British social anthropology, also encouraged women's involvement in anthropological research, proclaiming that "the man of the house . . . cannot do it all. If his wife sympathizes with his work, and is able to do it, really half of the work of investigation seems to me to fall to her" (550). As these statements suggest, the centrality of fieldwork meant that even women who lacked formal scientific training could draw upon their firsthand observations—often based on missionary work or travel with a husband employed in colonial administration—to authorize their participation in this emerging science. Many nineteenth-century women anthropologists, such as Alice Fletcher, Matilda Coxe Stevenson, Erminnie Smith, and Zelia Nuttall, were able to forge public identities as scientists, to secure funding for research travel, and to publish extensive and well-received scientific works (Visweswaran; Parezo; Lurie; Claassen).

But the initial welcome afforded to women had paradoxical effects during the interwar period. Many more women practitioners and students entered the discipline in the 1910s and 1920s, drawn to anthropology in part by the success of earlier high-profile women like Fletcher and Stevenson as well as by the well-known willingness of Franz Boas at Columbia to admit and mentor women students (Rossiter 151-53). But the perception of anthropology as accessible to women and amateurs undermined anthropology's still tenuous disciplinary status and unleashed fears of feminization that social scientists responded to with aggressively masculinized discursive practices and methodologies (63, 73). Thus women in anthropology in the 1920s and 1930s were required to grapple with an intensely professionalizing context if they wished to remain within rather than be written out of the discipline. (See Jordynn Jack's chapter in this collection for an analysis of the contradictory messages received by women in the physical sciences.)

In this chapter I describe some of the exigencies facing women anthropologists between the wars and analyze a range of rhetorical strategies women employed to resist their marginalization and to exert influence on their discipline. An astonishing number of women earned credentials, conducted research, served in professional organizations, and shaped their developing discipline during the 1920s and 1930s, including not only Ruth Benedict and Margaret Mead, the two most widely read anthropologists of the twentieth century, but also Elsie Clews Parsons, Gladys Reichard, Ella Cara Deloria, Ruth Underhill, Ruth Bunzel, Clara Lee Tanner, Zora Neale Hurston, Esther Schiff Goldfrank, Ann Axtell Morris, Erna Gunther, Hortense Powdermaker, and many others. Although the public arguments and scientific achievements of each of these women merit attention from scholars of rhetoric, in what follows I develop a concept of rhetorical community formation as a framework for understanding how women worked together to meet the exigencies of professionalization and to counteract their collective marginalization. After briefly describing the gendered implications of interwar professionalization, I offer two sets of analyses to clarify how community formation functions as a rhetorical strategy. First, I trace in the correspondence of many women anthropologists their efforts to actively shape a supportive and welcoming community for women. These documents suggest that women worked in the backstage of their professional lives to create networks analogous to the formalized professional networks that men were simultaneously developing—and often excluding women from. I then assess texts by archaeologist Ann Axtell Morris, whose two field autobiographies, *Digging in Yucatan* (1931) and *Digging in the Southwest* (1933), were enormously popular. Such popular texts certainly resulted in short-term rhetorical success for Morris, but their rhetorical significance can be understood differently, I argue, when analyzed in relation to the framework of community formation. Popularization, considered as a form of rhetorical recruitment, becomes a strategy for shaping disciplinary practice from a position of marginality.

Professionalization and Interwar Exigencies

During the 1910s and 1920s, not only anthropology but a range of newer social sciences found firmer footholds in the academy, pursued increasingly scientific research methods, and grew rapidly both in numbers and complexity of their institutions and specializations (Silverberg; Ross). This push toward professionalization was prompted in part through the emergence of new philanthropic foundations, such as the Rockefeller-supported Social Science Research Council (SSRC), the National Research Council (NRC), and the Carnegie Institution of Washington, all of which funneled millions of dollars into *scientific* social science research (Fisher). Anthropologists were eager to join sociologists, economists, and political scientists in securing the status and funding available to rigorous, academic, highly specialized professionals undertaking scientific research into an array of emerging social problems and concerns (Stocking 9–13).

These institutional transformations had rhetorical and gendered implications, particularly by generating an urgent need for what Thomas Gieryn has called "boundary work." Through boundary work, scientists distinguish between their practices—and the objective knowledge those practices ensure—and some "less authoritative residual nonscience" (5). Such distinctions reinforce the "link between 'science' and knowledge that is authoritative, credible, reliable, and trustworthy"

(30) and guard the power and prestige afforded to those who produce it. Interwar anthropologists undertook to define their discipline's legitimate practices and practitioners more strictly to establish a firmly *scientific* identity for anthropology—an identity that was in many ways threatened by anthropology's reputation as a welcoming science for women. When prominent anthropologist Alfred Kroeber wrote to Elsie Clews Parsons that "if ever Anthropology gets to be prevailingly a feminine science I expect to switch into something else" (13 Apr. 1929), he voiced a sentiment widely shared among his colleagues.

Despite these pressures, women during this period earned PhDs in increasing numbers, published prolifically, and won research grants from the Carnegie Institution, the Guggenheim Foundation, and the SSRC. The significant scholarship and teaching these women accomplished has been increasingly documented by feminist historians in anthropology, who note alongside these successes the pervasive gendered constraints that limited women's participation and subsequently erased many of their significant theoretical and methodological innovations (Lurie; Parezo; Gacs et al.). Importantly, while credentials and formal training were becoming more central to the discipline, women anthropologists were largely kept out of university positions where they could most readily influence the training of future professionals. As historian Margaret Rossiter points out, women faced substantial barriers in securing stable faculty positions (139): this generation of women anthropologists "built whole careers on little more than a series of temporary fellowships from the NRC and SSRC. In fact, there seems to have been a tendency . . . to give the fellowships to the women to 'tide them over' while the few jobs available went to the men" (272). One significant result of this pattern of exclusion was that, although women were being trained in graduate programs in growing numbers, they were not being employed by the few institutions that offered such training. Consequently, "the same institutions that granted degrees to women institutionalized unequal gender based employment policies" (Levine 134). These policies only exacerbated the tendency toward erasure of women's contributions to scientific life that so many feminist scholars have outlined.

Community Formation as Rhetorical Strategy

Amid these institutional changes and exclusions, there was one widespread, significant rhetorical practice by which women anthropologists counteracted their increasing marginalization and worked to construct a scientific community that would be as open to women in fact as it was in reputation. *Community formation* names a cluster of rhetorical strategies by which individuals construct themselves as a community and thus gain access to social and material resources. Specifically, *community formation* refers here to the efforts of women, often in the backstage of their professional life through correspondence and conversation, to mentor each other, forge intellectual networks, and construct relationships that could render the rhetorical space of professional science more congenial to women. (Sarah Hallenbeck's chapter in this collection on the Girl Scouts demonstrates how such strategies were taught to young women.)

Practices of community formation create what John Swales has called "sociorhetorical networks" that coordinate work through common goals (9). Nevertheless, collectives created through rhetoric inescapably include what Carolyn Miller calls both "centripetal and centrifugal impulses" that render rhetorical communities "fundamentally heterogeneous and contentious" (74). As an analytical framework, community formation emphasizes four dimensions of women's rhetorical practice during this period. First, this concept highlights *collectivity*: the creation between women of a sense of shared experience and shared purpose, counteracting perceptions of isolation. Second, "community" likewise suggests *stability* as a group undertakes to reproduce itself; in this instance, women who were prevented from directly training the next generation of professional anthropologists worked to establish a long-term congenial space for other women in the profession. In this sense, the concept of community formation draws upon the insights of genre scholars like Melanie Kill, who explores the rhetorical work involved in creating not only knowledge but also a community of practitioners who coordinate, evaluate, and legitimate that knowledge. Third, "formation" calls attention to the *activity* of forging a collective; communities are formed rather than found, through practices that are at least partially discursive. And fourth, "formation" likewise highlights the *particularity* of any community, which is shaped in particular ways around specific purposes and defined by a particular set of inclusions and exclusions.

These four dimensions of community formation illuminate the substantial but largely invisible work women undertook during the interwar period to ensure that other women would have access to the discipline's rhetorical spaces. Through analysis of correspondence retained in the Elsie Clews Parsons Papers and the Ann Axtell Morris

Family Papers, I locate a rich network of women engaging in social and intellectual exchange. The framework of community formation helps feminist scholars to understand those activities as rhetorical efforts that actively shape and reproduce a professional collective.

Collectivity

To counteract professional marginalization, women anthropologists worked to view their experiences as patterned and connected. This frequently entailed sharing news of other women's accomplishments, such as "Ruth Benedict was made Asst. Prof. at Columbia which is a grand scoop for feminism!" and "Bunny got a renewal of the Guggenheim fellowship . . . [and will] be taken on by Carnegie as a regular researcher next year" (Reichard, Letters to Parsons 17 Mar. 1931). Recognizing and naming patterns of gender discrimination also helped to create a sense of collectivity. When, for instance, Gene Weltfish, who had taught at Columbia along with her husband Al Lesser, was fired when her husband lost his teaching position, Reichard observed to Parsons, "it is a bit ironic that Gene Weltfish should not be allowed to lecture at Columbia any more because she is the wife of [Al] Lesser with whom she no longer lives" (11 Oct. 1939). Women also used backstage correspondence to counteract damaging rumors by sharing accurate accounts of discrimination. For example, Ruth Bunzel spent two years, from 1930 to 1932, setting up an ambitious interdisciplinary research project in Guatemala only to find herself replaced as project director by Sol Tax, a new male PhD who lacked her experience and qualifications. Although the anthropologists responsible for the decision, Alfred Kidder and Alfred Tozzer, circulated rumors about "improprieties" that led to her replacement—rumors that Bunzel said were "made up by someone out of whole cloth" (Bunzel to Parsons, 16 July 1934)—letters exchanged between other women anthropologists identified Bunzel's removal as gender discrimination. For instance, in a letter to Ann Axtell Morris, Reichard describes her frustration at professional slights and then notes: "I can't forget too that Carnegie promised Bunny [Ruth Bunzel] a job and then fell down on it. Things like that hurt one's faith" (5 Dec. 1932). In constructing a rhetorical community of women anthropologists, Reichard frames her professional struggles as more than individual disappointments. Women anthropologists were better able to perceive the barriers they faced as institutional rather than individual when they could link their disappointments with those of female colleagues.

Activity

There is ample evidence that women worked actively to include and recruit other women into their profession. Elsie Clews Parsons provided major funding for field research and subsidized publications by Gladys Reichard, Ruth Benedict, Ruth Underhill, Esther Schiff Goldfrank, Ruth Bunzel, Dorothy Keur, and many other men and women (Deacon; Zumwalt 279). But women's activity in shaping their discipline took less monetary forms as well. Correspondence between women anthropologists indicates the extraordinary degree to which these women read and responded to each others' manuscripts. Dozens of letters seek feedback on works in progress or accompany manuscripts being returned to their authors with suggestions. For instance, in an undated letter Underhill solicits suggestions from Parsons on her "Papago Ceremonies" manuscript before completing her own revisions; similarly, Benedict writes to Parsons requesting advice on a review she is writing: "I found it very difficult to write and I would be very grateful for any suggestions you might have about the review. There are so many points that might be taken up . . . and I wondered whether you would agree with the emphases in the one I enclose" (4 Nov. 1936). Women also questioned conclusions drawn in each others' published work, disagreed about substantive intellectual and methodological points, and shared data for comparison. For instance, Benedict writes at length to Parsons to challenge, congenially, some of the issues Parsons raised in a published review of Benedict's *Zuni Mythology*. Benedict concludes by noting, "it is such a rare chance to discuss field material with someone who knows the same tribe that I wanted to write you. Besides I thought perhaps you might have more comments to make than you could put in the review and I know they would be helpful" (19 June 1937). In many letters women share data for comparative purposes. Ruth Underhill notes in a letter to Parsons, "I have made some comparative notes for the appendix which may interest you, since they are focused on Papago and . . . resemblances to the Pueblos, particularly western ones, appear in great quantity" (3 Dec. [1938]), and then encloses several pages of comparative material for Parsons to use. These extensive editorial and intellectual exchanges actively construct a community of women working together on anthropological research.

Stability

Bonds among members of this community were also reinforced through correspondence, as women privately praised one another's scholarship. Many women distributed copies of their published works to colleagues, and appreciative notes flowed back and forth within this network. Underhill, for one, thanks Parsons for sending a copy of her monumental, two-volume *Pueblo Religion*, explaining, "I have scarcely had time to glance into it because I have been lending it to my students.... The book will be a boon to me in my teaching on the Southwest" (13 July [1939]). Reichard likewise requests a copy of Parsons's book for Elizabeth Sergeant, whom Reichard notes is "one of our most intelligent laymen and uses that kind of thing very well" (3 Aug. 1939). In a letter to Margaret Mead, Benedict notes appreciatively Powdermaker's positive response to Benedict's 1928 paper, "Psychological Types in the Cultures of the Southwest," an early example of the kind of analysis for which she soon became famous (Fowler 340). Thus, although few women attained faculty positions where they could shape future generations of their discipline, through their private circulation of scholarship and collaborative intellectual engagement, they formed alternative networks of support and influence.

Particularity

The community thus formed took particular shape, as Reichard's comment about Sergeant as "one of our most intelligent laymen" indicates. These networks primarily linked women professionals; true amateurs, like Franc Newcombe, Clara True, and Lucy Wetherill, were frequently subjected to criticism. Reichard, for instance, wrote to Parsons, "I do not think a thing of Mm. Lucy Wetherill.... She wrote a lot of sensational drivel in the S. Francisco papers last year.... I should distrust any of her data I am afraid" (17 Aug. 1923). By identifying Wetherill as sensationalist and untrustworthy, Reichard defines her own community of peers as sober and scientific in contrast. These women also assessed favorably other insiders' use of appropriate, reliable methods. For instance, Reichard writes to Parsons that according to the Zuni, Bunzel "never asked <u>questions</u>, she was just around with us," prompting Reichard to exclaim, "and <u>that</u> is my idea of the last word which can be said about a successful field worker" (28 Aug. 1941). Through such assessments, women anthropologists reinforced their status as qualified arbiters of scientific merit and validated certain practices, methods, and arguments.

Popularization as Rhetorical Recruitment

Women's popular anthropological writing during the 1920s and 1930s complemented, I argue, this broader practice of community formation in several ways. As anthropology professionalized during the 1920s, it became more isolated from nonspecialist audiences—an insular tendency that a number of early women anthropologists lamented and worked to counteract. Parsons, for instance, convinced dozens of prominent anthropologists to contribute short, readable sketches to her popular 1922 collection *American Indian Life*, which she hoped would distribute accurate information more readily than the "forbidding monographs" (1) anthropologists were increasingly writing. Feminist historians have argued that women write popular scientific texts for a range of purposes: to circulate alternative forms of knowledge, to gain access to crucial public audiences, and at times to challenge prevailing notions of legitimacy and authority (Gates and Shteir; Shteir). Further demonstrating what rhetorician Wendy Sharer has suggested of other women professionals during the interwar period, women anthropologists blended standard and innovative textual elements in their popular writing "to garner the ethos of rigorous researchers while also acting as advocates" (8) for social and institutional reform. Gladys Reichard and Ruth Underhill both wrote popular ethnographic novels that sharply critiqued federal Indian policy and boarding school education, bringing their specialized knowledge to bear on a topic of intense public interest during the 1920s and 1930s. In this way, women cultivated public support and countered their institutional marginalization by finding audiences—and students—to educate *outside* the discipline.

To demonstrate the community-building potential of popular anthropological writing, I analyze two exceedingly popular texts of the 1930s: Ann Axtell Morris's two personal narratives of archaeological discovery, *Digging in Yucatan* (1931) and *Digging in the Southwest* (1933). I focus on Morris's field autobiographies for two reasons. First, Morris's position relative to professional anthropology was typical during the interwar period. After completing a BA in history at Smith in 1922, she spent what she called a "gorgeous year" receiving formal field training at the American School of Prehistoric Archaeology in France (*Southwest* 13–14). She undertook field research and became well integrated into developing professional networks yet never attained a stable university or museum position. Instead, she primarily collaborated on Carnegie-funded expeditions with her archaeologist husband, Earl Halstead Morris, into whose reports her technical writing and field research were largely subsumed.

Second, I focus on Morris because it would be easy to read her successes as a scientific popularizer as primarily individual accomplishments with individual rewards. Her secondary status as an unpaid researcher working on her husband's digs limited Morris's access to formal channels of publication; in contrast, her field autobiographies ran to multiple printings, generated boxes of fan mail, and made her one of the most famous archaeologists of her day. The success of *Digging in Yucatan* thrilled the editor-in-chief of the Doubleday division that published the book, Helen Ferris, who encouraged Morris to begin her next volume at once (Letter to Morris, 1 May 1931). Reviews praised Morris's "zest and knowledge and humor" as well as her ability to "enable any one new to archaeology to understand what it is all about . . . and why archaeology is interesting and important" ("Finding America's Past"). That *Digging in the Southwest* was a selection of both the Junior Literary Guild and the Scientific Book Club suggests its appeal not just for the high-school readers targeted by her publishers but also for adults. Brisk sales of her books continued through the 1940s ("Ann Axtell Morris").

If read as rhetorical efforts to garner individual status, both books show Morris constructing an identity for herself as a legitimate archaeologist, not merely an archaeologist's wife. She emphasizes that her interest in archaeology preceded, rather than followed, her marriage (*Southwest* 12–16). She minimizes her secondary role in the digs her husband directed at Chichen Itza and Canyon del Muerto[1] and instead bolsters her authority as an independent researcher by highlighting her own work digging and interpreting data. Hence, she describes in detail a secondary excavation she directed, without pay, alongside the main Chichen Itza project, which had her "bossing my own gang of workers on my very own mound" (*Yucatan* 154). She also includes many photographs that visually reinforce her activity as a researcher: she grins at the camera while poised above a Basket Maker grave she has just uncovered (*Southwest* Fig. 11); she displays the results of her small Yucatan excavation in a photograph titled "I Proudly Exhibit the Beautiful and Fragmentary Sculptured Panel from My Temple to Dr. Morley" (*Yucatan* Fig. 25). This kind of textual evidence suggests the importance of popular publication as an outlet for countering her institutional marginality, using her substantial rhetorical abilities to establish, among her many readers at least, her identity as an archaeologist.

Yet crucial elements of these texts are overlooked in such an analysis. Using the framework of community formation, I suggest Morris's works functioned as rhetorical recruitment tools, complementing other women anthropologists' backstage efforts to create a welcoming community for women. As community formation, *Digging in Yucatan* and

Digging in the Southwest perform rhetorical work by actively directing young women toward avenues for legitimate participation in the developing discipline, working to construct and reproduce a collective that includes rather than marginalizes women.

That collective is depicted in Morris's texts as one that welcomes trained and knowledgeable women as equals. For both women and men who are "hard-boiled about facts" but who never "object to ants in the porridge, nor think of Indians as low-down dirty savages" (*Southwest* 22), archaeology offers clear avenues for entry into a warm community of "thoroughbred good sports, witty conversationalists, and loyal friends" (19). Morris characterizes herself as an example of archaeologists who were willing to share their knowledge with newcomers. She writes that although her first year among the archaeologists at Gallup left her "fairly lost beneath the torrent of unfamiliar words and strange ideas," she was quickly welcomed into "the sacred circle" (18), and now, having "acquired a magnificent technical vocabulary," her "initial and generalized ignorance of ten years ago has since given way to a large number of highly specialized and acutely detailed ignorances" (18). For those seeking scientific opportunity, the archaeological community is marked by their "untiring efforts to learn and their willingness to teach" (23). That this portrayal does not quite align with the reality of Morris's and other women's marginalized status does not negate its rhetorical significance. Indeed, this not-yet-realized vision of the welcoming community Morris describes recalls Carolyn Miller's characterization of a rhetorical community as a "virtual entity, a discursive projection, a rhetorical construct. It is the community as invoked, represented, presupposed, or developed in rhetorical discourse" (73). Thus viewing Morris's field autobiographies as a means of community formation suggests that through such imaginative acts, Morris simultaneously *projects* and actively *recruits* members into the kind of professional community she sought.

This invitation targets young women in particular when Morris emphasizes fieldwork as an escape from gendered constraints. Archaeology, Morris claims, "furnishes all the excitement of treasure-seeking decently concealed under the respectable cloak of science" (*Southwest* 12), and her many photographs reinforce this message of escape from gendered confinement as they depict Morris climbing cliff walls, standing atop the domed roof of a house still under construction, and cheerfully camping and excavating. One photograph in *Digging in the Southwest* shows Morris standing in front of a canvas tent, surrounded by rocks and rubble, with the exuberantly ironic caption "Woman's place is in the home!" These portrayals of fieldwork as offering women mobility and adventure suggest the *kind* of women Morris hopes to entice into her particular disciplinary community.

Woman's place is in the home!

Fig. 12.1. Ann Axtell Morris on a Carnegie-funded dig in Canyon del Muerto, Arizona, flouting gendered norms of domestic confinement. Photo courtesy of the Carnegie Institution of Washington.

These texts also actively invite young women into archaeology by providing procedural knowledge about disciplinary practice. As field autobiographies—that is, as personal narratives focused on fieldwork experiences—Morris's texts share discipline-specific knowledge and methodologies that would enable others to follow her lead into the field. As many reviews of her books observe, Morris is particularly adept at translating technical information concerning not only the content but also the *practice* of archaeology. One *New York Times* review of *Digging in the Southwest* notes that Morris explains "how the archaeologist goes about his work, the fundamental ideas which are always observed and the specific techniques that automatically come into play" (23). Reviews aimed at young adult readers emphasize the procedural knowledge to be gained from Morris's books; one notes that *Digging in the Southwest* will appeal particularly to readers with a latent interest in archaeology, for whom the book will not only "stir their enthusiasm" but will also "give them a realization of what it means to follow archaeology as a calling" ("New Children's Books" 16).

Using popularization as a strategy for recruiting and shaping a community, Morris *shares* access to technical knowledge rather than withholding insider information by treating it as too complex for non-specialists. She identifies the substantial specialized knowledge an archaeologist needs—knowledge of geology, botany, zoology, chemistry, as well as "the processes of preserving fragile specimens" (*Yucatan* 8)—yet she does not make acquiring such knowledge seem daunting. Morris, in fact, summarizes a great deal of complex information in both books, asserting that the "immediate result will be to make you, my gentle reader, quite as learned in the essentials as myself" (*Southwest* 38). Morris's field autobiographies educate audiences about the methods and practices of archaeology, not just the dramatic unearthing of rich buried treasures, and thus actively invite readers into her discipline.

Emblematic of these rhetorical recruitment efforts is Morris's extensive translation of insider chatter at the annual archaeological gathering at Gallup, New Mexico. Acknowledging that, for outsiders, "archaeologists' conversation sounds as mad as that of so many March Hares," she proposes and presents "a transcription of some of this chat" to demonstrate that "once their code is learned it is not difficult to see why people who engage themselves in such fascinating work spend all of their associated time together talking 'shop'" (*Southwest* 19). "For instance," Morris writes, "say that one enters the perfectly civilized dining room of El Navajo hotel," whereupon Dr. Morley immediately shares "all the main facts of the last season—'There's another cheese box under the Caracol, and Karl found a jade necklace, and I've just located a new Ahau, and there are more *garapatas* than ever'" (19). To help readers decode these "facts," Morris explains:

> Now none of this is true. The Caracol hasn't a cheese box under it—it's just the long-lost original foundation; Karl didn't find a jade necklace, because there is no true jade in America; no one could call the glyph Ahau new, since it was carved a good thousand years ago; and there couldn't possibly be any more *garapatas* (wood ticks) because we well knew that their population quota was full the previous season. (19)

Such translations display Morris's own familiarity with the discursive norms of this community, but they also make insider chatter more legible to prospective archaeologists.

Morris also models the questions and responses likely to excite or irritate professionals. She dismisses with a sigh the perpetual rumor of "a man who knows a man who knows where there's a pictograph of a man fighting a dinosaur" (20) but indicates the seriousness of Frank Robert's announcement that "he has found the burial ground of a village of round-skulled people who had with them the kind of pottery very definitely supposed to belong with the long-skulled people" (20). Morris explains that insiders find such a report "awfully upsetting, because Frank knows what he sees when he sees it, so there's no possibility of error. But it spoils some of our best theories dreadfully" (20). Here and throughout her texts, Morris introduces readers to the relative believability of claims, the major and minor disagreements over issues such as "the sequence of the early Southwestern culture periods" (21) that animate the community, and the foundational beliefs—such as the "fixed law of stratigraphy" (20)—upon which archaeological practice is based.

The community Morris constructs in these field autobiographies, which emphasize training and expertise, reflects the newly professionalized state of archaeology and anthropology between the wars. But her texts also respond productively to professionalization by alerting potential archaeologists to emerging requirements for participation in this discipline. Morris strongly discourages untrained archaeologists, arguing that "once [anyone] breaks ground in the study of a particular location, that site is ruined beyond all help for anyone else. If he misses a single observation, that fact, and it might be an invaluable one, is lost for all time. Hence, you see, the responsibility is tremendous" (*Yucatan* 6). Justifying her anti-amateur position by appealing to a researcher's responsibility toward "facts" themselves, Morris reflects the prevailing faith in empiricism and technical expertise. But her position can also be seen as a pragmatic recognition of changing institutional realities. Historians Nancy Parezo and Margaret Hardin have pointed out that some interwar publications such as the *Independent Woman* encouraged women who lacked specialized training to volunteer in museums as a way to gain entry into more demanding archaeological work (285)—a contention that was mostly misleading, for in the newly professionalized context, untrained amateurs, especially women or minorities, were almost never advanced to positions of authority or integrated into professional hierarchies. In contrast, Morris's pragmatic emphasis on formal training encourages interested readers to seek the credentials needed to enter the discipline.

Instruction in anthropological methods also promotes the goal of community stability; it serves as a mechanism for reproducing an inclusive anthropological community. Indeed, what evidence remains suggests that Morris's field autobiographies *did* recruit women to archaeology. Responding to Doubleday editor Dorothy Bryan's request for fan mail that could be quoted to promote a reprinting of her *Yucatan* book, Morris returns "a couple of letters from young female archaeologist fans" who "wanted to know where to go to college and what to take after they got there that would make them into full fledged archaeologists" (18 Mar. 1933). One such fan, fifteen-year-old Alice Ruth Bruce, wrote in 1937 for the *Washington Post*'s series "I Aim to Be ——" that Morris's autobiographies are "the most useful books" for a potential archaeologist. Bruce reports that she has already been, for seven years, a member of the New Jersey Archaeological Society and has requested materials from Columbia, "which has fine archaeological courses," acquainting herself with the entrance requirements for her chosen field. Bruce shows a remarkable degree of familiarity with the professional practice of anthropology: its apparatus of professional organizations, its assumed background knowledge in geology and history, and the importance of credentials and higher education for membership. Field autobiographies like Morris's responded to the burgeoning demand from young women for publications that would prepare them for positions in professional and public life. Emphasizing technical expertise, careful research, and intellectual training as requirements for entry into a discipline that offered women mobility and community under a "respectable" scientific cloak, Morris alerts "young female archaeologist fans" to the training they will need to participate as "full-fledged" members within a changing professional context.

Conclusion

Creating a community of women who funded, taught, and mentored one another can be seen alongside women's popular writing as two complementary responses to the exigencies of professionalization. Women's rhetorical work to construct a supportive community *inside* their discipline functioned as a behind-the-scenes counterpart to their rhetorical efforts directed at broad outside readerships. Both strategies offered women a way to broaden the community of meaningful participants. Women worked, in effect, to create the kind of discipline that Ann Axtell Morris claimed to participate in: one committed to knowledge rather than status and open to all qualified practitioners. Viewing popularization as a component of a broader strategy of community formation can, I suggest, help feminist historians better identify significant instances of collective, not just individual, rhetorical practice. It would be easy to minimize the long-term importance of Morris's field autobiographies: perhaps they were popular, but they haven't *lasted*. But using *community formation* as an analytical tool places achievements like Morris's in relation to a collective effort; together, the rhetorical work these women undertook becomes more difficult to discount.

Later, the dramatic disruptions associated with World War II and subsequent failures in institutional memory would make these women's contributions scarcely visible, to rhetoricians or anthropologists, during the second half of the twentieth century. Nevertheless, in multiple ways women anthropologists responded productively to the newly professionalized context of interwar social science. By cultivating popular interest, guiding other women toward avenues for legitimate entry, and supporting the work of women professionals already in the field, women anthropologists worked to convert their hard-won expertise into influence both within and outside their discipline.

Note

1. I acknowledge for their generous assistance in this research the archivists at the American Philosophical Society in Philadelphia; Dr. Inga Calvin, an archaeologist at the University of Colorado at Boulder, who is writing the first biography of Ann Axtell Morris; and Jonathan Pringle, archivist at the Museum of Northern Arizona.

In fact, as Inga Calvin points out, Ann's initial involvement in the Chichen Itza project was as a nanny for Sylvanus Morley's daughter and as a chaperone for Morley's unmarried secretary and bookkeeper, Edith Bayles (personal correspondence, 27 July 2008.) In *Digging in Yucatan*, Morris notes her boredom at not initially having her own project to work on but omits discussion of her nanny and chaperone duties.

B

> Why should they be our superiors? Have we not a mind like they? Do we not have a soul? Can we not think? Can we not love the same as they? Are they made of finer clay?—Jovita González, "Shades of the Tenth Muses"

"Have We Not a Mind Like They?": Jovita González on Nation and Gender

Kathy Jurado

The epigraph I begin with is taken from a short story by Tejana author and scholar Jovita González de Mireles[1] in which González imagines a conversation between Mexican-born Sor Juana Ines de la Cruz and the American poet Anne Bradstreet. Within the social landscape of González's South Texas at the turn of the century, Sor Juana's rhetorical question, "Have we not a mind like they?" echoes the sentiment of ethnic Mexicans along the U.S.-Mexico border experiencing racism through de facto Jim Crow segregation. It echoes as well the second-class citizenship conferred upon women in general. González's work as a writer and scholar in the 1930s challenged both these stereotypes by turning their unspoken assumptions on their heads. In a period when all Mexican subjects were rhetorically constructed as foreign, dirty, and ignorant, González's revised history instead identifies Anglo-Americans as the more recent immigrants, with Mexicans and Mexican Americans as their friends and teachers. In essence, in all her writing, González flipped the conventional script of anti-immigrant, xenophobic discourse that operates upon the axis of "foreignness," documenting instead a topsy-turvy world in which Mexican Americans belonged at the center.

González's body of work, which ranges from fiction to folklore to history, has been the focus of a handful of Latina/o scholars, such as José Limón, María Cotera, and Leticia Garza-Falcón. My interest, however, resides in the rhetorical strategies deployed in two documents that have remained largely absent from academic conversations on González's work: her master's thesis, "Social Life in Cameron, Starr and Zapata Counties" (published in 2006 as *Life along the Border)*, and the short story I began with, "Shades of the Tenth Muses" (published as part of the 2000 collection *Woman Who Lost Her Soul*), supplemented by her short memoir included in *Dew on the Thorn*.[2] My examination of these texts demonstrates a rhetorical reconfiguration of ethnic Mexicans and women as knowledge producers that challenges the racist and sexist discourses at the time. In other words, these works reflect a rearticulation of nation and gender from the perspective of a Mexican American woman living in the borderlands.

Background

Born on 18 January 1904 in Roma, Texas, a border town in the southeast corner of the state, folklorist Jovita González experienced life among the rapidly changing social and cultural landscape of southern Texas. A drastically shifting economy, a result of the newly constructed railroad and de facto segregation for ethnic Mexicans, shaped the social world she lived in. As a woman of Mexican ancestry, she came of age during a time when ethnic Mexicans struggled for incorporation into the national imaginary, which tested their allegiance to the nation and which only grudgingly brought women (Anglo and non-Anglo alike) into academia. This historical moment witnessed the height of the so-called Mexican Problem (Gutiérrez 56). Ethnic Mexicans were deemed "dirty" and characterized as lawless *bandidos*, among other things, in newsprint media. Meanwhile, the status of women, despite their acquiring the vote in 1920, remained strained regardless of racial background. For women of color, such as González, life along the border must have been experienced from the margins, an element she sought to challenge and rectify in her work.

Evident in her memoir in *Dew on the Thorn* as well as her thesis is the fact that González could trace her matrilineal ancestry to the original Spanish colonizers who established the first settlements in Nuevo Santander (in the general area that is the focus of her study) in the mid-1700s. This lineage of ancestral roots in Texas by ethnic Mexicans is a central theme in her thesis, evoked time and time again.

Such emphasis can be interpreted as an effort to refute the prevailing discourse of ethnic Mexicans as "foreigners" in Texas. González recounts her childhood fondly and remembers one aunt in particular, Tia Lola, who was an influential, feminist voice. She recalls memorizing poems in Spanish, such as "La Influencia de la Mujer," and reading the works of Sor Juana Ines de la Cruz. In 1910, her family relocated further north to San Antonio as the Mexican Revolution gripped the country, bringing death, chaos, and poverty that prompted a wave of immigrants fleeing across the border. The move away from the border was advantageous to González's education, as she wrote: "My father felt that the only heritage he could leave his children was an education . . . so after talking it over with Mother and grandfather, he decided that the family should move to San Antonio where we could be educated in English" (*Dew* xi).[3]

In the early 1920s González enrolled at the University of Texas but was forced to leave because, as she notes in her short memoir, financial troubles propelled her back home to San Antonio to teach. While González clearly had opportunities that exceeded the expectations of the average Mexican in Texas, as her academic endeavors reveal, it is also clear that this was not easy. "The following two years," she writes, "I taught at Encinal, as Head Teacher of a two-teacher school. After this experience I decided to go back to college. So I entered the summer school at Our Lady of the Lake in San Antonio" (*Dew* xii). Her memoir indicates that she often relied on grants to continue her studies, including a Lapham Scholarship to finance her MA.[4]

She received her bachelor's degree from Our Lady of the Lake College in 1927 and shortly thereafter entered graduate studies to pursue her master's at the University of Texas A&M, Corpus Christi. A mere five years after being forced to leave the University of Texas, she had published her first article (1927) and three years after that (1930) had completed her master's degree program. In 1930, she became the first Mexican American woman to be president of the Texas Folklore Society, a post she held for two years. González's academic success is evidenced by her publications in journals such as *Texas and Southwestern Folklore, Southwestern Review*, and the *Journal of the Texas Folklore Society*, all of which showcased her ethnographic abilities in collecting the folklore of Texas's Mexican communities.[5] She received a Rockefeller grant in 1934, which Sergio Reyna speculates may have funded her fiction writing (xii). By 1935, González had met and married Edmundo Mireles, another teacher. They eventually settled in Corpus

Christi and continued to teach until her retirement in 1966. She and her husband remained well-respected educators; together, they published a series of textbooks designed to teach children Spanish that were used "for many years in support of bilingual education in the southwestern United States" (Reyna xiii).

"Social Life" on the Border: Upending Nation

In order to understand the rhetorical impact of González's thesis, one needs to consider the role the sociocultural context played in shaping the ideas about Mexicans that González so vehemently disagreed with. The transition of the border from the proverbial "line on the ground" into the militarized border we know now is central to the racialization process that all ethnic Mexicans living in the United States then (and arguably still) had to negotiate. In her memoir, González describes a particularly poignant memory of a visit to her great grandmother Mamá Ramoncita before heading north for San Antonio:

> I have a clear picture of her lying in a four-poster bed her clear-cut ivory features contrasting with her dark sharp eyes.
> "Come, get closer to me, children, so I can see you better," she said. "Your mother tells me you are moving to live in San Antonio. Did you know that land at one time belonged to us? But now the people living there don't like us. They say we don't belong there and must move away. Perhaps they will tell you to go to Mexico where you belong. Don't listen to them.
> Texas is ours. Texas is our home. Always remember these words: Texas is ours, Texas is our home."
> I have always remembered the words and I have always felt at home in Texas. (*Dew* xi)

This fierce sense of belonging—a tangible undercurrent in all of her work, regardless of its genre—is not solely secured to the geographical reality of the newly established U.S.-Mexico border; it also speaks to the discursive construction of the national imaginary. Though xenophobia had influenced and propelled debates on immigration since the turn of the century, the so-called Mexican Problem of the early 1900s peaked in the 1930s with the inscriptions of Mexican immigrant bodies (and, subsequently, all ethnic Mexican bodies) as a public menace, outlaws, and foreigners.[6] González's master's thesis, "Social Life in Cameron, Starr and Zapata Counties," then, stands as an alternative history of Mexicans in the Texas region. The folklore she recorded in her detailed ethnography was, after all, documented proof of the longstanding roots of the ethnic Mexican community in Texas. Thus, one can view the submission of her thesis as a vehicle that inducts alternative scholarship into the archives of knowledge—archives previously dominated by biased, Anglocentric views.[7]

The sense of belonging imparted to González by her great grandmother is echoed in the first pages of her thesis. The introduction begins with a bold statement: "There exists in Texas a common tendency among Anglo Americans, particularly among Americans of one or two generations' stay in the country, to look down upon the Mexicans of the border counties as interlopers, undesirable aliens, and a menace to the community" (*Life* 41). This very first sentence articulates a provocative analysis of race, identity, and citizenship. The introduction sets a deliberate tone to her thesis and offers a fierce rebuttal to the implied rhetoric of Mexicans as "foreigners" in the United States. She goes on to ask of the reader who might have such an opinion to consider the following: that these "so called undesirable aliens" have lived in the state long before it was Texas, and "these people were here long before these new Americans crowded the deck of the immigrant ship" (41). The racist and racializing discourse of the era translated into the disenfranchisement of all ethnic Mexicans in the United States, regardless of citizenship—an ideology that González hotly contested, as evidenced in the focus of her thesis research, a detailed history of Mexican American life in three border communities. As Cotera has noted, González's work refused to "follow the accepted story line of Texas history," a fact that "placed González at odds with the version of history popularized by Barker, Walter Prescott Webb and even J. Frank Dobie" (*Native* 118). Indeed, González remembers her thesis adviser, historian Eugene C. Barker, as unenthusiastic about the nature or focus of her thesis, stating it was an "interesting but somewhat odd piece of work" (*Dew* xiii). It was the respected scholar Carlos Castañeda, a family friend and librarian of the University of Texas, who reportedly assured Barker that González's work would "be used in years to come as source material" (*Dew* xiii).

In an act of rhetorical strategy, González's first chapter refuses the figurative "border" separating Anglo-American history and Mexican history, blurring the two by beginning with a time that predates the acquisition of Texas and the Southwest in general. Instead of using the end of the Mexican-American War as the beginning of her historical timeline, she begins more than one hundred years earlier, in the 1700s, documenting the arrival of Spanish colonizers to the Texas area, then known as Nuevo Santander. González glosses over Anglo acquisition, highlighting instead the history of the Spanish-speaking community.

González's historical revisions are also starkly evident in her final chapter, "What the Coming of the Americans Has Meant to the Border People," in which she expands upon the implication made in her introduction by explicitly labeling Anglo-Americans as the unwanted invaders and foreigners: "The counties in which these people lived were run by Mexicans, and everywhere, with the exception of Brownsville, the Americans were considered foreigners" (*Life* 109). González goes on to note that the few "American" (read Anglo) families that lived along the border in the late nineteenth century adapted to the local environment and became "Mexicanized." In this way, she uses the academic discourse of her thesis to make visible a Mexican citizen subject that is neither "dirty" nor "foreign." Rather, she posits a Mexican subject with historical roots predating Anglo settlement by one hundred years and, thus, reclaims the oft-denied sense of belonging. She paints a somewhat romanticized picture of a time in which the Texas community lived in harmony with the few Anglos that chose to reside in the region and respectfully and successfully incorporated themselves into it. While not without its own occasional problematic reductions, González's thesis is also a testament to a sense of belonging for the Mexican community. Her thesis is an academic artifact, as the following examples will demonstrate, that radically inverts the rhetoric of Mexicans as a social problem and instead asserts the social value of Mexican culture and its historical presence in South Texas. It illustrates an active engagement on the part of González in offering rhetorical rearticulations of an upended history.

Such rearticulations are evident as well in her depiction of historical figures. In the first chapter, for instance, she tackles Juan Cortina, commonly thought of as an outlaw and *bandido* in American media, and instead offers a much more complex understanding. In Mexican history and culture, Cortina was a Robin Hood figure who helped the poor and heroically defied American imperialism. While she does not apologize for the raids that Cortina took part in, she does provide the historical contextualization and cultural differences in understanding that directly challenged the existing discourses circulating at the time about Cortina and, by extension, Mexicans. Rewriting Texas history in this way, as one might imagine, was no easy feat, a fact evidenced by the careful word choice and argumentation in her discussion of the Cortina Raids:

> Mexican as well as American, took advantage of the period of disorder to rob, sack and plunder the border towns. . . . During this reign of bloodshed Cortina was the self-appointed champion of the Mexican border ranchmen, who saw in him the leader that would free them from American domination and rule. . . . This Robin Hood of the Mexican border became naturally the idol of a certain element among the border Mexicans. (*Life* 55)

She makes sure to place blame equally on both Mexicans and Anglo Americans for participating in the border disturbances. However, her careful documentation not only redefines the *bandido* but also disassociates the vast majority of Mexicans from such an image.

González counters stereotypes with a third chapter composed almost entirely of demographic data of the counties in question. These statistics refute the discursive associations of ethnic Mexicans as lawless (perhaps, by extension, landless) *bandidos* and instead document the predominantly Mexican population as being landed gentry. The data not only reinforce the longstanding presence of the Mexican community in these areas, as evidenced by their numbers, but also place this population in the ranks of the landed elites. González provides a breakdown of the population in five categories: (1) Total property owners, (2) Mexican property owners, (3) Percentage of Mexican owners, (4) Non-Mexican owners, and (5) Percentage of non-Mexican owners. The percentage of Mexican landowners ranges from 72.9 percent to 99.38 percent (*Life* 71–72). Such overwhelming numbers are noteworthy because of the social landscape of the time, the implied rhetoric of Mexicans as foreigners in the land. Just six years prior to completing her thesis, two significant events in 1924 had further shaped the Mexican community as "foreign" and "Other": the establishment of the Border Patrol and the immigration restrictions reflected in the passing of the National Origins Act. Both actions reinforced the ideological discourse of Mexicans as a "problem." As Ali Behdad has noted, "The border is not just a territorial marker of the modern nation state, defining its geographical boundary, but an ideological apparatus where notions of national identity, citizenship and belonging are articulated. . . . The border is vested with tremendous symbolic power in defining the imagined community" (109). González's documentation of an overwhelmingly Mexican landed gentry thus functions as a response to the pejorative construction of Mexicans as landless foreigners.

She also uses data to counter the myth of Mexicans as dirty and ignorant. In one of her most intriguing chapters, "Social and Economic Life before the Development of the Lower Rio Grande Valley," González incorporates excerpts from a "little manuscript on manners and ethics" that was taught to Mexican Americans who acquired educations in Mexico. As her work makes clear, many Mexican Americans (or naturalized Americans of Mexican descent) had no option but to send their children to Mexican schools to be educated, particularly if they wanted their children to have the opportunity to pursue college in the future. Because of segregation, the American public schools that ethnic Mexicans were allowed to attend in no way compared to Anglo American public schools. As she puts it, "Public schools in the border have not been conducive to the mental development of the individual, much less to the potential improvement of the region" (*Life* 103). Thus, families who had the means would send their children to Mexico—and this, in turn, added another element of racial pride for what was a predominantly American-born stock of ethnic Mexicans.

Through various governmental entities, which included but were not limited to the Department of Labor and the United States Public Health Service, the bodies of Mexican immigrants were scripted as diseased and dirty, resulting in a myriad of associations that rendered them suspect and inherently foreign. The ethics and manners lessons from the "little manuscript" (presented in both Spanish and English) that are used by González, therefore, are interesting because they place ethnic Mexicans on par with the most cultured and elite Anglos, reflecting as they do the most refined manners. She begins with examples for young men when in the company of women: "Ladies must be given the utmost attention that is due their sex. We must give them the most comfortable seat, and never allow them to wait upon us at the table. And when we play a game with them we must excuse their mistakes and obey all their desires provided these are their place [sic], decorous and decent" (89). Another lesson elaborates on social courtesy at dances: "When at a dance he who is courteous and refined should first invite the ladies that have been ill treated by time, or who have any other defect" *(*89).

Beginning as she does with the lessons provided for young men, González tackles the threat that the Mexican male occupied in the American imaginary as a savage Other and a beast of burden. Such attitudes can be seen in the period transcripts of political debates over the question of the Mexican laborer, as when, for instance, a George P. Clemens of the Los Angeles Chamber of Commerce argued in 1929 that Mexicans were ideal for agricultural labor due to their "crouching and bending habits" while "the white is physically unable to adapt himself to them" (qtd. in Gutiérrez 47). Seen in this light, the image presented by González of an ethnic Mexican male as a dapper, dignified gentleman is quite revolutionary. "It must be remembered," González asserts, "that in old Texas Mexican towns such as Laredo, San Diego, Rio Grande City and Brownsville, there has always existed a group of educated, cultured Mexican families who have always been leaders in their communities" (104). Thus, her examples speak to a decorum that might be associated with the most elite southern hospitality. By incorporating this component on social mores and manners into her thesis, she has in effect provided a counterdiscourse to the ideological construction of Mexican males.

The effects of González's upside-down rewriting of history are strikingly evident in the penultimate chapter, "Border Politics," in which she presents what can safely be considered the first description of the newly established League of United Latin American Citizens (LULAC), today the largest and oldest Hispanic organization in the nation.[8] In fact, González lists all twenty-five principles proposed by the delegates to the new organization in 1929. Because LULAC has been, at times, a highly controversial organization within the Mexican American community, González's interpretation of LULAC's collective vision for Mexican Americans merits further critical analysis. As noted by several scholars, LULAC underscored American citizenship as part of their social identity as an organization (Gutiérrez 79–87; Iber and De León 230–33; Márquez 33). For some Mexican Americans, the idea of being incorporated into the social body of the United States was becoming more and more a point of frustration and contention between themselves and *los recien llegados*, the newly arrived Mexican immigrants. Among the most public and controversial stands that LULAC made as a newly formed organization, then, was to oppose Mexican immigration (Gutiérrez 79).[9] They were convinced inclusion in the national social body depended upon their ability to fit in while not forgetting their cultural heritage. Not surprisingly, such tactics provoked much controversy within the Mexican American community.

González's interpretation of LULAC's political ideologies provides a different reading from the norm. Whereas the organization has traditionally been seen as strictly assimilationist, it is clear from González's analysis that she understood LULAC to be engaging in a more nuanced, bicultural vision of citizenship. For her, assimilation did not "necessarily mean that Mexican Americans should forget their racial origin and their language" (*Life* 104), but instead that they become fluent members of both cultures. Her vision of bicultural citizenship is echoed in a passage from an anonymous source in her last chapter:

> It is our place and duty now to learn American ways, to send our children to American schools, to learn the English language, not that we are ashamed of our Mexican descent, but because these things will enable us to demand our rights and to improve ourselves. We understand our race, and when we are able to comprehend American ideas and ideals, American ways and customs, we shall be worth twice as much as they. (qtd. in *Life* 113)

In effect, her conceptualization of what is, in essence, a new "American" subject, much more fluid and multidimensional than the typically conceived unicultural American, anticipates contemporary debates and theorizations on ethnic Mexicans living within the United States. González's Mexican American subject is both modern and worldly, a native to South Texas enhanced by a bicultural subjectivity. As read by González, then, LULAC's primary focus was to make visible the erased Mexican American citizen-subject by public discourse and thereby to reclaim inclusion into the imagined social body of the nation. As such, LULAC served as a political representation of González's own scholarly work.

"The Tenth Muses": Upending Gender

While González used her thesis to upend prevailing ideas of Mexican foreignness and subservient status, conspicuously lacking from the work was any similar critical analysis of gender. It is likely that González found herself limited by the male-dominated academic world of the 1920s and 1930s. She therefore turned to fiction as another playing field in which to deploy rhetorical strategies, and her short story "Shades of the Tenth Muses" reads as a complex critique of gender assumptions for Mexican American women. Read together, then, both thesis and story employ similar rhetorical strategies of upending expectations by envisioning bicultural subjects who are, thereby, more than equal to their monocultural counterparts. (Elizabeth Wilkinson's chapter in this collection shows Gertrude Bonnin similarly using fiction to upend cultural expectations.)

"Shades of the Tenth Muses" often falls by the wayside among scholars of González in favor of her two larger works of fiction, *Caballero* and *Dew on the Thorn*. The story is, as Sergio Reyna has noted, the "only non-folkloric story she ever wrote" (xxv). In it, González imagines a conversation between Anne Bradstreet and Sor Juana Ines de la Cruz—two women who were each known as the "tenth muse" in their seventeenth-century, colonial settings. Bradstreet was the first Anglo-American woman poet of note; de la Cruz filled the same role in colonial Mexico. González reframes Mexican women through her imagined meeting of the Mexican nun and American poet. Cotera has noted that this imagined conversation is significant for its unequivocal gestures toward a "transnational feminist imaginary" (*Native* 2). While both "Shades" and her thesis invert dominant discourse about ethnic Mexicans and, in this case, women in particular, the story, by nature of its genre, gives González unlimited freedom to challenge pejorative constructions of Mexicans and women.

The story opens with the anonymous narrator describing her workplace, which is noticeably outside the domestic space of the home: she works in the "garage room" despite her family's "efforts to have [her] work in the house" (108). It is in this workspace that the spirits of Sor Juana Ines de la Cruz and Anne Bradstreet meet. In many ways, the evocation of the two poets' spirits echoes Virginia Woolf's "angel in the house" in that it is in her workspace that the narrator imagines these battling voices. Like Woolf, who was tormented by the "angel" that disturbed her thought process as she worked on her academic scholarship, the spirits of the poets evoke an internal battle that González may have struggled with as a Mexican American woman writer at the turn of the twentieth century. Regardless of the battle, what is clear is González's articulation of the tradition of women as producers of knowledge that spans centuries.

The women begin a conversation when Bradstreet, shocked by a framed prayer in the study, displays a face that reveals "terror and consternation" (109). Bradstreet, the Puritan poet, finds the prayer sacrilegious and blasphemous for its familiarity with God, while Sor Juana, the Catholic nun, finds her concern amusing and laughs outright. "You say you serve the Lord, don't you fear His wrath?" asks the spirit of Bradstreet, to which de la Cruz replies: "I have confidence in His love" (110). In this way, the banter between the women reveals at once their differences but, eventually, also their similarities. Upon realizing that both are called the "tenth muse," de la Cruz declares, "Then we should be friends, and know more of each other" (110). The imagined conversation carves out a fictive space in which two women from different cultures are able to bridge gaps that social norms and customs otherwise divide. González's womanist focus is bold and unapologetic, but between the two poets, González seems to favor the fiery candor and spirit of de la Cruz, which allows her a certain freedom to showcase radical feminist ideology. For example:

> "Did you ever want to get married?"
> "No, I can not say I ever did. Many suitors wooed and made love to me, but no one would I have. I always thought myself superior to any man."
> "You astound me, Juana."
> "Why should they be our superiors? Have we not a mind like they? Do we not have a soul? Can we not think? Can we not love the same as they? Are they made of finer clay?" (115)

González's intimate knowledge of both poets' work is apparent, and she wields this knowledge as an effective weapon, as when, for instance, she evokes the series of rhetorical questions in one of de la Cruz's most feminist-inspired poems, "You Foolish Men." If the two women represent competing versions of feminism, González makes it clear that de la Cruz retains the upper hand. Thus, her imagined Mexican American teaches her Anglo counterpart about equality, putting the two women in a relationship not just of friendship but also of teacher and student.

The symbolic possibilities within the story function on multiple levels. On one level, the conversation mirrors the cultural negotiations with Anglo expectations that Mexican American subjects navigate, as underscored in her thesis. On another level, the story speaks to a feminism that knows no borders in spite of differences, a testament to González's own knowledge of the feminist tradition of the two cultures she straddles. Indeed, while the Anglo community undoubtedly imagined a Latino culture where *machismo* reigned, González turns this preconception on its head with a story wherein the Latina teaches the New Englander about equality.

Conclusion

González's master's thesis and short story reveal rhetorical strategies that aimed to challenge the discursive construction of ethnic Mexicans and women at the turn of the century. The fact that both documents were unpublished in her lifetime, however, limited their impact upon the discourse of her day. Later historian Anne Firor Scott described the situation well when reflecting on her own book of southern life, *The Southern Lady: From Pedestal to Politics, 1830–1930*:

> It is difficult now to remember just how matters stood with respect to the history of women in 1959 when I began my first tentative explorations in that direction. A handful of scholarly works published in the 1920s and 1930s had made no impact whatever on those who swam in what they called "the mainstream.". . . Here and there, buried in journals were articles about particular aspects of women's past, and over the years there had been a considerable number of master's theses which had disappeared into libraries not to be seen again for many years. (240)

I would argue, however, that González's thesis is indeed significant when considered as a response to the racist and pejorative discourses circulating at the time about ethnic Mexicans living in the United States. It showcases a counterdiscourse that makes use of academia, the most effective venue to challenge such ideological constructions. González ushered a counterargument to racist history into the archives of knowledge and knowledge production—archives previously dominated by Anglocentric views. In so doing, the words from her family friend Dr. Castañeda ring true: "This thesis will be used in years to come as source material" (*Dew* xiii). Her short story likewise anticipated the theoretical questions at the core of women's studies, Latina/o studies, and cultural studies. Both works speak more strongly today than at the time of their production, but this is not unlike the status of many influential texts. Read together, González's thesis and story not only provide a rich and complex understanding of the U.S. national imaginary from the margins, but they function as rhetorical rearticulations of nation and gender that challenge and rectify misconceptions of otherwise voiceless communities.

Notes

1. The story was published posthumously in 2000 after its discovery by Latina feminist scholar María Cotera.

2. The works from González most often studied are her two historical novels, *Caballero* and *Dew on the Thorn* (published posthumously in the mid 1990s) and her research on folklore, published during her lifetime in the 1920s in various academic folklore journals.

3. Segregated schools in south Texas made it virtually impossible for ethnic Mexicans to achieve an education that rivaled their Anglo counterparts. González documents in chapter 4 of her thesis how "Mexican schools offered

better opportunities to the pupils" (*Life* 95). González notes how her older siblings had a "fairly good education in Spanish" (*Dew* xi), and this may speak to her father's choice to take the family north, far from the extreme segregation practiced along the border communities, in the hope of achieving a good education in English.

4. Leticia Garza-Falcón has noted that although contemporary press reports about González described her as landed elite from wealthy Spanish landowners, "her own eighteen-page handwritten memoir indicates otherwise" (Garza-Falcón 74).

5. González's published work was folklore, indicating her stronghold in the field of Anthropology. This is important, as Cotera notes, because it indicates a conscious choice by González to write her thesis through the history department at Texas A&M (*Life* 17).

6. The issue of the "Mexican Problem" most likely arose immediately after the Mexican-American War in 1848. It was certainly a central question in the decision to stop at the Rio Grande and not go further, for even land-greedy politicians had qualms about what to do with the "*mestizo* stock" of Mexico. Indeed, the question of race was so threatening to the Anglo American national imaginary that it challenged an equally powerful discourse, that of empire and acquisition.

7. Her fiction, particularly the novel *Caballero*, which was a collaborative effort with Eve Raleigh, reflects an unequivocal sense of ownership of the Texas borderlands. Perhaps not surprisingly, one of the possible titles suggested for *Caballero* was "All This Is Mine" (*Native* 200).

8. The formation of LULAC in 1929 was a result of a consolidation of three of the largest Mexican American organizations of this time: El Orden Hijos de America, El Orden Caballeros de America, and the League of Latin American Citizens, all of which were *mutualista* organizations (mutual aid societies) of the previous era in which citizenship was not a requirement (see Gutiérrez 82–85; Márquez 358). Comprised mostly of the middle class, their members typically included lawyers, teachers, and small entrepreneurs.

9. LULAC members believed that they had to make such a controversial decision in an effort to stop the Anglos' conflation of citizens and newly arriving (possibly undocumented) immigrants. LULAC also maintained a strong pro-assimilation stance.

14

"Exceptional Women":
Epideictic Rhetoric and Women Scientists

Jordynn Jack

In her 1926 handbook, *Fields of Work for Women*, Miriam Simons Leuck sums up the state of affairs for career women as follows: "Women are finding ever widening opportunities in the more desirable levels and are building for themselves a more equal road. The girl who possesses the courage to be a pioneer will frequently find that, by blazing the trail in one of these now uncharted vocational fields, she will attain more fame and fortune than lies in the safe, beaten track" (302). Leuck's pronouncement nicely encapsulates the epideictic tenor of advice published for women in the 1920s and 1930s, especially for women who wished to pursue careers in science. Popular texts about women in science spoke of expanding opportunities for those who possessed audacity and drive, often praising women pioneers, like Marie Curie or Florence Sabin, who indeed reached uncharted heights during that period.

The express purpose of epideictic rhetoric, according to Aristotle, is to accord praise or blame to a given person, his qualities and actions (book 1, chapter 9). Yet, as Gerard Hauser notes, epideictic does more than just commemorate individual exemplars; it also constitutes and reinforces shared values (5), or in Chaim Perelman and Lucie Olbrechts-Tyteca's terms, "increases adherence to the values it lauds" (50).

Cynthia Sheard has pointed out that epideictic rhetoric can also serve more transformative functions, invoking shared community values for the purpose of promoting alternative visions of that community (770). The epideictic texts in this study, press reports and career guides, reflect the ambivalent nature of epideictic rhetoric.

On the one hand, epideictic rhetoric about women scientists upheld common *doxa* regarding women, careers, and science. By praising the few women who reached the highest standards of scientific success, epideictic accounts shored up the image of science as an elite occupation, meant only for the smartest, bravest, and most persistent of individuals. In this way, they supported the myth of the "exceptional woman," which, Lois Cucullu argues, is a specifically modernist invention that produced specialists "who suppress others as less knowledgeable and who selectively credentialize others to sustain, extend, and reproduce their expertise" (174).[1] Whether or not the exemplars profiled in news reports or career guides *themselves* suppressed others, the profiles reinforce the message that only the unusually brilliant woman could hope to duplicate the success of a Marie Curie or Florence Sabin. On the other hand, by providing information for would-be scientists, these genres do challenge conventional *doxa* about women's career possibilities and open up space for readers to envision alternatives.

In this chapter, I examine how popular articles and career guides constructed the field of opportunity for women scientists between the wars. Both genres, I contend, were epideictic in nature. In the first section, I examine how newspaper and magazine articles profiled famous women scientists, chronicling their exceptional accomplishments and their simultaneous ability to maintain traditional feminine attributes, such as appearance, modest behavior, and motherhood. In the second section, I examine how career guides, while ostensibly deliberative in nature, helping young people to make choices about their future careers, were also epideictic in that they praise a given career path and the accomplishments scientists have made in it—or implicitly blame those readers who lack the drive, ambition, or requisite skills to succeed. Sometimes, writers of career guides also blame women themselves for their lack of advancement in scientific fields, siding with men who argued that women expected special treatment, shirked responsibility, or were generally incompetent. Thus, popular news articles created an image of the exceptional woman scientist, one that writers of career guides had to contend with in offering advice to would-be Curies or Sabins. I argue that the epideictic discourse in both of these genres rehearses and reinforces conventional values of femininity even as it praises women who rejected those values in favor of scientific careers.

Praise: The Exceptional Careers of Marie Curie and Florence Sabin

To examine how women scientists were presented in the popular media, I gathered articles about Marie Curie and Florence Sabin published in the *New York Times*, *Washington Post*, and *Time* magazine. I selected Curie and Sabin because they were the two most prominent women scientists in the United States between the wars, and the bulk of my analysis focuses on them. Curie, of course, was widely lauded for her Nobel prize-winning work on radium, while Sabin was praised for her work on the properties and origins of blood cells. As a point of comparison, I also searched for articles about other women scientists, including chemist Katherine Blodgett and mathematician Christine Ladd Franklin, and included articles that profiled them.

News articles that mention women scientists fall into three basic types. The first were reports of scientific findings, featuring women scientists as investigators. While these articles are epideictic in nature, as Jeanne Fahnestock has shown, they tend to evaluate scientific findings themselves, and scientists only to a lesser degree. A second type of article was the short note, which reported briefly (usually in one or two paragraphs) on a reception, award, or other accomplishment. In this essay, I focus on a third type of article that also reports on women scientists' accomplishments, but in a longer form; I am calling these "feature articles." These articles include profiles of women scientists, often based on interviews, accounts of award ceremonies, and, in Curie's case, a series of features that appeared in the news media when she visited the United States in 1921. Feature articles may include any combination of the following features: biographical information about the scientist, lists of awards and accomplishments, a description of the scientist's physical appearance, an account of the scientist's personality, and/or information about the scientist's personal life (hobbies, family, etc.).

The epideictic rhetoric used to describe Curie and Sabin positioned them as pioneers possessing unusual attributes for women, yet, at the same time, these accounts also invoked traditional tropes of femininity, perhaps to assure readers that these unusual and exceptional women were, nonetheless, still women. News features reported on both scientists' physical appearance: their dress, facial features, and hairstyles. These reports also pointed out that both scientists were modest or humble—key qualities not just for scientists but also for the ideal woman.

In addition, they recast both Curie's and Sabin's scientific research within maternal terms, as work stemming not just from scientific interests, but from feminine sympathies and moral concerns. In the nineteenth and early twentieth centuries, women scientists often drew upon maternal tropes in order to justify their entry into scientific spheres. For instance, the field of home economics was founded on the notion that women's domestic role could be professionalized and extended to the needs and development of society (Brown 359). While these women explicitly endorsed maternal tropes in order to advance their cause, neither Curie nor Sabin seemed to frame her work in maternal or feminine terms. By imposing this framework on their work, newspaper accounts repositioned women who might be understood as breaking with traditional concepts of femininity squarely in line with conservative gender ideologies.

Aristotle wrote that one of the key lines of argument available for epideictic rhetoric was to "point out that a man is the only one, or the first, or almost the only one who has done something, or that he has done it better than any one else; all these distinctions are honourable" (book 1, chapter 9). Indeed, in popular accounts, both Curie's and Sabin's accomplishments are frequently described as a litany of "firsts" and "bests" among women. In 1921, Curie visited the United States to receive a gram of radium, a gift from the Marie Curie Radium Fund, which was spearheaded by the society journalist and editor of *The Delineator*, Marie Mattingly Meloney. Due to Meloney's publicity efforts, the popular press began to tout Curie's accomplishments even before she arrived. The *New York Times* announced Curie's visit on 7 February, three months before her trip in May. The article positions Curie as *the* foremost woman scientist; she is described as a "leader of her sex in the scientific field" ("Radium Gift"). The article goes on to note that Curie "is the first woman to hold [the position of professor] at the Sorbonne, all precedents having been broken in order that Mme. Curie might lecture on radioactivity." This kind of rhetoric continued through a series of articles the *Times* published in the months leading up to her visit. An article from 27 February quotes a Dr. Robert Abbe extolling Curie's accomplishments and her exceptionality among women: "no other woman, by sheer force of energy and brainpower, has pursued a trail into an unknown jungle and brought to light such an unsuspected new factor in the world's make up, which has had such revolutionary influence in science" ("How Mme. Curie Discovered"). An article on 1 May declares that "the rise of this woman to the position of a leading scientist of the world is without parallel in history" ("Madame Curie's Genius"). Even before she visited, no one could be in doubt of Curie's primacy among *women* scientists. These articles never fail to make note of Curie's gender or of the fact that her accomplishments were unusual for that gender. The implicit comparison is not to other scientists, but to other *women* scientists, none of whom could match Curie's level of accomplishment.

Curie's actual visit was marked by even greater media fanfare. Her sojourn included a slew of public events and an accompanying slew of newspaper and magazine articles. In a dizzying whirlwind of appearances, awards, and receptions, Curie was feted by Smith and Vassar Colleges, the American Chemical Society, the New York Academy of Sciences, the American Association of University Women (AAUW), and many others. Curie's every step was recorded in the press. For example, Smith College awarded Curie an honorary doctorate in recognition of her scientific feats. At the ceremony, President William Allan Nellson deemed Curie the "first woman among women of all ages for the brilliance, magnitude and significance of her scientific discovery" ("Smith College"). In other words, her visit was an epideictic occasion, one in which Curie was positioned as "first" among women scientists.

In turn, Sabin was positioned implicitly and explicitly as the American counterpart to Curie. When Curie attended a reception hosted by the AAUW at Carnegie Hall, Sabin was chosen as spokesperson "as the greatest American woman scientist" ("Women" 1). Not surprisingly, the rhetoric of priority used to describe Curie was appropriated to laud Sabin's accomplishments, especially when she became the first woman elected to the National Academy of Sciences in 1925. In one profile in the *New York Times* Sunday magazine, Sabin's exploits are listed as follows:

> That she is the foremost woman scientist ever produced on this side of the world can scarcely be disputed. She was the first woman elected to a full professorship in an American medical school of the first rank. She was the first woman elected President of one of our leading scientific medical societies, the American Association of Anatomists. She was the first woman to be appointed a full member of the Rockefeller Institute for Medical Research. ("Academy of Sciences")

This litany of "firsts" was frequently repeated in popular articles and news reports. Another report, from *Time* magazine in 1939, described Sabin as the "first woman to graduate from the Hopkins [University], first woman to teach there, first woman member of the Rockefeller Institute, first (and only) woman member of the National Academy of Sciences" ("Rockefeller Retirements" 1). While these kinds of descriptions implicitly showed that women scientists could succeed in science at a very high level, they simultaneously set a standard few individuals of either sex would ever meet.

Both Curie and Sabin were formidable women, women who, given the choice, would probably emphasize their merit, scholarship, and equality with men over any explicitly feminine attributes. Penina Glazer and Miriam Slater write that female academics in the 1920s and 1930s "rarely saw themselves as persons who could bring special female qualities of nurturance or morality to the world of scholarship. They did not want to make public the concerns of the private sphere, such as health or child rearing" (65). Yet, perhaps in order to soften their images for a public audience, news reports frequently drew attention to their feminine qualities.

Indeed, contemporaneous accounts indicate that science continued its longstanding association with masculinity in the public mind, so that women scientists had to tread a fine line between demonstrating scientific rigor, on the one hand, and an appropriate level of femininity, on the other. Both male and female commentators enforced this opposition. For instance, a 1929 *New York Times* article quotes Mabel Walker Willebrandt (then assistant attorney general) in a national radio address on the topic of professional women; Willebrandt claims that women should enact gender neutrality or "fairness," and she disapproves of the fact that professional women—Marie Curie in particular—are almost always referred to *as women*. Nonetheless, Willebrandt insists that women should portray themselves "not by mannishness, [since] that only confesses weakness" ("Ignore Sex in Jobs"). Mannish behavior, Willebrandt claims, "is preposterous because it is parody"; presumably Willebrandt wants professional women to maintain some level of "femininity," whatever that might be. Similarly, when the psychologist and mathematician Christine Ladd-Franklin died in 1930, Dr. Cassius Jackson Keyser praised her ability in this way: "Hers . . . was an activity made possible by the union of a virile understanding with the finest intuitions and sympathies of woman" ("Dr. Ladd-Franklin Eulogized at Funeral"). Thus, gender was a salient variable for portrayals of women scientists, despite the insistence of many professional women that it was not important for their success.

Accordingly, newspaper reports frequently commented on women scientists' feminine appearance. *New York Times* articles frequently set aside a paragraph to describe Curie's looks—her "tall and slender" figure, "pale face," and "golden and abundant hair," for instance ("Radium Gift"), or her "high forehead" and piercing blue-grey eyes, which, according to one report, "have the clearness of youth with the penetration and depth of a profound thinker" ("Madame Curie's Genius"). During her visit to the United States, the *New York Times* described her as an "unassuming, motherly-looking scientist" dressed in a plain black suit and matching hat ("Mme. Curie Plans"). These accounts of Curie's appearance work to reassure readers that, despite her great scientific (read: masculine) accomplishments, Curie was still feminine in every way. One report states it baldly: "You will perhaps say that I describe a scientist of the other sex. Not at all. Mme. Curie is essentially womanly" ("Madame Curie's Genius"). In her 1939 profile of chemist Katharine Blodgett, Kathleen McLaughlin notes that she was "a petite researcher, a skimpy five feet tall," with a "tip-tilted nose," who "blended the impressive scholar with a dash of the pixie." Articles profiling Sabin variously describe her as "plain, blonde" ("Rockefeller Retirements") or "medium-sized and dark" ("National Academy" 1). While it is not unusual for reporters to comment on the physical appearance of those they are profiling, it is worth noting that the articles explicitly designate women scientists as "womanly," as a "pixie," or "motherly-looking"— terms which are definitely subjective, not factual descriptors.

A woman scientist's feminine appearance should be matched by a feminine demeanor, according to popular reports. In particular, newspaper journalists seemed to approve of modest, shy, or even girlish behavior. This tendency is nicely encapsulated in Kathleen McLaughlin's portrayal of Blodgett: "It is reassuring to the average, unscientific human to ferret out that the woman who calmly manipulates molecular films . . . is thrown into a shrieking panic on meeting face to face a common garter snake." McLaughlin notes favorably that Blodgett was a "phenomenal" listener and a shy talker, one who favored "keeping silence gracefully" unless directly questioned. Blodgett, she continues, is "puzzled at the publicity attracted by her achievement which, she carefully stresses, is as yet incomplete." Similarly, Dr. Robert Abbe notes approvingly that Curie did not name radium after herself, but chose a term that referred to the rays the element emitted since "knowledge, not fame, was her pursuit"

("How Mme. Curie Discovered"). Another article remarks, "There is nothing in the desire of self-advertisement about Mme. Curie. She is shy and sensitive to a degree" ("Madame Curie's Genius"). Sabin, likewise, is described as a "rather shy, distinctively feminine woman" ("Academy of Sciences"). One might object that perhaps Curie and Sabin actually *were* shy or that modesty is in fact a scientific value, not a feminine one. This may indeed be the case. Nonetheless, for reporters to mention this fact is a rhetorical choice that positions Curie and Sabin not as bold, intimidating women hoping to make a mark on the scientific world, but as humble servants to the pursuit of knowledge. And, as Margaret Rossiter has pointed out, modesty was a longstanding value attributed to women, who, since antebellum times, were expected to "be unobtrusive in public and take pains to camouflage any special talents" (75). Thus, by portraying Curie and Sabin as modest, newspaper articles were casting them in quite traditional terms.

Feature articles also note family duties with favor, since they demonstrated that women could simultaneously have a career and children. In the decades prior to Curie's rise to fame, women's educational opportunities had expanded significantly, mostly because proponents had argued that better education would help women fulfill their roles as wives and mothers. Yet, commentators still fretted that women's scientific careers prevented them from having children, leading to "race suicide" (Cope 217). In a report on women appearing in the guide *Who's Who in America* for 1926–27, Persis Cope decries the lower fertility rates among some professional women, praising "the mothers of six, seven, and in one case, twelve children, who have proved to the world that it is possible for a woman to engage in a highly successful career with-out sacrificing the most precious things in life" (218). Along these lines, popular reports also note Curie's motherly qualities with approval. When President Harding presented the gift of a gram of radium to Curie, he lauded her for her dedication to typically feminine duties as well as scientific ones:

> We lay at your feet the testimony of that love which all the generations of men have been wont to bestow upon the noble woman, the unselfish wife, the devoted mother. If, indeed, these simpler and commoner relations of life could not keep you from great attainments in the realms of science and intellect, it is also true that the zeal, ambition and unswerving purpose of a lofty career could not bar you from splendidly doing all the plain but worthy tasks which fall to every woman's lot. ("Radium Presented" 12)

Here Harding alludes to Curie's role as a wife and mother. Curie had two daughters with her husband and collaborator, Pierre; one of her daughters, Irene, went on to become a scientist and Nobel Prize winner herself. But Harding also recasts her scientific achievements as motherly gifts to all of humanity.

Alternatively, women's scientific endeavors were sometimes attributed to romantic, rather than motherly, motivations. In the 1925 *New York Times* profile, Sabin's research is cast in this equally feminine light. The article begins, "Susceptible as woman is to the appeal of romance—and adventure, too—it is not surprising that a woman who has just risen to eminence of a kind never before attained by any of her sex in America, should speak of the endeavor which led her there as a 'romantic adventure'" ("Academy of Sciences"). The article describes Sabin as a woman whose sense of romance and adventure led her to microscopic studies of the blood rather than "sensations stirred by the magic of a Summer night by music or by flashing steel and averted danger." By casting scientific exploits in the more feminine language of romance, the article reassures readers that Sabin did not transgress the boundaries of conventional gender roles, even if her type of romantic outlet (science rather than marriage) was atypical. Similarly, a 1930 article from the children's section of the *Washington Post* holds up Curie as an example to young readers, casting Curie's accomplishments in the florid language of adventure: "Just as the knights of old traveled the magic paths and into the valley of the unknown in which dangers waited to spring out on them, so this brave woman walked miles along the pathway of hard work until she came to the open sunshiny valley of knowledge with the beautiful flowers of discovery which she gathered to scatter about the world" ("Knights Are Given"). While this language of adventure might be seen as atypical to describe a woman's endeavor, the article concludes with a very traditional suggestion to young readers: that they not idle their summers away but, instead, draw inspiration from Curie's hard work and do something productive during the summer. In particular, the article recommends that "the girls can make dolls' dresses and the boys can have a wonderful time building a playhouse, making a ship or an airplane." Both of these examples assert that women scientists were motivated by a sense of adventure or passion, rather than the more sober, dispassionate pursuit of knowledge often attached to science.

Overall, these popular reports frame women scientists as *exceptional* women but as women nonetheless. While popular reports freely admitted that Curie's and Sabin's scientific talents are immense, they underscored that these talents did not prevent them from assuming conventional standards of feminine appearance and behavior. The tropes of modesty, appearance, romance, and motherhood recast the potentially controversial women scientists (and their activities) as inherently feminine. In this way, journalists softened the images of these formidable women, making them more acceptable to a public audience. At the same time, though, newspaper articles demonstrated to readers that women could and did find pleasure in science, that they could practice science without becoming "de-sexed," and that they could achieve in science on a par with men.

Blame: Gender Discrimination and the "Bootstraps" Rhetoric of Gender Neutrality

While newspaper articles portrayed women scientists as passionately pursuing scientific knowledge, they also created big shoes for future scientists to fill. In fact, Margaret Rossiter has argued that even Curie's highly publicized visit to the United States had little impact on women's employment or their reputations as scientists (100), especially because Curie created a standard for female scientists that was unattainable for most (127). In practice, scientific work for women continued to be stratified, with women being channeled into jobs deemed "women's work," including low-paying positions that men would not take, such as routine laboratory work, and positions that were connected to women's traditional areas of social service in some way, such as dietetics or child psychology (53). Women who wanted to contribute to scientific knowledge, rather than spending their time washing beakers or counting blood cells, pursued a strategy of over-qualification, internalizing the double standards that Curie and Sabin had been used to create (130). Perhaps influenced by these media portrayals, guidance handbooks for women seemed either to model the path to success on these exemplars or to offer an alternative route in science, one that seemed resigned to the reality that, for most women, scientific work would be more akin to factory or clerical work than to the impassioned pursuit of knowledge.

As a genre, career guides ostensibly responded to a recurrent rhetorical situation: the need of young women and men for help in selecting a career. In the 1920s and 1930s, these guides were usually written expressly for young men or for young women, so they usually highlighted careers already considered gendered. Career guides usually included the target audience in the title. For instance, Macmillan

"EXCEPTIONAL WOMEN"

and Harcourt Brace published a series of guides called "*The Young Man and . . . ,*" which included books about engineering, banking, law, business, and so on. Handbooks for women included titles such as *Vocations for Girls* (1939), *Jobs for Girls* (1930), and *Vocations for Women* (1933). Some texts addressed both male and female readers, such as Walter B. Pitkin's *New Careers for Youth: Today's Job Outlook for Men and Women from Seventeen to Thirty-Two* (1934). Aside from young men and women seeking career advice, vocational guides were sometimes addressed to guidance counselors, teachers, administrators, or even parents. For instance, Elizabeth Kemper Adams's *Women Professional Workers* (1921) was intended not just for students, but for teachers, administrators, and employers seeking a better understanding of available career paths for women (ix).

These books reflect the sex-typing of the disciplines into which male and female students were channeled. For instance, Helen Christine Hoerle and Florence B. Saltzberg include nursing, medicine, bacteriology, dietetics, and pharmacy in their career guide, *The Girl and Her Job* (1919), excluding the remaining sciences and engineering as options. While some guides included "science" as a general category, engineering was so strongly associated with men's work that it seldom appeared in guides for women. Of course, this reflects the educational opportunities open to women; most engineering schools remained male-only until World War II.

The authorship and organization of these texts varied. Some were written by a single author with expertise in vocational counseling, such as Kemper Adams, who was formerly a professor of education at Smith College. Kemper Adams offered an overview of several different fields of work for women, all based on interviews, surveys, and feedback she received from experts. Other texts featured separate chapters written by experts in each individual field; for her 1920 book, *Careers for Women*, Catherine Filene solicited profiles of professional occupations from leading women, who provided accounts of the educational requirements, career opportunities, and personal characteristics necessary for success. Still other career guides only appear under corporate authors, such as the New York City Bureau of Vocational Information's handbook, *Women in Chemistry*.

While career guides may not seem epideictic in nature, they readily partook of the topoi of praise and blame. They often praised careers themselves as particularly challenging, interesting, or open to women (and blamed those that were not). Authors of career guides also praised exemplars in each field. For instance, Doris Fleischman's *Outline of Careers for Women* (1928) noted that "there is no branch of science that has not been invaded by women" (457), mentioning Sabin by name and Curie by implication. Fleischman praises the feminist movement, in particular, for breaking down "the barriers that kept women from occupational fields which men had regarded as exclusively their own" (xi). Thus, career guides open up space for transformation in terms of women's representation in science and in society. For example, Kemper Adams hoped that the book might also reach men and women "who are considering the scope and nature of the professions and the implications of the new participation of women in the worlds of inquiry and affairs" (x). Indeed, Kemper Adams hoped that one day there would be no need for separate career books for men and women even though separate guides were still necessary in 1921, when women's status in the professional fields was still "somewhat indeterminate" (x). Kemper Adams states explicitly what other guidebooks seem to be arguing implicitly: that focusing on women's careers was still necessary given their relative newness to many fields, but that if women could prove themselves in these professions, gender equality would eventually become a reality. In this way, they serve a transformative epideictic function, constituting women's full participation in American society as a primary value.

At the same time, though, writers of career guides sometimes blamed women for their own lack of progress in the field, as I will show below. In this way, they conformed to conventional scientific values, such as meritocracy and gender neutrality, often offering these as the only solution to the sex discrimination that women still faced in science. Gender neutrality was a particularly pernicious value because it purportedly promised equal advancement to all, regardless of gender. In practice, though, women were continually denied opportunities for advancement at every stage, including admission to graduate programs in science, access to tenure-track jobs, and promotion to full professor. Yet, women were discouraged from raising issues of sex discrimination because scientific fields averred that there was no barrier to advancement for women, pointing to exemplars like Curie or Sabin as proof.[2]

Given this state of affairs, the advice given to young readers in these guidance books assumed that the best route toward change was through individual action. For instance, Kemper Adams notes that "not only for their own careers but for the sake of others who may follow, scientific women need to have unimpeachable qualifications, to expect no favors, and to show marked tenacity and courage" (328). Similarly,

Flora W. Patterson, a plant pathologist, admits that opportunities in her field were limited for women but holds out hope that "the exceptional woman may secure such a coveted position, and in time proving woman's efficiency the old-fashioned prejudice may be overcome" (qtd. in Filene 435). Echoing the epideictic tenor of popular accounts of Curie and Sabin, writers of career guides continued to place stock in "exceptional women," who seemed to offer the only path forward given the insistence on gender neutrality and meritocracy.

Given this larger goal, writers of career guides usually recommended hard work as the recipe for success. This argument is repeated throughout Filene's *Careers for Women*. For instance, physicist Margaret E. Maltby insists that "the opportunity for advancement in research depends entirely upon the character of the woman herself and her ability. There seems to be no prejudice against a woman, if she can do the work as well as or better than a man" (qtd. in Filene 432). Similarly, medical researcher Katherine R. Drinker writes, "Though it is, undoubtedly, more difficult for a woman than for a man of equal ability to attain a position of eminence in this field, if the character of her work is sufficiently distinguished practically no opportunity is closed to her" (qtd. in Filene 422). Advice such as this implies that emulating a Curie or Sabin offered the only path toward success. The suggestion was that women would have to be *exceptional* just to achieve a position that would be easily given to a male scientist of average ability.

Some writers were even more explicit in this regard, asserting that few women could hope to perform at the level required of a scientist. In this way, they upheld the notions of exceptionality that constructed science as the exclusive domain of a privileged few. Margaret Maltby, chair of the Physics Department at Barnard College, notes that women physicists are few and far between, both due to a lack of available positions and due to "the fact that few women have the combination of a constructive imagination, the mechanical skill necessary for the successful investigator, the mastery of mathematics—an essential tool of the physicist—and a broad knowledge of the principles and applications of a science that taxes the imagination and reasoning power, and that is mathematical because it is exact" (qtd. in Filene 430). In fact, Edith Johnson avows that only 4 percent of women were "capable, with proper training and experience, of more than ordinary accomplishments and sometimes brilliant attainments" (qtd. in Filene 18); only this small group of women might be "equal to, or even the peers of, their male competitors" (qtd. in Filene 19). Maltby and Johnson proclaim that only the most talented women should consider scientific careers given the prospects they faced and that other able (but not exceptional) women should consider more traditionally feminine careers. Indeed, if the likes of Curie and Sabin set the standard for all women scientists, it is little wonder that only 4 percent of women could even hope to enter the profession.

Sometimes, writers mentioned explicitly why many women failed to reach the standard set by the most eminent women in science. In her 1926 book, *Fields of Work for Women*, Miriam Simons Leuck notes that, while discrimination accounted for some of women's dissatisfaction with their careers, many professional women had a tendency to "shirk the actual responsibility" (14–15). Further, she warns that many women fell prey to the "dangers of egotism" (15), to "incompetency" (16), and to a general lack of discipline (20). Leuck counsels women not to expect special treatment and to avoid "office politics" (21), implying that women tended to depend on their feminine wiles for favors and to engage in gossip. In keeping with the epideictic mode of the guide book, Leuck praises those women who are willing to do "their work just a little better than the man at the next desk" (22), while blaming those who fail to live up to the standards set by the exceptional woman.

Similar concerns are echoed in a 1922 handbook produced by the New York City Bureau of Vocational Information, titled *Women in Chemistry*. The (unnamed) writer notes that while women brought some strengths to the field (such as conscientiousness and manual dexterity), common assumptions were that women were hampered by a lack of mechanical skill, a tendency to focus too much on the details and overlook the big picture (226), and an overall inability to "do original thinking" (227). Despite their willingness to admit that women faced such prejudices, the writer nonetheless advises women to "frankly face their limitations" and to work hard without "striving to be what they are not" (227). Women were strongly discouraged from expecting "special treatment" on the basis of their sex; quoting a practitioner in the field, the handbook maintains that women chemists should be "good sports," possessing "enough sense of fair play to expect to have her work judged by the same standards as a man's" (230).

Only in a few cases do writers offer an alternative to the "hard work" response to discrimination. Kemper Adams declares that women should "be on their guard against being used by employers to get expert work more cheaply done than by men, and should stand firmly for recognition and promotion on their record of work accomplished" (328).

Overall, though, the message to women is to keep their heads down, to work hard, and in fact to overachieve. As Leuck summed it up in her book, "Only the women now employed, by doing their work just a little better than the man at the next desk, can overcome this attitude in the end" (22).

Of course, the assumption that a few exemplary women could open opportunities for other women fails to address the institutionalized discrimination that prevailed in the interwar period. During the 1920s and 1930s, few women scientists attained the level of primacy Curie and Sabin earned in their respective fields. Rossiter sums up the plight of women scientists after 1910 as follows: "American society, and especially its university faculties, became far more willing to educate women in science than to employ them, and were almost adamantly opposed to advancing or promoting any but the most extraordinary" (xvi). Those women who did pursue careers in science often found themselves on the sidelines, mostly relegated to positions deemed appropriate for women (xvii). While science education was considered an appropriate field for women prior to the 1930s, even that area was gradually diminished, Watts argues, due to a backlash against women's "feminizing" influence on boys (150). Perhaps the only field in which women were well represented was home economics, but because the field itself was gendered feminine (and downgraded accordingly), the female "stars" of that field seldom received the kind of recognition or praise heaped on a Sabin or Curie.

Guidebooks reported facts about employment for women in the sciences, but they also tended toward the epideictic modes of praise and blame—lauding the exceptionally intelligent, persistent, and plucky women who could compete with men despite the male-dominated fields in which they worked and blaming those women who failed to live up to that standard. One can only imagine how young women might feel when reading about science careers in such guidebooks. While some might feel challenged to rise to the occasion, surely many other young women would feel discouraged. While the number of PhDs awarded to women in science did rise in the 1920s and 1930s, from about 50 to approximately 165 per year, the number of men earning PhDs also increased. Thus, women's percentage of the total number of PhDs earned actually fell after 1932, from a high of 15.5 percent to 11.5 percent (Rossiter 131). Thus, while the raw numbers showed an increase in women, proportionally, their representation did not dramatically increase. Presumably, few women would consider themselves "exceptional" enough to pursue scientific careers; it is not surprising, then, that women interested in science tended toward the more welcoming fields of home economics, social services, and nursing. In these female-dominated fields, a young woman would not need to consider herself exceptional to even have a hope of getting a job.

Epideictic Rhetoric and Women in Science

In 1935, the Association to Aid Scientific Research by Women disbanded. Formed in 1897, the association granted a research prize annually to assist a woman scientist, one that both Sabin and Curie had received. By 1935, however, the association believed their work to be finished. They passed a resolution voting to disband since "women are given opportunities to engage in Scientific Research on an equality with men, and to gain recognition for their achievements" (qtd. in Crawford 493). Certainly, if one took the exemplary women who won their annual prize as representative of the entire group, it would be easy to draw this conclusion. Yet, with the exception of home economics, the overall percentages of women in scientific fields were not "on equality with men." The association seemed to have fallen prey to the epideictic tenor of rhetoric about women in science, one that contended that the accomplishments of a few proved the field was fully open to women.

Prominent women scientists subscribed to this view as well; in 1935 Florence Sabin herself made a speech about women in science on the occasion of the M. Carey Thomas Prize at the fiftieth anniversary of the founding of Bryn Mawr College. Sabin admitted that "no great volume of scientific work has yet been done by women," but asked the following question: "is there any work by women, judged rigidly 'by the same standards as for men,' which is of such high quality that it marks a milestone in scientific progress? If we can say yes, then we shall argue that nature is not so prodigal of that grade of ability as to make it wise to waste any of it" (25). In other words, if a few women could be found to have made major contributions to science, then it was proven that women *could* be good scientists and that science itself was open to women. Sabin cited three women scientists in her speech, including Marie Curie, as an affirmative answer to her question. Of course, on an occasion such as this one, it is only fitting that Sabin should take an epideictic approach. Yet, her argument ultimately upheld the notion that the accomplishments of a few exceptional women could stand in for the group as a whole, many of whom struggled to achieve equal working conditions, let alone celebrity.

Part of the problem with the epideictic tenor of this rhetoric relates to the genre. News reports about scientific findings seek to celebrate scientific achievements while profiles tend to celebrate individual scientists. Neither type of article leaves much room for writers to question scientific institutions nor to advocate for changes to improve the lot of women scientists as a group. While ostensibly a forensic genre (one focused on facts), career guidebooks also assume an epideictic tone, either celebrating new and exciting opportunities or censuring those who fail to live up to the high standards required by scientific disciplines. Because epideictic genres serve to uphold dominant community values, they are ultimately invested in maintaining the status quo. Both newspaper reports and career guides support a view of science as an elite activity, one for which only a small proportion of women were suited. These texts also upheld conventional notions of femininity, praising great scientists like Curie for their motherly qualities and ultimately positioning those women who could compete on a par with men as aberrations.

Sabin's speech indicates that women scientists themselves assimilated the values promoted in these epideictic texts. As Evelyn Fox Keller has explained, "For women scientists *as scientists*, the principal point is that measures of scientific performance admitted of only a single scale, according to which, to be different was to be lesser. Under such circumstances, the hope of equity, indeed, the very concept of equity, appeared—as it still appears—to depend on the disavowal of difference" (236). This is why guidance books for young women encouraged their readers not to expect "special treatment," to be ready and willing to compete against men without drawing attention to their gender. Yet this advice belied the reality that men and women were not on an even playing field, not when women were continuously denied opportunities for advancement in nearly every scientific field. Given the preponderance of this type of rhetoric about women scientists, it is little wonder that women scientists would wait for decades to truly begin to address the systematic, institutional discrimination they faced.

Notes

1. Adrienne Rich also writes about the "Exceptional Woman," who receives "status and tenure" in the university but often at the expense of aiding other women or of exploring research areas connected to her interests as a woman (138).

2. For further analysis of how gender neutrality actually limited women's ability to draw attention to sex discrimination, see Jordynn Jack, *Science on the Home Front*.

15

"Long I Followed Happy Guides": Activism, Advocacy, and English Studies

Kay Halasek

In *The Resistant Writer*, Charles Paine argues that composition historiography has "concentrated too much on hero-villain dichotomies" and the insular intellectual culture of the university (xi). Leveling a similar critique, Jeff Rice exposes the tendency in composition historiography to create "grand narratives," "compress[ing] history into sweeping generalizations" (55). By seeking to articulate an origin and rationale for the discipline, composition historians, Rice argues, create a "mythic historic past" in which all that precedes a date (somewhere around 1963) is, at best, undertheorized and undisciplined (55).

In many of its earlier histories, composition studies also simultaneously wrote out, obscured, or marginalized women like Adele Bildersee and Helen Gray Cone, about whom I write here. The one existing treatment of Bildersee, by James Berlin, illustrates this tendency. In analyzing epistemological trends in twentieth-century writing instruction, Berlin identifies Bildersee's textbook *Imaginative Writing* (1927) as "one of the most popular expressionist textbooks of the twenties and thirties" (77) and then dismisses it as naïve in its foundationalist and apolitical notions of the self, suspect for its understanding of truth as attainable through personal enrichment, and complicit for its ties to "liberal culture, an aristocratic and elitist rhetoric that appeared in certain Eastern colleges" during this time (11). Berlin's claim that Bildersee's epistemology is expressivist in nature is not incorrect, but is—constructed as it is within the narrow confines of his argumentative purpose and historiographic method—problematically limited. Read in isolation from its author and institutional, historical, and cultural contexts and cast within Berlin's taxonomy, *Imaginative Writing* simply illustrates a particular epistemology or stands as a precursor to later creative writing pedagogies, but little else. Read, however, from a more panoramic view—within, through, and against biographical, institutional, historical, and cultural contexts—*Imaginative Writing* comes to mean something else, something more.

To demonstrate just what that "something else, something more" is, I first introduce a "sideshadowing" methodology that informs my historiographic approach. In answering the call from Paine to create "narratives that are more complex and that more accurately illustrate the relationships between culture and composition" (34), I found it necessary to construct both a research methodology and narrative form that simultaneously could account for and was accountable to Bildersee and Cone, the women about whom I was writing. I did not find these women using the conventional historical methods I'd learned in graduate school (and at times, honestly, it felt as though they had serendipitously found *me*), and, as it turned out, I could not adequately represent them using conventional historiographic narrative structures. In some senses, then, my primary objective in this chapter is to present this sideshadowing methodology and form. To achieve this end, however, I also demonstrate the methodology and form in action, using Bildersee and Cone as historical case studies, ultimately showing what a sideshadowing methodology yields about them—and about *Imaginative Writing*—that traditional historiographic methods and forms have excluded or elided.

A Sideshadowing Methodology: The Possibility of Possibility

In constructing a sideshadowing methodology, I borrow from Gary Saul Morson's *Narrative and Freedom*, which examines the nature of temporality in representing human history and concludes that "there are always a multiplicity of temporalities to consider" in every realm of human thought (3). Given this assumption, the historian must construct a historiographic methodology that allows for, even invites, alternative constructs of past events. "To understand a moment," Morson writes, is to consider "not only what did happen but also what might have happened," what other possibilities, people, conditions might "cast[ ] a shadow 'from the side,'" revealing other possibilities of a particular historical moment (119). In terms of composition historiography, Morson's work encouraged me to ask what methodologies I might employ in researching Bildersee and Cone that would allow me to move away from the "tendency to trace straight lines of causality" from one event to another (119) that characterizes Berlin's (and others') work.

The central informing characteristic of the sideshadowing methodology I present here is an emphasis on and valuing of the *peripheral*—insofar as peripheral means alongside the dominant (received) narrative, just at the seams of it, at the outermost range of its line of sight. The peripheral is that which is noticed only when we pay attention with what Bakhtin refers to as a "sidelong glance" (qtd. in Morson, "Who Speaks" 240). It's what we miss if we look only straight ahead, neglecting what is around the edges or in the corners, just beyond our immediate perception. In terms of Bildersee and *Imaginative Writing*, I asked myself what (or who) stood at the margins, on the edges, in front of, beside, and behind her and her work. To answer that question, I employed (and only later constructed and named) the peripheral methodological principles of *acknowledgment, attribution, relationship,* and *situatedness*.

It was Bildersee herself who prompted me to recognize *acknowledgment*, the first of the sideshadowing principles. Acknowledgment (through dedications or dedicatory epistles) of others—while in past centuries primarily a means of thanking patrons—is now for most authors (as it was for Bildersee in 1927) a means of recognizing those people who supported the author or to whom the book is metaphorically "given." Bildersee dedicates *Imaginative Writing* to her teacher, mentor, and department chair, Helen Gray Cone, acknowledging her with a dedication that reads, simply, "Long I Followed Happy Guides." The heartfelt dedication (taken from Emerson's "Forerunners") piqued my curiosity, leading me to research Cone, who in turn led me (through her acknowledgments) to other women writers and activists, including Jeannette Gilder.

Sideshadow: Gilder, sister of publisher and writer Richard Watson Gilder, stood in the center of an influential circle of journalists, agents, and writers, including Walt Whitman, who was a close friend. "Miss Gilder's Syndicate," her literary agency, provided support for writers in the city (Roberson 254). In addition to her journalistic writing and editing, Gilder wrote fiction, autobiography, and drama.

Following this line of inquiry, induced by the authors themselves, provided me a means of identifying and tracing the people with whom they expressed meaningful personal connections.

A second of Bildersee's colleagues, Blanche Colton Williams, came to my attention through a second sideshadowing principle—*attribution*. Attribution, the practice of crediting others for their implicit or explicit contributions to a work, traces not lines of causation but of professional or scholarly influence. Although not always clearly distinct from one another, attribution and acknowledgment emphasize slightly different elements of effect: attribution names (often literally, in print) professional indebtedness; acknowledgment notes influence of a somewhat more personal nature. While *acknowledging* a debt to Cone, Bildersee *attributes* to Williams a professional influence on *Imaginative Writing*. Williams commented on Bildersee's manuscript, and the chapters on short story writing in *Imaginative Writing* reflect Williams's goals in her own *Handbook on Story Writing* (Bildersee, *Imaginative* v).

> Sideshadow: Williams published the *Handbook on Story Writing* in 1917 and became department chair at Hunter in 1926. She published four biographies (of John Keats, George Eliot, Bess Aldrich, and Clara Barton); authored five books on story writing and reading (including mystery and detective fiction, Old English, and collections of student writing); authored, edited, or coedited another fourteen books between 1918 and 1941; and edited the O. Henry Memorial Prize for fourteen years. Williams's *Handbook on Story Writing* is also dedicated to Cone and recognizes Shirley V. Long, Williams's assistant, for her commentary on the manuscript (xiii).

The third peripheral characteristic of a sideshadowing methodology, *relationship*, takes into account those personal and familial relationships that bind the life of a historical subject and make the person's work possible. Relationships may, of course, also be attributed or acknowledged, as Cone's was by Bildersee and Williams—but this is not always the case because some relationships (those considered taboo, for example) could not be publicly recognized or were considered the province of the home, not the profession. Bildersee and Cone, for example, found their influences and drew their inspiration from different relationships: Bildersee from Cone and her own family, including her brother, Isaac, and sister, Dorothy; Cone, from her friends and classmates, especially Emma Klauser, with whom she undertook much of her service.

Sideshadow: Bildersee's sister, Dorothy, was also an alumna of Hunter College. A public school teacher like Klauser and administrator like her brother Isaac, Dorothy served as president of the New York Principals Association. Principal of PS 217, she was recognized professionally for her influential *Teaching in the Primary Grades* (1932). Dorothy led a WPA remedial reading program and pioneered tutorial programs for underprivileged students and in health education ("Dorothy Bildersee"). She, like Adele, served the city and its less affluent citizens through educational advocacy, a calling cultivated at the Normal School. Although their brother, Isaac, also served as a school administrator, he was a somewhat controversial figure in the New York City schools, where he served as a teacher and assistant superintendent. He issued in 1947 an order "forbidding the singing of Christmas carols that referred to the Nativity or the use of decorations that included religious symbols of any faith, such as those of the Jewish Hanukkah" ("Dr. Bildersee"; "Religious"). The order drew fire from every quarter and was overturned by the superintendent and mayor within four days ("School Carol" 39; "Pupils" 31). The Bildersees together created a family legacy of social service through education, one felt for decades in the New York City school system.

Sideshadow: Emma Klauser, a classmate and dear friend of Cone's, became a public school teacher after her training at the Normal School. May Cermak recounts the friendship as "one of the loveliest . . . I have ever known," and Klauser "one of the loveliest characters—sweet and gentle, yet forceful, keen, witty, and possessed of such a delightfully twinkling though quiet sense of humor and of a quaint whimsicality equally delightful. Truly, Miss Klauser and Miss Cone had much in common" (6). Klauser, also a poet, was a member of a Hunter alumnae committee that sponsored a meeting featuring Chauncey M. Depew (then president of the New York Central Hudson River Railroad Company and later a U.S. senator) on the topic of the "emancipation of women and her higher education" (Lindsay 7; "The Social World" 13). To say that the two were inseparable is perhaps an exaggeration, but historical documents and second person accounts of their relationship suggest that Cone and Klauser worked side-by-side much of the time. In recognition of their work at and dedication to the settlement house at Lenox Hill, for example, both women had a "table . . . dedicated in their memory" (Lindsay 6). Cone and Klauser continued their work and friendship for many years, likely until Klauser's death, which preceded Cone's. They lived together at E. 90th Street from at least 1912 to 1921, traveling together to Europe (along with Emma's sister, Ella, a music teacher, in 1921) on at least three occasions during that time. Cone makes no explicit acknowledgments of Klauser in her volumes of poetry, but her relationship with Klauser was, by all other accounts, a lifelong sustaining influence on Cone.

These sustaining relationships cultivated in Bildersee and Cone a sense of deep and abiding moral obligation to others. Locating, acknowledging, valuing, and narrating these relationships enrich our understanding of these women and their contributions to rhetorical and educational practice. We see not only the products of their service but also the people who forged their resolve and supported or influenced their work.

The fourth and final characteristic of a sideshadowing methodology is its *situatedness*, a seeking out of the "energy of the public sphere," the "experiences of the material and social world familiar" to the historical subjects (Heilbrun 108; Sutherland 28). Committed to situating Bildersee and Cone in their particular institutional, historical, and cultural moment, I necessarily had to enlarge the scope and nature of my historical inquiry to include (among other sources) the popular press (literary and women's magazines, newspapers), events of the day, society announcements, opinion and editorial letters, and alumni news. Reading Bildersee and Cone through such a situated approach brings multiple lenses (literary history, women's writing and authorship, English studies, social welfare advocacy, institutional history) and sites (classroom, synagogue, women's clubs, settlement houses) to the historical endeavor and enriches our understanding of them and this period in women's rhetorical and educational practice in America. Reexamining them with such a sidelong glance affords a reading that situates them and their work at once in the larger *and* more local educational, social, and cultural contexts in which they circulated. Such a rereading answers Lyotard's call for "'small narratives'" (Lather 156) and resists "grand narratives" and "sweeping generalizations" (Rice 55), affording us an understanding of English studies situated more fully in *its* cultural and social context, outside of the insular intellectual culture of the university about which Charles Paine warns.

Sideshadowing Narrative Form: Side Notes as the Sidelong Glance

Having articulated a sideshadowing methodology that valued the peripheral and employed the principles of acknowledgment, attribution, relationship, and situatedness, I still found myself struggling against the print narrative structures that typically inform historiography. I sought the means to represent (physically, on the printed page) these sideshadowing methodological principles—a form that did not confine Bildersee and Cone within the 8 ½ × 11-inch space. I wanted to construct an essay that realized what Patti Lather set out to accomplish in *Getting Lost: Feminist Efforts toward a Double(d) Science:* create a text that "is an enactment of its message" (156). I wanted to represent the understanding that mine is only one (and a not so final) word on Bildersee and Cone.

I (again, serendipitously) found models for a sideshadowing form through my leisure reading: Myla Goldberg's novel, *Wickett's Remedy*, and Patti Lather and Chris Smithies's *Troubling the Angels: Women Living with HIV/AIDS*. Both texts employ marginalia (either at the sides or foots of pages) as a means of representing multiple voices, viewpoints, information, and asides that gloss, question, or otherwise illuminate the main narrative. Fully understanding that the narratives about Bildersee and Cone I was weaving were necessarily limited and required me to select particular lines of inquiry, to give structure to what was, rather, a tapestry of stories, I opted to use side notes akin to Goldberg's and Lather and Smithies's to invite you to consider those other stories, those sideshadows on the periphery that allow you to see not only the main events but also accompanying and allied events. In other words, side notes—like those that appear above on Jeannette Gilder, Blanche Colton Williams, Dorothy and Isaac Bildersee, and Emma Klauser—are my attempt to represent the sideshadows—those "ghostly . . . might-have-beens or might-bes," those traces of history that retain "the possibility of possibility," that allow us to grasp "not only what did happen but also what else might have happened" or that happened beyond the frame of the narrative told (Morson 118, 119).

Such a resituating and refashioning of their histories demonstrates that these were women neither of solitary voice nor singular vision; these were women intimately engaged with classmates, friends, and family in collaborative civic and rhetorical action, women serving alongside others. In their civic and advocacy endeavors, the influence of experiences and relationships forged by family and at the Normal College were evident, even foundational, for both Bildersee and Cone.

The Narrative

Established in 1869, the Female Normal and High School in New York City was founded to "meet . . . a need for more and better teachers in the city's elementary schools" (Patterson 4). In fulfilling this mission, its curriculum included courses in the liberal arts and vocational training. Like other normal schools at this time, the Female Normal and High School was founded on the "idea and ideal" of democratic and universal public education (4, 7). Its students and alumnae led or participated in the free kindergarten and settlement house movements, helped to subsidize the college educations of young women unable to pay for their educations, founded literary societies and libraries, and embarked on careers in journalism and social service (57–58, 63). In short, the school was a site of educational and civic engagement, an institution that cultivated in students and faculty like Bildersee and Cone a commitment to improving themselves and those around them as both intellectuals and advocates for the public good.

Helen Gray Cone matriculated at the Female Normal School in 1873 and remained associated with the college until her retirement in 1926. Although now an obscure figure in American literary history, during her lifetime Cone was a beloved poet. A prolific writer, Cone was author of nine collections of poetry, and her work was widely anthologized in volumes devoted to nature poetry, poetry for children, and women in poetry. Her reputation as a poet, Amelia Josephine Burr suggests, would have been even more enhanced had she chosen to devote herself fully to her craft rather than to making poets of her students (4). In fact, her influence as a poet did not long survive her time, but her legacy survived through those students—among them Adele Bildersee, who most likely matriculated at the school in 1897, graduated in 1903, joined the Hunter College English faculty in 1907, and earned her doctorate from Columbia in 1932, completing a dissertation on state scholarship students at Hunter.

Sideshadow: Bildersee pursued one arm of her work in social advocacy through her dissertation, *State Scholarship Students at Hunter College of the City of New York*, which sought to determine whether continued allocation of state funds to support students of high academic standing was justified by the students' academic and civic achievements. Bildersee's conclusion was affirmative. She determined that scholarship students typically outperformed their classmates and fellow graduates, although not always to a statistically significant degree. Both undergraduate and graduate scholarship students persisted at a higher rate; were more likely to maintain good academic standing, take honors courses, and gain membership in honoraries; had higher GPAs; and won more awards. They participated in more extracurricular and social service activities and devoted more time to those activities (41–43, 81–82). Some of Bildersee's findings are particularly noteworthy in the context of her own involvement in social service. Respondents reported participating in departmental clubs, sororities, religious clubs, religious schools, settlement or war work, and other social services or programs such as Girl Scouts or Girl Reserves (60–62). The graduate cohort reported activities that included "protective and correctional work with children" and "recreational and educational club work"; work with such agencies as the YWCA, Council of Jewish Women, or welfare and relief societies; "propaganda for peace; [and] research in such problems as housing and unemployment" (63–64). Bildersee found that the students—and scholarship students in particular—were fulfilling Cone's charge to escape from isolation and take their place in a changing world.

A biblical scholar, Bildersee was also an active member of the New York Jewish community and published three books for young Bible and Hebrew students, her stated aim to make the subjects of study accessible to the young learner ("Dr. Adele" 34). *Imaginative Writing* was published in 1927, shortly after she left Hunter to become acting dean of the women's division at the merged Brooklyn campus of Hunter College and City College in 1926 (the same year Cone retired). Bildersee became the dean of the Women's Division in 1931 and was also director of admissions at the time of her retirement in 1954 ("Miss Bildersee" 23; "To Honor" 12).

> Sideshadow: Like her brother, Bildersee observed a definitive separation of church and state and strived—even in the face of strong opposition—to avoid even the appearance of institutional support of political candidates. Some seventeen years before her brother, in 1930, Bildersee herself made a very unpopular decision, preventing socialist politician Norman Thomas from addressing Brooklyn College's Social Science Club on "Why Politics Matters." As the *New York Times* reported in the wake of the event, several hundred young women went to hear Thomas ("Brooklyn College Girls" 21). When informed that the students had found a way to hear Thomas and asked about her decision to ban the lecture at Brooklyn College, Bildersee firmly upheld the right of the women to hear the speaker. Her decision was not a matter of his political views, she stated, but a matter instead of the appearance that the College supported his candidacy: Mr. Thomas "was forbidden to speak here because we do not feel that a candidate for office should make a political address in the heat of a campaign under the auspices of the college" (21). In short, she did not want Thomas to use the lecture as an occasion to promote his own interests, enlisting the authority of the college as he did. Bildersee remained politically active, even after her retirement. As a member of the Brooklyn Association for the United Nations, she worked to "build a strong and well-informed public opinion in support of the United Nations"—much as Cone had with the League of Nations nearly forty years earlier ("Plans Drive" 120).

As these short biographies suggest, both Cone and Bildersee were successful scholars and writers, but their published work, while recognized in their lifetimes, went largely unexamined by scholars in English studies for over sixty years. Cone is most remembered by scholars today for coediting with Jeannette Gilder in 1887 the two-volume *Pen-Portraits of Literary Women* and for her essay "Woman in American Literature," and Bildersee only for *Imaginative Writing*.

> Sideshadow: Cone and Gilder describe *Pen-Portraits* as a "presentation of the characteristics and surroundings" of selected authors, including Hannah More, Frances Burney, Mary Wollstonecraft, Mary W. Godwin, George Sands, George Eliot, Margaret Fuller, Maria Edgeworth, Jane Austen, Joanna Baillier, Lady Blessington, and Mary Russell Mitford.

What ultimately motivated a scholarly reflective critique of Cone's work was her 1890 essay, "Woman in American Literature," which articulates an early and powerful statement about the status of women writers and authorship. Scholars Elizabeth Ammons, Susan Williams, and Irene Visser, for example, turn to Cone's essay to discuss the developing understanding of women authors in the late nineteenth and early twentieth centuries. Ammons points out Cone's "vigorous protest against treating women separately" and her commitment to "sexual equality, not difference" (12). Williams confirms Ammons's claims and also argues that Cone's protestations against such difference confirm the presence of women's literature as a class of writing (29).

> Sideshadow: Jeannette Gilder shared Cone's opinions on women in literature, arguing for "putting men's work and women's work of the same kind side by side, and judging them not as sex work, but simply as work.... I do not believe in sex in literature and art. Every book should be compared with all other books of its kind, and so with every picture, statue, or musical composition" (399). An antisuffragette, Gilder also opposed women as preachers and lawyers and firmly states her distaste for women in politics, arguing that "it is too public, too wearing, and too unfitted to the nature of women" (399).

Visser articulates the central themes and claims of Cone's work and points to its significance on the continent. Although she acknowledges that the essay did little to introduce new female American authors to the Netherlands, Visser suggests that it invited the Dutch to investigate the challenges that faced their women writers during the same period.

> Sideshadow: Cone's essay was translated and published in the *Portefeuille* in 1891 and anthologized in Annie Nathan Meyer's *Woman's Work in America*. Meyer, a New York native, advocated throughout her life for higher education for women, ultimately succeeding in founding Barnard College (Meyer, "Higher Education" 64). Meyer, like Cone's coeditor, Gilder, was an antisuffragette, arguing "against the notion that women would purify politics" (Brody).

Most notable about Visser's analysis of Cone for my purposes here as I seek to enlarge the contexts in which I represent Cone (and ultimately

Bildersee) is Visser's understanding of Cone as "American poet, *educationist* and literary critic" (294; emphasis added). Cone was, as Visser suggests, fully aware of, called attention to, and sought to remedy the incapacitating effect that inadequate education had on American women writers (295).

> Sideshadow: Visser also points out Cone's concern about the exploitation of women authors by printers and publishers who often took advantage of their ignorance about contractual and financial matters (295). Given Cone's concern, it seems appropriate to note again her long-term professional and personal relationship with Gilder, who represented writers as they negotiated their publishing rights (Roberson 254).

For Cone, the history of women writing in the United States was one of intellectual isolation—a deplorable but correctable condition. "Weakened by an intellectual best-parlor atmosphere, with small chance of free out-of-door currents," Cone writes, women writers could do little more than produce inferior literature ("Woman" 922). The "defect," Cone notes, was not inherent in the women themselves; it was, rather, a result of cultural and educational conditioning: the "scattering, haphazard kind of education then commonly bestowed upon girls helped to bring about such conditions of things" (923). Education—sound, systematic, classical education like that Cone sought to provide the young women at the Normal School—would mitigate the circumstances. "Efficient work in literature, as in other professions" she continues, depends not "upon the actual amount of knowledge possessed, but upon the training of the mind to sure action, and the vitality of the spark of intellectual life communicated in early days" (923). This same philosophy informs Bildersee's text, which closes with a benediction for the student: "To go through life with senses alert and mind interested, to be able to get from books what the writer intended one to get, to be equipped to write when the call to write comes—it is not too much if one must pay for this with labor and pain" (*Imaginative Writing* 226). Cultivating the art of writing is laborious, but the fruits of that labor are manifold.

In addition to an "aimless education," women were subject to a "vagueness of demand" regarding the purposes of their writing (Cone, "Woman" 923). Like any writer confined to discursive tasks of little consequence or ill-defined purpose, women writers produced inconsequential, dull, ineffectual prose. If challenged to engage their minds in matters of intellectual merit, women would demonstrate their genius. Yet, having been denied such a role historically, women had been limited to the "cause of the domestic virtues and pudding"—the "cookery book" and the "polishing of furniture and the education of daughters" (923, 924).

> Sideshadow: Cone turned to her own writing as a means of engaging some of the most pressing cultural and social questions of her time, composing poems like "Arraignment" to protest war in the face of unparalleled human cost (Reilly 3). By all accounts an anglophile, Cone was particularly affected by World War I and its impact on England, an emotion that inspired much of her poetry during this period. "A Chant of Love for England"—recited in public forums and at war rallies in the United States, broadcast in England during the war, and reprinted numerous times afterwards—most fully represents Cone's deep belief in the power of literature as the lifeblood of a nation ("Cheer" 9). "A Chant of Love for England" is also anthologized in Lawrence F. Abbott's *Sixty American Opinions on the War*, a collection of excerpts of letters, essays, and speeches, among which Cone's is the only poem included. Published in England for an English readership, the volume was intended to "show how many friends we have in America" (v). "Keenly aware of social wrongs, observant, analytical of causes and aims," Cone "cherished a great faith in the success of our endeavors towards peace and justice" (Michels 3). An "untiring worker in the cause of world peace," Cone nonetheless realized that the peace that would follow "the Great War" would be achieved neither easily nor without loss (Stein 3). An active supporter of the Paris Pact, Cone succeeded in heading a group in 1928 that lobbied alumnae of the college to accept the resolution ("Paris" 26).

> Sideshadow: Cone's civic action was not limited to international affairs. She also supported workers' rights and actions against the exploitation of children and women laboring under horrifying conditions in New York City sweatshops. Her staff kept her abreast of conditions in the factories, including the 25 March 1911 fire at the Triangle Shirtwaist Factory that killed nearly 150 workers (Hahn 6). Although Cone apparently did not march in the 1909 shirtwaist makers' strike, she supported those who did—including colleague and college debate society adviser Sarah Rush Parks (Farrington, "A World" 6). Farrington (herself author of *The Essay: How to Study and Write It*) reports that, when asked about Parks's participation in the strike, Cone commented, "I am proud to know you stood such a test for others! If any one criticizes you, I will defend you" (6).

Although establishing women's colleges represented a step forward for women seeking to refine their intellectual and discursive skills, the general "advance in literature" among women was, in 1890, nearly negligible ("Woman" 930). Here Cone points again not to some defect in women but to an "unavoidable self-consciousness [that] hampers the first workers under a new dispensation" (930). That self-consciousness—along with inadequate training in the early years—crippled women as writers and speakers.

As early as 1908 (the year following Bildersee's appointment as an instructor to the English department), Cone stated in her departmental report a pointed concern over the inadequate preparation and training of students in literature, writing, and rhetoric, naming as "two vital needs" a "better preliminary training in elementary English, written and oral, and . . . a wider opportunity for the practice of higher composition and for the appreciative study of English literature than is afforded by our present arrangement of the course of study" ("Report," 1909 1). Echoing her sentiments in "Woman in American Literature," she acknowledges that the "deficiency is due rather to general conditions than to the defects of individual teachers or institutions" (1). The public educational system, focusing on meeting the demands of the Uniform Reading Lists imposed by the Harvard Committee of Ten, had consequently ignored essential practice in writing and rhetoric.

Cone staunchly maintained throughout her tenure as department chair (which lasted until the mid-1920s) the need for more focused training in writing and speaking.

> Sideshadow: The Hunter College Archives include Cone's annual departmental reports from 1908, 1911, 1913, 1914, 1916, and 1922 (all dated in subsequent years) and a report on a visit Cone made to Wellesley in 1911. The archives also include Williams's annual departmental reports from 1926 and 1929. The reports articulate a common concern that students' deficiencies in written and oral English demanded a great deal of the department's time and energies at the expense of work in more advanced subjects. "Instruction in speaking," I should note, did not mean instruction in rhetoric or oratorical training—although students in the college did eventually found a debating society under the guidance of Sarah Rush Parks.

At the same time, she also understood that the college had a broader mandate, a social responsibility to "escape[] from . . . isolation," and "take its place in a changing world" (Cone qtd. in Jones 5). The two educational goals, moreover, were not entirely separate for Cone. In an attempt to infuse the curriculum with an additional opportunity for writing, the department established in 1911 "English X," a required "essay to be submitted in the first term of the senior year" (Cone, "Report" 1912). Although never satisfied with the course or the students' performances, Cone attempted to tie the writing requirement to civic and social issues. Students were given a list of topics on which to write. One group, "Class II," was exclusively related to the study of English literature. Another group, "Class I," included such topics as "Cooperation between the City

Museums and the Public Schools," "A Study of the Flora of New York City in connection with the Nature-Study Curriculum in the Elementary Schools of the City," "Fuels of New York City," "Intensive Farming as an Occupation for Women," and "The Minimum Wage: A Study of Conditions, as revealed by the Massachusetts Reports and of Results, as seen from English [sic] and Australia" ("English X"). Students were, in effect, given the opportunity to investigate, through the senior essays, subjects related to their future work as teachers or to larger vocational, social, and economic challenges facing women.

> Sideshadow: At the time of my research, Hunter College Archives include no additional materials related to in-class or departmental assignments given by the faculty during Cone's tenure at the school. Given this, the assignment for English X stands as the only concrete contemporary evidence of the social and civic bent of the English and writing curricula during this time. As chair of the department in 1911, Cone would have contributed to determining the subjects for the assignment. Copies of the "Examination of Candidates" and "Examination of Seniors" from 1893 provide an additional glimpse into the expectations for admission and graduation just before the turn of the century.

That the English department generally and Cone in particular consciously constructed courses to situate the study of literature in a social context is confirmed by Williams as she recalls Cone's contributions to the Hunter curriculum. Cone's courses, Williams recalls, were created through a "thorough study and understanding of what all the world was doing for young women, . . . building wisely on her foundation a structure which has sufficed until today" ("From the Head" 2). Cone's pedagogy was not based solely on literature for its own sake—although, certainly, she strived to have students develop a love of literature, a charge that Bildersee later answered. Cone's pedagogy situated literature within and against the world into which her students were venturing. And for much of her career, that was a world that neither cultivated nor valued in them that "mind to sure action, and the vitality of the spark of intellectual life" ("Woman" 923).

> Sideshadow: The admiration of Cone's students long survived their teacher, as is demonstrated by 1926 graduate, Amelie Spiegel Rothschild, who recalls Cone's poetry class some eighty years after her graduation. Rothschild states simply, "I had a revelation in that class" (*At Hunter* 10). Patterson relates a similar testimonial from adolescent fiction writer August H. Seaman (69). Bildersee remembers Cone as "she gently led on those who were slow to enkindle, and the generous enthusiasm with which she encouraged and guided

those who had a spark that answered to her fire" ("Long" 7). In addition to her other duties, Cone sponsored the English Club, directed student plays, and mentored students preparing commencement essays as the only composition course at the time "required merely the preparation of a note-book filled with letter-forms" (Hess 4). Cone also established in 1915 (and Bildersee later led) the "Fellowship of Goodwill," a student organization whose aim was to "deepen in the life of the individual, and thus to spread in the life of the community, the spirit of GOODWILL to man, irrespective of difference in race or nationality, and all other distinctions which tend to become barriers" (Cone qtd. in Hahn 6). The Fellowship promoted "mutual encouragement and enlightenment" and promoted the "study of comparative literature" as a means of furthering global understanding, tolerance, and peace (Hahn 6). Cone and Bildersee took seriously the college motto, "*Mihi Cura Futuri,*" "Mine is the care of the future."

The answer to the question, "What ultimately motivated a scholarly reflective critique of Bildersee's work when it had gone unnoticed for nearly sixty years?" resides in a disciplinary desire in composition studies about which Jeff Rice writes. In an effort to create a tradition for the emerging discipline, historians often elevated one school of thought or set of pedagogical practices over others, demonizing them as naïve or complicit in some larger institutional or cultural machination. This is the case, as I explain at the outset of this chapter, with James Berlin, who dismisses Bildersee's *Imaginative Writing* as expressivist in nature. Also allied with aestheticism and progressive education, expressivism, Berlin argues, validates the experiences of the student and cultivates self-expression, situating the teacher as a guide who creates a productive learning environment but does not "instruct the student in the principles of writing" (13). The pedagogy that informs *Imaginative Writing* emphasizes self-expression by focusing on descriptive and narrative writing, and offers prose, poetry, and journalistic essays as models. Bildersee relies a great deal on George Herbert Palmer's *Self-Cultivation in English* and includes selections from Sherwood Anderson, Willa Cather, Joseph Conrad, Robert Frost, Ernest Hemingway, Sinclair Lewis, Amy Lowell, Anne Sedgwick, Robert Louis Stevenson, Sara Teasdale, and Oscar Wilde. Assignments include autobiography, short story, fairy tale, and one-act play rather than expository or argumentative prose.

Reading Bildersee through Berlin's lens enriches our understanding of these literary influences on *Imaginative Writing*; however, situating our reading of Bildersee within the context at the Normal School and through her relationship with Cone allows us to see that *Imaginative*

Writing extends Cone's pedagogical and social visions. Bildersee sought to cultivate students' ability to discern from fiction and essays the principles of sound writing that could then inform their own writing as they narrated their experiences and began to represent themselves and the world around them. (See Elizabeth Wilkinson's and Kathy Jurado's chapters in this collection for similar understandings of the motivational possibilities of creative writing.) Bildersee's approach is particularly well suited to a normal school, which sought to assist students in developing "simple and clear principles" rather than present to them "theories for their guidance" (Rideing 676). *Imaginative Writing* is not the comprehensive writing textbook with which contemporary students might be familiar. It contains no chapters on grammar and usage or citation formats. It does not purport to cover all elements or modes of writing, focusing instead on descriptive and narrative writing, as Berlin notes (77). The teacher is a "guide and advisor—collaborator, if need be" (Bildersee, *Imaginative* ix). The approach that informs her text is student centered, locating the authority and responsibility for learning with the student in collaboration with the teacher. Bildersee's goal is ambitious but clear: "encouraging" in the student "an interest in writing as a means of expressing what he has to communicate, in arousing in him a determination to write as well as he can, and in leading him in his efforts to master the technical difficulties of writing" (ix). This statement from the preface of *Imaginative Writing* demonstrates a more comprehensive purpose for writing than the expressivist end Berlin assigns to Bildersee, one that exceeds self-cultivation or self-expression. Her writing pedagogy values not only self-motivation and self-discipline but also the communicative function of audience-oriented writing. To limit it to an elitist or naïve ideology, as Berlin does, is to ignore its origins in and relevance to the educational, cultural, and gendered context of the Normal College, which valued both personal rhetorical agency *and* communicative purposes.

Imaginative Writing relies, understandably, on concepts and ideals that informed much of writing instruction during this time, namely, what Thomas Masters describes in *Practicing Writing* as individuality and transmission: an emphasis on developing students' abilities of self-expression and the abiding belief that by reading, analyzing, and imitating the work of the "masters," students will themselves benefit from the transformative effect of the literature and develop as writers (74, 101). As Berlin suggests, the pedagogy is also, not surprisingly given its publication in 1927, largely foundationalist in its epistemology.

For example, students are encouraged to "test" in one exercise the accuracy and comprehensiveness of their individual observations of a familiar local scene, "a city avenue or town street," by comparing their notes with one another. Such a collaborative activity sharpens students' observational abilities (24). Accuracy of observation and felicity of its verbal representation are crucial. One other notable expressivist element informs *Imaginative Writing*—a demonstrated and clear emphasis on the writing process and a willingness to set aside (if not dispense with entirely) concerns for grammar during those stages in the process when students generate new text. At one point, Bildersee encourages students, "Get to work: that is the important thing. Push the pencil doggedly across the paper, even if the words it writes are words for the wastebasket only. . . . Go back to the opening . . . and try again. Perhaps there is little—perhaps there is much—in your first effort that is worth salvaging" (45). At another, she prompts, "First, without thinking about the elements of style that we have lately been considering, let us write as rapidly as we can, trying to set the scene down just as it strikes us" (87).

Focusing on four pages in the one chapter (of twenty) that discuss figurative language, Berlin argues that Bildersee's text compels students to strive "of course, for the fresh and original" through metaphoric language (77)—a hallmark of expressivist rhetoric. On the contrary, Bildersee warns the student against moving too "far from the subject of his description" by using "far-fetched" figures, as doing so "will take the reader far afield too" (85). Her advice to the student writer, in contrast to Berlin's claim, is contextual and rhetorical, emphasizing the suitability of figurative language to the subject of the discourse and the needs of intended audiences. Also contrary to Berlin's claim that, as an expressivist, she believes the "basis of writing is a 'mystery' that can never be simply formulated," Bildersee seeks to demonstrate throughout *Imaginative Writing* that the "'strange illusion' that writing is easy for the elect and impossible for all else" (4) is nothing more than that—an illusion. Bildersee declares, "There is no one who can write without the 'straight work,' the 'persistence, care, discriminating observation, ingenuity, refusal to lose heart'" (6).

By limiting his analysis of Bildersee's text as expressivist, Berlin disparagingly claims that the "subject matter of the book is not writing, but the student" (77). Given Bildersee's dedication to students, one might wonder at Berlin's critique. The text, indeed, *does* foreground students—their lives, the complexity and pressure of the demands made on them by school, and their writing. Throughout *Imaginative*

Writing, Bildersee presents not only the writing of the "masters" but also the writing of Hunter students, usually selections that appeared in the pages of the *Echo*, a college magazine. Focusing on developing in students those skills she believes fundamental to their success, Bildersee encourages them to select for analyses and models "books written in [their] own generation or in a generation not too remote from [their] own" as styles of writing shift and contemporary models serve as the best means of determining current techniques (20). She also situates descriptive and narrative writing not as ends in themselves but as elements of a larger discourse, the autobiographical novel (40). The descriptions of a neighborhood, delicatessen, room, person at work, outdoor place, familiar persons, and routine activity are part of each student's autobiographical novel, what we would likely now refer to as memoir or life writing. (See chapters in this collection by Hephzibah Roskelly, Ann George, and Elizabeth Weiser for examples of how contemporaneous women were using memoir to further social activism.) By structuring the text in this fashion, Bildersee seeks to avoid the "feeling that what we write is in the nature of an exercise only, a discipline—it is, in its way, literature; and if it is written sincerely it will be read with attention and respect" (40). Students write to a reading audience about what they know.

> Sideshadow: The first twelve chapters of *Imaginative Writing* situate description and narration as elements in the autobiographical novel. The final eight chapters (on "narration with plot," dramatic plot, dramatic method, scene, opening and closing scenes) situate discursive elements in the forms of the short story, one-act play, historical romance, occult tales, and fairy and folk tales. A plot revolving around collision and conflict cannot, Bildersee notes, be written "on the scale of a novel" in the time remaining in a single academic term. She acknowledges that students "occasionally complete novels that they began in college courses" and "reach a much larger public than the college theme reader and the students' classmates. These, however, usually ripen during the long leisure of summer vacations" (114).

At the same time (and from a more local and immediate perspective), Bildersee's text might also be seen as a response to the call set out in Cone's 1908 departmental report for a "wider opportunity for the practice of higher composition and for the appreciative study of English literature than is afforded by our present arrangement of the course of study" (1). Bildersee introduces students to literature as a means of both improving their writing and inculcating in them (in rather Arnoldian fashion, admittedly) a refined sensibility for the finest in British and United States' culture.

> Sideshadow: Although many of Bildersee's examples of successful writing include selections of poetry and literary prose, many others are journalistic or expository in form and include selections from the *New York Times, Scribner's, Atlantic Monthly, Collier's,* and *Harper's Monthly.* Among those Bildersee cites as resources for young writers are poet Amy Lowell; humorist and newspaper columnist and editor Irvin S. Cobb; gothic writer, feminist, and literary critic Vernon Lee (Violet Paget); correspondent and diarist Lord George Allardice Riddell; Walter Bagehot, founder of the *National Review* and later editor-in-chief of the *Economist*; essayist and critic Logan Pearsall Smith (like Jeannette Gilder, a friend of Walt Whitman); Columbia professors Brander Matthews and John Erskine; columnist and critic Percy Lubbock; and William M. Tanner, author of *Essays and Essay-Writing* (1917) and *Composition and Rhetoric* (1922). Like Bildersee, Tanner advocated for "better English for immediate use, rather than the futile attempt to 'develop writers,'" as the goal of the writing textbook (iii).

Conclusion

By presenting and employing a sideshadowing historiographic methodology and narrative form based on the principles of acknowledgment, attribution, relationship, and situatedness, I sought in this essay to narrate the relationships and enlarge the contexts through which I presented Adele Bildersee and Helen Gray Cone. I sought to demonstrate the influence of the larger personal and cultural spheres in which their work took place; the significance of those spheres on their work, their lives, and the lives of those whom they taught and served; and the value of this kind of cultural and materialist study to understanding in a more complex and resonant fashion the history of English and writing studies. At the same time I sought to enact the ethical responsibility I have to the women whose lives I am narrating, "people whose experience it was [who] are no longer alive," who "did not always leave clear records of themselves" (Royster ix), celebrating the personal and professional relationships that made Bildersee's and Cone's work both meaningful and possible.

More specifically, I pledged that the sideshadowing methodology would show you "something else, something different" about Bildersee and *Imaginative Writing. Imaginative Writing* and Adele Bildersee may well hold notable positions in the history of creative or personal writing—but a sidelong glance, untethered from Berlin's expressivism (one that privileges the acknowledged, the attributed, the relational, the situated) reveals, as well, an author and text that are significant for their demonstrated commitment to students, writing instruction, and the normal school and its multiple missions to train teachers and prepare students for public service. *Imaginative Writing* is, as well, a testament, testimony, and gift: a testament to the Normal School and the values it instilled in its students and faculty; a testimony, a declaration to the colleagues, family, and friends who contributed to Bildersee's work; and a gift to Helen Gray Cone and us.

Note

I wish to acknowledge many individuals and institutions that assisted me in my research on this and other projects related to Hunter College. David Cooper and Marlies Danzinger directed me to William Omelchenko and Julio Hernandez-Delgado, who gave freely of their time, expertise, and the resources of the Hunter College Library and Archives. I am also indebted to the staff of the New York Public Library Rare Books and Manuscripts Collection. I am grateful, as well, for the financial support of The Ohio State University and the Elizabeth Gee Fund for Research on Women. I also wish to acknowledge the members of my writing group—Scott DeWitt, Beverly Moss, and Louie Ulman—to whom I owe a debt of friendship and thanks for their comments on my work. I also want to thank the students in my summer 2008 composition seminar at Ohio State University for their inspiring and challenging inquiries into the discipline and its history: Todd Alexander, Derek Boczkowski, Genevieve Critel, Jennifer Herman, Tim Jensen, Annie Mendenhall, Ryan Omizo, Paige Van Osdol, Julia Voss, and Tracey Ward. Finally, I wish to acknowledge the collection and series editors—Ann George, Elizabeth Weiser, Janet Zepernick, Cheryl Glenn, and Shirley Wilson Logan—for their incisive commentary and clarifying insight into this essay. "Long I followed happy guides."

WORKS CITED
CONTRIBUTORS
INDEX

Works Cited

Abbott, Lawrence F., ed. *Sixty American Opinions on the War.* London: T. F. Unwin, 1915. Print.
"Academy of Sciences Opens to a Woman." *New York Times* 17 May 1925: SM6. Print.
Addams, Jane. "Bayonet Charge" (or "The Revolt against War"). Elshtain, *Jane Addams Reader* 327–40. Print.
———. *Jane Addams: A Centennial Reader.* New York: Macmillan, 1960. Print.
———. *The Long Road of Woman's Memory.* 1916. Urbana: U of Illinois P, 2002. Print.
———. "A Modern Lear." *Jane Addams: A Centennial Reader* 31–34. Print.
———. "Our National Self Righteousness." *Jane Addams: A Centennial Reader* 442–48. Print.
———. *Peace and Bread in Times of War.* 1922. Urbana: U of Illinois P, 2002. Print.
———. *The Second Twenty Years at Hull House.* New York: Macmillan, 1930. Print.
———. *Twenty Years at Hull House.* 1910. New York: Penguin, 1960. Print.
Albertson, Chris. *Bessie.* New Haven: Yale UP, 2003. Print.
Alcorn, Marshall W. "Self-Structure as a Rhetorical Device: Modern *Ethos* and the Divisiveness of the Self." *Ethos: New Essays in Rhetorical and Critical Theory.* Ed. James S. Baumlin and Tita French Baumlin. Dallas: Southern Methodist UP, 1994. 3–35. Print.
"Along the Editor's Trail." *American Girl* Apr. 1925: 50. Print.
"Alumni News: A Century of Strong Hunter Women." *At Hunter* (Spring 2007): 10.
"Amelia Earhart Weds G. P. Putnam: Woman Flier and Publisher Wed." *New York Times* 7 Feb. 1931: 1. Print.
Ammons, Elizabeth. *Conflicting Stories: American Women Writers at the Turn into the Twentieth Century.* New York: Oxford UP, 1992. Print.
Anderson, Dana. *Identity's Strategies.* Columbia: U of South Carolina P, 2007. Print.
"Anderson Decries Our 'Speakeasy' Era." *New York Times* 7 Dec. 1931: 24. Print.
"Ann Axtell Morris." Obituary. *American Antiquity* 11.2 (Oct. 1945): 117. Print.
"Approve and Oppose Her." *New York Times* 2 Mar 1933. *New York Times Archive.* Web. 4 Mar. 2009.
Aristotle. *Rhetoric.* Trans. W. Rhys Roberts. New York: Modern Library, 1954. Print.
"At 50, Helen Keller Is Hailed as a Marvel of Attainment." *Kansas City Star* 22 June 1930: 4C. *Access Newspaper Archive.* Web. 11 Aug. 2008.
At Hunter Collection, 1914–2010. Archives and Special Collections, Hunter College Libraries, Hunter College of the City University of New York, N.Y. Print.

Atkinson, Ann J. "The Rhetoric of Social Security and Conservative Backlash: Frances Perkins as Secretary of Labor." *American Rhetoric in the New Deal Era, 1932–1945: A Rhetorical History of the United States.* Ed. Thomas W. Benson. East Lansing: Michigan State UP, 2006: 211–43. Print.

"Aviatrix Must Sign Away Life to Learn Trade." *Chicago Defender* 8 Oct. 1921: 2. Print.

Bacon, Josephine Daskam, ed. *Scouting for Girls: Official Handbook of the Girl Scouts.* New York: Girl Scouts of America, 1920. Print.

Baden-Powell, Robert. *Scouting for Boys: A Handbook for Instruction in Good Citizenship.* London: E. C. Horace Cox, 1908. Print.

Behdad, Ali. "INS and Outs: Producing Delinquency at the Border." *Aztlán: A Journal of Chicano Studies* 23.1 (1998): 103–13. Print.

Benedict, Ruth. Letters to Elsie Clews Parsons. Elsie Clews Parsons Papers. American Philosophical Society, Philadelphia, PA. Print.

Berlin, James. *Rhetoric and Reality: Writing Instruction in American Colleges, 1900–1985.* Carbondale: Southern Illinois UP, 1987. Print.

Bernardin, Susan. "On the Meeting Grounds of Sentiment: S. Alice Callahan's *Wynema: A Child of the Forest.*" *American Transcendental Quarterly* 15.3 (2001): 209–25. Print.

"Bessie Gets Away; Does Her Stuff." *Chicago Defender* 9 Sept. 1922: 3. Print.

"Bessie Smith's Revue." *Chicago Defender* 7 Aug. 1926, Nat. ed.: 8. Print.

Bible. Douay-Rheims American Edition, 1899. Print.

Biesecker, Barbara. "Coming to Terms with Recent Attempts to Write Women into the History of Rhetoric." *Philosophy and Rhetoric* 25.2 (1992): 140–61. Print.

Bildersee, Adele. *Imaginative Writing: An Illustrated Course for Students.* Boston: D. C. Heath, 1927. Print.

———. "Long I Followed Happy Guides." *Hunter College Bulletin* 8 March 1934: 7. Print.

———. "State Scholarship Studies at Hunter College of the City of New York." Diss. Columbia University, 1932. Print.

Bildersee, Dorothy. *Teaching the Primary Grades.* New York: D. Appleton-Century, 1932. Print.

Bix, Amy Sue. "Bessie Coleman: Race and Gender Realities behind Aviation Dreams." *Realizing the Dream of Flight: Biographical Essays in Honor of the Centennial of Flight, 1903–2003.* Ed. Virginia P. Dawson and Mark D. Bowles. Washington: National Aeronautics and Space Administration, 2003. 1–28. Print.

Bizzell, Patricia. "Opportunities for Feminist Research in the History of Rhetoric." *Rhetoric Review* 11.1 (1992): 50–58. Print.

Bonnin, Gertrude [Zitkala-Ša], Charles H. Fabens, and Matthew K. Sniffen. *Oklahoma's Poor Rich Indians: An Orgy of Graft and Exploitation of the Five Civilized Tribes—Legalized Robbery.* Philadelphia: Indian Rights Assoc., 1924. Print.

"Books." *Washington Post* 4 Nov. 1933: 12. Print.

Braddy, Nella. Foreword. *Midstream: My Later Life.* By Helen Keller. Garden City: Doubleday, 1929. ix–xxii. Print.

Brent, Doug. "Young, Becker and Pike's 'Rogerian' Rhetoric: A Twenty-Year Reassessment." *College English* 53.4 (1991): 452–65.
Brewton, Vince. "Helen Keller." *Dictionary of Literary Biography*. Vol. 303: *American Radical and Reform Writers*. Ed. Steven Rosedale. 2004. *Gale Literary Database*. Web. 13 Aug. 2008.
Brody, Seymour. "Annie Nathan Meyer." *Jewish Virtual Library*. American-Israeli Cooperative Enterprise, n.d. Web. 10 Aug. 2008.
"Brooklyn College Girls Evade Ban on Thomas; Hear Socialist Outside during Lunch Hour." *New York Times* 17 Oct. 1930: 21. Print.
Brooks, Evelyn. "Religion, Politics, and Gender: The Leadership of Nannie Helen Burroughs." *Journal of Religious Thought* 44.2 (1988): 7–22. Print.
Brooks, Van Wyck. "On Creating a Usable Past." *Dial* 66 (Apr. 1918): 337–41. Print.
Brown, Marjorie M. *Philosophical Studies of Home Economics in the United States: Our Practical-Intellectual Heritage*. Vol. 1. East Lansing: College of Human Ecology, Michigan State UP, 1985. 2 vols. Print.
Bruce, Alice Ruth. "I Aim to Be—" *Washington Post* 19 Sept. 1937: PY2. Print.
Bryant, Louise Stevens. "Educational Work of the Girl Scouts." Dept. of the Interior, Bureau of Education. Bulletin 46 (1921): 3–14. Print.
Bufwack, Mary, and Robert Oermann. *Finding Her Own Voice: Women in Country Music, 1800-2000*. Nashville: Vanderbilt UP, 2003. Print.
Bunzel, Ruth. Letter to Elsie Clews Parsons. 16 July 1934. Elsie Clews Parsons Papers. American Philosophical Society, Philadelphia, PA.
Burke, Kenneth. *Attitudes toward History*. 1937. 3rd rev. ed. Berkeley: U of California P, 1984. Print.
———. "Boring from Within." *New Republic* 4 Feb. 1931: 326–29. Print.
———. *Language as Symbolic Action: Essays on Life, Literature, and Method*. Berkeley: U of California P, 1966. Print.
———. *Permanence and Change: An Anatomy of Purpose*. 1935. 3rd rev. ed. Berkeley: U of California P, 1984. Print.
———. *The Philosophy of Literary Form: Studies in Symbolic Action*. 1941. 3rd rev. ed. Berkeley: U of California P, 1973. Print.
———. "Revolutionary Symbolism in America." 1935. *The Legacy of Kenneth Burke*. Ed. Herbert W. Simons and Trevor Melia. Madison: U of Wisconsin P, 1989. 267–73. Print.
———. *A Rhetoric of Motives*. 1950. Berkeley: U of California P, 1969. Print.
———. "Terministic Screens." *Language as Symbolic Action* 44–62. Print.
Burnier, DeLysa. "Erased History: Frances Perkins and the Emergence of Care-Centered Public Administration." *Administration and Society* 40.4 (2008): 403–22. <http://aas.sagepub.com> Web. 23 Apr. 2009.
———. "Frances Perkins' Disappearance from American Public Administration: A Genealogy of Marginalization." *Administrative Theory and Praxis* 30.4 (2008): 398–423. Print.
Burr, Amelia Josephine. "Poet to Poet." *Hunter College Bulletin* 8 March 1934: 4.
Burroughs, Nannie Helen. "Black Women and Reform." *Crisis* 10 (1915): 178–87. Print.
———. "Nannie H. Burroughs Says Hound Dogs Are Kicked but Not Bulldogs." *Afro-American* 17 (1934): N. pag. Print.

———. "What Must the Negro Do to Be Saved?" *Louisiana Weekly* 23 (1933): N. pag. Print.

———. "What the Negro Wants Politically." *From Megaphones to Microphones: Speeches of American Women, 1920–1960*. Ed. Sandra Sarkela, Susan Ross, and Margaret Lowe. Westport: Praeger, 2003. 46–47. Print.

———. "With All Thy Getting." *Southern Workman* July 1927: 301. Print.

Butler, Ellis Parker. Girl Scout News Bureau: Weekly Girl Scout Feature. 4 Jan. 1923. TS. Winthrop University Archives, Rock Hill, S.C.

Butler, Judith. "Imitation and Gender Insubordination." *Feminist Literary Theory and Criticism: A Norton Reader*. Ed. Sandra M. Gilbert and Susan Gubar. New York: Norton, 2007. 708–22. Print.

Cades, Hazel Rawson. *Jobs for Girls*. New York: Harcourt Brace, 1930. Print.

Campbell, Olive, and Cecil Sharp, eds. *English Folksongs from the Southern Appalachians*. New York: Knickerbocker, 1917. *Internet Archive*. New York Public Lib., 5 July 2007. Web. 3 Mar. 2009.

Carpenter, Cari. *Seeing Red: Anger, Sentimentality, and American Indians*. Columbus: Ohio State UP, 2008. Print.

Catholic Worker Movement. <www.catholicworker.org/index.cfm>. 1 Dec. 2008. Web. 5 Mar. 2009.

Cermak, May. "Her Interest in Social Service." *Hunter College Bulletin* 8 March 1934: 6.

Chapman, Margaret, and Marie E. Gaudette. *Girl Scout Handbook: Intermediate Program*. New York: Girl Scouts of America, 1947. Print.

"Cheer War Poems by Miss Marlowe." *New York Times* 27 May 1916: 9. Print.

Chiarello, Barbara. "Deflected Missives: Zitkala-Sa's Resistance and Its (Un)Containment." *Studies in American Indian Literatures* 17.3 (2005): 1–26. *Project Muse*. Web. 6 June 2010.

Child, Francis James. *English and Scottish Popular Ballads*. 1904. New York: Folklore, 1958. Print.

Christoph, Julie Nelson. "Reconceiving *Ethos* in Relation to the Personal: Strategies of Placement in Pioneer Women's Writing." *College English* 64.6 (2002): 660–79. Print.

Claassen, Cheryl, ed. *Women in Archaeology*. Philadelphia: U of Pennsylvania P, 1994. Print.

Clark, Gregory. "Kenneth Burke, Identification, and Rhetorical Criticism in the Writing Classroom." Conference on College Composition and Communication. Phoenix, AZ. 13 Mar. 1997. <www.cla.purdue.edu/dblakesley/burke/clark.html>. Web. 20 July 2009.

Cleveland, Reginald. "Woman Pilot Killed Racing at 200-Mi. Clip." *New York Times* 5 Sept. 1933: 1, 15. Print.

Cohen, Paula Marantz. "Helen Keller and the American Myth." *Yale Review* 85.1 (1997): 1–20. Print.

Cohen, Ronald, and Dave Samuelson. *Songs for Political Action: Folk Music, Topical Songs, and the American Left, 1926–1954*. Hambergen: Bear Family Records, 1996. Print.

Cone, Helen Gray. "Arraignment." *Scribner's Magazine* May 1888: 617–18. Print.

———. "A Chant of Love for England." Rpt. in *Hunter College Bulletin* 8 Mar. 1934: 7. Print.

———. "Report of the English Department (College)." Mar. 1909. MS. English Department Collection, 1908–56. Archives and Special Collections, Hunter College Libraries, Hunter College of the City University of New York. Print.

———. "Report of the English Department (College)." 1 Jan. 1912. MS. English Department Collection, 1908–1956. Archives and Special Collections, Hunter College Libraries, Hunter College of the City University of New York. Print.

———. "Woman in American Literature." *Century Illustrated Magazine* Oct. 1890: 921–31. Print.

Cone, Helen Gray, and Jeannette L. Gilder, eds. *Pen-Portraits of Literary Women by Themselves and Others.* 2 vols. New York: Cassell, 1887. Print.

"Conference Backs Social Security." *New York Times* 9 Apr. 1935. *New York Times Archive.* Web. 4 Mar. 2009.

Cook, M. Grant. "Helen Keller." Rev. of *Midstream*, by Helen Keller. *Times Literary Supplement* 16 Jan. 1930: 36. *TLS Centenary Archive.* Web. 13 Aug. 2008.

Cope, Persis. "The Women of 'Who's Who': A Statistical Study." *Social Forces* 7.2 (1928): 212–23. Print.

Cornell, Thomas, Robert Ellsberg, and Jim Forest, eds. *A Penny a Copy: Readings from "The Catholic Worker."* Maryknoll: Orbis Books, 1995. Print.

Cotera, María E. Introduction. *Life along the Border: A Landmark Tejana Thesis.* By Jovita González. Ed. María E. Cotera. College Station: Texas A&M UP, 2006. Print.

———. *Native Speakers: Ella Deloria, Zora Neale Hurston, Jovita González, and the Poetics of Culture.* Austin: U of Texas P, 2008. Print.

Cott, Nancy. "Across the Great Divide: Women in Politics before and after 1920." *Women, Politics, and Change.* Ed. Louise Tilly and Patricia Gurin. New York: Russell Sage Foundation, 1990. 153–76. Print.

Crawford, H. Jean. "The Association to Aid Scientific Research by Women." *Science* 76.1978 (1935): 492–93. Print.

Crow, Liz. "Helen Keller: Rethinking the Problematic Icon." *Disability and Society* 15.6 (2000): 845–59. Print.

Crowley, Sharon. *Toward a Civil Discourse: Rhetoric and Fundamentalism.* Pittsburgh: U of Pittsburgh P, 2006. Print.

Cucullu, Lois. "Exceptional Women, Expert Culture, and the Academy." *Rhetorical Women: Roles and Representations.* Ed. Hildy Miller and Lillian Bridwell-Bowles. Tuscaloosa: U of Alabama P, 2005. 158–86. Print.

Danisch, Robert. *Pragmatism, Democracy, and the Necessity of Rhetoric.* Columbia: U of South Carolina P, 2007. Print.

Davidson, Cathy N., and Ada Norris. Introduction. *Zitkala-Ša: American Indian Stories, Legends, and Other Writings.* By Zitkala-Ša. New York: Penguin, 2003. xi–xl. Print.

Davis, Angela. *Blues Legacies and Black Feminism: Gertrude "Ma" Rainey, Bessie Smith, and Billie Holiday.* New York: Pantheon Books, 1998. Print.

———. *Women, Race, and Class.* New York: Vintage Books, 1983. Print.

Davis, Richard Harding. Letter. *New York Times* 13 July 1915: B1. Print.

Day, Dorothy. "And Now a Note of Melancholy." *Catholic Worker* Nov. 1933. Rpt. in Day, *By Little and By Little* 54–55.

———. "A Baby Is Born." *Catholic Worker* Jan. 1941. Rpt. in Cornell, Ellsberg, and Forest 33–35.
———. *By Little and By Little: The Selected Writings of Dorothy Day*. Ed. David Ellsberg. New York: Alfred A. Knopf, 1983. Print.
———. "Catholics Have No United Front with William R. Hearst." *Catholic Worker* Jan. 1936. Rpt. in Cornell, Ellsberg, and Forest 20–21.
———. "Catholic Worker Celebrates 3rd Birthday; A Restatement of C. W. Aims and Ideals." *Catholic Worker* May 1936. Rpt. in the Dorothy Day Library on the Web. 15 June 2010.
———. "Days with an End." *Catholic Worker* Apr. 1933. Rpt. in the Dorothy Day Library on the Web. 15 June 2010.
———. "Editorial—Mid-Winter." *Catholic Worker* Jan. 1935. Rpt. in Cornell, Ellsberg, and Forest 18–29.
———. "Farming Commune." *Catholic Worker* Oct. 1938. Rpt. in the Dorothy Day Library on the Web. 15 June 2010.
———. *From Union Square to Rome*. Silver Spring, MD: Preservation of the Faith, 1938. Print.
———. *House of Hospitality*. New York: Sheed and Ward, 1939. Print.
———. "The Listener." *Catholic Worker* June–July 1933. Rpt. in Zwick and Zwick 24.
———. "Liturgy and Sociology." *Catholic Worker* Dec. 1935. Rpt. in the Dorothy Day Library on the Web. 15 June 2010.
———. "A Long Editorial but It Could Be Longer." *Catholic Worker* Feb. 1935. Rpt. in the Dorothy Day Library on the Web. 15 June 2010.
———. *The Long Loneliness*. New York: Harper, 1952. Print.
———. "Mary Is Fifteen." *Catholic Worker* May 1933. Rpt. in Cornell, Ellsberg, and Forest 4–6.
———. "Michael Martin, Porter." *Catholic Worker* Apr. 1937. Rpt. in Day, *By Little and By Little*. 81–82.
———. "Mysteries." *Catholic Worker* Dec. 1936. Rpt. in Day, *By Little and By Little*. 78–79.
———. "San Gennaro Festa Scene on Mott St." *Catholic Worker* Oct. 1939. Rpt. in the Dorothy Day Library on the Web. 15 June 2010.
———. "Scavengers." *Catholic Worker* Nov. 1933. Rpt. in Day, *By Little and By Little*. 57–58.
———. "To Our Readers." *Catholic Worker* May 1933. Rpt. in Cornell, Ellsberg, and Forest 3–4.
———. "Why Write about Strife and Violence?" *Catholic Worker* June 1934. Rpt. in Day, *By Little and By Little*. 62–63.
Deacon, Desley. *Elsie Clews Parsons: Inventing Modern Life*. Chicago: U of Chicago P, 1997. Print.
Denisoff, Serge. *Great Day Coming: Folk Music and the American Left*. Urbana: U of Illinois P, 1971. Print.
Des Jardins, Julie. *Women and the Historical Enterprise in America: Gender, Race, and the Politics of Memory, 1880–1945*. Chapel Hill: U of North Carolina P, 2003. Print.
Donawerth, Jane. Introduction. *Rhetorical Theory by Women before 1900: An Anthology*. Lanham: Rowan & Littlefield, 2002. xiii–xlii. Print.

"Dorothy Bildersee Dead at 86; Headed Principals Association." *New York Times* 4 Jan. 1972: 36. Print.

Dorothy Day Library on the Web. <http://www.catholicworker.org/dorothyday/>. Web. 15 June 2010.

Dos Passos, John. "Harlan: Working under the Gun." *New Republic* 2 Dec. 1931: 62–67. Print.

Downey, Aurelia. *Addresses for Woman's Day*. Washington: Nannie Burroughs Publ., 1976. Print.

Downey, Kirstin. *The Woman behind the New Deal: The Life of Frances Perkins, FDR's Secretary of Labor and His Moral Conscience*. New York: Doubleday, 2009. Print.

"Dr. Adele Bildersee Ex-Brooklyn Dean." *New York Times* 20 Nov. 1971: 34. Print.

"Dr. Bildersee Dies; Education Aide, 65." *New York Times* 24 Aug. 1952: 88. Print.

"Dr. Ladd-Franklin Eulogized at Funeral." *New York Times* 8 Mar. 1930: 11. *Historical New York Times*. Web. 7 June 2008.

Du Bois, W. E. B. "The Souls of Black Folks." *The Oxford W. E. B. Du Bois Reader*. Ed. Eric J. Sundquist. New York: Oxford UP, 1996. 97–240. Print.

Duke, David. *Writers and Miners: Activism and Imagery in America*. Lexington: UP of Kentucky, 2002. Print.

Earhart, Amelia. "Answers to Some Questions about Flying." *Hearst's International Combined with Cosmopolitan* Dec. 1928: 30–31. Print.

———. "Fly America First." *Hearst's International Combined with Cosmopolitan* Oct. 1929: 80–81, 134–36. Print.

———. *For the Fun of It: Random Records of My Own Flying and of Women in Aviation*. Chicago: Academy Chicago, 1932. Print.

———. "Mrs. Lindbergh." *Hearst's International Combined with Cosmopolitan* July 1930: 78–79, 196–98. Print.

———. "On What a Pilot Eats." Unpublished essay. [1935–37.] ID AEPb1f4i1. MS. George Palmer Putnam Collection of Amelia Earhart Papers. Purdue University Libraries, Archives and Special Collections, West Lafayette, IN.

———. "Try Flying Yourself." *Hearst's International Combined with Cosmopolitan* Nov. 1928: 32–35, 159–60. Print.

———. *20 Hrs. 40 Min.: Our Flight in the Friendship*. New York: Knickerbocker, 1928. Print.

———. "Vagabonding by Air." *Hearst's International Combined with Cosmopolitan* Dec. 1928: 28–29, 195–96. Print.

———. "Why Are Women Afraid to Fly?" *Hearst's International Combined with Cosmopolitan* July 1929: 70–71, 138, 140. Print.

Easter, Opal V. *Nannie Helen Burroughs*. New York: Garland, 1995. Print.

Eblen, Anna, and Colleen Kelley, eds. *Women Who Speak for Peace*. New York: Rowman, 2001. Print.

Editorial. *New York Times* 17 Sept. 1917: B2. Print.

Edwards, Ron. "Bessie Coleman, a Young Woman with the Right Stuff, Became a Flying Role Model for African Americans." *Aviation History* Nov. 1988: 8–10. Print.

Einhorn, Lois J. *Helen Keller, Public Speaker: Sightless but Seen, Deaf but Heard*. Westport: Greenwood, 1998. Print.

Elliot, Ralph. "Bessie Coleman Says Good Will Come from Hurt: Wants World to Know She Will Fly Again." *Chicago Defender* 10 Mar. 1923: 3. Print.

Elshtain, Jean Bethke. *Jane Addams and the Dream of American Democracy*. New York: Basic Books, 2002. Print.

———, ed. *The Jane Addams Reader*. New York: Basic Books, 2001. Print.

Elsie Clews Parsons Papers. American Philosophical Society, Philadelphia, PA.

Emerson, Ralph Waldo. "Forerunners." *Early Poems of Ralph Waldo Emerson*. New York: Thomas Y. Crowell, 1899. Print.

"English X." 1914. MS. English Department Collection, 1908–56. Archives and Special Collections, Hunter College Libraries, Hunter College of the City University of New York.

Enoch, Jessica. *Refiguring Rhetorical Education: Women Teaching African American, Native American, and Chicano/a American Students, 1865–1911*. Carbondale: Southern Illinois UP, 2008. Print.

Evans, David. "Bessie Smith's 'Back-Water Blues': The Story behind the Song." *Popular Music* 26.1 (2007): 97–116. Print.

"Examination of Candidates." 1893. MS. Archives and Special Collections, Hunter College Libraries, Hunter College of the City University of New York.

"Examination of Seniors." 1893. MS. Archives and Special Collections, Hunter College Libraries, Hunter College of the City University of New York.

Fahnestock, Jeanne. "Accommodating Science: The Rhetorical Life of Scientific Facts." *Written Communication* 15.3 (1998): 330–50. Print.

Faludi, Susan. "Second-Place Citizens." *New York Times* 25 Aug. 2008. *NYTimes.com*. Web. 11 Sept. 2009.

———. *The Terror Dream: Fear and Fantasy in Post-9/11 America*. New York: Metropolitan, 2007. Print.

Farrington, Dora Davis. *The Essay: How to Study and Write It*. Richmond: Johnson, 1924. Print.

———. "A World without a Seam." *Hunter College Bulletin* 8 Mar. 1934: 6. Print.

Feld, Rose C. "Back to the Kitchen? Woman Says 'No': She Is Determined to Hold Fast to Her Freedom, but Finds Herself Facing Obstacles." *New York Times* 9 June 1935. *New York Times Archive*. Web. 4 Mar. 2009.

Ferris, Helen. Letter to Ann Axtell Morris. 1 May 1931. MS. Elizabeth Ann Morris and the Morris Family Collections. Bayfield, CO.

Filene, Benjamin. *Romancing the Folk: Public Memory and American Roots Music*. Chapel Hill: U of North Carolina P, 2000. Print.

Filene, Catherine. *Careers for Women*. Boston: Houghton, 1920. Print.

"Finding America's Past." Rev. of *Digging in the Southwest*, by Ann Axtell Morris. *New York Times* 19 Nov. 1933: BR23. Print.

Fisher, Dexter. Foreword. *American Indian Stories*. By Zitkala-Ša. Lincoln: U of Nebraska P, 1985. Print.

Fisher, Donald. *Fundamental Development of the Social Sciences: Rockefeller Philanthropy and the United States Social Science Research Council*. Ann Arbor: U of Michigan P, 1993. Print.

Fleischman, Doris E. *Careers for Women: A Practical Guide to Opportunity for Women in American Business*. New York: Garden City, 1939. Print.

Foner, Philip S., ed. *Helen Keller: Her Socialist Years*. New York: International Publ., 1967. Print.
Fowler, Don. *A Laboratory for Anthropology: Science and Romanticism in the American Southwest, 1846–1930*. Albuquerque: U of New Mexico P, 2000. Print.
Frazier, E. Franklin. *The Negro Family in the United States*. Notre Dame: U of Notre Dame P, 2001. Print.
Friedan, Betty. *The Feminine Mystique*. 1963. New York: Norton: 2001. Print.
Gacs, Ute, Aisha Khan, Jerrie McIntyre, and Ruth Weinberg, eds. *Women Anthropologists: A Biographical Dictionary*. New York: Greenwood, 1988. Print.
Garza-Falcón, Leticia. *Gente Decente: A Borderlands Response to the Rhetorics of Dominance*. Austin: U of Texas P, 1998. Print.
Gates, Barbara T., and Ann B. Shteir, eds. *Natural Eloquence: Women Reinscribe Science*. Madison: U of Wisconsin P, 1997. Print.
Gay, Lucy. Letter to Miss Wales. 15 Mar. 1915. Julia Grace Wales Papers. Madison: State Historical Society of Wisconsin.
"General Johnson Takes Fling at Richberg." *New York Times* 22 Jan. 1935. *New York Times Archive*. Web. 4 Mar. 2009.
George, Ann, and Jack Selzer. *Kenneth Burke in the 1930s*. Columbia: U of South Carolina P, 2007. Print.
Gere, Anne Ruggles. *Intimate Practices: Literacy and Cultural Work in U.S. Women's Clubs, 1880—1920*. Chicago: U of Illinois P, 1997. Print.
Gieryn, Thomas. *Cultural Boundaries of Science: Credibility on the Line*. Chicago: U of Chicago P, 1999. Print.
Gilder, Jeannette. "Why I Am Opposed to Woman's Suffrage." *Harper's Bazaar* 19 May 1894: 399. Print.
Gilkes, Cheryl Townsend. *If It Wasn't for the Women: Black Women's Experience and Womanist Culture in Church and Community*. Maryknoll: Orbis, 2004. Print.
Glazer, Penina Migdal, and Miriam Slater. *Unequal Colleagues: The Entrance of Women into the Professions, 1890–1940*. New Brunswick: Rutgers UP, 1987. Print.
Glenn, Cheryl. *Rhetoric Retold: Regendering the Tradition from Antiquity through the Renaissance*. Carbondale: Southern Illinois UP, 1997. Print.
Goldberg, Myla. *Wickett's Remedy*. New York: Anchor, 2006. Print.
González, Jovita. *Dew on the Thorn*. Ed. José Limón. Houston: Arte Público, 1997. Print.
———. *Life along the Border: A Landmark Tejana Thesis*. Ed. María E. Cotera. College Station: Texas A&M UP, 2006. Print.
———. *Woman Who Lost Her Soul and Other Stories*. Ed. Sergio Reyna. Houston: Arte Público, 2000. Print.
Gornstien, Ken. "No Flight of Fancy: Bessie Coleman Earned Her Wings and Influenced a Generation of Black Pilots." *Northeastern University Magazine* 16.4 (1991): 19–21. Print.
Green, Archie. *Only a Miner: Studies in Recorded Coal-Mining Songs*. Urbana: U of Illinois P, 1972. Print.
Greenway, John. *American Folksongs of Protest*. Philadelphia: U of Pennsylvania P, 1953. Print.

———. "Aunt Molly Jackson and Robin Hood: A Study in Folk Re-Creation." *Journal of American Folklore* 69.271 (1956): 23–38. Print.
———. "Aunt Molly Jackson as an Informant." *Kentucky Folklore Record* 7.4 (1961): 141–46. Print.
Guthrie, Woody. "Hell Busts Loose in Kentucky." *Hard Hitting Songs for Hard Hit People*. Ed. Alan Lomax, Woody Guthrie, and Peter Seeger. New York: Oak, 1967. 139–40. Print.
Gutiérrez, David. *Walls and Mirrors: Mexican Americans, Mexican Immigrants, and the Politics of Ethnicity*. Berkeley: U of California P, 1995. Print.
Hagee, Alice Rogers. "Miss Perkins Talks of the Tasks Ahead." *New York Times* 7 May 1933. *New York Times Archive*. Web. 4 Mar. 2009.
Hahn, E. Adelaide. "The Fellowship of Goodwill: A Chapter in the Life of Helen Gray Cone." *Hunter College Bulletin* 8 March 1934: 6.
Handleman, Philip. "Armchair Aviator." *Yankee Wings* (Jan.–Feb. 1995): 20–22. Print.
Haraway, Donna. *Simians, Cyborgs, and Women: The Reinvention of Nature*. New York: Routledge, 1991. Print.
Harjo, Joy, and Gloria Bird, eds. *Reinventing the Enemy's Language: An Anthology of North American Native Women's Writing*. New York: Norton, 1998. Print.
Hauser, Gerard A. "Aristotle on Epideictic: The Formation of Public Morality." *Rhetoric Society Quarterly* 29.1 (1999): 5–23. Print.
Hayles, N. Katherine. "Flesh and Metal: Reconfiguring the Mindbody in Virtual Environments." *Data Made Flesh: Embodying Information*. Ed. Robert Mitchell and Phillip Thurtle. New York: Routledge, 2004. 229–48. Print.
———. *How We Became Posthuman: Virtual Bodies in Cybernetics, Literature, and Informatics*. Chicago: U of Chicago P, 1999. Print.
Heilbrun, Carolyn G. *Writing a Woman's Life*. New York: Ballantine Books, 1989. Print.
"Helen Keller Continues Her Remarkable Story." Rev. of *Midstream*, by Helen Keller. *New York Times* 27 Oct. 1929: BR5. Print.
"Here and There." *Mason City Globe-Gazette* 4 Feb. 1931: 18. *Access Newspaper Archive*. Web. 12 Aug. 2008.
Hess, Dorothea C. "Helen Gray Cone as Teacher." *Hunter College Bulletin* 8 March 1934: 4. Print.
Higginbotham, Evelyn Brooks. *Righteous Discontent: The Women's Movement in the Black Baptist Church, 1880–1920*. Cambridge: Harvard UP, 1993. Print.
Hine, Darlene Clark. *Hine Sight: Black Women and the Re-Construction of American History*. Bloomington: Indiana UP, 1994. Print.
———. "Rape and the Inner Lives of Black Women in the Middle West: Preliminary Thoughts on the Culture of Dissemblance." *Signs* 14.4 (1989): 912–20. Print.
Hoefer, George. "Bessie Smith." *The Jazz Makers*. Ed. Nat Shapiro and Nat Hentoff. Westport: Greenwood, 1975. 127–40. Print.
Hoerle, Helen Christine, and Florence B. Saltzberg. *The Girl and Her Job*. New York: Henry Holt, 1919. Print.
Hollis, Karyn L. *Liberating Voices: Writing at the Bryn Mawr Summer School for Women Workers*. Carbondale: Southern Illinois UP, 2004. Print.

Hopwood, Marion. "Woman Pilot Hits 200-Mile Clip." *Cleveland Plain Dealer* 2 Sept. 1932: 2. Print.
Horton, James Oliver. "Freedom's Yoke: Gender Conventions among Antebellum Free Blacks." *Feminist Studies* 12.1 (1986): 51–76. Print.
"How Mme. Curie Discovered Radium." *New York Times* 27 Feb. 1921: 7. *Historical New York Times*. Web. 7 June 2008.
Huber, Patrick. Rev. of *Pistol Packin' Mama: Aunt Molly Jackson and the Politics of Folksong*, by Shelly Romalis. *Southern Cultures* 7.4 (2001): 111–15. Print.
Hughes, Langston. "The Negro Artist and the Racial Mountain." *The Norton Anthology of African American Literature*. Ed. Henry Louis Gates and Nellie McKay. New York: Norton, 1997. 1267–71. Print.
Hunter, Tera. *To 'Joy My Freedom: Southern Black Women's Lives and Labors after the Civil War*. Cambridge: Harvard UP, 1997. Print.
Iber, Jorge, and Arnoldo De León. *Hispanics in the American West*. Santa Barbara: ABC-CLIO, 2006. Print.
"Ignore Sex in Jobs, Women Are Told." *New York Times* 30 Sept. 1929: 2. *Historical New York Times*. Web. 7 June 2008.
Inness, Sherrie A. "Girl Scouts, Camp Fire Girls, and Woodcraft Girls: The Ideology of Girls' Scouting Novels, 1910–1935." *Continuities in Popular Culture: The Present in the Past and the Past in the Present and Future*. Ed. Ray B. Browne and Ronald J. Ambrosetti. Bowling Green: Bowling Green State Popular, 1993. 229–40. Print.
Jablonski, Carol. "Declining Honors: Dorothy Day's Rhetorical Resistance to the Culture of Heroic Ascent." *Doing Rhetorical History: Concepts and Cases*. Ed. Kathleen J. Turner. Tuscaloosa: U of Alabama P, 1998. 191–206. Print.
Jack, Jordynn. *Science on the Home Front: American Women Scientists in World War II*. Champaign-Urbana: U of Illinois P, 2009. Print.
"Jack-knife." Weekly Girl Scout Feature: Girl Scout News Bureau. TS. 4 Jan. 1923. Winthrop University Archives, Rock Hill, S.C.
Jackson, Molly. "Molly Jackson Defines Folk Music Once and for All." Comp. Alex Luckey. *Kentucky Coal Mining Diva Aunt Molly Jackson: A Study of Folk Authenticity*. U of Virginia. May 2005. Web. 6 June 2008.
Jackson, Molly, and John Greenway. *The Songs and Stories of Aunt Molly Jackson: Stories Told by Aunt Molly Jackson/Songs Sung by John Greenway*. Liner Notes. New York: Folkway Records, 1961. Print.
Johnson, Edith. *To Women of the Business World*. Philadelphia: J. B. Lippincott, 1923. Print.
Johnson, Karen A. *Uplifting the Women and the Race: The Educational Philosophies and Social Activism of Anna Julia Cooper and Nannie Helen Burroughs*. New York: Garland, 2000. Print.
Johnson, Kristine. "Negotiating Radical Socialism and Orthodox Faith: Inclusive Rhetoric in the *Catholic Worker*." Rhetoric Society of America Conference. Westin Hotel, Seattle. 25 May 2008. Presentation.
Johnson, May Wright. "Bessie Smith." *Hear Me Talkin' to Ya: The Story of Jazz as Told by the Men Who Made It*. Ed. Nat Shapiro and Nat Hentoff. New York: Dover, 1966. 241–42. Print.

Johnson, Nan. *Gender and Rhetorical Space in American Life, 1866–1910*. Carbondale: Southern Illinois UP, 2002. Print.

Jones, Marguerite E. "Reminiscences." *Hunter College Bulletin* 8 March 1934: 5. Print.

Josephson, Hannah, and Matthew Josephson. *Al Smith, Hero of the Cities a Political Portrait Drawing on the Papers of Frances Perkins*. London: Thames and Hudson, 1969. Print.

Kehoe, Alice B., and Mary Beth Emmerichs, eds. *Assembling the Past: Studies in the Professionalization of Archaeology*. Albuquerque: U of New Mexico P, 1999. Print.

Keller, Evelyn Fox. "The Gender/Science System, or, Is Sex to Gender as Nature Is to Science?" *The Science Studies Reader*. Ed. Mario Biagioli. New York: Routledge, 1999. 234–42. Print.

Keller, Helen. "Blind Leaders." Nielsen, *Selected Writings* 55–66. Print.

———. *Midstream: My Later Life*. Garden City: Doubleday, 1929. Print.

———. "Put Your Husband in the Kitchen." *Atlantic Monthly* Aug. 1932: 140–47. Print.

———. "The Vaudeville Circuit, 1919–1924." Einhorn 106–8. Print.

———. "Why I Became an IWW." Foner 82–86. Print.

Kemper Adams, Elizabeth. *Women Professional Workers: A Study Made for the Women's Educational and Industrial Union*. New York: Macmillan, 1921. Print.

Kennedy, David M. *Freedom from Fear: The American People in Depression and War, 1929–1945*. New York: Oxford UP, 1999. Print.

Kill, Melanie. "Coordinating Networked Knowledge: Wikipedians, Genre, and the Pursuit of Digital Community." Rhetoric Society of America Conference. Minneapolis, 28 May 2010. Presentation.

Klingensmith, Florence. Letter to Unidentified Friend. Feb. 1932. MS. Ninety-Nines Museum of Women Pilots Collection. Oklahoma City.

"Knights Are Given Splendid Example of Mme. Curie." *Washington Post* 1930: JP5. Web. 7 June 2008.

Kroeber, Alfred. Letter to Elsie Clews Parsons. 13 Apr. 1929. MS. Elsie Clews Parsons Papers. American Philosophical Society, Philadelphia, PA.

Lather, Patti. *Getting Lost: Feminist Efforts toward a Double(d) Science*. Albany: State U of New York P, 2007. Print.

Lather, Patricia A., and Christine S. Smithies. *Troubling the Angels: Women Living with HIV/AIDS*. New York: Westview, 1997. Print.

Lawrence, Carol. "Julia Grace Wales: The Canadian Girl Who Has Won World-Wide Fame." *Woman's Century* (Dec. 1916): 8. Print.

Leo XIII. *Rerum Novarum*. Encyclical of Pope Leo XIII on Capital and Labor. 15 May 1891. Web. 12 Aug. 2007.

Lesser, Margaret. Letter to Ann Axtell Morris. 4 Jan. 1935. MS. Elizabeth Ann Morris and the Morris Family Collections. Bayfield, CO.

Leuck, Miriam Simons. *Fields of Work for Women*. New York: D. Appleton, 1926. Print.

Levine, Mary Ann. "Uncovering a Buried Past: Women in Americanist Archaeology before the First World War." Kehoe and Emmerichs 133–51. Print.

Lindsay, Jean S. "The Love for England." *Hunter College Bulletin*. 8 March 1934: 7. Print.

Lingenfelter, Mary Rebecca, and Harry Dexter Kitson. *Vocations for Girls*. New York: Harcourt, 1939. Print.

Lloyd, A. L. *Folk Song in England*. New York: International Pub., 1967. Print.

Locke, Alain. "The New Negro." *The New Negro*. Ed. Alain Locke. New York: Simon and Schuster, 1997. 3–16. Print.

Logan, Shirley Wilson. *"We Are Coming": The Persuasive Discourse of Nineteenth-Century Black Women*. Carbondale: Southern Illinois UP, 1999. Print.

Lomax, John, and Alan Lomax. *Our Singing Country: Folk Songs and Ballads*. New York: Macmillan, 1941. Print.

Long, Ray. "Powderpuffs for Men." *Hearst's International Combined with Cosmopolitan* July 1930: 1. Print.

Low, Juliette Gordon. "Girl Scouts as an Educational Force." Department of the Interior Bureau of Education. Bulletin 33 (1919): 3–8. Print.

Lurie, Nancy O. "Women in Early Anthropology." *Pioneers of American Anthropology*. Ed. June Helm. Seattle: U of Washington P, 1966. 29–81. Print.

Lynch, Timothy. *Strike Songs of the Depression*. Jackson: UP of Mississippi, 2001. Print.

"Madame Curie's Genius." *New York Times* 1 May 1921: 88. *Historical New York Times*. Web. 7 June 2008.

Marquez, Benjamin. *LULAC: The Evolution of a Mexican American Political Organization*. Austin: U of Texas P, 1984. Print.

Martin, George. *Madame Secretary, Frances Perkins*. Boston: Houghton, 1976. Print.

Marx, Karl. *Critique of the Gotha Programme*. 1875. Moscow: Progress Publishers, 1971. Print.

Masters, Thomas. *Practicing Writing: The Postwar Discourses of Freshman English*. Pittsburgh: U of Pittsburgh P, 2004. Print.

Mattingly, Carol. *Well-Tempered Women*. Carbondale: Southern Illinois UP, 1998. Print.

Maurin, Peter. "Easy Essays." Rpt. in *Cornell, Ellsberg, and Forest* 7–14. Print.

"May Day Is Quiet throughout World; 50,000 Parade Here." *New York Times* 2 May 1933: 1, 3. *Historical New York Times*. Web. 30 Sept. 2008.

McBride, Mary Margaret. "She's Only A Woman IN AIR BUREAU: Girl who Married Flying Teacher Works for Uncle Sam." *Pittsburgh Press* 19 Aug. 1934, Society sec.: 7. Print.

McLaughlin, Kathleen. "Creator for 'Invisible Glass' Woman of Many Interests." *New York Times* 24 Sept. 1939: 4D. *Historical New York Times*. Web. 7 June 2008.

Mead, Margaret. Introduction. *The Golden Age of American Anthropology*. Ed. Ruth Bunzel and Margaret Mead. New York: George Braziller, 1960. 1–13. Print.

Menand, Louis. *The Metaphysical Club*. New York: Farrar, Straus and Giroux, 2001. Print.

Meyer, Annie Nathan. "The Higher Education for Women in New York City." *Nation* 26 Jan. 1888: 64–68. Print.

———. *Woman's Work in America*. New York: Henry Holt, 1891. Print.

Michels, Anna W. "Helen Gray Cone's Taste in Literature." *Hunter College Bulletin* 8 March 1934: 3.
Miller, Carolyn. "Rhetorical Communities: The Cultural Basis of Genre." *Genre and the New Rhetoric*. Ed. Aviva Freedman and Peter Medway. Oxon, Eng.: Taylor, 1994. 67–78. Print.
Miller, Susan A. *Growing Girls: The Natural Origins of Girls' Organizations in America*. New Brunswick: Rutgers UP, 2007. Print.
"Miss Bildersee Appointed." *New York Times* 21 Jan. 1931: 23. Print.
"Miss Keller Seen as Symbol of Hope." *New York Times* 10 Apr. 1940: 33. Print.
"Miss Keller's Garden." *Aniston Star* 14 May 1930: 5. *Access Newspaper Archive*. Web. 12 Aug. 2008.
"Miss Keller Tells How Blind Progress." *New York Times* 6 Feb. 1913: 20. Print.
"Miss Perkins Cool under Green's Fire." *New York Times* 3 Mar. 1933. *New York Times Archive*. Web. 4 Mar. 2009.
Mitchell, Sally. *The New Girl: Girls' Culture in England, 1880–1915*. New York: Columbia UP, 1995. Print.
Mize, Sandra Yocum. "Dorothy Day: 'A Reason for the Faith That Is in Her.'" *University of Dayton Review* 23.1 (1994): 53–60. Print.
"Mme. Curie Plans to End All Cancers." *New York Times* 12 May 1921:1. *Historical New York Times*. Web. 7 June 2008.
Morris, Ann Axtell. *Digging in the Southwest*. New York: Doubleday/Junior Literary Guild, 1933. Print.
———. *Digging in Yucatan*. New York: Doubleday/Junior Literary Guild, 1931. Print.
———. Letter to Dorothy Bryan. 18 Mar. 1933. MS. Elizabeth Ann Morris and the Morris Family Collections. Bayfield, CO.
Morson, Gary Saul. *Narrative and Freedom: The Shadows of Time*. New Haven: Yale UP, 1994. Print.
———. "Who Speaks for Bakhtin? A Dialogic Introduction." *Critical Inquiry* 10.2 (1983): 225–43. Print.
Mournier, Emmanuel. *A Personalist Manifesto*. Trans. Monks of St. John's Abbey. New York: Longman, 1938. Print.
"National Academy." *Time* 6 May 1919: 1. *Time Magazine Online*. Web. 7 June 2008.
National Committee for the Defense of Political Prisoners. *Harlan Miners Speak: Report on Terrorism in the Kentucky Coal Fields*. 1932. Lexington: UP of Kentucky, 2008. Print.
"Negro Aviatrix Arrives." *New York Times* 14 Aug. 1922: 4. Print.
"New Children's Books." Rev. of *Digging in the Southwest*, by Ann Axtell Morris. *New York Times* 10 Dec. 1933: BR16. Print.
New York City Bureau of Vocational Information. *Women in Chemistry*. New York: Bureau of Vocational Information, 1922. Print.
Nielsen, Kim E., ed. *Helen Keller: Selected Writings*. New York: New York UP, 2005. Print.
———. *The Radical Lives of Helen Keller*. New York: New York UP, 2004. Print.
Paine, Charles. *The Resistant Writer: Rhetoric as Immunity, 1850 to the Present*. Albany: State U of New York P, 1999. Print.
Palmer, George Herbert. *Self-Cultivation in English*. Boston: Houghton, 1909.

Parezo, Nancy J., ed. *Hidden Scholars: Women Anthropologists and the Native American Southwest*. Albuquerque: U of New Mexico P, 1993. Print.
Parezo, Nancy J., and Margaret A. Hardin. "In the Realm of the Muses." Parezo 270–93. Print.
"Paris Pact Endorsed by Hunter Alumnae." *New York Times* 18 Nov. 1928: 26. Print.
Parsons, Elsie Clews. *American Indian Life by Several of Its Students*. 1922. Lincoln: U of Nebraska P, 1967. Print.
Patterson, Samuel White. *Hunter College: Eighty-Five Years of Service*. New York: Lantern, 1955. Print.
Pear, Robert. "Changing Stance, Administration Now Defends Insurance Mandate as a Tax." *New York Times* 18 July 2010. Times Reader Edition. Web. 18 July 2010.
Peirce, Adah, and W. W. Charters. *Vocations for Women*. New York: Macmillan, 1933. Print.
Peirce, Charles S. "What Pragmatism Is." *Selected Writings*. Ed. Philip Weiner. New York: Dover, 1958. Print.
Perelman, Chaim, and Lucie Olbrechts-Tyteca. *The New Rhetoric: A Treatise on Argumentation*. Notre Dame: U of Notre Dame P, 1969. Print.
Perkins, Frances. Interview by Dean Albertson. *Notable New Yorkers*. Columbia University Libraries Oral History Research Office, 2006. Web. 11 Aug. 2012.
Perkins, Frances. *The Roosevelt I Knew*. New York: Viking, 1946. Print.
Perkins, Lolita C. "Nannie Helen Burroughs: A Progressive Example for Modern Times." *Affilia* 12 (1997): 229–39. Print.
Piehl, Mel. *Breaking Bread: The* Catholic Worker *and the Origin of Catholic Radicalism in America*. Philadelphia: Temple UP, 1982. Print.
Pitkin, Walter B. *New Careers for Youth: Today's Job Outlook for Men and Women from Seventeen to Thirty-Two*. New York: Simon, 1934. Print.
Pittman, Coretta. "Black Women Writers and the Trouble with *Ethos*: Harriet Jacobs, Billie Holiday, and Sister Souljah." *Rhetoric Society Quarterly* 37.1 (2007): 43–70. Print.
Pius XI. *Quadragesimo Anno*. Encyclical of Pope Pius XI, On Reconstruction of the Social Order. 15 May 1931. Web. 12 Aug. 2007.
"Plans Drive to Aid U.N." *New York Times* 16 Oct. 1955: 120. Print.
"President Wilson to Get Woman's Plans for Peace." *St. Louis Post Dispatch* 13 Mar. 1915: N. pag. Julia Grace Wales Papers. State Historical Society of Wisconsin, Madison. Print.
"Pupils Can Carol Now." *New York Times* 9 Dec. 1947: 31. Print.
Quicke, J. C. "'Speaking Out': The Political Career of Helen Keller." *Disability, Handicap and Society* 3.2 (1998): 167–71. Print.
"Radium Gift Awaits Mme. Curie Here." *New York Times* 7 Feb. 1921: 10. *Historical New York Times*. Web. 7 June 2008.
"Radium Presented to Madame Curie." *New York Times* 21 May 1921: 12. *Historical New York Times*. Web. 7 June 2008.
"'Ravelings from the Green and Gold' at Camp Agnes Ann." TS. June 1925. Winthrop University Archives, Rock Hill, SC.
Reichard, Gladys. Collection. Museum of Northern Arizona, Flagstaff.

———. Letter to Ann Axtell Morris. 5 Dec. 1932. MS. Elizabeth Ann Morris and the Morris Family Collections. Bayfield, CO.
———. Letters to Elsie Clews Parsons. Elsie Clews Parsons Papers. American Philosophical Society, Philadelphia, PA.
Reilly, Joseph J. "From the Librarian." *Hunter College Bulletin* 8 March 1934: 1+. Print.
"Religious Carol-Singing Barred from 23 of Brooklyn's Schools." *New York Times* 5 Dec. 1947: 1+. Print.
Reuss, Richard. *American Folk Music and Left-Wing Politics, 1927–1957*. Lanham: Scarecrow, 2000. Print.
Reyna, Sergio. Introduction. *Woman Who Lost Her Soul and Other Stories*. By Jovita Gonzalez. Ed. Reyna. Houston: Arte Público, 2000. Print.
"Rhetorics and Feminisms: The Remix." Conference on College Composition and Communication, Lexington, 19 Mar. 2010. Panel Presentations.
Rice, Jeff. "The 1963 Composition Revolution Will Not Be Televised, Computed, or Demonstrated by Any Other Means." *Composition Studies* 33.1 (2005): 55–73. Print.
Rich, Adrienne. "The Eye of the Outsider: The Poetry of Elizabeth Bishop." *Boston Review* Apr. 1983: 15–17. Print
Rich, Doris. *Queen Bess: Daredevil Aviator*. Washington: Smithsonian Institution, 1993. Print.
Richards, I. A. *The Philosophy of Rhetoric*. New York: Oxford UP, 1936. Print.
Richison, Margie. "Florence Klingensmith: She Set a Dizzying World Record of 1,078 Inside Loops." *International Women Pilots Magazine/99 News* Mar./Apr. 2005: 8–9. Print.
Rideing, William H. "The Normal College of New York City." *Harper's New Monthly Magazine* 28 Apr. 1878: 672–83. Print.
Ritchie, Joy, and Kate Ronald. *Available Means: An Anthology of Women's Rhetoric(s)*. Pittsburgh: U of Pittsburgh P, 2001. Print.
Roberson, Susan L. "Jeannette Gilder." *Walt Whitman: An Encyclopedia*. Ed. J. R. LeMaster and Donald D. Kummings. New York: Oxford UP, 1998. Print.
"Rockefeller Retirements." *Time* 24 Apr. 1939: 58. *Time Magazine Online*. Web. 7 June 2008.
Romalis, Shelly. *Pistol Packin' Mama: Aunt Molly Jackson and the Politics of Folksong*. Urbana: U of Illinois P, 2000. Print.
Ross, Dorothy. *The Origins of American Social Science*. Cambridge: Cambridge UP, 1991. Print.
Rossiter, Margaret W. *Women Scientists in America: Struggles and Strategies to 1940*. Baltimore: Johns Hopkins UP, 1982. Print.
Royster, Jacqueline Jones. "To Call a Thing by Its True Name: The Rhetoric of Ida B. Wells." *Reclaiming Rhetorica: Women in the Rhetorical Tradition*. Ed. Andrea A. Lunsford. Pittsburgh: U of Pittsburgh P, 1995. 167–84. Print.
———. *Traces of a Stream: Literacy and Social Change among African American Women*. Pittsburgh: U of Pittsburgh P, 2000. Print.
Sabin, Florence. "Women in Science." *Science* 83.2141 (1936): 24–26. *Science Magazine*. Web. 7 June 2008.

Sarkela, Sandra, Susan Ross, and Margaret Lowe. *From Megaphones to Microphones: Speeches of American Women, 1920–1960*. Westport: Praeger, 2003.
"School Carol Ban Vetoed by Jansen." *New York Times* 7 Dec. 1947: 39. Print.
Schultz, Gladys Denny, and Daisy Gordon Lawrence. *Lady from Savannah*. Philadelphia: J. B. Lippincott, 1958. Print.
Scott, Anne Firor. *The Southern Lady: From Pedestal to Politics, 1830–1930*. Charlottesville: U of Virginia P, 1995. Print.
"The Screen." *New York Times* 19 Aug. 1919: 10. Print.
Seigfried, Charlene Haddock. *Pragmatism and Feminism*. Chicago: U of Chicago P, 1996. Print.
Sharer, Wendy. "Genre Work: Expertise and Advocacy in the Early Bulletins of the U.S. Women's Bureau." *Rhetoric Society Quarterly* 33.1 (2003): 5–32. Print.
———. *Vote and Voice: Women's Organizations and Political Literacy, 1915–1930*. Carbondale: Southern Illinois UP, 2004. Print.
Sheard, Cynthia Miecznikowski. "The Public Value of Epideictic Rhetoric." *College English* 58.7 (1996): 765–94. Print.
Shteir, Ann. *Cultivating Women, Cultivating Science: Flora's Daughters and Botany in England, 1760–1860*. Baltimore: Johns Hopkins UP, 1999. Print.
Silverberg, Helene, ed. *Gender and American Social Science: The Formative Years*. Princeton: Princeton UP, 1998. Print.
Singleton, Zutty. "I Remember the Queen." *Jazz Record* 58 (Sept. 1947): 10–11. Print.
Skinner, Carolyn. "Medical Interventions: The Rhetoric of Nineteenth-Century Women Physicians." 2010. MS.
Smith, Bessie. "Back-Water Blues." *Bessie Smith* Vol. 3: *"Preachin' the Blues." Original Recordings 1925–1927*. Naxos, 2004. CD.
———. "Dirty No-Gooders Blues." A. Davis, *Blues* 272. Print.
———. "Empty Bed Blues (Parts 1&2)." By J. C. Johnson. *Bessie Smith: The Collection*. Columbia, 1989. CD.
———. "It Makes My Love Come Down." *Empress of the Blues* Vol. 2, disc B: 1928–29. JSP Records, 2007. CD.
———. "Mama's Got the Blues." A. Davis, *Blues* 310. Print.
———. "Soft Pedal Blues." *Bessie Smith* Vol. 2: *St Louis Blues Original 1924–1925 Recordings*. HNH, 2003. CD.
———. "Washerwoman's Blues." By Spenser Williams. *Empress of the Blues* Vol. 2: 1926–33. JSP Records, 2007. CD.
"Smith College Gives Degree to Mme. Curie." *New York Times* 14 May 1921: 9. *Historical New York Times*. Web. 7 June 2008.
"The Social World." *New York Times* 20 May 1894: 13. Print.
Spack, Ruth. "Dis/engagement: Zitkala-Ša's Letters to Carlos Montezuma, 1901–1902." *MELUS* 26.1 (2001): 173–205. *JSTOR*. 10 Apr. 2005. Web.
"Starvation and War." *Wall Street Journal* 12 June 1917: A1. Print.
Stein, Elizabeth P. "Helen Gray Cone and the Shakespeare Society." *Hunter College Bulletin* 8 Mar. 1934: 3. Print.
Stocking, George W., Jr. "Ideas and Institutions in American Anthropology: Thoughts toward a History of the Interwar Years." *Selected Papers from the American Anthropologist, 1921–1945*. Ed. George W. Stocking Jr. Washington: American Anthropological Assoc. 1–74. Print.

Studer, Clara. "Women Can Fly Too." *Ninety-Niner* Sept. 1933: 1–2. Print.
Sutherland, Christine Mason. "Getting to Know Them: Concerning Research into Four Early Women Writers." *Beyond the Archives: Research as a Lived Process*. Ed. Gesa Kirsch and Liz Rohan. Carbondale: Southern Illinois UP, 2008. 28–36. Print.
Swales, John. *Genre Analysis: English in Academic and Research Settings*. Cambridge: Cambridge UP, 1990. Print.
Tanner, William M. *Composition and Rhetoric*. Boston: Ginn, 1922.
———. *Essays and Essay-Writing*. Boston: Atlantic Monthly, 1917.
Tedesco, Laureen. "Making a Girl into a Scout: Americanizing Scouting for Girls." *Delinquents and Debutantes: Twentieth-Century American Girls' Cultures*. Ed. Sherrie A. Inness. New York: New York UP, 1998. Print.
"They Take to the Sky: Group of Midwest Women Follow Path Blazed by Pioneer Bessie Coleman." *Ebony* May 1977: 88+. Print.
"Three Senses." Rev. of *Midstream*, by Helen Keller. *Time* 18 Nov. 1929: 80. Print.
"To Honor Two Brooklyn Deans." *New York Times* 8 May 1954: 12. Print.
Tompkins, Jane. *Sensational Designs: The Cultural Work of American Fiction 1790–1860*. New York: Oxford UP, 1985. Print.
Toulmin, Stephen. *The Uses of Argument*. Cambridge: Cambridge UP, 1958. Print.
"Transatlantic Girl Flyer Out Shopping in Borrowed Clothes: Miss Earhart Won't Go to Paris but Will Attend Ascot Races and Be Dinner Guest of British Air League." Id #: blflli20. 20 June 1928. N. pag. Print. George Palmer Putnam Collection of Amelia Earhart Papers. Purdue University Libraries, Archives and Special Collections, West Lafayette, IN.
True, Michael. "Jane Addams." *Nuclear Age Peace Foundation*. Nuclear Age Peace Foundation, n.d. Web. 10 June 2010.
Tylor, E. B. "How the Problems of American Anthropology Present Themselves to the English Mind." *Science* 4.98 (1884): 545–51. *JSTOR*. 1 June 2010.
Underhill, Ruth. Letters to Elsie Clews Parsons. Elsie Clews Parsons Papers. American Philosophical Society, Philadelphia, PA.
Van Vechten, Carl. "Memories of Bessie Smith." *Jazz Record* Sept. 1947: 6–7, 29. Print.
———. "Negro Blues Singers." *Vanity Fair* Mar. 1926: 67, 106–8. Print.
Visser, Irene. "American Writers in the Dutch Literary World 1824–1900." *I Have Heard about You: Foreign Women's Writing Crossing the Dutch Border, from Sappho to Selma Lagerlof*. Ed. Suzanna van Dijk, Petra Broomans, Janet F. van der Meulen, and Pim van Oostrum. Trans. Jo Nesbitt. Hilversum: Uitgeverij Verloren, 2004. Print.
Visweswaran, Kamala. "'Wild West' Anthropology and the Disciplining of Gender." Silverberg 86–123. Print.
Wales, Julia Grace. "Appendix A: International Plan for Continuous Mediation without Armistice." *Women at The Hague: The International Congress of Women and Its Results*. Ed. Jane Addams, Emily G. Balch, and Alice Hamilton. New York: Macmillan, 1916: 167–71. Print.
———. "Continuous Mediation, Mar.–April 1945." TS. Wales Papers. National Archives of Canada, Ottawa.
———. *Democracy Needs Education*. Toronto: Macmillan Canada, 1942. Print.

———."Graduate Study and the World We Live In." *American Association of University Professors Bulletin* 27 (Oct. 1941): 433–41. Print.

———. "The Legitimate Uses of Reading and Discussion in Freshman and Sophomore Composition." TS. Wales Papers. National Archives of Canada, Ottawa. Web.

———. Letter to Committee [International Committee of Women for Permanent Peace]. 5 June 1915. Wales Papers. National Archives of Canada, Ottawa. Web.

———. Letter to Louis Lochner. 31 Oct. 1917. Wales Papers. National Archives of Canada, Ottawa. Web.

———. *Mediation without Armistice: The Wisconsin Plan*. Madison: Wisconsin Peace Society, 1915. Print.

———. "Mediation without Armistice—Supplementary Notes." TS. Wales Papers. National Archives of Canada, Ottawa. Web.

———. "Pro, Not Anti: A Principle of Integration." *New Age* 8 Aug. 1940: 9–10. Print.

———. "Some By Ways of Peace Work, 1916–1918." TS. Wales Papers. National Archives of Canada, Ottawa. Web.

Ware, Susan. *Beyond Suffrage: Women and the New Deal*. Cambridge: Harvard UP, 1987. Print.

———. *Holding Their Own: American Women in the 1930s*. Boston: Twayne, 1982. Print.

Warnick, Barbara. "Lucie Olbrechts-Tyteca and *les Couples philosophiques*." National Communication Association, Chicago. Nov. 2007. Presentation.

Watts, Ruth. *Women in Science: A Social and Cultural History*. London: Routledge, 2007. Print.

Weiser, M. Elizabeth. "'As Usual I Fell On the Bias': Kenneth Burke's Situated Dialectic." *Philosophy and Rhetoric* 42.2 (2009): 134–53. Print.

Welch, Deborah. "Gertrude Simmons Bonnin (Zitkala-Ša)/Dakota." *The New Warriors: Native American Leaders since 1900*. Ed. R. David Edmunds. Lincoln: U of Nebraska P, 2001. 35–53. Print.

———. "Zitkala-Ša: An American Indian Leader, 1876–1938." Diss. U of Wyoming, 1985. Print.

Welsh, Herbert. "In Explanation." Preface. *Oklahoma's Poor Rich Indians: An Orgy of Graft and Exploitation of the Five Civilized Tribes—Legalized Robbery*. By Gertrude Bonnin, Charles H. Fabens, and Matthew K. Sniffen. Philadelphia: Indian Rights Assoc., 1924. 3. Print.

West, Cornel. *The American Evasion of Philosophy: A Genealogy of Pragmatism*. Madison: U of Wisconsin P, 1989. Print.

Wexler, Laura. "Tender Violence: Literary Eavesdropping, Domestic Fiction, and Educational Reform." *The Culture of Sentiment: Race, Gender, and Sentimentality in Nineteenth-Century America*. Ed. Shirley Samuels. New York: Oxford UP, 1992. 9–38. Print.

White House Interview, 12 Nov. 1915. TS. Wales Papers. National Archives of Canada, Ottawa. Web.

Willard, William. "Zitkala-Ša: A Woman Who Would Be Heard!" *WicazoSa Review* 1.1 (1985): 11–16. Print.

Williams, Blanche Colton. "From the Head of the English Department." *Hunter College Bulletin* 8 Mar. 1934: 1+. Print.

———. *A Handbook on Story Writing.* New York: Dodd, 1917. Print.

Williams, Susan. *Reclaiming Authorship: Literary Women in America, 1850–1900.* Philadelphia: U of Pennsylvania P, 2006. Print.

"Women." *Time* 28 May 1923: 7. *Time Magazine Online.* Web. 7 June 2008.

"World Labor Plans May Day Parades; Police Guard Here." *New York Times* 1 May 1933: 1, 3. Print.

Wright, J. B. F. "Precious Memories." Hymn 397. *Sacred Selections for the Church.* Ed. Ellis J. Crum. Kendallville: Sacred Selections, 1992.

Young, Richard E., Alton L. Becker, and Kenneth L. Pike. *Rhetoric: Discovery and Change.* New York: Harcourt, 1970. Print.

Zitkala-Ša [Gertrude Bonnin]. "An Indian Teacher among Indians. *Zitkala-Ša: American Indian Stories, Legends, and Other Writings.* Ed. Cathy N. Davidson and Ada Norris. New York: Penguin, 2003. 104–113. Print.

———. "Impressions of an Indian Childhood." Davidson and Norris. 68–86. Print.

———. "The School Days of an Indian Girl." Davidson and Norris. 87–103. Print.

Zumwalt, Rosemary Lévy. *Wealth and Rebellion: Elsie Clews Parsons, Anthropologist and Folklorist.* Urbana: U of Illinois P, 1992. Print.

Zwick, Mark, and Louise Zwick. *The Catholic Worker Movement: Intellectual and Spiritual Origins.* New York: Paulist, 2005.

Contributors

Risa Applegarth, assistant professor at the University of North Carolina at Greensboro, teaches undergraduate and graduate courses in rhetoric, writing, and genre. Her research has previously appeared in *Rhetoric Society Quarterly* and *College Composition and Communication*. She is currently working on a book manuscript titled "Other Grounds: Gender, Genre, and Science in American Anthropology."

Ann George, associate professor at Texas Christian University, teaches courses in rhetorical theory and criticism, composition, and style. She is coauthor of *Kenneth Burke in the 1930s* (2007) and is now working on a book manuscript "A Critical Companion to *Permanence and Change*." Her articles have appeared in *Rhetorica* and *Rhetoric Society Quarterly*.

Kay Halasek, associate professor at the Ohio State University, serves as a writing program administrator and teaches undergraduate writing and rhetoric courses and graduate courses in composition studies. She is currently completing a book project titled "Creating a Discipline: History, Historiography, and the Emergence of Composition Studies."

Sarah Hallenbeck, assistant professor at the University of North Carolina, Wilmington, teaches courses in professional writing, rhetoric of science, and feminist rhetorical history. Her work has appeared in *Rhetoric Review* and *Technical Communication Quarterly*.

Sara Hillin, assistant professor at Lamar University in Beaumont, Texas, has research interests that include feminist rhetorics and composition pedagogies. Her interest in the rhetorics of early pilots stems from a stint as a student pilot and a trip to the Ninety-Nines Museum of Women Pilots in Oklahoma City.

Jordynn Jack, associate professor at the University of North Carolina, Chapel Hill, is the author of *Science on the Home Front: American Women Scientists in World War II* (2009); her articles have appeared in *College English, College Composition and Communication, Rhetoric Society Quarterly, Rhetoric and Public Affairs, Rhetoric Review,* and *Quarterly Journal of Speech*.

Kathy Jurado earned her PhD in the University of Michigan's American Culture program. Her intellectual and research interests include Latina/o literature, contemporary American literature, immigration studies, popular culture, and third-world feminism.

Cassandra Parente, assistant professor at the Ohio State University, teaches traditional and service-learning courses in her research areas: literacy studies, rhetorical theory, writing, and research methods. She is currently working on a manuscript titled "Invisible Roots: Immigrants, Literacy, and Rhetorics of Silence," exploring post–World War II Italian immigrants' literacy practices.

Coretta Pittman, associate professor at Baylor University, focuses on the theoretical and cultural intersections of rhetoric, race, class, and gender. She has published articles in *Rhetoric Society Quarterly* and *Phoebe: Journal of Gender and Cultural Critiques* as well as chapters in two collections: *Agency in the Margins: Stories of Outsider Rhetoric* and *From Hip-Hop to Hyperlinks: Teaching about Culture in the Composition Classroom*.

Sandra L. Robinson is an independent scholar who earned her PhD in rhetoric at Texas Woman's University, in Denton. As an adjunct professor at Texas Woman's University, Robinson taught logic and critical thinking, philosophy and religion, women's studies, and communications. She currently teaches writing courses at the University of Phoenix.

Hephzibah Roskelly teaches courses in rhetoric and composition, American literature, and women's studies at the University of North Carolina at Greensboro. She is working on a study of nineteenth-century American women activists and their contributions to philosophical pragmatism.

Wendy B. Sharer, associate professor at East Carolina University, is coeditor of *Working in the Archives: Practical Research Methods for Rhetoric and Composition* (2009), author of *Vote & Voice: Women's Organizations and Political Literacy, 1915–1930* (2004), coauthor of *1977: A Cultural Moment in Composition* (2008), and coeditor of *Rhetorical Education in America* (2004).

M. Elizabeth Weiser, associate professor at the Ohio State University, is author of *Burke, War, Words: Rhetoricizing Dramatism* (2008), coeditor of *Engaging Audience* (2009), and has published articles in *Rhetoric Review*, *Philosophy and Rhetoric*, and the *International Journal of the Inclusive Museum*, among others. She is working on a book project titled "Who We Are: Global Museums and National Identities."

CONTRIBUTORS

Elizabeth Wilkinson, assistant professor at the University of St. Thomas, teaches Native American, American, and women's literatures. Her current project is an investigation of Gertrude Bonnin's rhetorical uses of silence, and she continues her research on the rhetoric of Native women, specifically in defense of land and culture rights.

Janet Zepernick directs the Writing Center and teaches rhetoric, research writing, and medieval literature at Pittsburg State University.

Index

AAUP bulletin, 25–26
AAUW (American Association of University Women), 13, 227
Abbe, Robert, 226, 229–30
Abbott, Lawrence F., 251
acknowledgment (sideshadowing principle), 242–43, 258
activity in community formation, 197, 199
Addams, Jane: "Bayonet Charge" speech by, 32–37, 38, 40; and Civil Liberties Union, 43; on connection between deprivation and violence, 38–39, 44–45; criticisms of and attacks against, 33, 35–37, 39, 41, 43–44, 45; death of, 46; on free speech, 43; future-oriented rhetoric of, 45–46; and Hull House, 32, 35, 38, 42, 44–46, 70; on immigrants, 42–43; and labor movement, 43, 47n4; memoirs by, 14, 36–46, 98–99; "Our National Self-Righteousness" speech by, 45; peace activism by, 1, 14, 19–21, 32–46; and Perkins, 70; pragmatic rhetoric used by, 34, 35, 37–42, 45–46, 47n1; and Progressive Party, 32; public respect for, 32–33, 38, 46; self-examination in memoirs by, 37–42; social workers trained by, 65, 66; speeches by, for federal Department of Food Administration, 38–39. *See also* Addams, Jane, works by
Addams, Jane, works by: general discussion, 47n3; *The Long Road of Woman's Memory* by, 35, 42; "A Modern Lear," 47; *Peace and Bread in Time of War*, 20, 33–34, 36–41, 43, 46; *Second Twenty Years at Hull House*, 33–34, 36, 39, 40, 42–45; *Twenty Years at Hull House*, 32, 42
aerocyborgs: Coleman as, 175, 177–83, 188–90; deaths of, while flying, 184–85, 188–89; definition of, 175, 176, 177; Earhart as, 175, 177–90; embodiment of, 176–83, 189–90; Klingensmith as, 175, 177–78, 183–85, 188–90; legacy of, 188–90; and "masculine" attire of, 178–80, 190n1; media attention and publicity for, 178–82, 184–85, 188, 189; photographs of, 178–80; and posthuman discourse, 175–76; rhetoric of, 177–82, 184–89
AFB (American Federation for the Blind), 101–2, 110
African American women: appropriate public behavior for, 144–45; in aviation, 15, 175, 177–83, 188–90; as blues singers, 144–57; and Cult of True Womanhood, 135–36; and culture of dissemblance, 134, 137; domestic work by, 135, 136, 152–53; education of, 129–31, 136, 141–42; and intraracial conflict, 153–54; moral superiority of, 130, 132–39, 144; nineteenth-century rhetoric of, 6–7; and politics of respectability, 134; in public and professional life in 1920s and 1930s, 1, 8, 10, 13; racism against and stereotypes of, 130–31, 133–35, 156; role of, in family life, 136; sexuality of, 136, 137, 145, 156; vulnerability of, to rape and domestic violence, 134, 136, 137; and woman suffrage, 137. *See also* African Americans; *and specific women*
African Americans: Burroughs on inner virtue for African American men, 138; double consciousness of, 146; flight school for, 182–83; and Harlem Renaissance, 144, 145, 148, 157, 157–58n2; and intraracial conflict, 153–54; and Jim Crow laws, 141, 143; migration of, to cities, 149–50; and New Negro, 143–44; racial uplift for, 14, 132–39, 144, 181–83. *See also* African American women; *and specific African Americans*

INDEX

Afro-American, 139–40
agency: of Burroughs, 129–31; limitations of celebrity as source of, 14; movement from agency to action by women, 5–8; transrhetorical agency of Gertrude Bonnin, 49–61
Albertson, Chris, 156
Alcorn, Marshall W., 145–46
Al Smith, Hero of the Cities (Perkins), 64
America (journal), 118
American Anthropological Association, 193
American Association of University Women (AAUW), 13, 227
American Civil Liberties Union, 1
American Federation for the Blind (AFB), 101–2, 110
American Federation of Labor, 73
American Girl, 85–86
American Indian Defense Association, 48
American Indian Life (Parsons), 201
American Indians. *See* Native Americans
American Writers' Congress, 126
Ammons, Elizabeth, 249
Anaganos, Michael, 110
Anderson, Dana, 117, 120, 128n3
Anderson, Mary, 1
Anthropological Society of Washington, 193
anthropology: accessibility of, for women, 193–96, 206–7; activity in community formation within, 197, 199; collectivity in community formation within, 197, 198; community formation within, 195, 196–200, 207–8; field guides in, 15, 201–7; particularity in community formation within, 197, 200; and popularization as rhetorical recruitment, 195, 200–208; professionalization and interwar exigencies within, 195–96, 208; stability in community formation within, 197, 199–200
Applegarth, Risa, 9, 15, 85, 193–208, 283
archaeology, 195, 201–7
Aristotle, 8, 223, 226
Armstrong, Louis, 143
Arnold, Matthew, 257–58
"Arraignment" (Cone), 251
Association to Aid Scientific Research by Women, 238

Astaire, Adele, 149
Atlanta Constitution, 134–35
Atlantic Monthly, 52, 53, 54, 62n5
attribution (sideshadowing principle), 242, 243, 258
Augustine, St., 120
Autobiographical rhetorical theory, 64–65, 68–77
aviation. *See* aerocyborgs
Ayer, Gertrude, 13

"Backwater Blues," 151–52
Bacon, Josephine Daskam, 83, 84, 89, 93n3
Baden-Powell, Lord Robert, 79, 81, 88–89, 92n1, 93n4
Baez, Joan, 174
Bakhtin, Mikhail, 242
Barker, Eugene C., 213
Barnacle, Mary, 163, 171
Barnard College, 235, 249
Barnett, Robert, 110
Barton, Clara, 97
Baruch, Bernard, 72
Batterham, Forster, 128n1
Batterham, Libbie, 128n1
Batterham, Lily, 128n1
Bayles, Edith, 208n1
"Bayonet Charge" speech (Addams), 32–37, 38, 40
Beard, Mary, 10–11, 13
Becker, Alton, 26–27, 30
Behdad, Ali, 215
Benedict, Ruth, 194, 198–200
Berdyaev, Nikolai, 122
Berlin, James, 240–41, 242, 254–56, 258–59
Berthoff, Ann, 8
Bessie Coleman Aero Club, 183
Bessie Coleman Aviators, 183, 189
Bethune, Mary McLeod, 1, 13
Bias-falling stance. *See* falling on the bias
bicultural identity, 49–50. *See also* transrhetorical agency
Biesecker, Barbara, 160
Bildersee, Adele, 15, 240–50, 252–59
Bildersee, Dorothy, 243–44, 246
Bildersee, Isaac, 243–44, 246
Bird, Gloria, 50
Bivens, Jason, 115
Bix, Amy Sur, 182
Bizzell, Patricia, 8

288

INDEX

Black women. *See* African American women
Blodgett, Katherine, 225, 229
Bloor, Ella Reeve ("Mother"), 13
blues music, 15, 143–57
Boas, Franz, 194
body: aerocyborgs' embodiment, 176–83, 189–90; of Marie Curie, 229; Keller's bodily performance, 98, 110–13; Bessie Smith's on-stage persona, 149. *See also* sexuality
Bonnin, Gertrude: and correspondence with one-time fiancé Carlos Montezuma, 51–52; cultural identity of, 49–50; as Dakota, and Dakota name of, 48, 49, 51–54, 62n1; education of, 49–53, 62n4; literary works by, 50–54, 62n1, 62n5; *Oklahoma's Poor Rich Indians* by, 14, 48–49, 54–61; as Other, 50, 53; purposive subjectivity and persuasive identification in rhetoric of, 9; sentimentalism used by, 50–51, 53–61; transrhetorical agency of, 49–61
border between U.S. and Mexico, 210, 212–18
Border Patrol, 215
boring from within, 98, 100, 101, 103, 108–9
Boston University, 86
Boy Scouts, 79, 81, 87, 88
Braddy, Nella, 98
Bradstreet, Anne, 209, 219–20
Bread for the World, 114
Brent, Doug, 23, 26–27, 30
Brewton, Vince, 113n1
Brockway, Howard, 162
Brooklyn College, 248
Brooks, Evelyn, 136, 138, 141
Brooks, Van Wyck, 4, 110
Brown, Marjorie M., 226
Bruce, Alice Ruth, 207
Bryan, Dorothy, 207
Bryant, Louise Stevens, 80, 82–84, 86
Bryn Mawr College, 7–8, 238
Bufwack, Mary, 162, 163, 174
Bumgarner, Samantha, 174
Bunzel, Ruth, 194, 198–200
Burke, Kenneth: on bias in language, 9; on boring from within, 98, 100, 101, 103, 108–9; on classifying of essence, 127; on conversational parlor, 11; Day compared with, 14; on falling on the bias, 115, 116–17; First American Writers' Congress speech by, 126; on idealism, 116; on identification, 23–24, 114, 115, 127; on indirectly communicative media, 177; marriages of, 128n1; on materialism, 116; on personalizing of essence, 127; on piety, 10, 98, 99–100, 112; on propaganda by inclusion versus propaganda by exclusion, 126; on terministic screen, 3, 11, 111–13; on tragic symbol, 188; Wales compared with, 14, 23–24
Burke, Kenneth, works by: *A Grammar of Motives*, 116; *Language as Symbolic Action*, 177; *Permanence and Change*, 99, 188; *A Rhetoric of Motives*, 23–24, 26, 99–100, 114, 127
Burnier, DeLysa, 63
Burr, Amelia Josephine, 247
Burroughs, Nannie Helen: agency of, 129–31; birth date of, 130; education of, 130–31; humor used by, 140–41; as moral entrepreneur, 130–32; on moral superiority of Negro women, 130, 132–39, 144; and National Baptist Convention Auxiliary Women's Convention, 131, 132, 141; and National League of Republican Colored Women (NLRCW), 140; and National Training School for Women and Girls, 129, 131, 136, 141–42; *On Their Way to the Slabtown District Convention* (play) by, 141; photograph of, 133; publishing company of, 131; and racial uplift, 14, 132–39, 144, 181; racism against, 130–31; and specializing in impossibility, 129, 142; violations of decorum by, 14, 130, 139–41; and *Worker* newspaper/magazine, 131–32
Butcher, Clara, 174
Butler, Ellis, 84, 85
Butler, Judith, 190n1

Caballero (González), 218, 221n2, 222n7
Call (Socialist Party), 97
Calvin, Inga, 208nn1–2
Campbell, Olive Dame, 162
Camp Fire Girls, 92n1
Caraway, Hattie, 1

Cardozo, Francis Lewis, 130
career guides, 15, 223, 224, 232–39
Careers for Women (Filene), 233, 235
Carnegie, Andrew, 102, 103
Carnegie Institution, 195, 196, 198, 201
Carpenter, Cari, 50
Carter Family, 174
Castañeda, Carlos, 213
Catholic Worker/Catholic Worker movement, 114, 116–28
Catt, Carrie Chapman, 6, 97
Cermak, May, 244
"Chant of Love for England, A" (Cone), 251
Chapman, Margaret, 92
Chestnutt, Charles, 137
Chiarello, Barbara, 62n3
Chicago Defender, 146–47, 180, 182
Chicago Tribune, 43
Child, Francis, 162
Christoph, Julie N., 150
Churchill, Winston, 185
Cicero, 64
citizenship: Girl Scouts' training for, 14, 80–87, 91, 92; and LULAC, 217–18, 222n9; Wales on democracy and world citizenship, 28–29
Civil Liberties Union, 43
Civil Rights movement, 140
Claassen, Cheryl, 194
Clark, Gregory, 23–24
Clemens, George P., 216–17
Cleveland, Reginald, 184
Cleveland Plain Dealer, 184
coal mining, 159–60, 164–68
Cohen, Paula Marantz, 110, 111, 113n1
Cohen, Ronald, 161, 167
Cold War, 10, 12
Coleman, Bessie, 15, 175, 177–83, 188–90
collectivity in community formation, 197, 198
College English, 25
Collier, Constance, 149
Colman, Penny, 63
Columbia University, 65, 86, 177, 194, 198, 207, 247, 258
Commonweal, 118
communally constructed truths, 8, 9
Communist Party, 117–22, 124, 166–67, 169, 171, 172–73
community formation, 195, 196–200, 207–8

Composer's Collective, 171
Composition and Rhetoric (Tanner), 258
composition studies. *See* English studies
Cone, Helen Gray, 9, 15, 240, 242–59
continuous mediation, 21–31
Cooke, M. Grant, 102
Coolidge, Calvin, 185
Cooper, Anna Julia, 130, 144
Cope, Persis, 230
Cornell, Thomas, 128n3
Cortina, Juan, 214–15
Cotera, María, 210, 213, 221n1, 222n5
Cott, Nancy, 2–3
Coughlin, Father Charles, 121, 122
Cowley, Malcolm, 128n1, 128n4
Crisis, 136–37, 148
Critique of the Gotha Program (Marx), 118
Crow, Liz, 107, 110, 113n1
Crowley, Sharon, 115, 128
Cucullu, Lois, 224
Cult of True Womanhood, 135–36
culture of dissemblance, 134, 137
Cunningham, Agnes "Sis," 173–74
Curie, Marie, 223–32, 234, 235, 236, 237, 238, 239
cyborgs. *See* aerocyborgs

Daily Worker, 117, 122, 169
d'Alvarez, Marguerite, 149
Danisch, Robert, 47n2
Daughters of the American Revolution (DAR), 13, 43–44
Davis, Angela, 129, 137, 148, 151–55, 157–58n2
Davis, Bette, 13
Davis, Richard Harding, 35–36
Dawes Act, 51
Day, Dorothy: and bohemian-conversion-devotion cycle, 117–18; and Burkean falling on the bias, 115, 116–17; and Burkean identification, 115, 127–28; and *Catholic Worker*/Catholic Worker movement, 114, 116–28; common-law husband and daughter of, 128n1; early journalist career of, 118; and intellectual underpinnings of *Catholic Worker*, 118–23; memoirs by, 116–17; and personalizing an essence, 127–28; and personalizing the abstract, 125–27; photograph of, 119; and propaganda by inclusion,

120; radical social theory translated for mainstream audience by, 1, 14, 114–16, 123–28; rhetorical stance of, 9, 114–17. *See also* Day, Dorothy, works by
Day, Dorothy, works by: *From Union Square to Rome*, 116–17, 120; *House of Hospitality*, 118, 120, 122; *The Long Loneliness*, 117, 118, 119, 121
Deacon, Desley, 199
"Death of Harry Simms, The," 172–73, 174n2
de la Cruz, Sor Juana Ines, 209, 211, 219–20
Delineator, The, 226
Deliverance (film), 104–6
Deloria, Ella Cara, 13, 194
Democracy Needs Education (Wales), 27–29
Democratic Party, 1, 13, 65–66, 74, 76, 140
Denisoff, Serge, 169
De Oratore (Cicero), 64
Des Jardins, Julie, 11
"Devil and the Farmer, The," 163
Dewey, John, 32, 34, 38, 44, 47n1
Dew on the Thorn (González), 210, 213, 219, 221, 221n2, 222n3
Dewson, Molly, 13
Dialogic Rhetoric movement, 26
Dickens, Charles, 55, 57, 59
Dickens, Hazel, 174
DiFranco, Ani, 174
Digging in the Southwest (Morris), 195, 201–8
Digging in Yucatan (Morris), 195, 201–8, 208n1
"Dirty No Gooders Blues," 155
Dobie, J. Frank, 213
Donawerth, Jane, 8
Dos Passos, John, 166, 168
Double consciousness, 146
Doubleday publisher, 98, 102, 108, 202, 207
Downey, Arelia, 131
Downey, Kirstin, 63
"Dreadful Memories," 166–67, 169
Dreiser Committee, 168, 169, 172
Drinker, Katherine R., 235
Du Bois, W. E. B., 143, 146, 147, 148, 157n1
Duke, David, 166

Earhart, Amelia: aerocyborg identity of, 177–78; aviation career of, 10, 15, 175, 177, 179, 188; birth year of, 177; criticism of, for "unfeminine" image, 178; death of, 177, 188; education of, 177; media attention and publicity for, 178, 180–81, 188; and Ninety-Nines Organization for Women Pilots, 189; photographs of, 178, 179; writings by and rhetoric of, 177–78, 185–88
Earlham College, 53, 62n3
Easter, Opal V., 139
Eastman, Max, 118, 128n4
Eblen, Anna, 43
education: of African Americans, 129–31, 136, 141–42; in anthropology, 194, 207; of Bonnin, 49–53, 62n4; of Burroughs, 130–31; of Earhart, 177; Female Normal and High School (New York City), 246–47, 250, 254–55, 259; flight school for African Americans, 182–83; of Jovita González, 211; of Mexican Americans, 211, 216, 221–22n3; of Native Americans, 49–53, 62n4; of Perkins, 65, 75; science education for women, 237; and Wales's continuous mediation, 24–29. *See also* English studies; *and specific universities*
Edwards, Ron, 180
Einhorn, Lois, 113n1
Elliot, Ralph, 182
Ellsberg, Robert, 128n3
Elshtain, Jean Bethke, 38
employment. *See* anthropology; science
"Empty Bed Blues" parts I and II, 155
Engels, Friedrich, 119
English studies: Cone and Bildersee in, 9, 15, 240–59; Cone on inadequacies of, 252, 257; critique of composition historiography, 240–41; New Rhetoric's approach to, 26–27; and sideshadowing methodology, 241–45, 258; and sideshadowing narrative form, 245–46, 258; social context of, 252–53; textbooks in, 240–41, 242, 243, 244, 248, 250, 254–59; Wales's continuous mediation, 24–29
Enoch, Jessica, 52
epideictic rhetoric: Aristotle on, 223, 226; of career guides, 233–36, 239; purpose of, 223–24; and women scientists, 223–24, 233–36, 238–39

INDEX

Essay, The: How to Study and Write It (Farrington), 251
Essays and Essay-Writing (Tanner), 258
ethos: Alcorn on, 145–46; of Coleman as black aviatrix, 181, 182; of Aunt Molly Jackson's folk music, 160–61, 164, 173; of Bessie Smith's blues music, 145–51, 154
Evans, David, 151
Everybody's Magazine, 62n5

Fabens, Charles H., 48–49, 61
falling on the bias, 115, 116–17
Faludi, Susan, 7, 12
"Farmer's Curst Wife, The," 163
Farrington, Dora Davis, 251
Fauset, Jessie, 143
Federal Insurance Contributions Act (FICA), 74
Feld, Rose, 71
Female Normal and High School (New York City), 246–47, 250, 254–55, 259
Feminine Mystique, The (Friedan), 3, 12
feminism: and employment opportunities for women, 234; First Wave Feminism, 3, 7; and Girl Scouts, 80; in 1940s and 1950s, 12; Second Wave Feminism, 3, 12; of Sor Juana Ines de la Cruz, 219–20; waves model of, 3; and woman's suffrage, 3, 7. *See also* gender
Ferber, Edna, 185
Ferguson, Miriam, 1
Ferris, Helen, 202
FICA (Federal Insurance Contributions Act), 74
field guides in anthropology, 15, 201–7
Fields of Work for Women (Leuck), 223, 236, 237
Filene, Benjamin, 162
Filene, Catherine, 233, 235
Fisher, Dexter, 49–50
Fisher, Donald, 195
Flanagan, Hallie, 13
Fleischman, Doris, 234
Fletcher, Alice, 194
flying. *See* aerocyborgs
Flynn, Elizabeth Gurley, 1
folk music, 159–74
Foner, Philip S., 113n1
Ford, Henry, 20–21, 102, 107, 113n3
Forest, Jim, 128n3

For the Fun of It (Earhart), 177, 184
Franklin, Christine Ladd, 225
Frazier, E. Franklin, 158n4
Friedan, Betty, 3, 12
Friends' Service Committee, 41
From Union Square to Rome (Day), 116–17, 120
Frye Bill, 61
Fuller Sisters, 173–74
fundamentalism, 115, 128

Gacs, Ute, 196
Garland, Jim, 168, 169, 174n2
Garvey, Marcus, 143
Garza-Falcón, Leticia, 210, 222n4
Gates, Barbara T., 201
Gaudette, Marie E., 92
Gay, Lucy, 31
gender: anthropology as career for women, 193–96, 198, 206–7; and aviation, 178–90; in blues music sung by Bessie Smith, 153–54; and Bonnin's section of *Oklahoma's Poor Rich Indians*, 49; and "bootstraps" rhetoric of gender neutrality in science, 232–38; Butler on gendering, 190n1; and career guides, 15, 223, 224, 232–39; Cone on women in literature, 248–52; and Cult of True Womanhood, 135–36; and cyborgs, 176–77; and domesticity ideal for woman, 6–7, 10, 12; exploitation of women authors by printers and publishers, 250; and family duties of women scientists, 230–31; femininity of women scientists, 225–26, 229–32, 239; and folk music, 161–63; gender neutrality and professional women, 228–29, 232–38, 239n2; Gilder on women in literature, 249; Girl Scouts and gender roles, 80–81; Jovita González on, 218–20; and "masculine" attire of aerocyborgs, 178–80, 190n1; Native American gender norms, 51–53; and peace activism, 30–31, 38; and politics of respectability, 134; and settlement movement, 38; sexism in workplace, 71; white model of domestic femininity, 51–53. *See also* African American women; feminism; white women
Gender and Rhetorical Space in American Life, 1866–1910 (Johnson), 6

292

General Federation of Women's Clubs, Indian Welfare Committee, 48
George, Ann, 1–16, 97–113, 126, 257, 283
Gere, Anne Ruggles, 80
Gerrard, Alice, 174
Gershwin, George, 149
Getting Lost (Lather), 245
Gilder, Jeannette, 242, 246, 248–49, 258
Gilder, Richard Watson, 242
Gilkes, Cheryl Townsend, 131
Ginzberg, Lori D., 3
Girl and Her Job, The (Hoerle and Saltzberg), 233
Girl Guides, 79, 80, 89
Girl Scouts: as "alternate public," 79–80; beginning of, 79; citizenship, cooperation, and collaboration training by, 14, 80–87, 91, 92; and democratic processes, 84–85, 92; and domesticity and homemaking, 80; feminist scholars on, 80; and Girl Scout Law, 82, 93n3; leadership training by, 86–87; legacy of, 81, 91–92; membership statistics for, 79; military terms and practices used by, 83–84, 86, 87; and obedience, 82–83, 86, 87; and preparedness, 81, 87–91, 93n4; and problem-solving skills, 85–86; as "protected enclave," 81; troop meetings of, 84–85; during World War I, 88
Glazer, Penina, 228
Glenn, Cheryl, 4, 5, 11
Gold, Mike, 118
Goldberg, Myla, 246
Goldfrank, Esther Schiff, 194, 199
González, Jovita: on assimilation, 217–18; biographical information on, 210–12; education of, 211; as educator, 211–12; on gender, 218–20; on Mexican Americans and U.S.-Mexico border, 15, 209, 212–18, 220; "Shades of the Tenth Muses" by, 209, 210, 218–20, 221n1; "Social Life in Cameron, Starr and Zapata Counties" (master's thesis) by, 210, 212–18, 220–21, 222n5; writings by, generally, 9, 15, 210, 211, 218–19, 221n2, 222n5, 222n7
Gornstein, Ken, 179, 180, 183
Grainger, Porter, 149, 152
Grammar of Motives, A (Burke), 116
Great War. *See* World War I

Green, Archie, 165, 170, 173
Green, William, 73
Greenway, John, 160, 165–69, 172
Grey, Sir Edward, 20
Grimke, Francis, 137
Guatemala, 198
Guggenheim Foundation, 196, 198
Gulick, Luther and Charlotte, 92n1
Gunning, Sarah Ogan, 174
Gunther, Erna, 194
Guthrie, Woody, 171
Gutiérrez, David, 217, 222n8
"Gypsy Laddie, The"/"Gypsy Rover," 161–62

Hahn, E. Adelaide, 251, 254
Halasek, Kay, 5, 15, 240–59, 283
Hall, Louise M., 86
Hallenbeck, Sarah, 14, 79–93, 141, 197, 283
Hamilton, Alice, 36
Handbook on Story Writing (Williams), 243
Handleman, Philip, 180
Haraway, Donna, 176–78
Hardin, Margaret, 206
Harding, Warren G., 230–31
Harjo, Joy, 50
Harlan Miners Speak, 168, 172
Harlem Renaissance, 144, 145, 148, 157, 157–58n2
Harper, Martha Matilda, 1
Harper's Monthly Magazine, 62n5
Harris, Marguerite Tjader, 13
Harvard Education Review, 30
Harvard University, 30, 177, 252
Hauser, Gerard, 223
Hayles, N. Katherine, 175–77
Health Care Reform Act (2009), 75
Hearst, William Randolph, 119
Hearst's Cosmopolitan, 177, 178
Hearst's International Combined with Cosmopolitan, 185–87
Heilbrun, Carolyn G., 245
Herbst, Josephine, 13
Hess, Dorothea C., 254
Hicks, Granville, 9
Higginbotham, Evelyn B., 134, 144
Hillin, Sara, 15, 175–90, 283
Hine, Darlene, 134, 136, 137
Hitler, Adolf, 46
Hoefer, George, 147
Hoerle, Helen Christine, 233

INDEX

Hollis, Karyn L., 6, 7
Holmes, Oliver Wendell, 40
home economics, 226, 238
Home to Harlem (McKay), 157n1
Hood, Adelyne, 173–74
Hoover, Herbert, 76, 140
Hopkins University, 228
Hopwood, Marion, 184
Horton, James Oliver, 135
House of Hospitality (Day), 118, 120, 122
How We Became Posthuman (Hayles), 175, 176
Huber, Patrick, 173
Hughes, Langston, 143, 157, 157n1
Hull House, 32, 35, 38, 42, 44–46, 65, 70, 75. *See also* Addams, Jane
"Hungry Ragged Blues," 165–66, 168, 169, 172
Hunter, Alberta, 144, 150
Hunter, Tera, 134–35
Hunter College, 243, 244, 247–48, 252–53, 257, 259
Hurst, Fannie, 185
Hurston, Zora Neale, 13, 157n1, 194
hybrid identity, 49–50. *See also* transrhetorical agency

"I Am a Union Woman," 167–68
ICWPP (International Congress of Women for Permanent Peace), 19–20, 33
idealism, 116
identification, 23–24, 114, 115, 127–28
Imaginative Writing (A. Bildersee), 240–43, 248, 250, 254–59
immigrants, 42–43, 121, 161, 212, 215–17
"Impressions of an Indian Childhood" (Bonnin), 51, 62n5
Independent Woman, 206
Indian Reorganization Act, 48
Indian Rights Association (IRA), 48
Indians. *See* Native Americans
Indian Service, 59–60
"Indian Teacher among Indians, An" (Bonnin), 62n5
Indigo Girls, 174
Industrial Workers of the World. *See* Wobblies (I.W.W.)
Inness, Sherrie, 80
Interior Department, U.S., 48, 82
International Congress of Women for Permanent Peace (ICWPP), 19–20, 33

"International Plan for Continuous Mediation without Armistice" (Wales), 22–23, 24, 28
IRA (Indian Rights Association), 48
"It Makes My Love Come Down," 155, 156
I.W.W. *See* Wobblies (I.W.W.)

Jablonski, Carol, 128n3
Jack, Jordynn, 15, 194, 223–39, 239n2, 283
Jackson, Aunt Molly: aesthetic experience used by generally, 9; birth year and birth name of, 159; childhood of, 159, 161, 162; children of, 174n1; and Communism, 169, 171, 172–73; concerts by, in New York City, 168–71; as cultural broker, 168–71; and emotional and artistic detachment from her music, 170–71; ethos of folk music by, 160–61, 164, 173; as folksinger, 15, 159–74; labor protest songs by, 165–74; leftist transformation of, from singer to symbol, 171–73; marriages of, 163; as midwife, 159, 164, 166; and mining, 159–60, 164–68; nickname of, 164; parodies of traditional songs by, 166–68; photograph of, 170; recording career of, 163, 166, 171
Jackson, Bill, 163, 167, 174n1
James, Henry, 98
James, William, 32, 34
Jim Crow laws, 141, 143, 209
Johnson, Edith, 235–36
Johnson, Hugh S., 71–72, 78n2
Johnson, J. C., 155
Johnson, James P., 148
Johnson, Karen A., 131, 135
Johnson, Kristine, 128n3
Johnson, May Wright, 143, 148
Johnson, Nan, 4, 6, 7, 10
Jordan, David Starr, 20, 31
Journal of the Texas Folklore Society, 211
Jurado, Kathy, 15, 49, 209–22, 255, 284

kairos, 160, 162–63
Keller, Emily, 63
Keller, Evelyn Fox, 239
Keller, Helen: on American culture, 106–10; on birth control, 108–9; bodily performance by, 98, 110–13; and Burkean boring from within, 101,

294

103, 108–9; and Burkean piety, 98, 99–100, 112; and Burkean terministic screen, 111–12; as feminist and socialist, 97–100, 102–4, 108–10, 112, 113n1; film (*Deliverance*) of life of, 104–6; humor as rhetorical strategy of, 101, 113n3; on industrialism, 107, 108; limitations of celebrity as source of rhetorical agency for, 14, 100, 110, 113n2; as lobbyist for American Federation for the Blind (AFB), 101–2, 110; *Midstream* by, 98, 102–13, 113n4; photographs of, 110, 111; physical disability of, 100, 101, 104, 111; and piety-impiety conflict, 99–106, 110–13, 113n2, 113n4; public image and public misperceptions of, 97–98, 103, 104, 113n4; *Story of My Life* by, 98; and Wobblies (I.W.W.), 97; on writing autobiography, 103
Keller, Helen M., 86
Kelley, Colleen, 43
Kelley, Florence, 70
Kemper Adams, Elizabeth, 233, 234, 236
Kennedy, David M., 121
Keur, Dorothy, 199
Kidder, Alfred, 198
Kill, Melanie, 197
King, Rev. Martin Luther, Jr., 114
Klauser, Ella, 244, 246
Klauser, Emma, 243–44
Klingensmith, Florence, 15, 175, 177–78, 183–85, 188–90
Kroeber, Alfred, 196

Labor Department, U.S., 1, 7, 63, 70–78, 216
labor movement: Addams's support for, 43, 47n4; and Communist Party, 166–67; Cone's support for, 251; and miners, 166–68, 171; and Perkins, 73; and Wobblies (I.W.W.), 43, 97
Ladd-Franklin, Christine, 228
Lakoff, Robin, 189
Lane, Layle, 13
Lange, Dorothea, 13
Language as Symbolic Action (Burke), 177
Lardner, Ring, 185
Larkin, Margaret, 171
Lather, Patti, 245, 246
Lawrence, Daisy Gordon, 88
"Lay the Lily Low," 167

Leadbelly, 171
League of Nations, 42, 248
League of United Latin American Citizens (LULAC), 217–18, 222nn8–9
League of Women Voters, 82
Ledford, Lily May, 173–74
"Legitimate Uses of Reading and Discussion in Freshman and Sophomore Composition, The" (Wales), 25
Lenin, V. I., 109
Leo XIII, Pope, 120, 121
L'Esprit, 122
Lesser, Al, 198
Leuck, Miriam Simons, 223, 236, 237
Levine, Mary Ann, 196
Lewis, Sinclair, 185
liberalism, 115
Library of Congress, 166, 171
Life along the Border (González), 210, 221–22n3
Limón, José, 210
Lincoln, Abraham, 86
Lindberg, Mrs. Charles, 185
Lindsay, Jean S., 244
Lloyd, A. L., 160, 163
Lochner, Louis P., 20, 31
Locke, Alain, 143–44, 148
Logan, Shirley Wilson, 5, 6, 133, 181
Lomax, Alan, 163, 171
Long, Ray, 185, 188
Long, Shirley V., 243
Long Loneliness, The (Day), 117, 118, 119, 121
Long Road of Woman's Memory, The (Addams), 35, 42
Louisiana Weekly, 138–39
Low, Juliette Gordon, 79, 80, 81, 92, 92nn1–2
Lowe, Margaret, 140
LULAC (League of United Latin American Citizens), 217–18, 222nn8–9
Lurie, Nancy O., 194, 196
Lynch, Timothy, 160, 166, 167, 168
Lynn, Loretta, 174

Macy, Anne Sullivan, 101, 102
Madame Secretary, Frances Perkins (Martin), 66
Maltby, Margaret E., 235–36
"Mama's Got the Blues," 154
Maritain, Jacques, 122
Márquez, Benjamin, 222n8

Martin, George, 64, 66
Marx, Karl, 118, 119, 122, 124. *See also* Communist Party
Mason, Otis, 193
Masses, 118
Masters, Thomas, 255
materialism, 116
Mattingly, Carol, 3, 6
Maurin, Peter, 117–24, 126
McBride, Mary Margaret, 189
McDaniel, Hattie, 1
McKay, Claude, 157n1
McLaughlin, Kathleen, 229
Mead, Margaret, 13, 193, 194, 200
media: on aerocyborgs, 178–82, 184–85, 188, 189; on Earhart, 178, 180–81, 188; on scientific findings, 239; on Bessie Smith, 151; on women scientists, 15, 224–32. *See also specific newspapers and magazines*
Mediation without Armistice (Wales), 22, 23
Meloney, Marie Mattingly, 226
Menand, Louis, 40
Mexican Americans, 15, 209–18, 221, 221–22n3, 222n6
Meyer, Annie Nathan, 249
Michels, Anna W., 251
Midstream (Keller), 98, 102–13, 113n4
Miller, Carolyn, 197, 203
Miller, Susan A., 80, 88
Mills, John, 163
mining, 159–60, 164–68
Mireles, Edmundo, 211–12
Mitchell, Joni, 174
Mitchell, Sally, 80
Mize, Sandra Yocum, 128n3
"Modern Lear, A" (Addams), 47
Monroe, Harriet, 13
Montezuma, Carlos, 51
Montgomery Advertiser, 134
Moonshine Kate, 173–74
Morley, Sylvanus, 208n1
Morris, Ann Axtell, 194, 195, 197–98, 201–8, 208n1
Morris, Earl Halstead, 201–2
Morson, Gary Saul, 241–42, 246
Mournier, Emmanuel, 122
"Mr. Cundiff Turn Me Loose," 159
M Street School, 130
music. *See* blues music; folk music
Muskogee Phoenix, 55–57

NACW (National Association of Colored Women), 13, 137
Nannie Helen Burroughs Press, 131
Nannie Helen Burroughs School, 141–42
Narrative and Freedom (Morson), 241–42
National Academy of Sciences, 227
National Association of Colored Women (NACW), 13, 137
National Baptist Convention Auxiliary Women's Convention, 131, 132, 141
National Committee for the Defense of Political Prisoners, 168
National Consumers' League, 65, 70
National League of Republican Colored Women (NLRCW), 140
National Miners Union (NMU), 166–68, 171
National Organization for Women, 3
National Origins Act, 215
National Peace Conference, 32
National Recovery Administration, 66, 71–72
National Research Council (NRC), 195, 196
National Training School for Women and Girls, 129, 131, 136, 141–42
Native Americans: abuse and exploitation of women and children in *Oklahoma's Poor Rich*, 48–49, 53–61; congressional hearing on, 61; Dawes Act on, 51; education of, 49–52; Oklahoma land rights for, 14, 48–49, 54–61; and women's roles, 51–52
"Negro Artist and the Racial Mountain, The" (Hughes), 157
Neharkey, Millie, 55–58
Nellson, William Allan, 227
Neutral Conference of Experts, 20–21, 24
New Age, 27
Newcombe, Franc, 200
New Deal, 63, 66, 71–72, 74–75, 77–78, 123, 173. *See also* Roosevelt, Franklin D.
Newman, Meredith, 63
New Masses, 118
"New Negro, The" (Locke), 143–44
New Rhetoric: anticipation of, by women, 3, 5, 8–9; canonical theories of, 6, 8–9; communally constructed truths as aim of, 8, 9; on dialogue,

8, 9; on language, 8, 9; on persuasive strategies, 6; and teaching of reading and composition, 26–27; Wales's continuous mediation compared with, 23–24, 26–27
news media. *See* media
New York Call, 118
New York Herald Tribune, 170
New York School of Philanthropy, 65
New York Times: on Jane Addams, 35–37; on banning of Norman Thomas's lecture at Brooklyn College, 248; on Curie, 226–27, 229–30; Earhart's articles for, 177; on Aunt Molly Jackson, 169; on Keller, 100, 101, 102, 105; on Morris's *Digging in the Southwest*, 204; on professional women, 228; on Sabin, 227, 229, 231; on sexism in workplace, 71; on Bessie Smith, 151; on women aviators, 182, 184; on World Labor Day (1933), 117
Nielsen, Kim E., 110, 113n1
Nineteenth Amendment, 3, 7
Ninety-Niner, 184–85
Ninety-Nines Organization for Women Pilots, 189
NLRCW (National League of Republican Colored Women), 140
NMU (National Miners Union), 166–68, 171
NRC (National Research Council), 195, 196
nuclear weapons, 23, 24
Nuttall, Zelia, 194

Odets, Clifford, 171
Odetta, 174
Oermann, Robert, 162, 163, 174
Oklahoma Bar Association, 61
Oklahoma's Poor Rich Indians (Sniffen, Fabens, and Bonnin), 14, 48–49, 54–61
Olbrechts-Tyteca, Lucie, 8, 9, 223
Old Curiosity Shop, The (Dickens), 55, 57, 59
Omlie, Phoebe, 189
On Their Way to the Slabtown District Convention (Burroughs), 141
Other: African Americans as, 134; Bonnin as, 50, 53; Day on, 126; Mexican Americans as, 215, 216–17
Our Lady of the Lake College, 211

Outline of Careers for Women (Fleischman), 234
Owens, Avie, 174

pacifism. *See* peace activism
Paine, Charles, 240, 241, 245
Palmer, George Herbert, 51, 254
Parente, Cassandra, 15, 149, 159–74, 284
Parezo, Nancy J., 194, 196, 206
Parker, Dorothy, 1
Parks, Sarah Rush, 251, 252
Parsons, Elsie Clews, 194, 196–201
particularity in community formation, 197, 200
Parton, Dolly, 174
Pasachoff, Naomi, 63
pathos, 125
Patterson, Flora W., 235
Patterson, Samuel White, 246, 253
peace activism: by Addams, 1, 14, 20–21, 32–46; by Cone, 251; educational sites for rhetorical innovation for, 24–29; by International Congress of Women for Permanent Peace (ICWPP), 19–20, 33; Neutral Conference of Experts during World War I, 20–21, 24; opposition to women's peace activism, 10; by Wales, 9, 14, 19–31; and Wales Plan during World War I, 19–21, 28, 31; and Wales's continuous mediation, 21–31
Peace and Bread in Time of War (Addams), 20, 33–34, 36–41, 43, 46
Pear, Robert, 75
Peirce, C. S., 32, 34, 46
Pen-Portraits of Literary Women (Cone and Gilder), 248–49
Penn, William, 109
Perelman, Chaim, 9, 223
peripheral, 242
peripheral methodological principles, 242
Perkins, Frances: autobiographical rhetorical theory of, 64–65, 68–77; education and early career of, 65, 75; on fitting in and being one of the boys, 65, 68–73; on harnessing power of information, 65, 75–77; as labor secretary in Roosevelt administration, 1, 63, 70–78; multiple and shifting role of, in *The Roosevelt I Knew*, 74; and National Consumers' League,

Perkins, Frances (*continued*)
65, 70; as New York State industrial commissioner, 66, 76; as New York State labor commissioner, 66, 76; on perpetual apprenticeship, 65, 73–75; photograph of, 70; political memoir of Roosevelt administration by, 14, 64, 66–77; public identity of, 10; and Al Smith, 64, 65–66, 75–76; and Social Security, 63, 66, 74–75
Perkins, Lolita, 130
Perkins Institute for the Blind, 110
Permanence and Change (Burke), 99, 188
personalism, 122
personalizing an essence, 127–28
personalizing the abstract, 125–27
Phaedrus (Plato), 64, 74
Phillips, Frank, 185
Pickford, Mary, 102
Piehl, Mel, 118
piety, 10, 98, 99–106, 110–13
Pike, Kenneth, 26–27, 30
pilots. *See* aerocyborgs
Pittman, Coretta, 8, 14–15, 130, 143–58, 284
Pittsburgh Courier, 136
Pittsburgh Press, 189
Pius XI, Pope, 120, 121
Plato, 64, 74
Platt, George Foster, 105
politics of respectability, 134
popularization, 195, 200–208
Post, Marjorie Merriweather, 1
poverty: and *Catholic Worker*/Catholic Worker movement, 114, 116–28; of Native Americans in *Oklahoma's Poor Rich Indians*, 14, 48–49, 54–61. *See also* Hull House
Powdermaker, Hortense, 194
Powell, William, 183
Practicing Writing (Masters), 255
pragmatism, 32, 34, 35, 37–42, 45–46, 47nn1–2
"Precious Memories," 166–67
Prejean, Sr. Helen, 114
Pringle, Jonathan, 208n1
"Pro, Not Anti: A Principle of Integration" (Wales), 27
professions. *See* anthropology; science
Progressive Party, 32
propaganda by exclusion, 126
propaganda by inclusion, 126

Public Health Service, U.S., 216
Pueblo Religion (Parsons), 200
Pyle, Gladys, 1

Quadragesimo anno (Pius XI), 120, 121
Queen Bess: Daredevil Aviator (Rich), 181
Quicke, J. C., 113n1

racial uplift, 14, 132–39, 144, 181–83
racism: against African American women, 130–31, 133–35; in aviation, 180–83; Burroughs on fighting, 139–40; and Jim Crow laws, 141, 143, 209; against Mexicans Americans, 209, 212–13, 215–17, 221
Rainer, Luise, 171
Rainey, Gertrude "Ma," 144
Raleigh, Eve, 222n7
Rally, 86
Ransom, John Crowe, 9
Reece, Florence, 173
Reichard, Gladys, 194, 198–201
Reilly, Joseph J., 251
relationship (sideshadowing principle), 242, 243–45, 258
Republican Party, 1, 100, 140
Rerum novarum (Leo XIII), 120, 121
Resistant Writer (Paine), 240
Reuss, Richard, 171
Reyna, Sergio, 211, 219
rhetoric: anticipation of New Rhetoric by women, 8–9; and movement from agency to action by women, 5–8; new methodologies for research on, 5, 15; in nineteenth century by women, 6–7; overview of women's early-twentieth-century rhetoric, 3–13; and popularization, 195, 200–208; and underestimation of hegemonic definitions of "women's place," 9–11. *See also* New Rhetoric; *and specific women and their works*
Rhetoric: Discovery and Change (Young, Becker, and Pike), 15, 26–27, 30
rhetorical community, 203
Rhetoric of Motives, A (Burke), 23–24, 26, 99–100, 114, 127
Rhetoric Retold (Glenn), 4
Rice, Jeff, 240, 245, 254
Rich, Adrienne, 239n1
Rich, Doris, 181, 182

Richards, I. A., 9
Richison, Margie, 184
Riddle, Almeda, 174
Rideing, William H., 255
Ritchie, Jean, 174
Ritchie, Joy, 161
Roberson, Susan L., 242, 250
Robert, Frank, 206
Robertson, Ben, 170
Robinson, Betty, 1
Robinson, Sandra L., 14, 90, 129–42, 144, 181, 284
Rockefeller, J. D., 102, 195
Rockefeller Institute, 228
Rogerian rhetoric, 14, 27, 30
Romalis, Shelly, 160–69, 171, 173, 174nn1–2
Roman Catholic Church. *See Catholic Worker*/Catholic Worker movement
Ronald, Kate, 161
Roosevelt, Eleanor, 13
Roosevelt, Franklin D., 14, 64, 66–77, 78n1. *See also* New Deal
Roosevelt, Theodore, 32, 33, 39
Roosevelt I Knew, The (Perkins), 14, 64, 66–77, 78n2
Roskelly, Hephzibah, 14, 21, 32–47, 98–99, 257, 284
Ross, Dorothy, 195
Ross, Nellie Tayloe, 1
Ross, Susan, 140
Rossiter, Margaret, 196, 230, 232, 237
Rothschild, Amelie Spiegel, 253
Royster, Jaqueline Jones, 6, 16n2, 174, 181, 258
Rukeyser, Muriel, 13

Sabin, Florence, 1, 223–32, 234, 235, 236, 237, 238, 239
Saltzberg, Florence B., 233
Samuelson, Dave, 161, 167
Sarkela, Sandra, 140
Schlafly, Phyllis, 97
Schlossberg, Helen, 97
"School Days of an Indian Girl" (Bonnin), 53, 62n5
Schultz, Gladys Denny, 88
science: and "bootstraps" rhetoric of gender neutrality, 232–38; Burke on scientific language, 9; career guides on, 15, 223, 224, 232–39; Curie's career in, 223–32, 234, 235, 236, 237, 238, 239; epideictic rhetoric and women scientists, 223–24, 233–36, 238–39; family duties of women scientists, 230–31; femininity of women scientists, 225–26, 229–32; gender neutrality and women scientists, 228–29, 232–38, 239n2; media representation of women scientists, 15, 224–32; romantic motivations of women scientists, 231; Sabin's career in, 1, 223–32, 234, 235, 236, 237, 238, 239; women's adoption of scientific worldview to counter gender or racial stereotypes, 10. *See also* anthropology
Scott, Anne Firor, 11, 80, 84, 220–21
scouting. *See* Boy Scouts; Girl Scouts
Seaman, August H., 253
Second Twenty Years at Hull House (Addams), 33–34, 36, 39, 40, 42–45
Seeger, Charles, 171
Seeger, Pete, 171
Seeing Red (Carpenter), 50
segregation. *See* Jim Crow laws
Self-Cultivation in English (Palmer), 254
Selzer, Jack, 126
sentimentalism, 50–51, 53–61
Sergeant, Elizabeth, 200
settlement movement. *See* Hull House
sexism. *See* gender
sexuality: of African American women, 136, 137, 145, 156; in blues music sung by Bessie Smith, 154–56; and folk music, 161–62; of Bessie Smith, 15, 149
"Shades of the Tenth Muses" (González), 209, 210, 218–20, 221n1
Sharer, Wendy B., 2–3, 6, 14, 19–31, 33, 80, 81, 125, 201, 284
Sharp, Cecil, 162
Sheard, Cynthia, 224
Shteir, Ann B., 201
sideshadowing methodology, 241–45, 258
sideshadowing narrative form, 245–46, 258
Siegfried, Charlotte Haddock, 47n1
Silverberg, Helene, 195
Simians, Cyborgs, and Women (Haraway), 176
Singleton, Zutty, 150
situatedness (sideshadowing principle), 242, 245, 258

Sixty American Opinions on the War (Abbott), 251
Skinner, Carolyn, 7, 16n2
Slater, Miriam, 228
Smith, Al, 64, 65–66, 75–76
Smith, Bessie: audience reaction to, 150–51; birth year of, 146; blues music of, 9, 15, 143–57; death of, 149; ethos of blues music of, 145–51, 154; hopelessness and despair as theme of, 151–53; Langston Hughes on, 157; intraracial conflict as theme of, 153–54; opposition of, to race- and class-based forms of oppression, 15; performance and recording career of, 146–49, 157–58n2; photographs of, 147, 149; public identity of, 10; "roughness" of, 147–48; sexual freedom and exploration as theme of, 154–56; unconventional sexual self of, 15, 149
Smith, Clara, 144
Smith, Elinor, 188
Smith, Erminnie, 194
Smith, Mamie, 144
Smith College, 227, 233
Smithies, Chris, 246
Sniffen, Matthew, 48–49, 61
Snyder, Homer P., 61
"Social Life in Cameron, Starr and Zapata Counties" (González), 210, 212–18, 220–21, 222n5
Social Science Research Council (SSRC), 195, 196
social sciences. *See* anthropology
Social Security, 63, 66, 74–75
Socialist Party, 97, 117, 118
sociorhetorical networks, 197
"Soft Pedal Blues," 156
"Soft-Hearted Sioux, The" (Bonnin), 53, 62n5
Solidarity, 97
"Some by Ways of Peace Work" (Wales), 24–25
Southern Agrarianism, 119, 128n4
Southern Lady, The (Scott), 221
Southern Workman, 138
Southwestern Review, 211
Southwestern U.S., 195, 201–7
Spack, Ruth, 51–52
Spence, Lucille, 13
SSRC (Social Science Research Council), 195, 196

stability in community formation, 199–200
Stanford University, 20
Stanley, Roba, 174
Starr, Ellen Gates, 32, 38
Stebbins, Grant C., 55–56
Stechie, Ledcie, 55, 58–60
Stein, Elizabeth P., 251
Steinem, Gloria, 6
Stevenson, Matilda Coxe, 194
Stewart, Jim, 163, 164, 174n1
Stocking, George W., Jr., 195
Stone, Harlan F., 74
Story of My Life (Keller), 98
Stowe, Harriet Beecher, 54, 59
Studer, Clara, 183, 184–85
stunt flying. *See* aerocyborgs
subjectivity, 9
Sullivan, Anne. *See* Macy, Anne Sullivan
Sutherland, Christine Mason, 245
Swales, John, 197
Swanson, Claude, 70–71

Tanner, Clara Lee, 194
Tanner, William M., 258
Tate, Allen, 128n4
Taubman, Howard, 66
Tax, Sol, 198
teaching. *See* English studies
Teaching in the Primary Grades (D. Bildersee), 244
Tedesco, Laureen, 80
temperance movement, 6
Tennessean, 151
terministic screen, 3, 11, 111–13
Terrell, Mary Church, 130, 144–45
Terror Dream, The (Faludi), 12
Texas A&M University, Corpus Christi, 211, 222n5
Texas and Southwestern Folklore, 211
Texas Folklore Society, 211
Texas State Board of Education, 97
Thomas, Norman, 248
Time magazine, 102, 225, 228
Times Literary Supplement, 102
Toiler, 97
Toulmin, Stephen, 9
Toward a Civil Discourse (Crowley), 115
Tozzer, Alfred, 198
transrhetorical agency, 49–61
Treaty of Versailles, 40, 46
"Trial Path, The" (Bonnin), 62n5

Troubling the Angels (Lather and Smithies), 246
True, Clara, 200
Tubman, Harriet, 97
Twain, Mark, 102
20 Hrs. 40 Min.: Our Flight in the Friendship (Earhart), 177
Twenty Years at Hull House (Addams), 32, 42
Tylor, Edward, 193

UMWA (United Mine Workers of America), 166
Uncle Tom's Cabin (Stowe), 54, 59
Underhill, Ruth, 194, 199, 201
unions. *See* labor movement; *and specific unions*
United Mine Workers of America (UMWA), 166
United Nations, 30
universities. *See* English studies; *and specific universities*
University of Chicago, 34, 44
University of Colorado at Boulder, 208n1
University of Texas, 211, 213
University of Wisconsin, 19, 31

Van Vechten, Carl, 148, 149, 150, 157–58n2
Vanity Fair, 147–48
Visser, Irene, 249–50
Visweswaran, Kamala, 194

Wagner, Robert, 75
Wagoner, Alice, 87
Wales, Julia Grace: Burke and New Rhetoric compared with, 14, 23–24, 26–27; continuous mediation principles by, 21–31; and educational sites for rhetorical innovation, 24–29; on free cooperation without compromise, 27; and International Congress of Women for Permanent Peace (ICWPP), 19–20; peace activism by, 9, 14, 19–21; rhetorical practices of, generally, 2, 14; textbook (*Democracy Needs Education*) by, 27–29; on United Nations Charter, 30; and Wales Plan for peace during World War I, 19–21, 28, 31
Walker, Ruby, 156
Wall Street Journal, 36

Wallen, Shade E., 56
Ware, Susan, 16n1
Warnick, Barbara, 16n4
"Warrior's Daughter, A" (Bonnin), 53, 62n5
Washington Bee, 130
Washington Post, 207, 225, 231
"Washwoman's Blues," 152–53
Waters, Ethel, 148
Watts, Ruth, 237
"We Are Coming" (Logan), 6
Webb, Walter Prescott, 213
Weiser, M. Elizabeth, 1–16, 16n3, 114–28, 257, 284
Welch, Deborah, 61
Well-Tempered Women (Mattingly), 6
Wells, H. G., 98
Wells-Barnett, Ida B., 144–45, 181
Welsh, Herbert, 48
Weltfish, Gene, 198
West, Cornel, 40, 45
Wetherill, Lucy, 200
Wexler, Laura, 52
Wharton School of Finance and Commerce, 65
"Which Side Are You On," 173
White Buffalo Woman, 51
Whiteman, Jordan, 59, 60
white women: and Cult of True Womanhood, 135; and domestic femininity, 51–53; nineteenth-century rhetoric of, 6–7; in public and professional life in 1920s and 1930s, 1, 7–8, 10, 13. *See also* gender; *and specific women*
Whitman, Walt, 109, 242, 258
Who's Who in America, 230
"Why I Am a Pagan" (Bonnin), 54, 62n5
Wickett's Remedy (Goldberg), 246
Wiggins, Ella Mae, 173
WIL (Women's International League), 43–44
Wilkinson, Elizabeth, 14, 48–62, 125, 218, 255, 285
Willebrandt, Mabel Walker, 228
Williams, Blanche Colton, 243, 246, 252, 253
Williams, Spencer, 152
Williams, Susan, 249
Wilson, Howard E., 30
Wilson, Woodrow, 20, 24, 31, 34, 40, 69, 70, 141
Witness for Peace, 114

WMU (Woman's Missionary Union), 131–32
Wobblies (I.W.W.), 43, 97
"Woman in American Literature" (Cone), 248–52
Woman suffrage, 3, 7, 66, 82, 116, 137, 249
Woman Who Lost Her Soul (González), 210
Woman's Missionary Union (WMU), 131–32
Woman's Work in America (Meyer), 249
women. *See* African American women; feminism; white women
Women in Chemistry, 233, 236
Women Professional Workers (Kemper Adams), 233, 234, 236
Women's Bureau, 125
Women's International League (WIL), 43–44
Women's International League for Peace and Freedom, 32, 35, 40
Women's National Democratic Club, 13
Women's Speakers' Bureau, 13
Women's Trade Union League, 13
Woodward, Ellen Sullivan, 13
Woolf, Virginia, 219
Worker newspaper/magazine, 131–32
Worker's Music League, 171
working class. *See Catholic Worker*/Catholic Worker movement; labor movement
Works Progress Administration, 66
World Center for Women's Archives, 10–11
World Tomorrow, 44–45
World War I: Addams's peace activism during, 33, 34–41; Allied naval blockade during, 36; and Cone, 251; England during, 251; Girl Scouts during, 88; Neutral Conference of Experts for peace during, 20–21, 24; and Treaty of Versailles, 40, 46; U.S. entry into, 21, 24, 40; Wales Plan for peace during, 19–21, 28, 31; Wilson's pacifist stance at beginning of, 34, 40
Wright, J. B. F., 166–67
writing instruction. *See* English studies
Wyman, Loraine, 162

"You Foolish Men" (de la Cruz), 220
Young, Richard, 26–27, 30
"Young Woman's Blues," 153–54
Yucatan, 195, 201–7, 208n1

Zepernick, Janet, 1–16, 63–78, 125, 285
Zumwalt, Rosemary Lévy, 199
Zuni Mythology (Benedict), 199

Studies in Rhetorics and Feminisms

Studies in Rhetorics and Feminisms seeks to address the interdisciplinarity that rhetorics and feminisms represent. Rhetorical and feminist scholars want to connect rhetorical inquiry with contemporary academic and social concerns, exploring rhetoric's relevance to current issues of opportunity and diversity. This interdisciplinarity has already begun to transform the rhetorical tradition as we have known it (upper-class, agonistic, public, and male) into regendered, inclusionary rhetorics (democratic, dialogic, collaborative, cultural, and private). Our intellectual advancements depend on such ongoing transformation.

Rhetoric, whether ancient, contemporary, or futuristic, always inscribes the relation of language and power at a particular moment, indicating who may speak, who may listen, and what can be said. The only way we can displace the traditional rhetoric of masculine-only, public performance is to replace it with rhetorics that are recognized as being better suited to our present needs. We must understand more fully the rhetorics of the non-Western tradition, of women, of a variety of cultural and ethnic groups. Therefore, Studies in Rhetorics and Feminisms espouses a theoretical position of openness and expansion, a place for rhetorics to grow and thrive in a symbiotic relationship with all that feminisms have to offer, particularly when these two fields intersect with philosophical, sociological, religious, psychological, pedagogical, and literary issues.

The series seeks scholarly works that both examine and extend rhetoric, works that span the sexes, disciplines, cultures, ethnicities, and sociocultural practices as they intersect with the rhetorical tradition. After all, the recent resurgence of rhetorical studies has been not so much a discovery of new rhetorics as a recognition of existing rhetorical activities and practices, of our newfound ability and willingness to listen to previously untold stories.

The series editors seek both high-quality traditional and cutting-edge scholarly work that extends the significant relationship between rhetoric and feminism within various genres, cultural contexts, historical periods, methodologies, theoretical positions, and methods of delivery (e.g., film and hypertext to elocution and preaching).

Queries and submissions:
Professor Cheryl Glenn, Editor
    E-mail: cjg6@psu.edu
Professor Shirley Wilson Logan, Editor
    E-mail: slogan@umd.edu

Studies in Rhetorics and Feminisms
Department of English
142 South Burrowes Bldg.
Penn State University
University Park, PA 16802-6200

Other Books in the Studies in Rhetorics and Feminisms Series

A Feminist Legacy
The Rhetoric and Pedagogy
of Gertrude Buck
Suzanne Bordelon

Regendering Delivery
The Fifth Canon and
Antebellum Women Rhetors
Lindal Buchanan

Rhetorics of Motherhood
Lindal Buchanan

Conversational Rhetoric
The Rise and Fall of a Women's
Tradition, 1600–1900
Jane Donawerth

Feminism beyond Modernism
Elizabeth A. Flynn

Evolutionary Rhetoric
Sex, Science, and Free Love in
Nineteenth-Century Feminism
Wendy Hayden

Liberating Voices
Writing at the Bryn Mawr Summer
School for Women Workers
Karyn L. Hollis

Gender and Rhetorical Space
in American Life, 1866–1910
Nan Johnson

Appropriate[ing] Dress
Women's Rhetorical Style in
Nineteenth-Century America
Carol Mattingly

The Gendered Pulpit
Preaching in American
Protestant Spaces
Roxanne Mountford

Rhetorical Listening
Identification, Gender, Whiteness
Krista Ratcliffe

Feminist Rhetorical Practices
New Horizons for Rhetoric,
Composition, and Literacy Studies
Jacqueline J. Royster
and Gesa E. Kirsch

Vote and Voice
Women's Organizations and
Political Literacy, 1915–1930
Wendy B. Sharer